Political Liberalization in Brazil

About the Book and Editor

The civilian government inaugurated in Brazil in March 1985, following twenty-one years of military rule, is the culmination of a slow process of liberalization that has brought greater freedom of political expression, organization, and activity. How the Sarney government responds to the challenges it faces and the institutional choices it must make will shape Brazil's political evolution for years to come. Should Brazil develop a democratic system, it would be the third most populous democracy in the world. Political trends in Brazil are therefore of considerable significance to Latin America and the United States. In this comprehensive analysis of the forces pushing democratization forward, those opposing it, and the contradictions created by the ad hoc nature of the dynamics between the two, the contributors examine the legacy of two decades of authoritarian rule, the choices facing the civilian government, and possible future developments.

Wayne A. Selcher is College Professor of International Studies at Elizabethtown College in Pennsylvania. He is the editor of *Brazil in the International System: The Rise of a Middle Power* (Westview, 1981).

Political Liberalization in Brazil

Dynamics, Dilemmas, and Future Prospects

edited by
Wayne A. Selcher

Westview Press / Boulder and London

Westview Special Studies on Latin America and the Caribbean

This Westview softcover edition was manufactured on our own premises using equipment and methods that allow us to keep even specialized books in stock. It is printed on acid-free paper and bound in softcovers that carry the highest rating of the National Association of State Textbook Administrators, in consultation with the Association of American Publishers and the Book Manufacturers' Institute.

Copyright © 1986 by Westview Press, Inc., except Chapter 4, © 1986 Robert A. Packenham.

Published in 1986 in the United States of America by Westview Press, Inc.; Frederick A. Praeger, Publisher; 5500 Central Avenue, Boulder, Colorado 80301

Library of Congress Cataloging-in-Publication Data
Main entry under title:
Political liberalization in Brazil.
  (Westview special studies on Latin America and the Caribbean)
  Includes index.
  1. Political participation—Brazil. 2. Brazil—Politics and government—1985– . I. Selcher, Wayne A., 1942– . II. Series.
JL2481.P65 1986   323'.042'0981   85-11556
ISBN 0-8133-0263-3 (soft)

Printed and bound in the United States of America

(∞) The paper used in this publication meets the requirements of the American National Standard for Permanence of Paper for Printed Library Materials Z39.48-1984.

6   5   4   3   2   1

Contents

Tables and Figures

Figures

Acknowledgments

The editor would like to thank the Howard Heinz Endowment for research support granted to make possible the compilation of this volume and the completion of Chapter 2. Elizabethtown College also defrayed a portion of the research and preparation expenses.

The original inspiration and encouragement for this book came from colleagues Enrique Baloyra, Bolivar Lamounier, and Amaury de Souza. Suggestions shared among the contributors moved it toward its ultimate form, and their cooperation kept the enterprise progressing. Howard Kroesen and Tom Leap worked out methods of electronic transfer of some of the manuscripts. Alice Knouse, to whom I owe a large debt of gratitude, set it up on the word processor and labored patiently and well through repeated revisions and slippery deadlines. Sharon Patrick furnished timely auxiliary typing assistance. Finally, the staff at Zug Memorial Library provided its usual fine reference support.

Wayne A. Selcher

Introduction

Wayne A. Selcher

While most U.S. observers of Latin America were focusing attention on the tragedies of violence in Central America, Brazil, a much more significant actor in its own right, underwent a successful and peaceful transition from military rule to representative political institutions. It is rare in the developing world for an authoritarian regime to turn over power gradually and stably to a democratically elected successor, as happened in Brazil. If Brazil, with its 138 million inhabitants, develops a democratic system in both form and public policy, it will be the third most populous democracy in the world, after India and the United States. As part of a democratic trend in Latin America, future political developments in this second most populous nation of the hemisphere are therefore of considerable significance to Latin America, the United States, and the study of transition from military dictatorship toward representative forms of government and the rule of law.

The Rationale for Liberalization, 1974–1979

Military rule was installed by coup in Brazil in April 1964 as a reaction to internal disorder under the leftist government of President João Goulart. For most of the next decade civilian political expression and freedoms were curtailed as the military attempted to purge from society those elements it considered subversive. Excesses of repression and violent opposition were experienced most sharply from 1967 to 1974.[1]

The evolution of Brazilian politics from 1974 to March 1985, in contrast, shows a gradual, begrudgingly and, for the most part, paternalistically granted trend toward greater freedom of political expression, organization, and activity. The process of liberalization proceeded largely within the control of an essentially military regime increasingly desirous of ridding itself of most of its political power, but still afraid of the consequences of genuinely competitive and responsive civilian governance. This approach-avoidance reaction and the constant testing of limits by the opposition entailed some threats and setbacks and a more uncertain and prolonged decompression than, say, in Spain or Portugal. Yet it was relatively stable, contrasted to patterns elsewhere in South America.

1

During the presidencies of Emílio Garrastazú Médici (1969–1974) and the less repressive Ernesto Geisel (1974–1979), the authoritarian regime was backed by the consensus of the armed forces' high command, and it did not tolerate interference from Congress or the judicial branch. Military control was exercised through the naming of a general as president, the enactment of a series of dictatorial institutional acts and national security laws, and the oversight of the National Security Council and National Intelligence Service (SNI), as well as through physical repression. An artificial two-party system was maintained, with strait-jacket effects in the short run. Sociopolitical conflicts were suppressed and postponed rather than resolved, while the emergence of new civilian political leadership was hindered by the bureaucratic-military alliance that monopolized the centralized political process.

This alliance, consolidating power steadily since the coup of 1964, thrived on the enhanced role of the state under Médici and Geisel. It derived its initial political power from technical competence, shared values, esprit de corps, quasimonopoly of certain development skills, and similar views of the nation-building process.[2] The power of this alliance stifled broader political development because of its technocratic emphasis on national planning and state intervention by trained civilian bureaucrats and military officers in the administration, supposedly exempt from interest group and other partisan pressures. The system emphasized government effectiveness in promoting macroeconomic development and order for legitimation purposes rather than political representativeness. In essence it represented a modernization of the flexible patrimonial order, or dedication to unification and centrally controlled change through bureaucracy that has characterized elitist rule in Brazil for generations.[3]

Liberalization was initiated by Geisel in 1974 as a process of *distensão* (decompression), a reaction to social (and especially middle- and upper-class) disaffection with government policies, which raised a legitimacy question that had to be dealt with on the political level. The regime leaders had not invested much effort in creating legitimation for a long-term or deeply institutionalized authoritarian model, preferring to justify certain arbitrary actions while still keeping a minimum of democratic rhetoric and referring to the system itself as "exceptional." In principle this left open a search for a less harsh and more democratic normality, even as authoritarian practices became routinized.[4]

Declining growth after the 1967–1973 "economic miracle" cut the prime rationale for an authoritarianism then already waning in public acceptance. Dreams of national grandeur became increasingly less cred-ible. Violent opposition had been crushed, making the national security state more difficult to justify. Rapid socioeconomic diversification since 1964 necessitated an approach to governance that protected the economic model by basing political legitimacy on less costly and more subtle means than repression of interests and persons deemed undesirable or subversive. Further, overly centralized decisionmaking by a small group

had generated its own law of diminishing returns, which Bolivar Lamounier terms a "black hole effect," a "loss of flexibility, rationality,
and efficiency because of the absence of proper channels of support
and feedback."[5]

Governance based on concessions and compromise, rather than rule
by fiat, along with a clearly limited liberalization to allow some consultation with civil society became both necessary and feasible. This
was made possible by a change of consensus within the military
leadership—a change toward some of the original ideals of the 1964
coup, such as acceptance of more democratic ideals (however limited),
military rule as a condition of exception, and opposition to military
involvement in repressive brutalities uncharacteristic of the institutional
traditions. The nonpersonalistic exercise of the presidency under the
dictatorship involved consultative soundings of the high command on
major issues. By 1974, the imperatives of governance and the deep
involvement of the military command in political decisions and (especially) presidential succession were beginning to factionalize the armed
forces into quasiparties enough to pose a conceivable threat to their
hierarchical unity and discipline should authoritarian rule continue in
its then current form.[6] (Yet the slow process of extraction from power
would in itself give rise to internal conflicts.)

The extent of support for the opposition in the 1974 legislative elections
surprised the government but gave more weight to Geisel's calculated-
risk strategy from within for engineering a planned, controlled, and
evolutionary transition to a somewhat more competitive system through
piecemeal but credible reforms at the margins of power. As conceived
and supervised by presidential adviser and political architect General
Golbery do Couto e Silva, the objective was to relieve repression and
pressure at the edges slowly, by stages, and without a schedule. A
reliable base of support for the government in the increasingly relevant
electorate was to be created so that the establishment's control of the
center of decision making, particularly the national executive and economic policy, was not threatened in the longer run. The goals of the
bureaucratic-authoritarian regime were not to be affected, but its grip
on power was to be adjusted to changing circumstances brought on by
national development. Fully competitive democracy, supposedly the
ultimate value, was to be postponed vaguely and indefinitely until the
country had accumulated sufficient capital, basic industry, and political
maturity to be able to afford to redistribute wealth (i.e., to be able to
"deal with the social question").

In the interim, at first under the label of "relative democracy," ad
hoc procedural devices (*casuísmos*) came to be used pragmatically to
divide and blunt the advance of the opposition, minimize the spontaneous
and unexpected, and defuse the extremists of left and right.[7] To maintain
maneuvering space and long-run progress by means of a precarious
balance, the regime repeatedly found it necessary to resist the demands

of, alternately, the hardliners and the reformers, in and out of government. Liberalization measures alternated with consolidation measures in a metaphor of diastole and systole. To be successful, the system had to be flexible enough to accommodate the political elites important at any given point, yet dependable enough to ensure control from the Presidential Palace. Concessions, then, had to be yielded slowly and reluctantly. Clearly, attenuated authoritarianism or, at best, a limited pluralism under central control but with a workable level of legitimacy was the original goal, not full democracy.

Such was the logic of the plan, and it functioned rather effectively from the regime's point of view (although with some surprises) through the end of the Geisel government. Yet subsequent events escaped official control, and the smooth flow of liberalization as well as its intended circumscribed character were greatly modified by the course of events. Once the decision to liberalize had been made, and the authoritarian state plainly regarded as one of exception, the government was judged ever more widely by its willingness to complete the transition. Despite the hesitations and reversals, the dynamic of the process turned out to be a liberalizing trend because the government continued to seek broader consent from society and because the opposition exerted constant and nonviolent pressure. Governmental strategems to restrict, delay, and stall were counteracted by persistent and increasingly effective opposition efforts to expand, speed up, and restart. The result of this push-pull dynamic was a continual redefinition of the "limits" of *abertura* (political opening), its mechanisms, its set of participants, and its objectives.[8]

What began as a "transition from above" eventually became a more negotiated and inclusive "transition through transaction" (as the term is used in Chapter 5) because of unforeseen consequences and circumstances, as well as inconsistencies within the scheme itself. Consequently, the course of liberalization, worked out step by step, was replete with unexpected twists, ironies, ambiguities, contradictions, and dilemmas. Not the least of these was the fact that President João Figueiredo, who presided over the final phase of the transition to civilian government, was selected out of the directorship of the National Intelligence Service (SNI), the repressive side of the regime.

Abertura as a Process

The intent of this volume is to present an analytical evaluation of the process of political liberalization, starting in the latter part of the Geisel presidency, emphasizing the period of President João Figueiredo (1979–1985), and advancing some speculation on potential developments for the "New Republic" begun on March 15, 1985. The contributors to this volume provide a comprehensive analysis, based on their ongoing studies of Brazil's political opening as it was unfolding, of the forces pushing liberalization forward, those that opposed it, and the restrictions imposed by the ad hoc nature of the dynamics between the two. Rather than taking a chronological approach, the authors concentrate on the dynamics, contradictions, dilemmas, and trends of *abertura* as a flow of political (rather than economic) events. Chapters 1 and 5, in particular, place the Brazilian experience within the general literature on transitions from authoritarian to representative rule. A bibliography on each topic is provided in the notes for each chapter. The first five chapters reflect events until late 1985, while the sixth chapter looks into the future from the circumstances of early 1986.

In the first chapter, Baloyra examines the early to intermediate stages of liberalization through a model of the six basic contradictions every political system must manage. Within the paradigm of authoritarian deterioration and breakdown, his conclusions highlight the uncertainty and open-endedness of the Brazilian process of transition and illustrate the ever-decreasing ability of the military to control the process once it committed itself to respect some basic procedural norms. Particularly crucial in motivating further liberalization in 1977–1981 was the style of the political management of the growing contradictions between the military as institution and the military as government, and between the military and the rest of the society.

Selcher then examines why the smooth flow of liberalization under Figueiredo was hindered and its future course made questionable by a number of contradictions or dilemmas, political predicaments caused by the piling up of unaddressed issues for the next government to solve. The shorter-run difficulties of *abertura* were attributable to a crisis of central authority and strategy in the face of a fairly united and insistent opposition and congressional reassertion. The deeper-lying difficulties were attributable to persistent structural imbalances in Brazilian society among social classes and among regions. Such imbalances widened as short-term tactical maneuvering repeatedly sidetracked key opportunities to build solid political institutions for the longer run, which threw a greater burden onto the civilian government.

Fleischer concentrates on the role of the Congress as a major force in pushing for widening liberalization and as a key arena for expansion of representation, including growth in strength and determination of the opposition parties and the break-up of the official party. The origins of this role are examined in a comparison of the backgrounds and political orientations of deputies and senators elected in 1978 and in 1982, showing the political results of regional and party differences. The formation of new party blocs within Congress is analyzed as a movement causing deterioration in legislative-executive relations and the defeat of the official candidate for the presidency in the January 1985 electoral college.

Packenham, in surveying the Brazilian literature about Brazilian politics, finds that a major shift in the substance and terms of the theoretical discourse about politics in the Brazilian intellectual culture occurred during the tenure of the military regime. Intellectual interpretations were dominated by Marxist perspectives during the first decade of the period, but new tendencies toward greater acceptance of the forms and practices of pluralistic liberal democracy have emerged with political liberalization. He describes some major trends and issues in the changing analysis, reasons behind and implications of the shift in central tendencies, and factors that support and oppose continuation of the recent trends.

Share and Mainwaring, developing a model of political transition through transaction, compare Brazil and Spain, the most significant contemporary cases of the phenomenon. Although the two cases are noted for their relatively low level of violence and high degree of stability during decompression, the authors argue that such transitions are difficult to achieve, require certain prerequisites, and entail some political, economic, and social costs. In developing this theme, Share and Mainwaring examine why authoritarian elites undertake democratic transition, which conditions make such a transition possible, and what costs and benefits are associated with managed transitions.

Schneider completes the collection with speculations on Brazil's political future. Starting from the interaction of political, economic, and social developments, he arrives at a series of alternative political scenarios resulting from a comprehensive set of economic contexts for the 1986–1988 period. Combined with examination of the power, alignments, and orientations of twenty-nine political actors—analyzed back to 1960 and projected under each alternative context—these scenarios lead to quantitative probabilities for the different possible political situations for the years ahead rather than just qualitative assessments regarding "stability" or "instability."

Challenges to the New Republic: From *Abertura* to Democracy?

The consensus of the volume is that *abertura* succeeded in creating political institutions supportive of further democratic development. *Abertura* showed surprising resiliency and passed successfully through several major tests, the final being the indirect presidential election of January 1985. Even with the severity of the national problems, sufficient consensus and moderation still exist among the majority of political actors to make possible a more democratic system that can resist extreme rightist and leftist pressures.

The victory of civilian Tancredo Neves signified a "New Republic" and an end to over two decades of rule by generals, vindicated by the peaceful transfer of power to Vice-president José Sarney on March 15, 1985. (President-elect Neves was too ill to take office and subsequently died on April 21.) Yet the legacy of severe economic recession, management of the $100 billion foreign debt, realignment of the party system, grassroots movements for change, a turning-point constituent assembly, and other difficulties continue to challenge the political system. The new government faced an upsurge in demands, with a precarious ability to govern and a weak economy. As Sarney himself said in a major address to the nation in July 1985, "I have inherited the greatest political crisis in Brazilian history, the largest foreign debt in the world, and the greatest internal debt and inflation we have ever had."[9]

More than the previous military government, the Sarney administration will have to respond to internal pressures on the foreign debt issue and to the "social debt" owed to the millions in the poorest classes, which have experienced the greatest deprivations. There is considerable social agreement that this response will be one of the most important measures of the quality of the democratic institutions of the New Republic. The large income disparity could threaten political stability and points up the political and social limits to economic austerity when a large percentage of the population fails to earn a survival wage. Those previously excluded from even a modest standard of living must be given a stake in society. Social and political stability under civilian rule, as well as social justice, depend upon social reforms and an economic adjustment that encourages economic growth, reactivation of stagnant industrial plants, and domestic capital accumulation. In this sense, longer-term resolution of the foreign debt issue and success in foreign trade will be crucial for Brazil's democracy and its relations with the United States. Ultimately, Brazil's debt will have to be handled politically as part of a system of international financial reform. In the meantime, a narrowly orthodox monetarist financial view of Brazil based upon quarterly statements would endanger its social fabric and its broader shared interests with the United States and the rest of the Western world.

Notes

1. The bureaucratic-authoritarian political system of this period was best analyzed in Alfred Stepan (ed.), *Authoritarian Brazil: Origins, Policies, and Future* (New Haven: Yale University Press, 1973). At that time, few, if any, close observers foresaw the process of political liberalization that is the topic of this present volume.

2. Alexandre de S. C. Barros, "The Changing Role of the State in Brazil: The Technocratic Military Alliance," paper presented at the sixth annual meeting of the Latin American Studies Association, Atlanta, Georgia, March 25–28, 1976, p. 11.

3. Riordan Roett, *Brazil: Politics in a Patrimonial Society*, Rev. ed. (New York: Praeger, 1984), especially pp. 35–47 and 96–122.

4. Sérgio Henrique Abranches, "Crise e Transicão: Uma Interpretacão do Momento Político Nacional," *Dados* 25, no. 3 (1982): 317–323.

5. Bolivar Lamounier, "Opening Through Elections: Will the Brazilian Case Become a Paradigm?" The "black hole" analogy was used by Golbery himself in a July 1980 speech to the National War College (ESG) in Rio.

6. Walder de Góes, "Sôbre a Gênese da Abertura Política," paper prepared for the Sixth Annual Meeting of the Associacão Nacional de Pós-Graduacão e Pesquisa em Ciências Sociais, Nova Friburgo, RJ, October 1982, pp. 3–6.

7. These case-by-case modifications of the rules to benefit the holders of power did not always attain the desired results, as shown by David V. Fleischer, "Contitutional and Electoral Engineering in Brazil: A Double-Edged Sword, 1964–1982," *Inter-American Economic Affairs* 37, no. 4 (Spring 1984): 3–36.

8. A useful overview of the debate during this period is found in Marcus Faria Figueiredo and José Antônio Borges Cheibub, "A Abertura Política de 1973 a 1981: Quem Disse o Quê, Quando-Inventário de um Debate," *Boletim Informativo e Bibliográfico de Ciências Sociais,* no. 14 (Second Semester 1982): 29–61.

9. "Sarney Arma seu Jôgo," *Veja,* July 31, 1985, p. 22.

1

From Moment to Moment: The Political Transition in Brazil, 1977–1981

Enrique A. Baloyra

Democratic Transition: The Theoretical Crucible

Conceptual Models of Brazilian Politics

Scholarly interpretations of the Brazilian authoritarian regime of 1964–1985 may be grouped into three major types. Despite their more obvious differences these three perspectives share one implicit assumption concerning the nature of political authoritarianism in contemporary Brazil, namely, that the military regime would be long-lasting. As a matter of fact, comprehensive and very sophisticated analyses of the military regime were published when the dynamics of liberalization described in this essay were already set in motion. We are dealing, therefore, with a process that took the scholarly community somewhat by surprise, and one that was viewed with skepticism and suspicion by some.

The Continuity Paradigm. A first group of students of authoritarian Brazil emphasizes the degree to which the regime drew upon precedent. These scholars believe in the continued relevance of a corporative model that evolved between 1930 and 1945[1] and consisted of a bureaucratic state sustained by the patronal political authority of the public sector.[2] There are vast similarities between this *Estado Nôvo* of Getúlio Vargas and the post-1964 regime.[3] Therefore, according to these scholars contemporary Brazilian politics may best be interpreted as an attempt to adapt a basically authoritarian polity to the minimal exigencies of formal democracy.[4] Two implications of this interpretation are that the installation of a military regime in 1964 was a restoration of sorts and that attempts to reconcile authoritarian and democratic forms have produced two structurally similar regimes: "strong" democracies (*democraduras*) and "benign" authoritarian regimes (*dictablandas*).[5] This interpretation presupposes additional complications since analysts must determine whether the outcomes of particular episodes forecast the prevalence of one tendency—*dura* or *blanda* (hard or soft line)—over the other. We find this dilemma in Ronald Schneider's treatment of the manipulated democracy of Humberto Castelo Branco, the Castelo dictatorship, and Costa e Silva's failure to humanize the regime.[6] This dilemma is also latent in Peter Flynn's evaluation of the Geisel government, which he believed to be rent by the internal contradictions of authoritarian control.[7]

Recent cases of transition in Mediterranean Europe and in South America suggest that if a political regime is to change from dictatorship to democracy then, at some point in time, the government constituted under authoritarian auspices will stop acting arbitrarily and cease to engage in systematic and severe deprivations of human rights. In a transition to democracy, restraint ultimately prevails over arbitrariness and recklessness. James Madison believed that "good government" means the absence of tyranny and that tyranny is the systematic and severe deprivation of basic civil liberties. Kalman Silvert developed this further when he defined democracy as "the process of the contained use of reason operating through accountable institutions."[8] Combining Madison's and Silvert's definitions we arrive at a relatively universal and culture-free view of "good government," a designation identified with democracy in Brazil and in other Iberic and Iberoamerican countries in recent years.

Despite the very elegant and pertinent reservations advanced by those suscribing to the continuity paradigm, it is possible to identify and utilize relevant criteria to mark the transition from tyranny to good government in Brazil. I will focus on when and how Brazilian military governments began to use their public powers with more restraint, how this enabled intermediary institutions to reassert themselves, and how the military lost control of the process in ultimately being confronted by two distinct choices: a costly involution and retreat toward authoritarianism or a full-fledged transition to democracy.

The Paradigm of Breakdown. An alternative point of view also acknowledges the momentum of corporatist precedent, but emphasizes the interplay of a series of causal elements that bring about discontinuity. One of the leading proponents of this paradigm, Guillermo O'Donnell, wrote about an "elective affinity" between democratic breakdown and the "deepening" of industrial capitalism in South America.[9] O'Donnell's formulation has been questioned in the case of Brazil.[10] But even his critics recognize that the Brazilian regime of 1964–1985 may have been the paradigmatic case of bureaucratic-authoritarianism.[11] One finds some elements of the continuity paradigm in the work of Alfred Stepan, but he does not treat corporatism as culture. Instead Stepan views a corporatist installation as a defensive policy response undertaken by the elite.[12]

Among those subscribing to the paradigm of breakdown, Ronald Schneider is undoubtedly the most explicit and exhaustive, going to considerable lengths to discuss the applicability of different models of modernization and political development to the emergence of the Brazilian military regime.[13] One finds a critical utilization of the literature of comparative politics by O'Donnell and Stepan that is far from a simplistic rehash of structural-functional theories gone awry in South America. Their theoretical inspiration is derived from the seminal contributions of Juan Linz, which the scholars in this group reformulated to develop a series of analytical models that describe how democracies deteriorate and fall.[14] Although some of these models proffer useful insights, one must apply them very carefully in the case of authoritarian Brazil as it is not clear when the regime broke down.

The Paradigm of Rupture. The third approach is quite a contrast to the other two. It brings together a heterogeneous group of authors sharing the belief that the "new style of authoritarianism" resulted from a fundamental rupture with the past. Where others saw crises of government or of regime, these scholars see a crisis of the state itself, which is engendered by late, dependent, and peripheral capitalism. Responding to this crisis, a new class alliance is formed by the more internationalized sectors of the bourgeoisie, the military, and representatives of transnational enterprises. This coalition seeks to promote a new phase of capitalism through the exceptional state.

One conspicuous element within this third perspective is that, despite the very similar causal factors identified by individual scholars, opinion was almost evenly divided between those who considered the new regimes fascist and those who viewed them as something else. Luis Maira suggested that the new authoritarian regimes of South America should not be considered fascist since they lacked key definitional characteristics associated with classical fascism.[15] Vania Bambiria and Theotônio dos Santos countered that the question was not how many such characteristics a particular case had but, instead, how many of the *essential* characteristics were present and operative.[16]

Totalitarian or Authoritarian? To be sure, key elements of classical fascism were absent from the new authoritarianism in South America. But this debate reflected a deeper concern about the nature of these regimes. At issue was the extent to which the regimes were so close to totalitarianism that they could not be expected to evolve, deteriorate, and decay peacefully. Regardless of this disagreement, scholars in this group believed that since the new authoritarian regimes had been inaugurated through a fundamental rupture of extant patterns of state-society relations they would not break down except through a rupture of the relations they had created.

In the case of Brazil there is a virtual unanimity that the *inauguration* of the regime came during its most repressive phase, more than four years after the *installation* of the military government. This delay suggests that either there was considerable disagreement within the military about which project to implement or a complete absence of a project at the time of installation. More important, one must ask what the military sought to consolidate following that inauguration. It is difficult to reconcile the interpretation that it tried to consolidate a fascist regime with the subsequent facts of *abertura* (political opening). Whereas 1968–1974 has been viewed as an unintended or inevitable "descent into dictatorship," 1974–1985 has been described as a "liberalization" that became a democratic transition. Therefore decompression (*distensão*) in its original conception may be viewed as an attempt to return the regime to the configuration of 1964–1968. This would imply that the military recognized that the repressive phase of 1968–1974 could not, in itself, become the regime. In other words, it sought to consolidate a regime that was not a total rupture with the past.

The Analytical Framework

This chapter is a contextual analysis of the behavior of the Brazilian military from 1977 to 1981. It discusses three key events: the selection of General João Baptista Figueiredo as the new president of Brazil in December 1977; the *pacote de abril* (April package) of 1977; and the political reform of October 1978. The focus is on the contradictions affecting the authoritarian regime and on the relationships among (1) the military government, (2) the high command of the Brazilian armed forces, (3) the political parties and the Congress, and (4) the civil society. The discussion traces the changing configuration of the regime during the last two years of Ernesto Geisel's presidency and the first two of Figueiredo's. The analysis seeks (1) to describe how the carefully controlled *distensão*, or decompression, that the military had envisioned became a less manageable *abertura*, or political opening to democracy; and (2) to identify the conditions that made this possible.

The Contradictions of Authoritarian Control in Brazil

Six basic contradictions of political organization are inherent in all forms of domination. These result from interactions among four loci of political activity: the state, the government, the political community, and the society. By *state* I mean the scheme of political domination used to invest a government with public power and to legitimize how that power is to be used to regulate social and economic relations. *Government* refers to a network of public officials dependent on a chief executive, the members of which participate in the policymaking process and depend, for their tenure in office, upon the tenure of the chief executive and/or his ability to govern effectively. The *political community* consists of groups and individuals who enjoy citizens' rights. Finally, *society* is a network of institutions through which groups and individuals participate in economic production and distribution, exchange values among them-selves, and relate to one another in relatively stable and predictable ways.

Interactions among these four arenas of political activity create con-tradictions that must be addressed by individuals, groups, and institutions. Democratic regimes are built on the premise that these inevitable contradictions can be managed, whereas totalitarian and authoritarian regimes seek to eliminate them altogether. The kinds of dominant contradictions affecting different regimes and different forms of the state vary with the mode of production, the political culture and political tradition of the nation, and the cleavage structure of the society. Contradictions are not simply acute cases of "interest conflict," but relatively permanent and insoluble dilemmas of politics. All societies and forms of the state, not just the capitalist ones, are subject to contradictions.

Each contradiction concerns the relationships among the actions taking place in the four basic loci of political activity. These relationships involve the allocation of a given value (citizenship, power, or sovereignty) or determine the appropriateness of a function that relates the values (ideology, leadership, or legality). State and society confront each other over their relative autonomy. Issues debated at the societal level may be displaced toward the political community and thereby become activated. This may or may not be connected to changes in the criteria defining the notion of citizenship and the groups and individuals to which it applies. Actors in the government and in the political community seek to prevail in questions of public policy. The government may or may not be able to function within the parameters of its own legality and within the sphere in which its decisions are binding on the society. In turn, state institutions may find it difficult to justify their actions vis-à-vis the society and the political community. As a result of these contradictions, government and regime may or may not be considered legitimate, as judged by extant ideological standards. A graphic representation of the theoretical framework that I have discussed in very succinct form is presented in Figure 1.1.

This simplified representation of the dynamics of political contradictions presupposes a parsimonious number of recursive relationships and a structural rather than a more rigidly causal scheme. Five assumptions may be made about these contradictions in capitalist societies: (1) the primary contradiction is between state and society, that is, between hegemony and autonomy; (2) the government is the most unstable element in the configuration, given the disruptive impacts of the market, the business cycle, and political competition; (3) the state is the most stable element; (4) relations among the government, the society, and the political community are the more crucial ones in defining the nature of the regime; and (5) relations among the state, the government, and the political community are the main loci of activity in a process of transition from one type of regime to another. The last two assumptions presuppose that the state is the most relevant causal actor providing for the stability of the regime, whereas the society becomes an important causal factor in the dynamics of change. In other words, state and society are relevant agents of stability and change, respectively.

Some additional observations are necessary. First, it is imperative to qualify the appropriate categories of political objects. For example, sociologist Fernando Henrique Cardoso has recommended that the term

FIGURE 1.1
The Contradictions of Political Domination

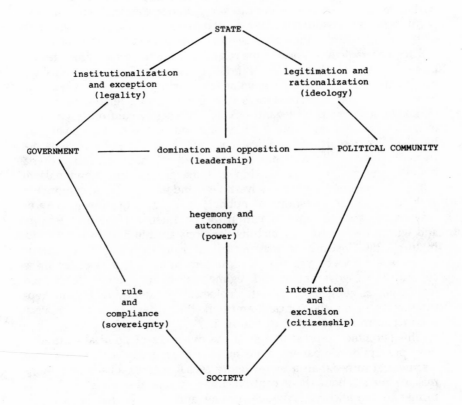

NOTE: The figure does not totally conform to the principle governing the
        graphic representation of causal relationships. For the sake of
        parsimony, relevant exogenous variables, such as mode of production and
        political culture, are not specified. Therefore the model depicted
        here is not hierarchical and is represented as an "underdetermined" set
        of relationships. Given that this is a general model, no direction of
        causality is specified, and the relationships depicted are assumed to
        be recursive.

"bureaucratic-authoritarian" be applied to the regime, not the state.[17] A
related problem concerns the characterization of a regime in terms of
only one supposedly dominant feature. Corporatist installation, national
security ideology, technobureaucratic coalition, and *desenvolvimentista*
(loosely, progrowth) orientation certainly describe important facets of
a regime but could be misleading if elevated to the status of an overall

characterization. Third, even though it seems logical to assume that regimes are characterized by an overall congruence, this may not be the case. Kalman Silvert suggested that

> a lack of fit among elements within social situations is the usual case, and "harmony" is rare. Legal systems only loosely describe behavior, morality, and power relations. Members of social classes do not have similar ideologies or even more basic values. . . . We need a word other than the negatively weighed *disjunction* to describe our normal inconsistency.

He added that

> institutional differentiation does not occur evenly or uniformly as societies "develop." . . . A major problem involves the nature of social synthesis, the ways in which a seeming lack of "fit" among major social units is given sense within a synthetic ordering of the entire situation.[18]

Cardoso may have been thinking along these lines when he illustrated one aspect of the disjunction found in the Brazilian authoritarian regime. It would be incorrect, he observed,

> to suppose that the state apparatus operates as a *unified whole* in Latin America. The absence of a party that could bind the system together and of a truly totalitarian ideology prevents the technobureaucracy and office holders from becoming committed to the military ideology of state grandeur. . . . These features make the functioning of bureaucratic-authoritarian regimes less consistent than it looks at first glance.[19]

This is especially important in a case like Brazil's, where the heterogeneity of the society and the diversity of norms that guided individual and group behavior under the regime created a very fluid situation. Irrespective of the regime's authoritarian nature and of the objectives of government policy, gaps emerged between the blueprint for government action and the outcomes of government initiatives. These gaps increased the incoherence of the regime, particularly after the election of 1974 and during the transition period from controlled *distensão* to the more chaotic and uncertain stage of *abertura*.

The Brazilian Model of Authoritarian Domination

When referring to Brazil during 1964–1985 I am talking about a capitalist state of exception in which a military government exercised dictatorial rule, assisted by a coalition of elites whose collaboration was sought because of their presumed expertise, functional relevance, and ideological compatibility with a strategy of legitimation based on the doctrine of national security and on a model of national development inspired by a mixture of neo-liberal and neo-mercantilist doctrines. The authoritarianism of the regime was manifested in three types of inter-actions: (1) in the virtual representation and controlled participation of groups and individuals in a political community restricted to the pro-pertied and managerial classes; (2) in the ad hoc and arbitrary nature of the policymaking process, and (3) in the use of intimidation and repression, whenever necessary, to overcome the opposition of members of that community and/or the resistance of those excluded from it. The basic elements defining the regime are *dictatorial rule by a military government in a capitalist state of exception.*

There is almost unanimous agreement in the literature that the structure of the regime did not crystallize until the passage of Institutional Act No. 5 in December 1968.[20] However, relatively soon after the coup on March 31 and April 1, 1964, in the very first Institutional Act issued by the military, there was an unequivocal declaration of the kind of regime that the military had in mind:

> The Revolution is not seeking to legitimize itself through Congress. Rather, it is the latter which receives legitimacy from this Institutional Act, by means of the exercise of that Constituent Power inherent in all revolutions.[21]

Changes brought about by Institutional Act No. 2 of October 24, 1965, granted the president powers to suspend Congress and govern by decree, enabling him to issue "complementary acts" as deemed necessary and broadening his power to decree a state of siege. The act allowed the president to fire civil servants; to remove elected officials, declaring them *cassados* (without rights of political participation); and suspend a person's political rights for ten years. Institutional Act No. 2 also increased the executive's control over government expenditures, eased the procedure to amend the constitution, packed the Supreme Court and the Federal Appeals Court, extended the jurisdiction of military tribunals to cases of individuals charged under the National Security Act, and instituted the indirect election of the president by Congress.[22]

On December 13, 1968, the exceptional character of the state became more accentuated with passage of Institutional Act No. 5. Whereas Institutional Act No. 1 created the *poder constituinte* of the government in putting the state above the society, and Institutional Act No. 2 put the presidency beyond congressional restraint, Institutional Act No. 5 put the office of the presidency above the law. In this case the law was the government's own constitution of 1967, which turned out to be too confining. Institutional Act No. 5 allowed the president to recess legislative bodies, cancel elective mandates, suspend political rights and consti-tutional guarantees, set aside the right of habeas corpus, and confiscate property. Complementary Act No. 38, issued jointly, recessed Congress indefinitely.[23]

Institutional Act No. 5 formalized the exceptional nature of the state, but as early as April 9, 1964, the military had set out to create a presidential dictatorship. More powers were added through new institutional acts, but these only gave the exceptional state more definitive form. This gradual appropriation of power, which resulted in the inauguration of the regime in December 1968, is depicted in Figure 1.2. The figure describes the unfolding of these authoritarian features, tracing how, at first, the military proclaimed its nondelegated domination of the state (Institutional Act No. 1); then granted unconditional power to the military president (Institutional Act No. 2); and finally elevated him above the law (Institutional Act No. 5). The military sought to legitimize the regime through the ideology of "national security" and through the results of the economic policies of the regime. Finally, it managed to exclude labor and the popular classes from the political community, but these elements eased their way back in after 1977.

The one common characteristic of the military governments of 1964–1985 is the state of exception that began with the enactment of Institutional Act No. 1, on April 9, 1964, and ended with the swearing-in of Vice-president-elect José Sarney as acting president on March 15, 1985. During those years the Brazilian authoritarian regime may have been more or less imbued by the doctrine of national security, more or less concerned with the "internal enemy," more or less limited in its external sovereignty by dependent capitalism, and more or less embarked on monetarism or developmentalism. A genuine democratization in Brazil did not require the end of *desenvolvimentismo* nor a major change in the position of the domestic bourgeoisie within the power bloc. The process may have left intact the ideology of national security, and it certainly will not result in a society where expertise is no longer needed. But it had to produce the breakdown of the state of exception and of the presidential dictatorship created in 1964.

One must seek the origins of the Brazilian *distensão* in the results of the election of 1974, which repudiated the policies of the administration of Emílio Garrastazú Médici; in the increasing discontent with the shortcomings of the economic model; and in the growing realization within the military that it could not consolidate the regime except through a liberalization of the very harsh conditions imposed by Médici. *Abertura* later came about as a result of the military's inability to manage *distensão* as a process of controlled liberalization.

The Military Conundrum

A New Contradiction

Traditionally the Brazilian military has fulfilled the role of a *poder moderador* (moderating power), which, under the constitutions of 1891, 1934, and 1946, put it at the crossroads of two important contradictions

FIGURE 1.2
Political Contradictions in the Brazilian Regime, 1964-1985

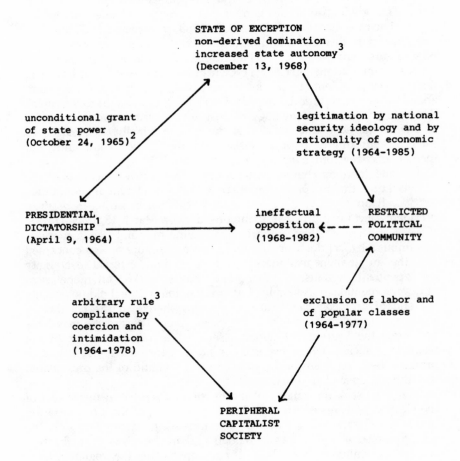

STATE OF EXCEPTION
non-derived domination
increased state autonomy[3]
(December 13, 1968)

unconditional grant
of state power[2]
(October 24, 1965)

legitimation by national
security ideology and by
rationality of economic
strategy (1964-1985)

PRESIDENTIAL
DICTATORSHIP[1]
(April 9, 1964)

ineffectual
opposition
(1968-1982)

RESTRICTED
POLITICAL
COMMUNITY

arbitrary rule[3]
compliance by
coercion and
intimidation
(1964-1978)

exclusion of labor and
of popular classes
(1964-1977)

PERIPHERAL
CAPITALIST
SOCIETY

[1]By Institutional Act No. 1
[2]By Institutional Act No. 2
[3]By Institutional Act No. 5

involving state-government relations and state-society tensions (see Figure 1.1).[24] The military owed the president obedience within the limits of the law (*obediência dentro dos limites da lei*), which gave it the opportunity to decide whether the president himself was acting within those limits. The military did not interpret this law on its own, but also by taking into account the exigencies put to it by groups and individuals, as in the crises of 1930 (against Washington Luís), in 1945 and 1954 (against Getúlio Vargas), and in 1961 and 1964 (against João Goulart). Traditionally the right to overthrow a president did not imply the right to assume power for a prolonged period.

The doctrine of national security had a profound impact on the redefinition of this role through "a new professionalism of internal security and national development."[25] The military theorists from the National War College (Escola Superior de Guerra—ESG) were not left alone to decide how to evolve a new legitimacy for this new role. Their technocratic allies provided "positive foundations of the legitimacy of the regime . . . given by the quality of the exercise of power, that is, by its actions especially in the economic area; during a first stage, by the *rationality* of the decisions and . . . (later) by its results in terms of economic development."[26]

But once in control of the government, military presidents and their colleagues at the Planalto Palace in Brasília realized that they were confronted by a new contradiction in Brazilian politics, namely, their relationship with the military institution. One can trace the evolution of the Brazilian regime in terms of this contradiction. In essence, the new contradiction between the military in the barracks and the military in the government resulted from the very installation of the regime in April 1964. The attempt to monopolize public power created a duality of state and governmental functions for the military. This duality would have divided it no matter how popular or legitimate the governments because the dictatorship created a tension between a government that had to manipulate discipline and hierarchy to control a state institution (the military) and that very state institution that could not, under any circumstances, perform the functions of an official party without destroying itself in the process. This contradiction made the new Brazilian regime relatively unstable, particularly in relation to the question of presidential succession.

I suggest that between 1964 and 1968 actors within the military institution had some leverage over the military government. Castelo Branco had to capitulate to the demands of radical nationalists and hardliners and enact Institutional Act No. 2. Similarly, President Artur da Costa e Silva had to go back on his promise to respect Congress and not only suspend Congress but also enact Institutional Act No. 5. Then, during the tenure of Emílio Garrastazú Médici, who exercised his exceptional powers in full, power began to shift back toward the president and his advisers (known as the Planalto group). This more advantageous position in their relations with the military institution gave presidents Geisel and Figueiredo the opportunity to impose a controlled political liberalization on their more recalcitrant colleagues. Geisel began *distensão* to arrest the deterioration suffered by the regime under Médici and to prevent its breakdown. This process became an *abertura* under Figueiredo.

But Geisel and Figueiredo invested most of their influence in this process and had relatively little left over to govern effectively.

The Geisel Succession

The nomination and indirect election of General João Baptista Figueiredo to the presidency of Brazil illustrate how the "institutional contradiction" operated to destabilize the military government. I propose that 1977–1978 provided the only opportunity when the Planalto group could select the new president, manage the tensions within the military to prevent serious divisions, and neutralize rival coalitions combining officers and politicians. I also suggest that many of the actions of Geisel and of Figueiredo are more understandable if placed within the context of these overriding concerns.

In early 1977 four officers were mentioned as possible successors of Geisel: Figueiredo, who was head of the National Intelligence Service (Serviço Nacional das Informações—SNI); Army Minister General Sílvio Frota; Second Army Commander General Euler Bentes Monteiro; and Supreme Military Court Judge General Rodrigo Otávio Jordão Ramos. Only the SNI chief and the army minister were taken seriously; Generals Bentes Monteiro and Jordão Ramos appeared more inclined to support a genuine process of democratic transition.

General Figueiredo had a solid position. He had been chief of staff of the Third Army and also of the SNI, where he had been a close collaborator of General Golbery do Couto e Silva, the founder of the ESG. He had been chief of the military cabinet and secretary general of the National Security Council (Conselho de Segurança Nacional—CSN) during the presidency of Médici. When General Golbery became head of Geisel's civilian household and Figueiredo head of the SNI, both men worked together closely. Therefore Figueiredo had ties both to Sorbonnists like Golbery and to the hardliners.

General Sílvio Frota was certainly not a *castelista* (a supporter of the ideas of General Castelo Branco, first president after the 1964 coup, a moderate who supported military intervention limited in time and depth of change). He was relatively close to the more hardline element, but he was not one of them. Geisel had chosen him to succeed a bona fide hardliner, General Dale Coutinho, in part to prevent the nomination of another hardliner by the army high command. As commander of the First Army, Frota had opposed the use of torture and, after the murders of Vladimir Herzog and Manuel Fiel Filho, he stood by Geisel when the president fired Second Army Commander General Ednardo D'Avila Melo, whose troops were responsible for the murders. Frota wanted to become the irresistible candidate of the *institution*, a tactic utilized successfully by Costa e Silva but unsuccessfully by Costa's Minister of Interior General Afonso Albuquerque Lima. Apparently President Geisel believed that Frota lacked what it took to run "the club," that is, the 110 or so generals in active service. During 1977 Geisel sought to develop support for Figueiredo gradually and to delay the announcement of his decision in order to avoid the role of lame duck.

Frota counted on the endorsement of General Antônio da Silva Campos, chief of Army Intelligence (the Centro de Informações do Exército—CIE); Army Secretary General Ênio Pinheiro; Army Chief of Staff Fritz Azevêdo Manso; First Army Commander José Pinto de Araújo Rabello; *castelista* generals like Arnoldo Calderari and Ariel Pacca de Fonseca; and officers in the line of promotion to *general de exército* like César Montagna. Much of this support was "soft," as events demonstrated later, but it was a barometer of military discontent with the perceived arrogance, prepotence, and corruption of the Planalto group. Criticism of the Planalto group focused on Golbery, Press Secretary Humberto Esmeraldo Barreto (a close confidant of Geisel), and Professor Heitor de Aquino (Geisel's private secretary). Military discontent was exacerbated by the fact that Figueiredo was a three-star general (*de divisão*) and relatively low in the order of promotion to four-star (*de exército*). His selection was interpreted as a political decision and resented as a hierarchical transgression.

The Planalto group also had to worry about Frota's civilian support. Some ARENA (National Renovating Alliance) congressmen, led by Marcelino Linhares, the government party's deputy leader in the Chamber, were asking for the participation of the military high command in the selection of the official candidate. They were very concerned with the outcome of the 1978 congressional elections and saw the Frota candidacy as an opportunity to have an impact on the politics of succession and to prevent a repeat of the electoral fiasco of 1974. Linhares infuriated Geisel when he accused the Planalto of wanting to prevent the high command from participating in the succession process—a charge repeated later by ARENA Senator José de Magalhães Pinto. Geisel described Linhares and his ARENA colleagues in a speech as *vivandeiras impenitentes* (literally, unrepentant camp followers).

The Planalto group wanted to give the army minister sufficient latitude to avoid making him a victim and as little as possible so that Frota's "institutional" candidacy could be blocked. Above all, the Planalto group wanted to prevent a serious rift between itself and the military institution and to thwart any civilian interference that could exacerbate this contradiction. It was concerned with signs of discontent in the barracks, such as the "colonels' movement." In April 1977 some officers tried to approach President Geisel at the Vila Militar in Rio to present him with a letter requesting a return to the barracks. The letter accused "a group in government" of using charges of subversion to protect their own interests. Geisel refused to acknowledge the document. In May the group adopted the name Movimento Militar Democrático Constitucionalista (MMDC), the same name as was used by the São Paulo (*paulista*) movement that led a revolt against Getúlio Vargas in 1932, and issued a manifesto signed by 110 middle-level officers asking for democratization, a freely elected constituent assembly, political amnesty, judicial independence, due process, abolition of the institutional acts, and a provisional government organized along corporatist lines. It repeated its attacks against a corrupt *cúpula*—i.e., the Planalto—that was using the army as a praetorian guard.

Frota's chances depended, in part, on his ability to unify the different currents of military discontent, but he needed time plus the support of pivotal figures. On October 12, taking advantage of the fact that some of Frota's supporters were out of town, Geisel summoned the army minister to the Planalto Palace and demanded his resignation. When Frota refused, Geisel fired him. Returning members of the high command went straight back to the palace to witness the swearing in of Frota's replacement, Third Army Commander General Fernando Belfort Bethlem, a strict disciplinarian.

Frota's immediate options were very narrow. He tried to rally support at Army Headquarters, but a coup was out of the question. Geisel had effective military control of the capital, having placed his nephew-in-law, General Roberto Franca, in charge of the strongest armored brigade in town. Frota's best hope was to maintain his candidacy, presenting himself as the victim of the same group that was generating so much discontent within the ranks. He flew to Rio, where he was well received by colleagues who commiserated with him. But Frota went public, circulating a list of ninety-nine "communists" in high places, mounting a frontal attack on the government, and questioning the legitimacy of the military government—instead of challenging Geisel's right to punish him for participating in the succession process as an "institutional" candidate.[27] This challenge exposed the raw nerve of the dominant contradiction of the regime, enabling Geisel to present Frota's actions as indiscipline and threatening to the integrity of the institution.

The fact that Frota did not pursue his candidacy after his removal implies that his movement was rooted in the military institution and that it responded to attempts by officers to make the government accountable to the institution. To be sure, he had some support in ARENA and in business circles but once removed from his post, once cut off from his base of power in the Army Ministry, he was absolutely useless to his supporters, who had to look for another alternative to Figueiredo.

General Hugo Abreu, chief of President Geisel's military household, was a veteran of the antiguerrilla campaign of 1972–1974 in the Araguaia region. He had joined Frota and Justice Minister Armando Falcão in demanding stern treatment for those advocating a more genuine liberalization. He had been Frota's point man within the Planalto Palace and, unable to prevent Frota's downfall, Abreu stayed on, trying to block Figueiredo's nomination from within. Therefore Abreu was not exactly a democratic "aperturist." On January 1, 1978, Abreu stated his objections to the Figueiredo candidacy in a lengthy report. Shortly thereafter Geisel summoned him, and, in the presence of Golbery and Barreto, the president told Abreu that Figueiredo was the official candidate. While Abreu circulated his report around Army Headquarters trying to rally support for the move to block Figueiredo, Geisel started to poll the high command by phone. By late afternoon on January 4, Geisel had commitments from all armed forces ministers and from most of the generals with full voting rights. Geisel made his choice public, and Abreu resigned.

Abreu's January 1978 report and October 1978 letter to *O Estado de São Paulo* addressed the issue of corruption first, referring alternately to a "highly corrupt establishment group" and to "an oligarchy compromised with the hidden interests of multinational groups." The fight against corruption had been a paramount concern of the military conspirators of 1964. That objective, according to Abreu, had been compromised and a more "democratic" consultation was required if the revolution were to survive. His report had insisted that it was technically impossible to promote Figueiredo before the ARENA convention. The implication was that military hierarchy would be compromised for the sake of political expediency, and, worse still, that it would be compromised to create the candidacy of a man who had been spying on his fellow officers.

With Frota and Abreu gone, Trade and Industry Minister Severo Gomes tried to promote the candidacy of General Bentes Monteiro. Gomes delivered a few nationalist speeches at the ESG but, like Frota, he went public trying to rally support for Bentes among the business community and *paulista* circles. He was forced to resign in February 1978, and Bentes retired quietly in March, amid the protests of those nationalists around him who were still infuriated by Gomes's firing.

The Bentes candidacy did not really gather momentum until ARENA nominated Figueiredo in April 1978. Discontent generated by the imposition of Figueiredo, the firing of Frota, and the dismissal of Abreu made some officers turn to the MDB (Brazilian Democratic Movement) to ask the opposition party to launch a military candidate. The three names suggested by these officers to the MDB included Abreu, a hardline nationalist; General Jordão Ramos, a legalist; and General Pacca de Fonseca, a *castelista* (moderate) nationalist. These variegated choices underline the great ideological disarray and political confusion among these officers but do not belittle the significance of their action. In fact, they were asking the opposition to nominate a military man against a military government.

Bentes took a route different from Frota's. In May 1978 he made his move. In order to present a contrast to Figueiredo, who had told the ARENA convention in April that he was not a democrat, Bentes declared himself a democrat, in favor of the rule of law and of direct elections for all posts. He promised that he would serve for only three years, and he made it clear that he wanted to become the presidential candidate of the opposition MDB. The MDB, therefore, found itself having to choose between an ambiguous *distensão* offered to them by the military government and a more generous *abertura* offered by a dissident military officer who wanted to be its presidential candidate. Following a great deal of maneuvering, including attempts to form a coalition with the ARENA faction of José de Magalhães Pinto, the MDB leadership offered Bentes the presidential nomination in early August.

The Bentes campaign had the flavor of an electoral conspiracy and was an important precedent in several respects. First, the candidacy itself was an ominous development for the Planalto. The short and long of it was that officers in active service had gone outside (military) institutional channels to present the candidacy of an officer who advocated the end of the regime. Second, the succession process itself could not be counted on to avoid similar occurrences in the future. Nothing could prevent ARENA members of the electoral college from going over to the opposition, joining with the MDB to form a majority coalition, and electing an opposition candidate. Finally, the government had hoped that once committed to certain institutional practices, such as relatively competitive elections, it could manipulate them in its favor. But as early as 1977 Geisel found it necessary to enact the *pacote de abril* and to create the *senadores biônicos* to prevent a repetition of the electoral disaster of 1974 and supposedly to put the fate of the regime beyond the reach of dissident officers and party politicians.

The Context of the Pacote and the Political Reforms

At the time of the Frota firing, President Ernesto Geisel issued a stern warning: Brazil was only a "relative democracy." In December 1977 Geisel declared that the main obstacles to democratic improvement in Brazil were the intransigence of sincere revolutionaries and the irresponsibility of the opposition.[28] These statements identify the sources of Geisel's basic problems at the time, within the military and in the political community, on the issue of succession and on the question of the *distensão*, respectively.

To be sure, the political evolution of Brazil between 1977 and 1981 suggests that some elements of a democratic transition were in place. More specifically, there was a serious effort to discontinue the institutionalized practice of violent political repression that had dominated the administration of Emílio Garrastazú Médici, and the government was trying to prevent further abuses along this line. As a result of this, a new context was emerging in which the government seemed committed to more civilized treatment of the opposition but not to the point of sharing power. The actions of the Geisel government provoked irritation among hardline military elements, who saw little value in fair treatment for "defeated adversaries" and believed that such treatment created expectations within the opposition for further improvement. Both hardliners and oppositionists sought to influence the course of the *distensão*.

Geisel's strategy sought to maximize the control of the Planalto group over decompression to prevent a breakdown of the regime, either as a result of an inopportune confrontation with the hardliners or a takeover of the process by the opposition. In order to accomplish this he could have tried to create a transitional coalition but, evidently, he disliked the choice of available partners: the "sincere revolutionaries" in the barracks and the "irresponsible politicians" in the Congress. Lacking this support coalition, as well as a tacit a priori agreement with the opposition about the parameters of the transition, Geisel had to confront a generic dilemma of these processes all by himself. That is, he faced the problem of how to evolve more democratic institutional practices from a basically authoritarian blueprint. The *pacote de abril* of 1977 and the political reforms of 1978 illustrate how Geisel floundered with this plan.

These two initiatives were intimately related since they were but two aspects of Geisel's strategy for *distensão*. The *pacote* showed Geisel's unwillingness to allow the opposition to play a more important role in the process of transition. The political reforms of 1978 revealed his desire to end the more unsavory aspects of the arbitrary rule of the military regime. The *pacote* subordinated the outcome of the 1978 elections to the *distensão* proposed by Geisel. Geisel wanted a measured and gradual restoration of rights that would not be accelerated by a Congress with increased powers and/or dominated by the opposition, and he wanted to prevent his colleagues from becoming too divided over the scope and nature of the transition. Finally, he was trying to accomplish these objectives while engineering his own succession, the only president to do this successfully during the period from 1964 to 1985.

During the early months of 1977 Geisel was faced with an increasing number of demands to end the state of exception. Many of the groups in the political community participated in this campaign. Given the limitations of the electoral process and the inability of ARENA and the MDB to become real agents of intermediation and interest representation, these groups had to address the government directly. This would ultimately create the effect that the Planalto group was trying to avoid in the first place, namely, a direct confrontation with societal groups outside the "legal" political community and in a context of political activation.

The Role of the Business Community. The Brazilian bourgeoisie was split on the question of *distensão*. Some of the business community came out in favor of democratization. Representatives of powerful national groups like Cláudio Bardella, chairman of the Associação Brasileira da Indústria de Base, were incensed by the firing of Trade and Industry Minister Severo Gomes, who had advocated changes in the economic model favorable to the domestic sector of the national bourgeoisie. Nationalist military figures also had asked for greater official attention to the domestic market. In Gomes's case the demand for economic change appeared to be linked to a demand for a genuine *abertura*. This was an option that could become attractive to a bourgeoisie chafing under the orthodox economic policies of Finance Minister Mário Henrique Simonsen, basically hostile to statism (*estatização*), and worried about the denationalization of industry and the deteriorating economic situation. However, one must not exaggerate the extent to which the bourgeosie was prepared to present a project of its own as an alternative to military domination. According to Eli Diniz, even the "new" entrepreneurs were only seeking to increase their bargaining power and not to challenge the military regime.[29]

Some *paulista* businessmen took their case directly to the military. In February 1977 Papa Júnior, Chairman of the São Paulo Chamber of Commerce, followed up a visit to Figueiredo by issuing a statement claiming that most industrialists supported a return to democracy. In March Einor Kok contacted Second Army Commander General Dilermando Gomes Monteiro to express similar views. Luís Eulálio Bueno Vidigal, president of the Association of Vehicle Parts and Components Manufacturers (SINDIPECAS) and a friend of Antônio Delfim Neto, declared that the country could not be run like a barracks in times of economic difficulty. In August Roberto de Abreu Sodré, former ARENA governor of São Paulo, took advantage of a trip to Rio Grande do Sul to lecture Third Army Commander Belfort Bethlem on the need for *abertura*. Belfort invited Sodré to speak to his senior staff officers.

The military did not take these entreaties lightly. In August many of the speeches delivered at Army Day celebrations were very combative. Third Army Commander General Mário Ramos de Alencar reminded businesspeople that, "We try to give you the necessary tranquility and order so that you can invest and produce." General Dilermando repeated the Sorbonnist conception of the social pact in more direct language: "While you create wealth, the army creates security."[30] First Army Commander General José Pinto de Araújo Rabello expressed concern about the divisive impact that the calls for *abertura* were having on the armed forces. Following Sodré's visit, Belfort Bethlem circulated a private document in which he lamented "the media campaign aimed to demoralize the authorities" with *civilista* calls for a return to the barracks.[31]

Others in the business community were more audacious in promoting the presidential candidacy of one of their own, Senator José de Magalhães Pinto. This candidacy was legitimized in terms of the candidate's identification with the objectives of the revolution. In 1964, as governor of Minas Gerais, he had been a leading civilian figure in the coup against Goulart. He was owner-president of the Banco Nacional, Brazil's third largest bank. He had been a close collaborator of Costa e Silva, serving as foreign minister from 1967 to 1969. His influence had declined during Médici's term, but he had made a comeback with his election to the Senate in 1970. He had been president of the Senate and of Congress from 1975 to 1976. In sum, Magalhães felt that these credentials, plus the importance of his native Minas Gerais in Brazilian politics, made him a leading civilian aspirant to succeed Geisel.

In December 1977 industrialist José Ermírio de Moraes, head of the VOTORANTIM industrial group, stated that Magalhães should be allowed to campaign. This came at a time when the senator was criticizing the government, calling for direct elections to all posts and for a return to the rule of law, and insisting that he was running as a candidate of the revolution.[32] Magalhães, therefore, was appealing to the core coalition of the regime while challenging the *castelista* social pact by questioning state supremacy on economic matters. Magalhães's candidacy could have benefited from the fallout of former Frota supporters and from dissident elements within ARENA, like those led by Herbert Levy and by Paulo Pimentel. But once ARENA endorsed Figueiredo, Magalhães's only option was to compete with General Bentes Monteiro for the nomination of the MDB, a role that hardly suited the banker.

A third group of businesspeople remained on the sidelines. Mavericks like Paulo Maluf, who in 1984 followed the strategy utilized by Magalhães and became the nominee of the PDS (Democratic Social Party), remained aloof from these initiatives. He had just become chairman of the São Paulo Chamber of Commerce and would later become governor of the state. People around Delfim Neto were waiting for some indication about the role of their man in the Figueiredo administration. Finally, men who had flourished during the "economic miracle," like septuagenarian Theobaldo de Nigris, chairman of the Federação das Indústrias do Estado de São Paulo (FIESP), made some half-hearted noises about democratization but fell into step quickly.

In summary, although the pressure from business was not to be taken lightly, attempts to create an *aberturista* nationalist coalition did not attract massive support from the high command and the top business organizations. Business opposition to *estatização* alienated the *castelistas*, while demands for democratization alienated military hardliners.

The Role of Other Social Actors. The demands of other groups in and out of the political community lacked the clout that business could wield as junior partner in the official coalition. Their efforts to redefine their relationships with the government were laced with demands for democratization. Because of their relative powerlessness, the foreclosure of the electoral option, and the confrontation between the MDB and the government over the *pacote* and the political reforms, these groups were spurred into a direct confrontation with the government. The government ultimately entertained many of their demands, but the exertions of these groups were resented very deeply by the hardliners since they dealt with the end of the state of exception and with the return of the rule of law. Therefore, the government wanted to move as carefully as possible.

Early 1977 saw a flurry of demands for *abertura*. In February a group of intellectuals sent a strongly worded petition to Justice Minister Armando Falcão asking for an end to censorship. But censorship would not be eased until June 1978, and the Falcão Law (*Lei Falcão*) restricting free debate remained in full force during the election campaign of 1978. Also in February 1977 the Brazilian Lawyers' Association (Ordem dos Advogados do Brasil—OAB) condemned the continued use of torture. In March, many lawyers and judges came out against Geisel's blueprint for judicial reform, demanding reinstatement of habeas corpus for political crimes and asking for guarantees that judges would not be retired under Institutional Act No. 5. In April the new OAB chairman, Raymundo Faoro, challenged the notion that Institutional Act No. 5 empowered the president to amend the constitution. The OAB was very critical of the 1978 political reforms. Dalmo Dallari, chairman of the Archdiocese of São Paulo's Comissão de Justiça e Paz termed the reforms "a political retreat." In October 1978 the OAB was outraged by a clause in the new national security bill that allowed police to keep secret their notification to a military court that an arrest had been made. Godofredo da Silva Teles, a prominent lawyer, termed this "totalitarian, obscurantist and monstrous, devised by a small elite that proclaims itself the center of national intelligence."[33]

In reality these reforms were very modest and cautious advances, not retreats, and the rule of law was gradually coming back but at a glacial pace. The lack of even a tacit understanding between government and opposition on this and other matters rarefied the context of these ambiguous initiatives, increased tensions, and demonstrated that a transitional coalition linking government and opposition actors in favor of democratization had not crystallized at the time. It would only crystallize later, during 1983–1984, leaving the Planalto Palace out in the cold.

Relations between the Catholic Church and the government remained very strained. In February 1977 the fifteenth assembly of the National Conference of Brazilian Bishops (Conferência Nacional dos Bispos Brasileiros—CNBB) issued a document, "Christian Demands of a Political Order," which was very critical of the doctrine of national security. In February 1978 the Comissão de Justiça e Paz raised the issue of amnesty, which was taken up by the CNBB. In March the comissão issued a report, "Violence Against the Meek," denouncing the institutionalized use of torture. In April the CNBB issued another condemnation of national security. These pronouncements by the Church increased tensions between hardliners and legalists within the military institution.

In essence the Church, the OAB, and the intellectual and scientific organizations affected *distensão* in an indirect way. Their moral condemnations focused on one of the crucial aspects of the transition, the end of the exceptional state, and put the Planalto on the defensive. The government did not want to lose control of the agenda, but it could not tolerate an onslaught of rightist violence against these organizations. Unable to suppress these organizations' demands altogether, the government tried to tone them down and to neutralize the impact of the more problematic individuals within the legal framework of a regime that still was authoritarian.

During 1977 military officers like General Dilermando Gomes Monteiro and General Diocleciano Cerqueira Lima asked politicians to stop the demands for amnesty and for a constituent assembly. ARENA Senator Jarbas Passarinho, a retired officer, asked the opposition not to push the army, since this could be counterproductive. The government showed its ugly side; activists were picked up, threats were made, there were *cassações* (suspensions of political rights) of some individuals and some journalists were charged under the national security statute. But the Planalto Palace remained in a difficult position. If *distensão* were to be made credible, Geisel could not simply repress these individuals and suppress the institutions standing behind them. But to allow them a prominent place in the political community would infuriate the hardliners and provoke an outbreak of violence.

The Role of Excluded Groups. Labor and the students represented a very different type of challenge for Geisel. Although the government may have grieved over the activism of the Church, the OAB, the Brazilian Society for the Advancement of Science (SBPC), and human rights organizations, the activities of more "subversive" organizations were met with undisguised anger and hostility. Their very right to organize, to become participants in the restricted political process in Brazil, remained well beyond the most generous bounds of tolerance that could be found in the Geisel administration. If the demands of other groups provoked discord among the military, labor and student activism literally made them see red. If the basic strategy of Geisel was to deal with everyone from a position of strength in order to prevent interference with his blueprint for an orderly and very gradual *distensão*, that strategy assumed that groups that had never accepted the legitimacy of the military government would not be allowed to play any role in the political process. They were to remain excluded.

Efforts by the student movement to reassert itself were not very successful. Initially the response of the military government was relatively restrained, and state governors were allowed to deal with the student demonstrations of May 1977 while Justice Minister Falcão and General Hugo Abreu monitored the situation. Hardliners like Air Force Minister Brigadier Araripe Macedo and General Abreu saw the hand of Communist subversion behind the student demonstrations. More level-headed individuals like General Dilermando believed that there was no direct threat to national security. The students were seeking to restore their national association, the União Nacional dos Estudantes (UNE), banned since 1964, and they rebuffed the conciliatory gestures of some state governments. Their protest strikes of June and September were unsuccessful; finally the federal government yielded to hardline pressure and there was a crackdown. In June a number of student leaders were charged under the national security statute; an additional thirty were indicted in August. UNE was not reconstituted until June 1979.

Labor, the other major "subversive" group in civil society, experienced similar difficulties but came out of the confrontation with renewed vigor.

Labor unions had been tolerated by the regime but, following a practice going back to the *Estado Nôvo*, only under the control of the official and acquiescent *pelego* leadership, which had little to gain from either a very militant defense of sectoral demands or any attempt to link these to a process of democratization. But the *pelegos* had to watch for the inroads made by dissident and more militant labor leaders who, in the words of one of the most prominent of them, Luís Inácio da Silva (Lula), wanted the workers to make money, not history.

The labor conflicts of 1977-1978 centered on protests about government manipulation of the official index of inflation and on dissidents' attempts to engage in limited free-trade unionism at the expense of the officially controlled *pelegos*. Labor's Office of Statistics and Socioeconomic Studies (DIEESE) had found the official index unreliable on the side of systematic underestimation of the level of inflation. These criticisms prompted Finance Minister Mário Henrique Simonsen to admit that his predecessor, Delfim Neto, had manipulated the index.

Nevertheless, trade unionism remained very limited. Labor leaders were allowed to visit Brasília in September of both 1977 and 1978. The first meeting produced a promise by Finance Minister Simonsen to exchange inflation data with labor's DIEESE. The second meeting was a humiliating setback. The government not only rebuffed labor's demand for the abolition of the strike statute but also passed Decree No. 1632 making strikes more difficult. In addition, government officials let it be known that they would not tolerate a continued presence of labor leaders in the federal capital. One must bear in mind that these labor representatives were the docile *pelego* leaders supported by the government and that the humiliation they suffered was not a governmental concession to military hardliners but a natural result of a *castelista* vision of the social pact in which labor's role was to be subservient to the state.

The government's lack of respect for even its own labor leadership proved to be counterproductive. In October 1978, with labor already declared persona non grata in Brasília, about 250,000 engineering and metallurgical workers went on strike in Rio de Janeiro and São Paulo, demanding a wage increase of at least 70 percent. The strike succeeded not only because of the intensity of the demand and the discipline with which the strikers closed ranks and hunkered down, but also because the leadership, including the *pelegos*, had no choice but to join the strike movement in order not to lose control of their unions. In short, although the labor question had relatively little direct impact on the crisis of succession, the military government wanted to maintain a tight control over the labor movement to keep it out of the political community. But labor's isolation from the government, the social circumstances of the workers, the support that their strikes began to receive from other social actors, the economic importance of some of the sectors affected by renewed labor activism, and the availability of alternative leadership brought about one of the most serious challenges facing Figueiredo during his first months in office.

The Politics of Uncertainty: The Pacote and the Political Reforms

There is little doubt that one important concern of the Geisel administration during the succession crisis of 1977-1978 was to prevent the emergence of a relatively independent center of political power, whether in the society (around demands for change in the economic model), in the political community (in the manner of strong opposition candidates and a cohesive MDB that could cause a repeat of the 1974 debacle), or within the military (acting out of concern for their own institutional integrity). The firings of Frota and Abreu involved the prevention of breakdown originating in the "dominant contradiction" of the regime. The *pacote de abril* of 1977 and the political reforms of 1978 sought to decompress government-society and government-political community contradictions without regime breakdown.

Geisel announced his intention to engineer some "democratic improvements," but his unwillingness to allow anyone outside the command group to participate in the design and implementation of *distensão* belied his intention. Moreover, Geisel gave proof that he was prepared to act arbitrarily to set *his* version of liberalization in motion. Geisel's "insider's dilemma" was not unique. His was a key dilemma confronting any authoritarian government in the early stages of a transition, namely, how to evolve democratic practices from an authoritarian blueprint. To make matters worse, Geisel tried to accomplish this without a previous pact or even a tacit agreement with the opposition, as have done *all* his military colleagues who have launched processes of transition to democracy in South America recently.

The MDB had an "outsider's dilemma" of its own, common to any opposition looking at the preliminary stages of a process of transition conducted from above. At issue here is whether (1) to take the government at its word and accept its commitment to a transition that has not been negotiated or (2) to force the government, regardless of its real intentions, to deliver a process of transition to democracy. The difficulty of this choice is compounded by the need to anticipate whether government threats about a retreat to the status quo ante are real.

Geisel wanted to obtain a commitment from the MDB to his version of *distensão*, but this version remained very ambiguous through the succession crisis—at least through the summer of 1978. This ambiguity had its advantages, and it kept everyone guessing, including the hardline element, but it also had certain costs. The MDB found it difficult to commit itself to a project of transition for which no clear blueprint or timetable existed. In addition, Geisel's first few moves were not very auspicious. His entreaties to the MDB were linked to a design to make opposition gains more difficult in the elections of 1978. To compound the problem, Geisel showed little flexibility and resorted to constant threats.

During March 1977 ARENA's Petrônio Portela, president of the Senate, and Ulysses Guimarães, of the MDB, consulted with each other frequently on the matter of the political reforms. The atmosphere between MDB and ARENA leaders was very cordial, but Portela found it necessary to warn his interlocutor that the military would neither accept direct gubernatorial elections in 1978 nor risk losing control of Congress. The MDB countered with demands for the restoration of habeas corpus, immunity for the judiciary, and a series of other changes to the state of exception that could be brought about gradually. But Geisel and the Planalto group insisted on subordinating the rules of the 1978 elections to the question of *distensão*. The government threatened with *cassações* (denials of individual political rights) and new institutional acts if the opposition refused to accommodate its demands.

The confrontation that ARENA and MDB moderates wanted to avoid materialized when the government failed to obtain the required two-thirds majority to pass the first two reform bills submitted to Congress. These were constitutional amendments involving the judiciary and were viewed by the opposition as obstructionist measures designed to make judges and parliamentarians more vulnerable to federal government pressure. The Planalto was adamant in its attempt to control two branches of government that were supposed to become more independent under a genuine *abertura*. Despite government threats the congressional delegation, or *bancada*, of the MDB refused to change its position and called the government's hand.

On April 1 Geisel recessed Congress and later that day, in a televised speech, attacked the MDB with charges that it was trying to act like a minority dictatorship. The next day the MDB published a strong rebuttal, accusing Geisel of trying to turn Congress into a rubber stamp: "In no democratic country does the rejection of a government project by parliament become a reason for decreeing the recession of the legislative power."[34] In turn, the government hardened its position, announcing that *vereadores* (municipal council members) would be included in the state electoral colleges that would select the new governors and that the terms of incumbent *vereadores* would now run through 1982. Geisel was worried about the possibility that five lame-duck legislatures seated in 1974 would elect MDB governors in their states. He wanted to avoid having to share power with opposition governors, something that Figueiredo had to live with and that definitely changed the configuration of the regime after the 1982 elections. High-level talks continued despite the hostile rhetoric and the increasing distance between government and opposition. But the government's offer was not very generous; in exchange for approval of the proposed reforms the government would create a collegiate body, a Council of State dominated by the Planalto, to administer Institutional Act No. 5. In other words, in exchange for opposition support for measures that would make exceptionalism less violent, the government would be prepared to share the practice of exceptionalism with the opposition. The opposition interpreted this as a return to the days of the empire.

On April 14 the reforms were made public. The principal changes included continued indirect elections for governors (through state electoral colleges loaded with *vereadores*), continued indirect elections for one-third of the Senate, changes in the size of the state delegations to the Chamber of Deputies (discriminating against the larger states), a simple congressional majority for the passage of constitutional amendments, extension of the *Lei Falcão*, a one-year extension of Figueiredo's term, and a postponement of the proclamation of the new president by the electoral college to October 1978.[35] Reaction to these obstructionist measures, which quickly became known as the *pacote de abril*, came not only from the opposition but also from within the military. The televised appearance of Alencar Furtado and Ulysses Guimarães, and the *cassações* of Furtado and of Marcos Tito, another MDB deputy, killed the chances of any understanding. In August ARENA president Francelino Pereira leaked a timetable for constitutional reform that included further ARENA-MDB talks, a second stage in which the official nominee would join the deliberations, and a post-electoral stage for Congress to vote additional changes. The MDB wanted to handle the political reforms through a constituent assembly and remained aloof.

In March 1978 Geisel spoke to Congress. He averred that the *pacote* had been his outstanding achievement and that the senators elected under the new electoral law would bring brilliant individuals (called *biônicos* or "bionics" by a sarcastic public) to the Senate. ARENA senator Teotônio Vilela was as critical of the speech as were his MDB counterparts, who simply walked out of the Chamber when Geisel accused "a minority alienated by political passion" of creating the obstructions which made the *pacote* necessary.[36] The tone of the speech surprised ARENA as much as it did the MDB and undermined a new Portela attempt to renew the dialogue.

Geisel's speech, coming from a man who appeared sincere in his desire to end torture and violence, offers further evidence of the ambiguous and contradictory nature of the government's blueprint for *distensão*. Supposedly, gradual reforms would end violations of human rights and the systematic use of violence by the government. This would restore legitimacy to the regime and increase public confidence in the military's commitment to "democratic improvements." The more favorable climate resulting from this experience would, in turn, create conditions in which the military would be able to share power gradually, without the interference of partisan passions. But this was an idealistic scenario which, even under optimal conditions, would be difficult to live up to. In addition, Geisel's version of *distensão* could also be interpreted as an attempt by the Planalto to buy the military revolution a renewed lease on life. This would have meant the consolidation of a presidential dictatorship made possible by a weak Congress and a subservient judiciary. The opposition wanted no part of this.

Another issue was whether the government was prepared to act within a framework of limited powers. Geisel's inflexibility and his draconian measures in 1977-1978 did not bode well in this sense, nor did the precedent of thirteen years in which the military had found it impossible to rule without appropriating ever more powers and without using arbitrarily those it already had. Maybe the opposition was asking for things that Geisel could not deliver—too much, too soon—but the government's early gambit was a contradiction in terms.

In June Portela introduced the government's draft bill for party reorganization without opposition endorsement. The MDB's André Franco Montoro introduced a bill restoring direct elections with the endorsement of 38 senators, including 10 from ARENA, and of 138 deputies. An infuriated Geisel vowed to use Institutional Act No. 5 if Montoro's bill passed. Portela spent most of his time trying to delay consideration of Montoro's bill and appealing directly to the Brazilian Lawyer's Association (OAB), the National Conference of Brazilian Bishops (CNBB), the Brazilian Press Association (ABI), and some prominent individuals to support the government's draft. But he could not engage the interest of the MDB. The *emedebistas* wanted to repeal the *pacote de abril* and to handle the political reforms through a constituent assembly because, according to Montoro, the 1967 constitution itself was authoritarian, not just the institutional acts.

Congress reconvened in August, greeted by warnings from General Ariel Pacca de Fonseca, Army Chief of Staff, that the political climate was similar to that of December 1968.[37] But Portela had done his homework. The secretary to the subcommittee in charge of the government bill, ARENA Senator José Sarney, allowed little discussion and swept aside a host of opposition amendments. In September the government bill passed by a vote of 241 to 145. The measure reduced the duration of states of emergency from ninety to sixty days, subject to the approval of a newly created constitutional council. Some requirements for the creation of new parties were eased a bit. *Cassações* were made more difficult. Although major irritants like the *Lei Falcão* and the *senadores biônicos* were left intact, the bill included a number of significant discontinuities. Article 153 of the constitution of 1967 was abolished, eliminating the more severe penalties for "warfare" against the state. Article 185 was amended, limiting the duration of *cassações* to ten years (although *cassados* could not participate in elections until 1982). The package reintroduced habeas corpus for political offenses and abolished the president's power to recess Congress. A new restriction on the president's power to suspend citizens' rights was less generous; it enabled the minister of justice to suspend the political rights of defendants until a verdict of innocence was returned. Congressional approval was not required for the declaration of a state of siege, with a maximum duration of sixty days. Finally, a two-thirds majority of both houses was required to amend the constitution.[38]

A comparison of the Geisel reforms with previous attempts to institutionalize the regime suggests that the political reforms of 1977-1978 tried to limit the use of arbitrary rule although, in essence, the regime continued to be authoritarian. The reforms sought to make utilization of the dictatorial powers of the presidency less necessary. The October reform aimed at a return to the 1967 constitution, a document that the opposition believed authoritarian. That document was designed as a bulkhead sheltering the executive from two organic problems of Brazilian politics: Congress and the political parties. Likewise, the new requirements for the legalization of political parties showed remarkable continuity with previous efforts to rationalize (Complementary Act No. 4 of November 20, 1965) and reorganize them (Complementary Act No. 54 of May 19, 1969). Therefore, in 1978, the military remained mystified by political parties and by Congress and uncertain as to how to deal with them. Fourteen years in power apparently had taught them little in this regard.

The statements by senior officers comparing the atmosphere of 1978 with that of 1968 suggest a great irony. In December 1968 Institutional Act No. 5 put the president above the law after the military discovered that being above Congress was not enough. In 1978 Geisel wanted to bring his own powers under the rule of law, albeit protected by the safety net provided by a reformed judiciary and a collegiate use of exceptionalism. Castelo Branco ended his tenure under Institutional Act No. 2, which expired as Costa e Silva came to office under the 1967 constitution. Castelo had misgivings about Costa and may have wanted to build a relatively orderly *dictablanda* before his successor took office. Geisel rescinded Institutional Act No. 5 before Figueiredo came to office in an apparent effort to return to Castelo's *dictablanda*.

However, the intimidating manner in which Geisel secured passage of the reforms made the regime less legitimate and may have accelerated its deterioration. Despite his intention to make the regime less arbitrary, he failed in his threatening style to engage the support of the opposition, which remained suspicious and uncertain as to whether the *distensão* would be but another attempt to legitimize the national security state rather than a harbinger of an *abertura* that could culminate in the inauguration of a democratic regime. The opposition took nothing for granted, kept its own counsel, and fought hard to bring about the latter on its own terms.

The outcome of the congressional election of November 15, 1978, must be termed a defeat for the Geisel government. Despite the *Lei Falcão*, despite the machinery of the government behind the electoral promises of the ARENA candidates, and despite other body blows aimed at the opposition, the MDB held together and its infrastructure delivered the vote. In addition, a study by David Fleischer suggests that the government's "victory" was Pyrrhic since Geisel could have kept control of at least one of the two chambers without the *pacote* and, more importantly, without alienating the opposition.[39] However, as has been the case in most of the recent processes of transition to democracy in South America, the Geisel government wanted to maximize certainty, and to give itself a wide safety margin. This insecurity and the overkill that it produced were among the legacies of *castelismo* and one of the constants that characterized the entire period of military rule in Brazil. At bottom there was a misunderstanding of democratic politics by the military that it had failed to correct after fourteen years in power.

The direction of change in Brazil at the time of Figueiredo's inauguration seemed to be carrying the regime toward an *abertura* produced by attempts by actors in the society and in the political community to extend the limits of *distensão*. Figueiredo himself exemplified the profound contradictions of *castelismo*: a search for legitimation versus a tendency to act without restraint. Shortly after his victory, the president-elect promised a political opening, vowing that he would "arrest and break" anyone who dared to oppose this. "The game will go on," he added, "but if the opposition goes beyond established limits, I will pick up the ball and put a stop to it."[40] In retrospect, he obviously was quite wrong.

The New Administration

In January 1979, shortly before his inauguration, President-elect João Baptista Figueiredo promised Brazilians that he would concentrate on four objectives: progress with freedom, order with democracy, peace with justice, and state security with individual safety.[41] Figueiredo did not want a full-fledged democratization at the time, especially if this included an opposition government in Brasília in the near future. General Golbery do Couto e Silva suggested as much in a July 1980 speech at the ESG. In his speech Golbery described what Brazilians had begun to call the *abertura* as a process of decentralization that sought to rectify the "excesses of centralization" begun in 1968. This was necessary, Golbery told his military audience, because economic pressures and social unrest could find an outlet in protests against "undisguised authoritarianism" and create a polarization that would lead to "dangerous radicalizations."[42] The Planalto, therefore, wanted to utilize *abertura* to increase the legitimacy of the regime, to divide the opposition, and to thwart the consolidation of the MDB as a solid opposition front. Golbery believed that the prevention of polarization was indispensable to allow *abertura* to bring about a "more progressive and democratic style of life."[43] Whereas Ernesto Geisel had been satisfied with a "relative democracy," João Figueiredo may have felt the need to work toward a "mitigated representative democracy."[44] But like Geisel before him, Figueiredo found that he could neither keep this process of change under control nor could he go back.

The Government and the High Command

Figueiredo's first set of military promotions favored a group known as the *oficialidade germânica* (Germanic corps) of the classes of 1936–1939. This group included the president's brother General Euclides de Oliveira Figueiredo, the new commander of the Vila Militar in Rio; General Milton Tavares de Souza (Miltinho), head of the CIE under Médici, promoted to four-star and named chief of the Second Army; General José Luís Coelho Neto, a leader of the hardline element stationed in Rio, promoted to three-star; and General Walter Moniz, a close collaborator of Coelho, designated head of the military school. Completing the roster of possible and certain opponents of *abertura* were the new Army Minister General Walter Pires de Albuquerque; General Newton de Oliveira e Cruz, head of the SNI central office; Navy Minister Maximiano da Fonseca; Navy Chief Admiral Barroso; Army Personnel Department head General Antônio Carlos de Andrade Serpa; and Third Army commander General Antônio Bandeira.

Although many of these hardliners had supported Frota and Abreu, they eventually switched to Figueiredo during the succession crisis. Many had backgrounds in intelligence. Figueiredo's appointments through April 1981 seemed to favor these elements while using "discretion" in promoting close associates and friends over unknown quantities. This resulted in a heavy concentration of hardliners in Rio and in São Paulo, and they gave Figueiredo considerable trouble early in his presidency, challenging him openly and forcing him to slow down *abertura*. But, despite their early successes during 1979–1981, they failed to stop *abertura*. Therefore, it would appear that *abertura* continued despite unfavorable developments within the military institution, not because military aperturists had prevailed in 1979.

The Cabinet

Figueiredo's first cabinet was heterogeneous. It included "Médici men" Delfim Neto (Agriculture), César Cals (Mines and Energy), Eliseu Rezende (Transportation), and Mário Andreazza (Interior); Geisel holdovers like Golbery (Head of the Civilian Household), Major Heitor Aquino Ferreira (Secretary General of the Presidency), Mário Henrique Simonsen (Planning), and Carlos Rischbieter (Finance); and ARENA luminaries like Petrônio Portela (Justice). The presence of so many "heavy-weights" in the cabinet made the early going rough. There were conflicts over the economic model between *realista* fiscal conservatives like Simonsen and Rischbieter, and Delfim and the pro-growth *desenvolvimentistas*. The issue was decided relatively early in favor of the latter. The faction most favorable to *abertura* consisted of Portela, Murilo Macedo (Labor), Eduardo Portela (Education), and Brigadier Délio Jardim de Mattos (Air Force), a personal friend of Figueiredo. The members of this group supported a generous version of amnesty, maintained frequent contact with the opposition, and provided the main voices of reason and moderation. They had to confront the *realistas* who wanted to give top priority to economic matters, and were overwhelmed by the *desenvolvimentistas*. Figueiredo, Golbery, and Aquino provided the *castelista* continuity.

By December 1980 six members of the original cabinet were gone. Simonsen and Rischbieter left because of disputes over economic policy. Petrônio Portela died on January 6, 1980. Eduardo Portela resigned in October 1980 after Delfim vetoed his plan to give a 48 percent pay increase to striking faculty and teachers. Health Minister Mário Augusto Jorge de Castro Lima resigned in October 1979 to protest a decision to distribute birth control pills indiscriminately. Social Communications Minister Said Farhat was dismissed in December 1980 when his ministry was disbanded. Their departure was interpreted as a triumph of the "Médici men" and a setback for *abertura*. This impression was reinforced by the pattern of promotions in the army, by the government's hardening attitude toward its opponents and its crackdown on labor, by a feeling that Figueiredo had all but capitulated to right-wind demands to slow down or stop *abertura*, and by the resignation of Golbery on August 6, 1981.

I have no quarrel with this view except to emphasize that *abertura* moved on despite the predominance in the cabinet of "Médici men" who epitomized the values promoted by the regime since 1964. But they did not dominate the government. If anything, the Planalto remained very divided throughout the Figueiredo presidency.[45] Golbery and General Octávio Medeiros, SNI chief, remained notoriously at odds. When Golbery left, the Planalto group became even more fragmented. His responsibilities were divided among Medeiros, João Leitão de Abreu (who became his formal successor despite Medeiros's opposition), and Figueiredo himself. Medeiros and General Danilo Venturini, head of the military household, gradually overshadowed presidential secretary Heitor Aquino but could not overcome Leitão. When Figueiredo became ill in September 1981, Leitão, overcoming the opposition of Medeiros, mobilized support for the interim presidency of Vice-president Aureliano Chaves, and then took care of official business himself until Figueiredo's return in November. When Figueiredo took another medical leave in mid-1983, Chaves became much more assertive; Medeiros's star was declining, and the process of presidential succession could no longer be controlled by the Planalto, even after Figueiredo's return. In summary, although the Figueiredo cabinet was dominated by Médici men, the Planalto lost the coherence it had enjoyed under Geisel. If *abertura* continued, it was not because of bonhomie, but because cleavages inside the government contributed to force Figueiredo to treat *abertura* more as a genuine formula for political transition than as a blueprint to reequilibrate the regime in a new position of dominance.

"President João" and His Blueprint

In essence, Figueiredo's government preserved the division of labor of the *castelista* social pact between military officers providing security (using the slogan "Progress with freedom") and technocrats and entrepreneurs creating wealth ("Order with democracy"). The first team, headed by Delfim Neto, dealt with economic adversity and the subsequent business discontent and labor activism. Golbery managed the second team, which covered relations with the political community and the opposition. However, some of Golbery's luster was eroding because Figueiredo did not follow his advice on several occasions. Golbery's inability to anticipate the full implications of every attempt by the government to forestall electoral gains by the opposition underlined the uncertainties of *abertura* and the deteriorating position of the government. SNI chief Medeiros coordinated the team handling "National security with individual safety." This task involved state-society relations and was extremely sensitive, as it concerned dismantling the state of exception—a process started when Geisel abolished Institutional Act No. 5—and reestablishing presidential authority over the security apparatus. Hardliners, assisted and encouraged by Medeiros and his allies, resisted the effective exercise of that authority and directly attacked social actors trying to operate within the confines of the last of Figueiredo's desiderata: "Peace with justice." This was an arena in which economic issues and human rights issues were contested and in which the Planalto was on the defensive.

The Figueiredo desiderata may be superimposed on the overall configuration of the regime (see Figure 1.2) to describe the dynamics at hand in more graphic form. This has been attempted in Figure 1.3, in which each of the desiderata is treated as a specific instance of the contradictions of authoritarian domination and is related to Golbery's strategy of controlled political transition. The figure highlights the changes in the regime, but two constants remained as a result of the military's continued adherence to its strategy of legitimation. One was a continued emphasis on security and order, and the other was a deference to the regime's version of economic rationality.

Some of the relevant actors confronting one another over these issues are identified in the figure. They challenged Figueiredo's blueprint for *abertura* and in so doing had a decisive impact on the process. Human rights activists and relatives of victims of torture insisted on bringing their cases before the courts, testing the meaning of *peace with justice*. The labor and student movements, contrary to what Golbery expected, did not fade away. Labor agitation sought to take advantage of *progress with freedom*. Hardliners reacted against political activists and through several bombings literally attempted to blow up the *abertura*. Entrepreneurs chafing under the increasingly austere policies of Delfim Neto asked for democratization. A very resilient MDB proved to be stronger

40

FIGURE 1.3
The Abertura Under Figueiredo

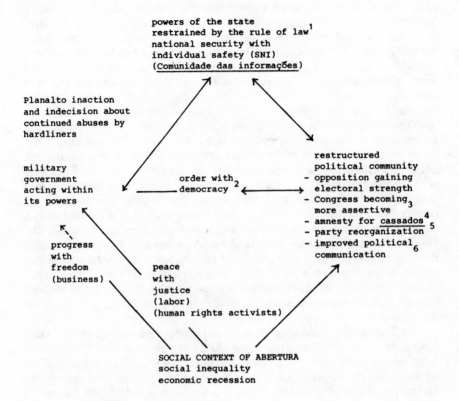

powers of the state
restrained by the rule of law[1]
national security with
individual safety (SNI)
(Comunidade das informações)

Planalto inaction
and indecision about
continued abuses by
hardliners

military
government
acting within
its powers

order with
democracy [2]

restructured
political community
- opposition gaining
  electoral strength
- Congress becoming[3]
  more assertive
- amnesty for cassados[4] [5]
- party reorganization
- improved political[6]
  communication

progress
with
freedom
(business)

peace
with
justice
(labor)
(human rights activists)

SOCIAL CONTEXT OF ABERTURA
social inequality
economic recession

[1]Drawing upon the reform of October 1978.

[2]Drawing upon the pacote de abril and the measures of
November 1981 and June 1982.

[3]Defeating government draft bills.

[4]Lei de anistia of August 28, 1979.

[5]Party reform bill of November 1979.

[6]Lei Falcão abolished in July 1979.

than anticipated and made the "mitigated democracy" less orderly. Finally, members of the PDS formed a coalition with the opposition, thereby helping to put an end to the military's version of a controlled and limited transition.

Progress with Freedom

The society that João Figueiredo set out to govern on March 15, 1979, had two dominant characteristics: an extraordinarily complex and dynamic network of economic interactions and increasing socioeconomic inequality. Complexity made economic policymaking more difficult. Inequality made it more sensitive.

By 1981 Brazil had 306 of the 500 largest enterprises in Latin America; 900 state enterprises generating 40 percent of all investment, employing 1.4 million people, and providing indirect employment to an additional 4.2 million; 109 sectoral associations affiliated with the top industrial association (FIESP) of one state (São Paulo); huge domestic conglomerates with interests in many different economic sectors; at least 25 weapons manufacturers, many of whom had multimillion dollar export contracts; an automotive industry that turned out 1.13 million units in 1979; a world-record foreign debt of about US$55 billion in June 1980; a debt, at that time, of US$4.7 billion with *one* foreign bank (Citicorp of New York); and the fastest-growing market in the world.

Given the military's strategy of legitimation, the ability to continue to manage the economy successfully was vital for the government. Balance-of-payment problems and triple-digit inflation threatened the legitimacy of the regime. A simultaneous solution to these issues was difficult since it had to reconcile competing demands and vastly different policy strategies. Basically, the government had to decide between a recessionary strategy of stabilization that could be costly at the time of the 1982 elections or a more incremental one that might not be acceptable to the international banking community.

Brazil's balance-of-payments problems had developed despite the phenomenal performance of Brazilian exports from 1977 to 1981. Delfim subscribed to the *desenvolvimentista* view that balance-of-payments problems are essentially a problem of balance of trade that can be corrected with aggressive export promotion. This he did, and he was relatively successful. But in early 1980 Delfim had to set aside his optimism and give priority to a policy of stabilization. Delfim spent most of 1980 trying to make his ad hoc program of stabilization work, taking with one hand what the other had given. He pushed export promotion but cut back on export subsidies and public investment. He allowed interest rates to go up but then had to run all over the place to placate entrepreneurs. He quarreled with foreign bankers and denounced the inflexibility of the IMF but sent Finance Minister Ernane Galvêas to Washington for a preliminary inquiry. He held secret talks with labor leaders, looking for a two-year moratorium on wage demands. Finally, he put together a package that enabled him to meet all 1980 foreign exchange requirements. But despite this remarkable performance Delfim could not prevent the coming recession.

There was much business discontent with this situation. In June 1980 the PMDB's (Party of the Brazilian Democratic Movement) Saturnino Braga proposed a new social pact. In December 1980 thirty-two prominent citizens issued a manifesto asking for an alternative economic model. Bankers blamed the government for the high rates of interest. Economists like Luíz Carlos Bresser Pereira claimed that the situation was intolerable. But no unified challenge came from the private sector. Many companies depended on federal government contracts. Others were trying to weather the storm through the largesse of key figures like São Paulo governor Paulo Maluf, who was trading contracts for promises of future support. Finally, the austerity program of the government put most of the burden on labor, not management.

The Brazil that João Figueiredo set out to govern in March 1979 also harbored great social inequalities. First, there were the increasing disparities in income. From 1960 to 1977 the share of the poorest 50 percent of the population declined from 17.4 percent to 13.1 percent, while the share of the wealthiest 10 percent increased from 39.6 percent to 51 percent.[46] Second, income differentials in the countryside were exacerbated by land tenure patterns and by differential access to credit. In March 1980 a study by the CNBB's Comissão Pastoral da Terra (CPT) showed that 0.8 percent of the landowners controlled 42.6 percent of the land.[47] Conflicts about land tenure became more common, and the SNI intervened in them.[48] Third, unemployment remained a major problem.[49] In February 1980 Labor Minister Murilo Macedo called the situation "worrisome" and argued that if unemployment were not to increase even further, the economy had to grow at the rate of 7 percent from 1980 to 1985. But this desideratum collided with the views of the monetary authorities who had suggested that, if the problem of the balance of payments were going to be resolved, the economy could not grow by more than 6 percent per year. Then there was the perennial problem of the Northeast. The nine states in the region, with about one-third of the country's population, took in only 10 percent of the national income in 1979.[50]

The view that social inequality engenders revolution is, at best, incomplete. But the need to reconcile growth and austerity, on the one hand, and the potential for political mobilization created by public awareness of growing economic inequalities, on the other, put Figueiredo in a more vulnerable position than his two predecessors had been. He had to face a mobilized and angry labor movement intent on regaining the terrain lost to inflation and to government neglect of its interests. There were 150 strikes of some importance during the first nine months of 1979. This activism alarmed the hardliners, who demanded swift reaction. Given their similar views about the labor movement, hardliners and the Planalto acted in unison to defuse this challenge. Generals Miltinho and Coelho Neto dealt directly with strikers in their states.

The next year there were only two significant strikes, one by dock-workers in Santos and another by metalworkers of the engineering unions of São Paulo. The second ended in disaster when rank-and-file pressure forced the leaders to ignore a labor court's initial ruling favorable to the unions and to hold out for more benefits. After forty-one days some workers had returned to work, and the federal government moved in, intervened in the unions, charged the leaders under the national security statute, and fired without severance pay about one thousand workers identified as ringleaders by management.

This defeat cooled off the movement but made it stronger because it led to important changes in tactics by the *autêntico* (purist) unionists who turned their attention to building up the Workers Party (Partido dos Trabalhadores—PT). The government could not take advantage of the situation to clobber the movement into total submission and destroy it altogether. The more severe aspects of a government proposal on social security were defeated by Congress. Management opposed Delfim's attempt to discontinue the twice-a-year wage adjustments. In addition, the government never made much headway punishing trade unionists. In 1980 Murilo Macedo reinstated leaders who had been sacked for their role in the 1979 strikes. The Planalto prosecuted the leaders of the 1980 metalworkers' strike, but their trial turned out to be a major embarrassment for the Planalto.

In sum, although the government had to contend with pressures from management and labor, one cannot really assign a crucial role to the social context that prompted their activism. Economic difficulties contributed to the deterioration of the regime but were not decisive in bringing about change. Instead, the interplay between government policies and social context presented the government with some difficult choices: Change the economic model to save the regime, delay further changes of the regime to insure the success of the economic strategy, or sacrifice both in order to make an orderly transition possible.

Peace with Justice and National Security with Individual Safety

The two objectives of peace with justice and national security with individual safety dominated debate from 1979 to 1981, as they provided the substantive background to three issues: the scope and nature of inquiries into human rights abuses, amnesty, and the relative autonomy of the so-called intelligence community (*comunidade das informações*). On October 28, 1978, a young federal judge, Márcio José de Morais, had a decisive impact on the transition from *distensão* to *abertura*. The judge found that, in October 1975, government agents acted illegally in arresting journalist Vladimir Herzog and in taking him to the DOI-CODI interrogation center of the Second Army in São Paulo, where he was tortured. De Morais found no evidence that Herzog committed suicide, and he ruled that Herzog's widow was eligible for indemnity since the government was at fault. Justice Vice-minister Roberto Battendieri called the decision "strange and unprecedented." General Ednardo D'Avila Melo, the commander of the Second Army at that time, was more direct: "Herzog was not a political detainee," he said, "he was just a Communist."[51]

The experience of recent cases of transition to democracy in South America shows that a military institution trying to extricate itself from control of the government will do everything to cover its tracks and to prevent retribution for its abuses of authority. The military perceives inquiries and prosecutions as threats to its institutional integrity. In Ecuador and in Peru the military refused to allow any inquiries by outsiders. In Argentina the Radical government of Alfonsín prosecuted the commanders of three different military juntas and a host of other officers. This unusual move created serious strains for the new democratic regime but the military did not react to the trials by undermining the authority of the government.

In Brazil, the *comunidade das informações* was aroused by this challenge. Members of many of its branches—including officers associated with OBAN (Operação Bandeirantes), those within the DOI-CODI (Divisão de Operações Internas—Centro de Operações de Defesa Interna), branches of the CIE (Centro de Informações do Exército) and the CIE itself, CENIMAR (Navy Intelligence) operatives, agents of CISA (the Centro e de Informações e de Segurança da Aeronaútica), and SNI members—had serious reservations about *abertura*, and were resolutely opposed to amnesty and to inquiries of any kind.

It is not clear how much *abertura* was threatened by attempts to address these issues. But there is little doubt that amnesty, the return of the exiles, and inquiries into human rights abuses were important steps in the transition from *distensão* to *abertura*. Moreover, hardline reaction to these steps and the consequences thereof were significant components of the process of transition in Brazil, a process that involved a series of confrontations between democratic aperturists and obstructionists of different stripes. Despite the modest results afforded by airing these issues, the precedent of other cases shows that there is no transition unless violent obstructionism is neutralized. The extreme and violent actions undertaken by hardliners seeking to put these issues to rest contribute to their own downfall. This was also the case in Brazil.

The political climate grew tense during May 1979 following testimony before Congress by some victims of torture. MDB purists (*emedebistas autênticos*) outvoted their moderate colleagues 69-57 to set up a parliamentary commission of inquiry into torture. MDB moderates did not want to put *distensão* through such a severe strain, while the *autênticos* complained that the MDB was not obliged to help the government save face. Most inquiries into torture, however, were being conducted by the press, by the Brazilian Committee for Amnesty (Comitê Brasileiro pela Anistia), and by victims or relatives of victims who had initiated judicial actions against their former captors. These had already provoked violent reactions and threats by hardliners.

Figueiredo took up the question of amnesty in February 1979, asking Petrônio Portela and Attorney General-designate Clóvis Ramalhete to prepare a draft bill. The Supremo Tribunal Militar (STM) had been reviewing cases tried under the national security statute. Hardline pressure delayed the introduction of the bill until June and, to the chagrin of Portela and of STM Judge Jardim de Mattos, prevented a more generous version. Two amendments were defeated, one introduced by ARENA's Djalma Marinho covering all political prisoners and another including torturers under the *crimes conexos* (related crimes) section of the draft. Once the MDB congressional bloc secured inclusion of labor leaders and became convinced that no more concessions were forthcoming, the MDB deputies voted for the government bill. Figueiredo signed it the same day, August 22.[52] The amnesty excluded "those who had resisted by arms," but most political prisoners were released through the sentence review process conducted by the STM. The amnesty covered 4,682 Brazilians who had been *cassados* between April 1964 and April 1977, including 1,261 military officers and enlisted men.

A rightist terrorist campaign began shortly thereafter. Between August 1979 and May 1981 a total of forty-one bombing attacks took place. Targets of violence were leftist media (journalists, printing shops, newsstands, and editorial offices), returning exiles, offices of opposition parties, striking workers, lawyers, human rights activists, and victims of torture. Figueiredo moved to isolate violent hardliners through transfers and retirements. Despite this cautious policy the Planalto did not try to disguise the intent of the terrorists. In August 1980, following the bombing of the OAB headquarters in Rio, Figueiredo vowed that "four, twenty, or a thousand bombs exploding over our heads will not change our policy." In a rare interview Golbery warned that the bombing campaign was being conducted against the government and against *abertura*.[53] Neither of them elaborated on who was behind the campaign. In September Figueiredo flew to São Paulo "to visit his old friend Miltinho." The real purpose of the visit was to give a stern warning to Colonels Leo and Cyro Etchegoyen, the Second Army's chief of staff and chief of intelligence, respectively. They had masterminded the kidnapping of Dalmo Dallari, a Catholic activist lawyer, and agents under their command had used indiscriminate violence against striking workers. The Second Army was quieter after the visit.[54]

Despite this modest success Figueiredo had not been able to make much headway toward restructuring the intelligence community as he had promised. Only the CISA had been dismantled and only because of the direct intervention of Air Force Minister Jardim de Mattos. In April 1981 journalist Hélio Fernandes, himself the target of a bombing, warned that a parallel government was trying to end *abertura*. On the night of April 30 a bomb exploded in a car occupied by two agents of the DOI-CODI unit of the First Army. The car was parked in the Riocentro complex, outside a theater where a folk music festival was going on, organized by leftist groups to celebrate May Day. The explosion killed one of the car's occupants, an army sergeant. Several bombs were found in the wreckage, which was filmed by television crews at the scene.[55]

The incident put Figueiredo in a difficult position. First Army Commander General Gentil Marcondes Filho claimed that his officers were on duty at the time. Third Army Commander General Antônio Ferreira Marques delivered a virulent speech in which he attacked amnesty and the inquiries. Apparently army opinion crystallized around the need to cover up the incident, even if it had been provoked by hotheads of the intelligence community. In addition to Golbery, who came out in favor of a full inquiry, Figueiredo's best source of support for such a move was the opposition. On May 7, the presidents of the six opposition parties issued a joint statement supporting an inquiry. But Golbery and the opposition could not counterbalance the weight of the army high command and of the *comunidade*. Colonel Luís Antônio do Prado Ribeiro, appointed by Figueiredo to carry out the investigation, resigned while the inquiry was still in its preliminary stages. He was replaced by Colonel Job Lorena de Sant'Anna, the public relations officer of the First Army.

The lack of any visible progress in the inquiry deepened the discontent among those officers who had been dismayed by the incident. Junior officers at the First Army were conducting a parallel investigation. Air Force Minister Jardim de Mattos and Navy Minister Fonseca openly criticized the army for the incident and asked for the dismantling of DOI-CODI. Despite this growing discontent and despite Golbery's resignation, the inquiry got nowhere. But the *comunidade* was alarmed and pressed for a quick resolution. In October the STM voted 4 to 3 to end all the proceedings on the case. However, this only served to intensify tensions within the military. STM Judge Admiral Júlio de Sá Bierrenbach denounced the cover-up publicly. He was berated by Army Minister Pires de Albuquerque and by General Carlos Alberto Cabral Ribeiro. Navy Chief of Staff Admiral José Geraldo Theophilo de Aratanha came to Bierrenbach's defense. A still convalescing Figueiredo had to intervene to calm tempers. He got a retraction of sorts from Pires, and Bierrenbach dropped plans to sue Pires and Cabral Ribeiro. But the admiral maintained that Colonel Lorena had falsified the evidence.[56]

The Riocentro incident had two distinct and opposite impacts on *abertura*. One was negative and marked by Figueiredo's inability or unwillingness to deal with the incident through the courts and to use it to put the *comunidade* on a short leash. It was obvious that the armed forces could not afford to air its dirty linen in public. However, Riocentro, as did similar incidents in other processes of transition, had an indirect impact favorable to *abertura* by worsening the conflicts inside the Planalto and within the military. In essence, the hardliners' campaign of violence embarrassed the institution and eventually turned military opinion against them. This increased their isolation and allowed Figueiredo, who knew as much about the moles of the *comunidade* as they did about him, to pick their allies apart through retirements and transfers into bureaucratic jobs in Brasília. In December 1980, using new legislation that strengthened the president's hand in dealing with dissident officers, Figueiredo eased General Bandeira into retirement. Miltinho died in June 1981. Ferreira Marques, Gentil Marcondes, and Coelho Neto were replaced in July 1981. Once the furor over amnesty had blown over and once it was clear that the inquiries were not such a direct threat to them, most officers were not very sympathetic to the use of intimidation and violence by the *comunidade*. Once outside Planalto, Golbery went on the offensive to block General Medeiros's presidential bid and to force Figueiredo to bring the *comunidade* under control.

In sum, because of the mischief of some and despite the haplessness of others, the military eventually put its own house in order. The Riocentro incident helped bring this about by driving home the need to control hardline violence. Had this not been the case, military reaction to the results of the 1982 election would have been very different, and Aureliano Chaves might not have been able to become interim president for the second time in 1983. By hook and by crook, the former cop (Figueiredo) proved to be better at outlasting and outwitting the violent extremists of the *comunidade* than the master strategist (Golbery) who bowed out early. Justice was not served—seldom is justice served in situations of transition—but the hardliners were neutralized and restraint ultimately prevailed within the military.

Order with Democracy

Essentially, from 1979 to 1981 President Figueiredo was trying to preserve a quintessential feature of the Brazilian military regime. Although the presidency had "descended" from the lofty heights to which it had been elevated by institutional acts, the descent had stopped well above Congress and above civil society. It also had to be kept well beyond the reach of the opposition, although, beginning in 1980, military figures within the Planalto and elsewhere were already talking about the desirability of a civilian figure to succeed Figueiredo. But they needed control of the Congress to disguise the presidential dictatorship. The departure of Golbery had left the Planalto without its most experienced political operator, and his absence probably accelerated the government's loss of control of the Congress.[57]

Figueiredo's unwillingness to give up the *decurso de prazo*, which turned government drafts into legislation unless Congress acted upon them before a certain period of time, and his refusal to yield on issues like parliamentary immunity, open votes on presidential vetoes, and executive power to pass economic legislation by decree were not just a matter of personal obstinacy but a profound legacy of *castelismo*. In the Sorbonnist conception a strong executive was as necessary for the normal functioning of government as sound economic policy was to the security of the state. Figueiredo's refusal to yield on the question of "sovereignty" was congruent with the belief that there is no other Prince than the state in Brazil.[58]

To the Sorbonnists, politics was, after all, a question of state, and Figueiredo was no less horrified by the prospect of having to deal on equal terms with the legislative branch, rebellious by nature, than was Costa e Silva. The desire to maintain the presidential dictatorship and to keep it under wraps ultimately would not be very successful, however, and efforts to have "order with democracy" would inevitably produce disorder. This desire to maintain presidential dictatorship was behind the Planalto's preliminary moves on the constitutional question, Golbery's design for the new configuration of the party system, and the effort to maintain the opposition at bay in both houses of Congress. For a while the government was able to have its way, but Figueiredo's failing health, the military's growing apprehension about efforts to remain in power, and the inability to get the economy out of recession undermined this project.

The "Mexican Model"

The question of the "Mexican model" emerges here, as it provided a precedent in which a "party of the revolution" had settled the issue of presidential succession and, as a result of this, had been able to evolve a benign authoritarianism or a *dictablanda*. Two things happened in the Mexican case which were absent in Brazil. According to Juan Felipe Leal, the origins of the contemporary Mexican state must be sought in the differentiation of functions between the military bureaucracy of the federal armies and a government bureaucracy which originated in them and finally created a party of the revolution. This evolved over a series of crises of presidential succession in which candidates had to take the death-defying leap from "General" to "Mr. President."[59]

In Brazil's *castelista* division of labor, the political function fell on the military, but Brazilian military presidents never came to power by virtue of their control of the official party machinery. The function of the official party in Brazil was to produce ceremony, not candidates. Factional politics inside the military institution produced candidates disconnected from the machinery of a party without power. This, in turn, prevented them from "going civilian" without losing out. All along, the military institution remained the primary constituency of the government; the role behavior of the military presidents reflected this perception. Mexicanization could not take place without military "políticos" becoming exclusively the latter and without a party to make this possible. Neither of these conditions were present in Brazil.

In the Mexican formula the "Party of the Revolution" (PRI) has a social base of support that includes a peculiar alliance between labor, the peasantry, and middle-class bureaucrats. Given the exclusionary nature of the military regime, ARENA-PDS could only provide a rural-based electoral machinery that was dominant in the more backward states but that could not deliver the urban working-class vote. The cleavage structure emerging in the late seventies and early eighties in Brazil and the demographic trends accompanying it made this very difficult. The best the Planalto could hope for was to divide the opposition with the party reorganization of 1979-1980 and then engage in *casuísmos eleitorais* (tinkering with election rules) to protect its congressional majority.

Golbery hoped that the reform would fragment the MDB and make very difficult the crystallization of a nationalist coalition joining military nationalists, dissident factions of the bourgeoisie, and middle- and working-class elements. He also wanted to offer a partisan alternative and lure former PTB adherents (*petebistas*) out of the MDB. But the reform backfired; the MDB-PMDB did lose some strength as a result of the reorganization, but the PP (Popular Party)-PMDB fusion in November 1981 restored the system to a two-party dominant, not a true multiparty system. This was confirmed by the results of the 1982 election.

In addition, the old *udenista* and *pessedista* factions in the PDS fought very bitterly over control of the party at all levels. Figueiredo had to intervene in a number of disputes between these factions during the reorganization stage. In January 1981 Djalma Marinho challenged the Planalto's candidate for speaker of the Chamber. The government had to exert all its influence to get Nelson Marchezan elected to the post, threatening the PDS contingent and darkly auguring that *abertura* would be imperiled seriously if the government did not get its way. As the PDS became more unruly, the government became less able to control Congress. Without a comfortable margin there, and with the governorships of the largest states in the hands of the opposition, the necessity to impose order through the presidential dictatorship became more peremptory. However, the changing context of the *abertura* made this more difficult, even in the area of economic policy.

But the principal problem of the PDS lay with the military and with its conception of the role that the "party of the revolution" would play in the model. The "Mexicanization" of that party and of that model required that the PDS, not the military institution, become the official party. From 1964 to 1984 the Brazilian military could not bring this about. This failure, coupled with its desire to maintain the respectability of the regime by holding fairly competitive elections, was another effective cause of the transition. In the end, the military could not act like a political party without tearing itself apart, and its visceral distaste of "politics" kept it from allowing ARENA-PDS to play a prominent role. This being the case and with the logic of electoral competition allowed to take its course, it was only a matter of time before the military would decide to orchestrate a dignified and orderly retreat.

Conclusion

Because the Brazilian regime was the most successful of the bureau-cratic-authoritarian regimes of South America, a failure to consolidate itself in power is noteworthy. Because the Brazilian case included a transition without an explicit blueprint and without a pact, it will be analyzed and debated for some time. Many Brazilian scholars agree that a crisis of legitimacy was one of the taproot causes of the transition. National security and economic efficiency could not legitimize the regime despite "the miracle" and the successful internal war against subversion.[60] The military had no ideological substitutes for national security and economic efficiency. The crisis of legitimacy was aggravated by the government's inability to cope successfully with deteriorating economic conditions. From 1974 to 1982, legitimation through elections gave the Planalto a respite and enough time to resolve conflicts among military factions and to isolate violent obstructionists.

But these observations alone do not explain why the transition to democracy in Brazil took longer than in any other South American country. One alternative explanation is that the Planalto designed *distensão* primarily for *continuísmo* (staying in power), and that it did not plan to allow an opposition government until after a few elections. Although 1979–1981 is perceived as a time during which the liberalization was put on hold, it was precisely during this period that the Planalto gave some substantive content to the process. It was then that the limited *distensão* became an expanding *abertura* that eventually no one actor would be able to control.

The Brazilian case also illustrates the open-endedness of a process of democratic transition and the predominance of political factors. It would be hard to explain this process in terms of the cultural revisionist and fundamental rupture paradigms. However, the transition has not done away with the factors identified by such paradigms as obstacles to national political development or further democratization. I suggest that the antidemocratic values of many political actors and the bottlenecks of the exchanges between the domestic and external sectors of the Brazilian political economy can undermine the ultimate consolidation of a democratic regime in that country. However, political transitions and regime inaugurations are produced by many acts of political will by many different people. There is nothing deterministic or heroic about them.

By the same token it is easy to second-guess the Planalto strategists. Their basic problem was not one of faulty tactics or flawed execution. Their fundamental problem was that they sought to become respectable and to gain popular approval without shedding their *castelista* conceptions. They clung to these in a context in which their domination was deteriorating, and they wanted to maximize certainty in a process characterized by ambiguity. The last Planalto group may have left power convinced that government instability is a threat to national security. In conclusion, we cannot credit the Brazilian military itself with designing and implementing a genuine process of transition to democracy. However, it does deserve credit for finally allowing its initial project to become a democratization.

Acknowledgments

I am indebted to Ambassador John Crimmins and to professors Thomas Skidmore, David Fleischer, and Gary Wynia for their comments on and criticisms of the first draft of this essay. This volume's editor, Professor Wayne Selcher, contributed greatly to the distillation and refinement of many of the ideas presented here. I dedicate this essay to the memory of my colleague Frank Munger, who passed away on the day I finished its first draft.

Notes

1. See Kenneth P. Erickson, *The Brazilian Corporate State and Working-Class Politics* (Berkeley: University of California Press, 1977), pp. 15–26.

2. Riordan Roett, *Brazil, Politics in a Patrimonial Society* (New York: Praeger, 1978), pp. 42–47.

3. Thomas E. Skidmore, "Politics and Economic Policy-Making in Authoritarian Brazil, 1937–1971," in Alfred Stepan (ed.), *Authoritarian Brazil; Origins, Policies, and Future* (New Haven: Yale University Press, 1973), pp. 39–42.

4. Philippe C. Schmitter, "The Portugalization of Brazil?" in Stepan, op. cit., p. 185.

5. Ibid., pp. 185–186.

6. Ronald M. Schneider, *The Political System of Brazil* (New York: Columbia University Press, 1971), Chapters 4–6.

7. Peter Flynn, *Brazil, A Political Analysis* (Boulder, Colo.: Westview Press, 1978), Chapter 11.

8. Kalman H. Silvert, *Essays in Understanding Latin America* (Philadelphia: ISHI Publications, 1977), p. 12.

9. Guillermo O'Donnell, *Modernization and Bureaucratic Authoritarianism* (Berkeley: Institute of International Studies, 1973), pp. 89–106.

10. José Serra, "Three Mistaken Theses Regarding the Connection Between Industrialization and Authoritarian Regimes," in David P. Collier (ed.), *The New*

Authoritarianism in Latin America (Princeton, N.J.: Princeton University Press, 1979), especially pp. 101 and 113–148.

11. Ibid., p. 102, and Guillermo O'Donnell, *El estado burocrático autoritario* (Buenos Aires: Editorial Belgrano, 1982), pp. 60–62 and Chapter 2.

12. Alfred Stepan, *The State and Society, Peru in Comparative Perspective* (Princeton, N.J.: Princeton University Press, 1978), p. 47.

13. Schneider, op. cit., pp. 8–21 and 334–356.

14. I am referring to Juan J. Linz's seminal piece, "An Authoritarian Regime: Spain," in Erik Allardt and Yrjo Littunen (eds.), *Mass Politics, Studies in Political Sociology* (New York and London: The Free Press, 1970), p. 253.

15. Luis Maira, "Notas para un estudio comparado entre el estado fascista clásico y el estado de seguridad nacional," in Hugo Miranda (ed.), *El control político en el Cono Sur* (Mexico: Siglo XXI Editores, 1978), pp. 45–65.

16. Vania Bambiria and Theotônio dos Santos, "Dictadura militar y fascismo en Brasil," in Miranda, op. cit., p. 171.

17. Fernando Henrique Cardoso, "On the Characterization of Authoritarian Regimes," in Collier, op. cit., p. 40.

18. Silvert, op. cit., p. 113 and 117–118.

19. Cardoso, op. cit., pp. 48–49, emphasis added.

20. Fernando Henrique Cardoso, "La cuestión del estado en Brasil," *Revista mexicana de sociología* 37, no. 3 (julio–setiembre, 1975): 612–613; Flynn, op. cit., pp. 418–423; Schneider, op. cit., pp. 266–274.

21. Flynn, op. cit., p. 326, citing Mario Victor.

22. Schneider, op. cit., p. 72.

23. Ibid., p. 274; Flynn, op. cit., pp. 422–423.

24. Alfred Stepan, *The Military in Politics* (Princeton, N.J.: Princeton University Press, 1971), p. 75.

25. Alfred Stepan, "The New Professionalism of Internal Warfare and Military Role Expansion," in Stepan (ed.), *Authoritarian Brazil*, p. 47.

26. Celso Lafer, *O Sistema Político Brasileiro: Estrutura e Processo* (São Paulo: Editôra Perspectiva, 1975), p. 75.

27. *Latin America Political Report* (October 21, 1977), p. 323.

28. *Latin America Political Report* (December 9, 1977), p. 383.

29. Eli Diniz, "Empresariado e Transição Política no Brasil: Problemas e Perspectivas," paper delivered at the XI International Conference of the Latin American Studies Association, Mexico City, September 29–October 1, 1983, pp. 22–26.

30. *Latin America Political Report* (September 9, 1977), pp. 278–279.

31. *Latin America Political Report* (October 28, 1977), p. 331.

32. *Latin America Political Report* (December 23, 1977), pp. 394–396.

33. *Latin America Political Report* (October 27, 1978), pp. 343–344.

34. *Latin America Political Report* (April 8, 1977), pp. 105–106.

35. *Latin America Political Report* (April 22, 1977), pp. 114–116.

36. *Latin America Political Report* (March 10, 1978), pp. 78–79.

37. *Latin America Political Report* (August 25, 1978), p. 264.

38. *Latin America Political Report* (September 22, 1978), pp. 292–293.

39. David V. Fleischer, "Renovação Política—Brasil 1978: Eleições Parlamentares sob a Égide do 'Pacote de Abril,'" *Trabalhos em Ciências Sociais*, Série Sociologia 24 (Brasília: Fundação Universidade de Brasília, 1980), pp. 29–33.

40. *Latin America Political Report* (October 20, 1978), p. 324.

41. *Latin America Political Report* (January 26, 1979), p. 30.

42. "A Abertura, por Golbery: Documento—A Conferência Secreta da ESG," *Veja*, (September 10, 1980, pp. 3–4.

43. Ibid., pp. 4 and 6.

44. Bolivar Lamounier and José Eduardo Faria (eds.), *O Futuro da Abertura: Um Debate* (São Paulo: Cortez Editôra, 1981), p. 35.

45. *Latin America Regional Reports, Brazil* (March 13, 1981), p. 8.

46. For a more optimistic view see Guy Pfefferman and Richard Webb, "The Distribution of Income in Brazil," *World Bank Staff Papers*, no. 356 (September 1979). See Paulo Singer's critical review of this study in *Latin America Regional Reports, Brazil* (April 25, 1980), pp. 6–7. See also *Latin America Weekly Report* (March 28, 1980), pp. 6–7.

47. *Latin America Weekly Report* (March 21, 1980), pp. 5–6. See also *Latin America Weekly Report* (August 29, 1980), p. 5.

48. *Latin America Regional Reports, Brazil* (January 4, 1980), pp. 6–7.

49. *Latin America Weekly Report* (May 23, 1980), p. 7.

50. *Latin America Regional Reports, Brazil* (March 14, 1980), p. 4.

51. *Latin America Political Report* (November 3, 1978), p. 337.

52. *Latin America Political Report* (August 24, 1979), pp. 259–263.

53. *Latin America Regional Reports, Brazil* (September 12, 1980), pp. 1–2.

54. Ibid.; see also *Latin America Regional Reports, Brazil* (August 8, 1980), pp. 1–2.

55. *Latin America Weekly Report* (May 15, 1981), pp. 1–2.

56. *Latin America Regional Reports, Brazil* (October 16, 1981), p. 1.

57. For a more complete discussion of these dynamics see David Fleischer's chapter in this volume.

58. Cardoso, "Cuestión del estado," op. cit., p. 602.

59. Juan Felipe Leal, "The Mexican State: 1915–1973, A Historical Perspective," *Latin American Perspectives* 2, no. 2 (Summer 1975): 48–63.

60. Lamounier and Faria, op. cit., pp. 33–50.

2

Contradictions, Dilemmas, and Actors in Brazil's *Abertura*, 1979–1985

Wayne A. Selcher

General João Figueiredo, inaugurated president in March 1979, continued on the political liberalization course that his predecessor Ernesto Geisel had set, now under the name of *abertura* (opening) but in substantially changed circumstances as public demands for more democracy grew. Figueiredo had both sufficient democratic convictions and enough support in the military to isolate those who still sought to prolong military rule, including those who would do so by violence. With General Golbery do Couto e Silva as his mentor and endowed with a six-year term (expediently extended from five), Figueiredo's personable image and accomplishments in the first year led to a public atmosphere of political exuberance, optimism, rising expectations, and political progress. During Geisel's last months in office, he had eliminated some of the harsher legal instruments of the dictatorship, particularly Institutional Act Number 5. Many of the most arbitrary remaining features of the authoritarian regime were removed by Figueiredo in rapid succession and without backlash during 1979. The government successfully (albeit in some cases halfheartedly) preempted some of the opposition's causes, such as an implicitly unrestricted amnesty, freedom for political prisoners, tolerance of the banned National Student Union (UNE), greater toleration for strikes, and semiannual wage adjustments for inflation.

The widely welcomed party reform of December 1979 ended the dictatorship's imposed two-party system, but the new government's primary intention was to split the opposition Brazilian Democratic Movement (MDB) into several weaker parties through ruptures on the right and left wings. Rules on organization and voting, on the other hand, were designed to encourage a workable aggregation of forces (four or five parties) rather than an inoperably large number of small parties. Golbery also sought to end the pro and con nature of the two-party system and to create a basically centrist party culture to promote evolutionary change. The result was a more representative and generally accepted multiparty system, with the net effect of creating more options on the left. The opposition ranks, more affected than the official Democratic Social Party (PDS) by the changes, had to pay much attention to rapidly cultivating a constituency, organizing, and differentiating themselves from each other as well as from the government. This led to their begrudging acceptance of the government's postponement of municipal elections from 1980 to 1982, with the extension of the mandates of those officials already in office. In all, the system proved rather effective from 1979 to 1982 in engaging as participants both the newer elites resulting from the development process and the former political figures returning under unconditional amnesty.

Contradictions and Dilemmas of *Abertura*

During 1980 and into 1981, however, Figueiredo's initially strong popularity was challenged by less inhibited political activity, the death of imaginative Minister of Justice Petrônio Portela, anti-*abertura* violence from the right, the restrictive effects of the foreign debt, and mounting economic recession. As time went on, a constant sense of impending major shifts and growing complexity dampened the national spirit of self-confidence, raised the political stakes, soured the president's mood, and accentuated the inherent problematical contradictions and dilemmas of *abertura* that plagued the rest of Figueiredo's administration.

A more representative system of expression of interests naturally stimulates increased demands for equity and liberty as a reaction to the authoritarian regime's emphasis on growth and order. The nation was now a more politically mobilized society, with blatantly unequal opportunity in which the richest 10 percent of the population earned 47.7 percent of the income, while the poorest 60 percent earned but 19.6 percent of the income (1980). So *abertura*, carried to its logical democratic consequences, went beyond intra-elite institutional reform to open a larger social reform question of lower-class economic participation.[1] Few in the middle- and upper-classes that controlled politics were yet willing to deal with that long-postponed conundrum. Significantly, the Figueiredo government did not give up ultimate control over economic policy nor did it tie economic *abertura* to political *abertura*. (The government, however, did dispense favors in the paternalistic tradition to shore up support as seemed expedient.)

Political repression was at its height during the period of most rapid economic growth. Ironically, in what at first glance seemed a sort of perverse inverse proportionality, political liberalization under Figueiredo occurred during, and was made more difficult by, the building of Brazil's worst economic crisis (1981–1983) since the Great Depression. Brazil's international credit flagged, and it was no longer possible after 1980 to stave off recession through foreign borrowing. A task to tax the national political institutions was to manage a political opening while balancing authoritarian and democratic forces in an economic recession of unforeseeable severity and duration in a socioeconomically polarized society without provoking instability through political polarization. The government was coping both with challenges to its own authority and with potential threats to the existing social order.

A greater range and number of parties, factions, and interest groups (enumerated in Chapter 6) began to question the extent to which change could be officially controlled or channeled and to what extent a transition process would be allowed to spread only limited participation and benefits. With the attenuation of authoritarianism, more independent political trends arose to shape the agenda, some of them intensified by the feeling of uncertainty and by economic necessity. In this sense, economic crisis pushed political liberalization. The government became so saddled with economic discredit that tangible progress toward democracy, that is, toward its own removal from office, became its chief basis for legitimacy.

During the years of dictatorship and economic growth, the government was able to regard its economic policy as a technocratic matter above general political consultation. Allocation policies and effects were determined by a narrow range of actors. Economic crisis in a more open system, however, greatly increased the intensity of economic demands being made by a widening variety of actors, including previously repressed groups (such as labor and peasants), antistatist national entrepreneurs, and international actors such as the International Monetary Fund (IMF) and foreign creditors. *Abertura* both permitted and was made more complicated by the reactions of the groups affected by the government's austerity measures, measures that were adopted at IMF behest to maintain national creditworthiness and to attack the problem of payment of the foreign debt. The whole economic model came into serious question, with stakes heightened by the role of the state and of subsidies and controls in the economy.[2] Interpenetration of the political and economic realms created much more difficulty for government control of both sectors than when they could be kept separate. The speed of change once the two became interdependent outran governmental ability to anticipate challenges early enough to cut them short through political gimmickry (*casuísmos*) and paternalism or clientelism.

Opposition parties and groups were able to operate more freely as support for them spread and governmental attention focused increasingly on short-run tactical, rather than strategic, political purposes. The number of arenas of effective political competititon increased. In time, the amount of effort that the government put into frustrating the opposition and its own dissidents on the succession question seriously hindered its ability to administer the country. This diversion of attention, combined with the pace of change, multiplied recourse to short-term *saídas*, or quick fixes, which resulted in missed opportunities to build solid political institutions for the longer run. Attacks on worsening and broader socioeconomic problems challenging national stability were postponed until the next government. Unaddressed issues such as land tenure, population growth, and inflation piled up, presenting more urgent choices later on.

Recourse to elections created a serious dilemma for the government, as noted by Bolivar Lamounier.[3] The government used a series of contrived elections in the two-party system of 1966–1979 as a formalistic legitimation technique while depriving such elections of substantive policy consequences. The elections consistently went against the government and in effect turned into plebiscites on (and increasingly against) the whole system. Yet, given the government's declining electoral prospects and standings in the polls (carefully monitored by the National Intelligence Service—SNI), to allow the results of the elections to be faithfully mirrored in decisional outcomes would work to undercut the regime. The series of elections since 1974 generated upward expectational dynamics. Many factors increasingly weighed against an indefinite extension of liberalization on official terms, that is, of reduced but not eliminated authoritarianism with formalistic concessions to democratic practices. Pressure grew to end the gradualist and imposed phase by creating a constituent assembly, which would initiate authentic redemocratization.

The government, by simultaneously working to ensure the credibility of elections while loading the mechanisms to control results, was also undercutting the credibility of the party system through which it hoped to mobilize enough support to rule and eventually perhaps to turn power over to the politicians. The regime, more used to suppressing or manipulating the poorly institutionalized party system than working through it in good faith to develop it as an instrument of representation, first preferred to rule through a dominant party, à la Mexico. ARENA (National Renovating Alliance, then the official party) proved incapable of this role in the mid-1970s. The government decreed party reform in 1979 mainly to divide the opposition, to divert some dissatisfaction from itself, and to try (unsuccessfully) for a "loyalist" centrist party with which it could cooperate on a long-term basis. It was ill equipped tactically, especially after 1981, to operate within the more complex and uncertain multiparty system growing out of its own rules changes.

Public preferences in policy and candidates diverged increasingly from those acceptable to the government. Unable to create a "loyal" (i.e., docile) opposition, the government, with its zero-sum reasoning, found it difficult to accept the legitimacy of the authentic opposition and the idea of free alternation in power. The military regime's hardliners found only a fine line, if any, between opposition to key official policies and "challenging the regime" (contestar o regime), one of their taboos.

Figueiredo had to pay considerable attention to his "inner public," the military and security apparatus, more so after losing his following in the general public. Dissension over the flow of abertura and its very desirability continued at a low but troublesome level both within and between the army and the intelligence community, requiring his constant attention. Military fear of exposure for earlier repressive actions was only partially allayed by the governmental interpretation that the 1979 amnesty applied to excesses by all sides. Excesses of the police and security forces, as well as official corruption, still seemed beyond full legal accountability. Few expected major recriminations at the conclusion of *abertura*, but there was no certainty regarding what investigations and enforcement policies the next government might undertake, spurred by public opinion and a critical press.

As Congress slowly gained more power, the difficulties in moving from measured concessions with some reversals, through the phase of negotiations within the official PDS and the opposition, and on to more open and autonomous patterns of alignments raised doubts about the government's ability to govern without resort to gimmickry or measures of exception bordering on intimidation. Divisions within the administration, economic factors running out of government control, occasional government truculence toward the opposition, and intimidating rumors of *fechamento* (political closing) reinforced these doubts and underlined the vulnerability of *abertura*.

After the setbacks of 1981, Figueiredo became more open to the counsel of hardline advisers, such as SNI chief General Octávio Medeiros, a chief adversary of Golbery (who left office in August 1981). Faced with opposition insistence on a quicker pace of liberalization, the government characteristically asserted that the only real alternative to its own pace was chaos, radicalization, or an authoritarian involution. Ironically, the government's public credibility in fulfilling further the pledge of *abertura* depended upon its abandonment of the power resources to which it was most accustomed, just when it needed to institute unpopular economic measures demanded by the international financial community.

The ability of the Planalto group to diminish the state of exception and arbitrariness was not complemented by a timely ability to initiate a building of democratic practices. At the same time that social momentum was mounting toward what came to be called "the principle of consent" (of the governed), making it ever less likely that *abertura* could be reversed at acceptable cost, Figueiredo and his advisers continued to govern in a style increasingly out of tune with the trends of national opinion. They showed low sensitivity to or empathy with emerging political currents in civil society, nor were they able to come up with a workable alternative political and economic model to replace what was obviously failing. They were thus also ever less able to achieve Golbery's original objective of assuring the continuity in power of the "revolutionary coalition." Meanwhile, an uncensored press picked away at government scandals, foibles, and discrepancies between word and deed.

The November 1982 General Elections
as a Turning Point

Abertura in the form of a pragmatic bargaining process among unequals, still with unilateral changes in the rules, passed successfully through several severe tests in 1981, including a peak in antiliberalization, rightist terrorism. The government lost its principal manager of liberalization in August 1981 when Golbery, already on the defensive, resigned in protest over obvious and successful military pressure against a full official inquiry into the April 30, 1981, explosion outside a leftist popular-music concert at the Riocenter, an incident in which rightist military intelligence operatives were clearly implicated. (Ironically, although Golbery previously had been portrayed by the opposition as a sinister and undemocratic *éminence grise*, his resignation was mourned by nearly all the opposition, because it seemed a victory for hardline security elements.) His successor, João Leitão de Abreu, proved less capable as a strategist and tactician. On the positive side, the temporary assumption of the presidency by civilian Vice-president Aureliano Chaves after Figueiredo's heart attack in September was widely taken as a sign of military support for normalization.

The *direct* municipal, congressional, and gubernatorial elections of November 1982, the widest since 1962, became the next crucial test, given their role in measuring government popularity nationally, affecting the regime's ability to rule in Brasília and the key states, and determining in large measure the composition of the electoral college that would choose the next president. The very willingness to allow such broad elections and to abide by their results, in a period of economic hardship and after postponement of municipal elections from 1980 to 1982, showed the regime's dedication to maintaining a credible electoral schedule and an atmosphere in which an electoral opposition could survive.

The optimisitc spirit of the opposition was diminished, however, by the implacably imposed electoral "package" of November 1981, a retaliation for congressional defeat of an earlier piece of electoral legislation. The measure weakened the opposition parties' chances just as and because their collective standings in the polls looked strong. As always, government rules were applied to restrict apparent opposition strengths and to help rehabilitate the waning official PDS. Party alliances were prohibited, straight-ticket voting made mandatory, and all parties were required to submit candidates for all posts within a state in order to present a slate. The minority parties had weak to nonexistent structures in many of the slightly over four thousand *municípios*, unlike the PDS and the PMDB (Party of the Brazilian Democratic Movement). Given these constraints, the small and largely business-based Partido Popular (PP), which the government had hoped to use to build a progovernment center coalition, merged with the PMDB (from which many of its founders had come). In effect, long-run official hopes riding on the emergent PP were sacrificed to more immediate concerns about the PDS.

An additional electoral measure instituted a more complicated ballot without party and candidate names, requiring the voters themselves, still within the straight ticket, to write in all their candidates (a possible total of six) separately by name or number. The chief purpose of this *voto vinculado* (tied vote) was to increase the potential for strong local candidates or patronage givers to pull in the top of the ticket with them, on balance a benefit to the official party because of its more nearly nationwide presence in municipal office and its local and national patronage and machine advantages. The complicated ballot also required parties to spend considerable time teaching their adherents how to cast a valid party vote.

Constitutional Amendment 22, which went into effect on June 24, 1982, further improved the government's position in the elections and throughout Figueiredo's term. In essence, it set up a system to further overrepresent in the electoral system and the enlarged Chamber of Deputies the less-populated and less-developed states in which PDS strength lay, at the expense of major states in which opposition gains seemed certain. (São Paulo in particular was hard-hit by such measures.) The purpose of these devices was to save face from a clear electoral repudiation, to safeguard a viable legislative position, and, above all, to guarantee PDS control of the electoral college.[4]

Voting Patterns

Occasional overdrawn government warnings against opposition "radicalization" and implied threats about a possible "impasse" had some intimidating effects but did not prevent the unfolding of a lively and orderly campaign, with legally restricted television and enthusiastic mass-meeting outreach, and the calm realization of what were nearly universally regarded as very fair elections by Brazilian standards. All governors and the one-third of federal senators up for election were elected by simple majorities and all the federal deputies and state legislators by proportional representation. The party-strength results, as mediated by the electoral system, are shown in Table 2.1. (Also see Table 3.8.) The following outstanding patterns can be noted.

1. With only 41.5 percent of the total valid party vote, the government PDS gained 12 of the 22 elected governors (54.5 percent), 15 of the 25 senators (60 percent), 235 of the Chamber of Deputies seats (49 percent), and 52.8 percent of the seats in the electoral college.

2. With 58.5 percent of the total valid party vote, the opposition won the governorships of ten major or leadership states, representing 60 percent of the population and 75 percent of the GNP, largely in the Center-South. The most important of these were São Paulo, Rio de Janeiro, Paraná, and Minas Gerais. The opposition

TABLE 2.1
Party Vote Standings in the Brazilian General Elections of
November 1982

Party	Office			
	Governor	Senator	Federal Deputy	State Deputy
PMDB	39.6%	37.8%	36.5%	35.8%
PDS	37.3	36.5	36.7	36.0
PDT	5.4	5.1	4.9	4.8
PTB	4.2	3.9	3.8	3.7
PT	3.3	3.2	3.0	2.9
Blank	7.5	10.2	10.9	11.9
Void	2.7	3.3	4.2	4.9
TOTAL	100.0%	100.0%	100.0%	100.0%

Source: Superior Electoral Court (TSE) data reported in Diário
         da Justiça, November 28, 1983, pp. 18,682–18,686.

Note: Total votes cast, including blank and void, were 48.48
        million, out of an eligible electorate of 58.62 million,
        showing a low rate of abstention (17.3%).

swept control of the urban areas. The PMDB alone won governance
of 75 of the 100 largest cities in the nation, the PDS 17, the PDT
(Democratic Workers Party) 4, the PTB (Brazilian Labor Party) 2,
and the PT (Workers Party), 1. (No municipal elections were held
in Brasília.) The opposition won city council majorities in 19 of
the 23 state capitals and extended its control of municipalities
from 12.7 percent to 34.8 percent of the total of 4,085.[5]

3. As measured by total valid party vote for federal deputy by region,
   electoral support for the official PDS fell at 36.7 percent nationally,
   but approached or exceeded 50 percent only in the less-developed
   Northeast (64.7 percent) and North (47.7 percent).[6] Nine of the
   12 PDS governors were elected from the Northeast and North.
   Nationally, PDS success was inversely correlated with degree of
   urbanization and with degree of development. In the state of São
   Paulo, for example, the PDS won only 22.5 percent of the valid
   party vote for federal deputy, and the PMDB found strong municipal
   support. Even in the Northeast, the PMDB won council majorities
   in seven of the nine capital cities (except Aracajú and São Luís),
   while overwhelming PDS majorities were rolled up mainly in the
   interior.

4. If results are seen as a national poll on the bases of support between the two chief and only really national parties, both the PDS and the PMDB maintained very nearly the same distribution of their national vote percentages by states for their Chamber of Deputies cohorts as their predecessors ARENA and the MDB had in the elections of 1978. In 18 states and territories, largely the least populated and least developed, the variation between elections was within 1 percent for either party. With the minor exception of Ceará, all of the seven examples of greatest competition were in the industrialized and socially diversified Center-South, which experienced more multilateral contests involving a more fragmented opposition. The chief variations were:[7]

PDS		PMDB	
Rio Grande do Sul	(+4.7%)	Rio de Janeiro	(−10.3%)
São Paulo	(−4.0%)	São Paulo	(+5.5%)
		Paraná	(+2.1%)

5. The three smallest parties—PDT, PTB, and PT—gathered 11.7 percent of the vote for federal deputy but had very limited success geographically. Only the PDT elected a governor (Leonel Brizola, Rio de Janeiro). Using national Chamber of Deputies vote totals, the geographical concentration of party support by state is clear, as Rio Grande do Sul, Rio de Janeiro, and São Paulo stick out as the most competitive. The PT had a more national vote presence than the PDT and PTB, although often at a very low level.

States	Parties		
	PDT	PTB	PT
Rio de Janeiro	66.0%	27.4%	9.6%
Rio Grande do Sul	29.0		
Minas Gerais			7.2
São Paulo		69.8	71.3
Percentage of party's national vote total for federal deputy	95.0%	97.2%	88.1%

6. Rather few blank and void ballots were cast, and the abstention rate (17.3 percent) was the lowest in over twenty years. The high participation was apparently the result of widespread dissatisfaction with the status quo, coupled with the large number of offices to be filled and a sense that electoral power was now an effective instrument for change.

The results were ambiguous enough at various levels to provide both government and opposition with reason to celebrate, thus enhancing the legitimacy of the non-zero-sum electoral process. Neither side received a crippling setback, yet more of a balance of electoral power was struck between the two forces. PDS control of nearly two-thirds of the municipal governments, over half of the state governments, two-thirds of the Senate, and 52.6 percent of the electoral college, as well as near-control (a simple majority) of the Chamber of Deputies was balanced against the weight of the governorships and other gains made by the opposition, including its stronger showing in the vote totals, the larger cities, the modern regions of the country, and the middle class.

Political Effects of the Elections

The elections marked a clear and pivotal stage in the lessening of the government's ability to control *abertura*. Results clearly rewarded the moderate and pragmatic candidates and culled extremists or ideologues of left and right, providing a conciliatory political atmosphere in spite of the urgency of the issues. Hardline warnings of "dangerous radicalization" lost general credibility. The opposition received an institutional and legitimacy base much larger than before. (Previously, the opposition had only one governor, Chagas Freitas of Rio de Janeiro, a clientelistic politician amenable to Brasília's style of governance.) The national government, dependent in large measure on political rigging and administrative favoritism for its victories, had to meditate seriously on its declining electoral support and the disadvantages of future direct elections. Manipulative *casuísmos* now held doubtful utility in controlling electoral outcomes. The PDS found support nationwide, but the role of the Northeast as PDS bastion markedly raised that region's political capital and value of participation in the liberalization and succession processes.

Beyond the above mixed regional patterns, at the national aggregate level no sharp political cleavages were revealed, providing evidence that cultural, ethnic, rural-urban, and even class voting determinants were far from absolute. The election neither revealed a politically polarized society nor served to set group staunchly against group.[8] Yet social-class effects on voting have been noted in electoral and survey analyses over time. One study, for example, showed that in the city of São Paulo in elections from 1966 to 1978, the ratio of votes given to ARENA relative to those given to the MDB declined as one scanned results from the richest zones of the city downward to the poorest. Similar results were found in PDS/opposition vote ratios in 1982, although heterogeneity of incomes and votes within each zone preclude the deduction of a linear relationship between income levels and oppositionist voting.[9] Middle-class dissatisfaction with the regime and the economy was a major contributing factor to PMDB victories, especially in the Center-South where the middle class is most influential. The message for change was clear in the campaign, the results, and the aftermath. Even PDS candidates in urban regions had to base their campaigns on a change-oriented theme more than in 1978.

Opposition rhetoric and successes were such as to give further credence to the thesis that neo-Marxism, strong in opposition intellectual thought from 1964–1974 was further giving way with *abertura* to a more moderate or compromising reformist attitude more compatible with representative democracy. This change turned the center of attention away from a polarizing and combative class interpretation of politics toward discussion of national problems such as the building of representative institutions, alternation in power, democratic principles, pluralism, evolutionary change, and protection of minorities. (The political evolutions of Leonel Brizola of the PDT and Fernando Henrique Cardoso of the PMDB are prime examples of this more general shift.) The opposition was careful not to antagonize the radical right within the military and adapted to the political manipulations, hoping for continued expansion of participation even while working through (and against) a weighted system.

The election led to talk of a political truce, national conciliation, consensus, a social pact, and closing the gap between government and the opposition. Alternation in power was clearly down the road if *abertura* progressed, yet the rise to leadership of more "trustworthy" opposition figures and PDS control of the electoral college that would choose the next president gave the government more time to broaden its social base, should it desire to and find that possible.

The election campaign, with intensive press coverage and polling, stimulated a broad and effervescent public debate on pressing national issues—notably, unemployment, inflation, personal security, housing, health care, and corruption—and spread political education, awareness, and probably rising expectations. Strongly nationalistic appeals and political violence were rare in spite of the urgency of the issues. The vote expressed a desire for change and gave credibility to *abertura*, parliamentary and electoral procedures, and democratic ideals for many groups. With low rates of abstention and few blank or void ballots, the electorate also showed a sophistication sufficient to handle the cumbersome electoral procedures, especially remarkable because so many millions of young voters were participating for the first time.

The two major parties—PDS and PMDB—certified their dominance of the system, each with a substantial vote in every state. Absence of a PDS absolute majority in the national Chamber of Deputies endowed the smaller parties with disproportionate bargaining power there. The smaller parties, although saddled with the restrictions of the November 1981 electoral "package," demonstrated a following within a short time, a role which promised to grow. Their continued existence over the next several years was made possible only by the suspension until after the 1986 elections of an exigent constitutional provision requiring a threshold of 5 percent of the national vote total cast for the Chamber of Deputies, distributed in at least nine states, with a minimum of 3 percent of the vote in each of the nine.

Election results lent support and viability to the opposition strategy of forcing continually broader negotiations by showing the government that it could not govern and control the succession by itself and by encouraging a dialogue with all sectors of the opposition in making important national policies, modifying the constitution, and selecting the next president. The stage was thus set for coalition politics, broader institutional reforms, and a civilian candidate for president.

The election brought in many new leaders at all levels and brought some important changes (direct and indirect) in political fortunes to established individual careers. Outstanding cases of those who gained in national prominence include the following:[10]

1. Leonel Brizola—PDT governor of Rio de Janeiro and presidential aspirant in case of direct elections
2. Roberto Campos—former ambassador (to London and Washington) and minister of planning (under Humberto Castelo Branco), PDS federal senator from Mato Grosso
3. Fernando Henrique Cardoso—PMDB federal senator from São Paulo and opposition intellectual
4. Severo Gomes—PMDB federal senator from São Paulo and ex-minister of industry and commerce from the Geisel years
5. Marco Maciel—PDS senator from Pernambuco, ex-governor, and vice-presidential hopeful
6. Antônio Carlos Magalhães—PDS former governor of Bahia and presidential aspirant
7. Paulo Maluf—PDS former governor of São Paulo, wheeler-dealer federal deputy (SP) with a national record number of votes, and a leading presidential contender
8. Nelson Marchezan—PDS leader in the Chamber of Deputies (RS)
9. André Franco Montoro—PMDB governor of São Paulo, a former senator elected with business support and backed by a social democratic intellectual team
10. Tancredo Neves—lifelong conciliatory politician, PMDB governor of Minas Gerais, PMDB-PDS centrist "bridge," former senator, and presidential hopeful

Official Reaction

The government interpreted the results of the elections as legitimate (albeit lamentable) indicators of the political forces in civilian society and as providing parameters for further developments. Figueiredo had campaigned heartily and heavily, with a personable image, and was surprised by the extent of opposition victories. At first he took the loss as an affront. The head of his military household, General Rubem Ludwig, convinced the government to treat the opposition governors in a manner more cordial than formalistic aloofness. The military as an institution was publicly acquiescent toward the election results, and Figueiredo squashed an isolated and quixotic plan by a few disgruntled and mostly retired generals in Rio to keep Brizola from taking office.

The March 15, 1983, gubernatorial inaugurations were widely regarded as the end of the absolute power of the regime installed in 1964 and as an opportunity to broaden political participation more quickly. The military used the occasion to stay in the barracks and stress its disengagement. The opposition governors were now able to control important states without federal intervention, while PDS governors in the Northeast became more assertive in their demands on Brasília because of their enhanced roles as party stalwarts. With a fresh mandate and buoyed by the spirit of the elections, the Congress and the PDS became more assertive toward the executive as well.

The government had a propitious moment to recoup its losses by building credibility through an imaginative spirit of conciliation and change. Figueiredo, however, made no significant policy shifts and limited himself to offering a "truce" to the opposition, an ambiguous term that implied at least a prior state of belligerency on the government's part. As far as economic policy and the role of the "economic trio" (Planning Minister Antônio Delfim Neto, Treasury Minister Ernane Galvêas, and Central Bank President Carlos Langoni) were concerned, it was as if the elections had not occurred. Wider participation in decisions was becoming crucial to build consensus in both the political class and the public for economic austerity measures that were to be taken under IMF insistence on dealing with the debt issue. Figueiredo was used to handing out *abertura* milestones and fought hardliners who wanted to delay the elections, but the results showed a new phase in which negotiations with the opposition were now more necessary. His pronouncements became less authoritarian, but he found it difficult to change political style and increasingly lost effectiveness because of that.

A Crisis of Central Authority: 1983

By mid-1983 Brazil began to suffer seriously from what Brazilians call *desgovêrno*—disorienting misgovernment. Figueiredo's immediate problems in 1983 proved overwhelming for him and his government—floods in the South, continuing drought and hunger in the Northeast, serious economic recession with growing unemployment, inflation of 200 percent per year, a foreign debt of $90 billion with $3 billion arrears on interest by the end of 1983, and sporadic social disturbances endangering a narrow and controlled political-class solution.

The inauguration of ten opposition governors proved to be one of President Figueiredo's least pressing problems. These men, well aware of the degree of concentration of state resources in the federal government and the delicacy of the political moment, immediately rejected the idea of an oppositionist front. They moved cautiously to avoid confrontation and to give the president no grounds for accusing them of aggravating national problems. With resources scarce, they were willing to think realistically small and to work for marginal gains such as tax reform to benefit the states, reduction of the role of state companies, and decentralized administrative control. Power moderated their style, as well as tarnishing their image somewhat. They closed ranks with Brasília to condemn and repress public disturbances, a wild card which could threaten the gentlemen's agreement that *abertura* had become. Governors Tancredo Neves (MG) and Leonel Brizola (RJ) were more firm with the first mob action of April 1983, which was caused by economic hardships, than was André Franco Montoro (SP), but the latter became less timid after reprimands from President Figueiredo. The federal government stalled on reforms to benefit state governments because the opposition would be strengthened thereby. As the months passed, the opposition governors and ultimately the PDS governors became important actors in broadening the succession process.

Because economic matters were not Figueiredo's strong suit, he allowed minister of planning Antônio Delfim Neto to dominate that area and to be both disciplinarian and lightning rod for criticism, resulting in poor central policy coordination among ministries. Delfim Neto oscillated between progrowth policies and austerity measures because of contradictory pressures from the domestic front and the IMF. Bickering and short-term coping and fending were the result of the lack of a coherent central plan. Economic abuses and overruns went unpunished. There was during 1983 and 1984 the widespread impression of a reactive government in disarray, a crisis of authority without economic, political, and financial control, and without new approaches. There was also the image of a government marking time until the end of its term, without the competency, public support, or power of decision to solve the mounting problems, a government that within a year frittered away the national image of responsibility vital to the country's economic future. Negative contrasts were drawn with Mexico's relative ability at the time to put its economic affairs in order. The consequent loss of a sense of governmental direction, in a country dominated by the state, deprived the political sectors of a feel for where things were heading, causing a degree of uncertainty not recently known in Brazil. "Long-range planning" became preparation for the next month.

Figueiredo did not wear well as a politician toward the end of his term because he did not have a taste for working within the party politics that he helped to bring about. His authoritarian background and hierarchical preferences were out of synchronization with civilian politics and with the changing balance of executive-legislative power sharing. His style became defensive and less effectual after he was stung by the results of the November 1982 elections, peeved by opposition criticisms and the drop in his public popularity, and deeply irritated by defections from his party (which he was continually less able to control). His distaste for politics, complicated by coronary problems and subsequent bypass surgery in the United States (July 1983), was a major cause of the crisis of leadership and sense of drift in the government as his term drew to a close.

The president was constantly plagued by a dilemma; on one hand, at sixty-five, he gave indications of a desire to retire and relieve himself of the burdens of leadership, yet, on the other hand, his sense of dedication to a satisfactory succession compelled him to remain. The more overwhelmed he became, the stronger was the tendency to hold onto Delfim Neto obsessively as the key to his economic policy, and not to change ministers generally (out of a sense of loyalty). Carlos Langoni, president of the Central Bank, and Hélio Beltrão, the popular social welfare minister, both resigned to protest the degree of centralization of economic policy and the unworkability of Delfim's goals. The economic czar himself remained untouchable, and he went on to make a series of agreements with the IMF that were repeatedly renegotiated because Brazil did not fulfill them.

Vice-president Aureliano Chaves's successful but cautious exercise of the presidency during Figueiredo's six-week absence for surgery and recuperation was well received by broad segments of the civilian and military leadership as he was well regarded as serious, reasonable, trustworthy, and approachable by all camps. Yet Golbery's assertion that Figueiredo had neither will nor health to govern, or the suggestion by top military advisers Délio Jardim de Mattos and Walter Pires de Albuquerque (and many civilians) that the president take a prolonged break for recuperation and leave Chaves to deal with the debt renegotiation, negotiations with the opposition, and controversial antiinflation measures only spurred him to return to office more quickly.

Presidential civilian staff chief Leitão de Abreu's role as political coordinator among the ministries and vis-à-vis the politicians was seriously impeded by his imperious or indifferent attitude toward the PDS leadership and the rank and file, an aloof style more in keeping with his same role in the Médici government. In contrast to Golbery's practice, Leitão sidelined the minister of justice as a chief political strategist for the government. Leitão and General Octávio Medeiros (head of the National Intelligence Service) fell out over Leitão's record as strategist, causing problems of coordination between the civil and military staffs as Leitão consolidated influence as chief political planner, assumed functions that Figueiredo dropped, and helped to thwart Medeiros's presidential ambitions.

Because Leitão served as a de facto linchpin of the administration, these considerations did not bode well for a broadening of the government's political base in Brasília. They also opened up space for successful maneuvering by the legendary and still influential Golbery on the shape of the regime and the succession question in a direction different from Figueiredo's preferences, as politicians streamed to him for advice and he made veiled statements to the press. The initiative thus passed to the political parties and social groups as a national social consensus for a broad-front negotiation emerged and grew strong.

The Major Political Parties' Roles in *Abertura*

Political parties in Brazil have been weak historically in performing the classic functions of interest aggregation and translating voter preferences into public policy. Most parties have served limited patronage clienteles, have been largely nonideological and only weakly programmatic, and have operated principally to mobilize votes for specific leaders. As much of the population was effectively excluded from the political process, parties originated in the legislature or were created by the executive rather than emerging from the grassroots. State control and manipulation of parties was the norm rather than the exception. During the military regime, party weakness in the linkage or mediatory function between government and citizenry or between executive and legislative branches was further intensified by measures to limit effective opposition, govern around the parties, reduce the frequency and significance of elections, and distort the representation system to favor ARENA and the PDS.

This repeated malapportionment of the electoral system to the disadvantage of more developed areas was used mainly to counteract (but only on a stop-gap basis) one of the dominant trends of Brazilian electoral outcomes since 1945—the gradual and almost linear decline in voter support for conservative parties, which draw heavily on the traditional Brazilian population and thus on a declining demographic base.[11] Urbanization, mobilization of the lower-class vote, education, and socioeconomic development generally have presented challenges that conservative parties in Brazil have been unable to meet. Beyond electoral manipulation, dissension among opposition elements served somewhat to delay the policy effects of this electoral trend, carried forward more effectively in practical consequences by the 1982 elections than by those that preceded them.

As Lamounier and Rachel Meneguello have observed, opposition party success despite the antiparty measures of the dictatorship served in some senses to counteract in the public mind the cynicism usually felt toward parties. The prodemocracy and rule-of-law opposition rhetoric of the period, the organizational resistance it demanded, the focus on enhancing electoral legitimacy, and the trend away from party proliferation and localism toward two electoral centers and national party identification are paradoxically positive legacies for effective party governance under democracy.[12] It remains to be seen, of course, whether these conditions of the transition persist under a more competitive civilian regime.

The 1982 election campaign, the results, the events that occurred soon afterward provided a clearer picture of the programs and follower profiles of the five principal parties of the Figueiredo term and of the key roles they played in the ensuing outcome of *abertura*.

Partido Democrático Social (PDS)

The PDS, the party run by the government rather than the party running the government, suffered from years of being taken for granted and manipulated as a mouthpiece of the executive. It was a reflection of the administration and a distributor of patronage through clienteles rather than a creator of ideas. The president of the party was named by the president of the republic, not elected. Because of the party's subservience to the executive, it participated until late 1983 in the continued subordination of Congress, its logical base for more autonomy. The PDS lost in public image during its complete identification with an increasingly unpopular government (over whose policies it had no control) and its descendence from ARENA, the imposed official party of the dictatorship. The PDS still suffers from a history of dwindling electoral support and during *abertura* had few young national stars other than Deputy Nelson Marchezan, Senator and later Minister of Education Marco Maciel, and Governor Esperidião Amin (SC).

PDS victories in November 1982 owed much to government electoral engineering and distribution of largesse. After the election, patronage favors were cut off in areas that suffered PDS losses, which weakened the party's clientelist machines there. Nor did the party receive any recompense at the federal level to offset their losses in the states and cities. During early 1983, the party was already experiencing dissidence in Congress along two major lines: (1) the "participationist" faction, which was discontented with PDS "manager" Leitão de Abreu and wanted more voice, and (2) various factions supporting several would-be candidates for president in 1985 rather than waiting to hew to Figueiredo's lead. Subsequent proliferation of would-be official candidates just multiplied divisions within the party.

PDS members first elected to Congress in 1982 were especially unhappy in a subservient role after the energetic campaigns many of them undertook. With eyes on the presidency, Deputy Paulo Maluf (SP) encouraged the dissent. The government's offers of positions to entice the thirteen PTB deputies into coalition in the Chamber from May to August 1983 incensed the neglected party. The newly created, prorenovation "participationist" slate elected 35 percent of the national directorate in July 1983 but received no seats on the executive commission. (PDS president José Sarney, however, nearly lost his post.) Northeast PDS politicians began demanding more government attention to drought and poverty problems in their region. The rank-and-file PDS leaders in the cities clearly were becoming more socially responsive than they were previously and increasingly critical of government policies they saw as advancing inequity and threatening to transform an economic crisis into a social crisis.

Because demands for *abertura* within the PDS went essentially unresolved, government control of the PDS faded during 1983, and in 1984 the ranks suffered desertion to a centrist coalition that ended the

PDS electoral college majority and threatened to doom the party to minority status. Neither Figueiredo nor Leitão de Abreu proved adept at healing the growing dissidence. Both seemed more indignant or bored than conciliatory, demanding unconditional loyalty in styles more appropriate to the pre-1979 political scene, even though Figueiredo's nationwide travels during 1983 and 1984 to hold onto succession showed greater consultation and consensus building than previously. The change was too little, too late.

All these flaws, combined with a vulnerable simple majority in the Chamber of Deputies, created serious problems of congressional relations for the executive and complicated the transition to the succession, the selection process itself, and the post-1985 reliability of the PDS as an effective vehicle for those who try to govern and legislate through it. The party's national electoral future will be heavily affected by the intraparty dispute between those representing old-style clientelism typical of the interior and the less-developed regions and those advocating more progressive styles and policies more attuned to modern Brazil and the party's roots in the Center-South (roots heavily disadvantaged by the military regime's electoral manipulations).

Partido do Movimento Democrático Brasileiro (PMDB)

The PMDB is a reformist, broad-spectrum, programmatic party with a heavily urban base, centered in the middle class and the upper levels of the working class, and led by liberal professionals. Among Brazilian parties, it is the one most similar to the Western organizational-mediator-style party. It is a lineal descendent of the MDB, but the 1979 party reform caused some of the MDB followers and politicians to bolt to the other four opposition parties. The small and short-lived Partido Popular (PP), a probusiness party based in São Paulo and Minas Gerais, merged with the PMDB in 1982, which gave impetus to a moderating trend and a centrist appeal within the party. This was further enhanced by the victory of moderates in the national directorate elections in December 1983. The PMDB is not personalistic (unusual and still somewhat of a disadvantage in Brazil) and constantly labors against potential splits in its diverse ranks because it is more of an agglomeration or a "rainbow" than a united party. It suffered during *abertura* from a reactive oppositionist stance. The affiliates of this party constituted a spectrum from Minas Gerais Governor Tancredo Neves (a frequent interlocutor with the Presidential Palace and the PDS) to Miguel Arraes (Northeast leftist firebrand during the Goulart period). Public opinion polls showed it to have a basically centrist yet reformist image.

The presence of a few leftist and Communist former bêtes noires in the party and its resistance to co-optation because of its reformist and programmatic nature annoyed political strategists in the Presidential Palace, who constantly hoped to hatch a scheme to split off some co-optable followers. The defeat of the clientelist Chagas Freitas-faction candidate of the PMDB in the Rio gubernatorial race (Miro Teixeira) was a particular blow because that declining wing of the party had been congenial to the government in Brasília.

The PMDB had built reliable electoral bases since 1974 and served as the main benefactor of the antigovernment vote in November 1982. Under the slogan "Hope and Change," it played up its position as the most established and best-known alternative to the PDS. The "old warrior" advantages will weaken with time as the party system becomes more competitive. The party came out of *abertura* in good shape, but it lost adherents as new center and left parties were formed after March 1985. Overall, power has accentuated disparities within the party, especially between the pragmatic local and state officeholders, on one side, and the more "authentic" national directorate, plus some federal deputies and senators, on the other.

The party's political program in 1983-1984 clustered around a number of largely procedural and prodemocracy demands with uncertain substantive outcomes—an elected constitutional convention, direct election of mayors of state capitals, direct election for president, independence of the judicial branch, more power for Congress, and a moratorium on foreign-debt payments. The program also was critical of foreign multinationals and state enterprises. During the latter phase of *abertura*, the accommodationist style of the PMDB and its focus on Congress as the appropriate forum for national negotiations on the political future facilitated the formation of a broad-front opposition movement to decide the presidential succession.

Partido Democrático Trabalhista (PDT)

The PDT is still largely a personal vehicle of Leonel Brizola, who formed it when the Supreme Electoral Tribunal denied him the use of the famous PTB initials, which harkened back to the Getúlio Vargas years. Its base is almost completely limited to the states of Rio de Janeiro (where Brizola is governor) and Rio Grande do Sul (his native state). In Rio de Janeiro, the PDT drew votes well in working-class areas and within the middle class. It won a simple majority in the state assembly and a majority the city chamber, but its candidates fared poorly in comparison to those of the PDS and the PMDB in the interior. Brizola, the effective party head, is not party president and gets along poorly with the party's congressional delegation. The PDT has been working on its internal organization and "socialist option," as developed by Brizola in collaboration with West European democratic socialist parties during his long exile. (Mário Soares of Portugal and Willy Brandt of West Germany were particularly important contacts.) Brizola has therefore attracted more intellectual support for his administration than is usual for a governor and may in the future more clearly declare socialist tendencies.

His initial gubernatorial relations with the conservative military (including some retired generals) were uneasy because of his leftist and antimilitary reputation of twenty years earlier and his current socialism. Consequently he tried to protect his fragile availability as a presidential candidate by cultivating a reasonable, constructive, and cooperative image as governor, striking compromises and launching low-cost community action projects to achieve a respectable record. His ultimate ambition is the presidency. Surveys during 1983 showed him to be the strongest candidate by far in a direct election in spite of lack of a national party base. By late 1984, however, his popularity had been so badly tarnished by the realities of governance that he was among the least popular of the major governors in the public opinion polls.

Partido Trabalhista Brasileiro (PTB)

Small as it is, the PTB illustrates the power of a label and the power of negotiation of small parties on which the PDS hoped to rely for support on crucial issues. The party, in keeping with its trading on the still mystical image of Getúlio Vargas, was born in the shadow of its leader, Vargas's grandniece Ivete Vargas. She assumed control in 1980 from a minority position in a "newcomers versus oldtimers" dispute with Brizola, thanks to friendship with Golbery and federal desires to disadvantage Brizola by giving the label's symbolism to a "trustworthy" party. From May to August 1983, the PTB entered into an opportunistic and tempestuous coalition with the PDS in the Chamber of Deputies, to attempt a PDS-PTB majority. The hard-bargaining Ivete broke off the coalition when insufficient moderately proworker legislative changes and federal positions for a patronage network were forthcoming.

The failed PDS-PTB coalition, soon swept aside in significance by PDS defections, was symptomatic of the government's inflexible approach to the increasingly autonomous party politics that eventually undercut its power and pulled succession from its grasp. As the PTB started out closely tied to Ivete's dynamic person and did not find a firm electoral constituency, its future was placed in serious jeopardy by her death in January 1984.

Partido dos Trabalhadores (PT)

The PT is unique among parties in Brazil today in being based authentically on the workers' movement rather than on either the middle or upper class. It is not a paternalistic party or a creation of the government to control the labor movement. Its origin goes back only to the 1978 ABC region metalworkers strikes in São Paulo in which its leader, Luís Inácio da Silva (Lula), then a union president, attained fame. The party is militantly prolabor and takes a purist "class party" stance toward cooperation with other parties because of their poor records on workers' questions. Through cooperation with the more assertive labor unions (the *nôvo sindicalismo*) and the Catholic Church's Ecclesiastical

Base Communities (CEBs) and workers' pastorate (the *pastoral operária*), the PT established directorates and candidate slates for 1982 in all states but Alagoas. In many cases these were little but skeleton organizations, yet their existence represented quite an accomplishment when contrasted to the PTB's failure to achieve a candidates' roster in thirteen states and the PDT's failure in eleven.

The PT's organizational inexperience and combative spokespersons for its separateness cost it dearly in 1982. Ironically, it did not even win mayoralties in the ABC region but only five local council seats and nine seats in the state assembly because the worker vote was aimed at changing the state government and went to André Franco Montoro (PMDB). Lula's candidacy for governor did not seem credible to workers as an anti-PDS choice, especially after he made several television appearances in which he attacked the other opposition parties on nearly the same basis as he did the PDS. The mandatory straight-ticket vote and the party's exclusivity badly hurt the local PT candidates. In São Paulo state, the party received 9.9 percent of the gubernatorial vote and 9.0 percent of the vote for federal deputy. In Rio de Janeiro, the PT candidate for governor received only 2.8 percent of the vote and candidates for federal deputy only 2.6 percent of the vote.

The São Paulo-centered party's bases are heavily urban—the ABCD regions' workers, middle-class leftist intellectuals, and parts of the masses influenced by liberation theology. It has a significant middle-class–voter component. The party is bifurcated into a practical political-action wing (largely industrial workers) and a theoretical intellectual wing with neo-Marxist tendencies (with numerous university student radicals and professors). The more militant adherents subscribe to class-struggle ideology. During *abertura*, the PT remained much more a nucleus of activists and enthusiasts than a mass party, emphasizing social action and building its bases more than electoral strength aimed at 1982.

The Influence of Public Opinion and Social Actors on *Abertura*

A very high rate of urbanization, higher levels of literacy and education, *abertura* itself, the economic crisis, and the atmosphere of the elections mobilized many groups and gave rise to associational pluralism, intermediate groups, and social movements that make Brazil's political system increasingly complex and harder to predict. Elite-level groups were the main players. A number of professional organizations, such as the Brazilian Lawyers Association (OAB) and the Brazilian Press Association (ABI), were in the forefront of the drive for further political liberalization, as was the National Student Union (UNE). The press began investigative reporting, disclosing scandals, pointing out errors and incongruities, expanding and deflating the hyperactive rumor mill, fueling debates, and picking up causes (for example, state enterprises by the *Estado de São Paulo* and police abuses by the *Jornal do Brasil*).[13]

Significant growth in mass organization has been registered in the labor movement, the peasant movement, the base communities of the Catholic Church, and in neighborhood associations, but the labor movement has had the clearest national political impact so far. No exclusive ties with parties have developed for any of these incipient collective movements, although they all appeal to progressive tendencies. Three parties claimed to speak primarily for labor during the transition, for example, and more were legally recognized in 1985. The emerging pattern of relationships between social movements and parties and between social movements and the government will become more important in articulation of the interests of the poor and the disadvantaged. These networked urban movements are a major innovation because they do not owe their existence to the government and resist elitist politics and the traditional paternalistic style of control. They are still a bit wary of institutionalization, even within their own movement, and they value autonomy. They are therefore a challenge to the state's domination of civil society and to the controlled and limited agenda usually characterizing Brazilian politics.

Their political significance is in the long-run effect of the raising of their members' political consciousness regarding the causes of inequities and domination, in the development of participation and organizational power, and in the encouragement of democratic political and social action to defend group interests. They sought during *abertura* to resist a narrowly negotiated "political class" or intra-elite consensus, a formalistic limited democracy to consolidate gains heavily for the middle and upper classes. In the process, more aspiring political participants were trained and more issues insistently raised. In the medium and longer runs, the ability of government to ignore or manipulate grassroots promobilization groups will likely diminish, whereas the groups' capabilities to bring new demands to the system and to expand the agenda effectively are likely to grow.[14]

Public Opinion

Public opinion polling in the metropolitan capitals flourished with *abertura* and the election period, providing a reading of the changing national mood, but analysis of that mood's diffuse impact is more problematical.[15] Direct elections made the politicians take articulate public opinion somewhat more seriously than before. Mass opinion still counts for little, short of outbreaks of disruptive behavior. Middle-class opinion, on the other hand, has been significant (although seldom unified) because of the role this approximately 20 percent of the population plays as a source of national creative power and political and economic recruitment. The middle class was, on balance, a strong supporter of *abertura* but by 1983 felt unconsulted, badly pressed in purchasing power by the economy, insecure, and cynical in the face of a government abounding with revelations and rumors of unpunished irregularities and corruption.

Political confusion in the face of national problems gave little cause for hope or trust in the government.

After the euphoria of the 1982 elections, in which the economy was a major issue, public opinion turned glum during the deepening recession in 1983. Gloomy economic forecasts and fears of impending disaster proliferated. Used to a record of strong growth for decades, middle- and upper-class Brazilians found it difficult to adjust to a serious economic downturn and the prospect of lower economic expectations for an extended period. Regarding issues, the three chief concerns expressed in a May 1983 national sample of twelve metropolitan areas were unemployment (44.3 percent), income levels (16.3 percent), and inflation (15.5 percent), whereas only 7.2 percent expressed concern about the foreign debt and a mere 1.1 percent about the process of democratization. A declining standard of living in the near future was expected by 58.5 percent, and three-quarters of the population saw solutions as "distant" or "very distant." A plurality of 39.6 percent blamed the economic crisis on government policies.[16] There were few supporters of further austerity measures. Blame earlier reserved for adverse international economic circumstances and the IMF apparently was being shifted to the Figueiredo government. Many felt that the government was more concerned with the IMF and foreign bankers than with the economic well-being of Brazilians.

Considering the severity of its economic condition, the mass public was more passive or patient than reactive or unruly, as if not desiring to trigger a violent reversal of liberalization, leery as it was of past government excesses. Sporadic lootings and burnings by mobs in early 1983 warned decisionmakers that further aggravation of both economic and political conditions could set the stage for more frequent and serious episodes, which could threaten public order and provoke the military to forceful reaction. These anomic outbursts were limited in number and in damage done but produced a strong psychological effect, as did the serious and longer-term increase in street crime.

The Figueiredo government became constantly more unpopular with the general public and politically isolated. The president's personal popularity hit its height in late 1979, fell through 1980, recovered a bit in 1981, but fell continually after early 1982. His initial reputation as champion of liberalization wore thin, and the public became ever less willing to separate him from its harsh evaluation of his government. In July 1984, his national opinion poll rating hit −44 percent, the lowest of his term to that point.[17] (Planning Minister Delfim Neto was even more unpopular). As a result, in March 1985 Figueiredo left office a resentful man who felt his contributions were not appreciated by the politicians or the public at large.

In a rather rapid turnaround, the latter half of 1984 saw a revival of the more typical national self-confidence, bouyancy, resilience, and faith in the future. There was a feeling that the worst had passed and the bottom had not fallen out nor had the social fabric torn. The upswing in optimism was caused by signs of economic recovery, the evolution of a national spirit of political consensus, and hope for a broadly acceptable civilian candidate for president now that the military regime gave signs of being on its last legs.

The massive, energetic, and peaceful public demonstrations in many cities from January to April 1984 in favor of direct elections for president ("*Diretas Já!*"), were unsuccessful in attaining enough congressional votes to achieve that goal. They did serve as irrefutable proof to opponents of liberalization that public opinion across an impressive spectrum demanded a representative civilian president, a continuation of the transition, and major economic changes through a change in government. The principle of consent of the governed, of public consultation, was clearly defended. In those demonstrations national symbols such as the flag and the national anthem, regarded sceptically by many during the dictatorship, again became objects of civic pride.

Major Business and Industry Executives

The large national entrepreneurs were an important part of the civilian revolutionary coalition in 1964 and initially benefited from the economic model it implanted. Their discontent, clear by the late Geisel years, challenged the terms of the politically narrow base of the "security and development" style of authoritarian capitalism that had relied on the partnership of the military, the technocrats, national industrial capital, and foreign capital.[18] The overoptimistic Second National Development Plan (1975–1979) implied a growing role for the state in the economy. With increased national indebtedness, lower rates of economic growth, and the self-sufficient aloofness of the economic technocrats, the major entrepreneurs criticized first the distortions of the economic model and then the political system behind it. In trying to open the political system for themselves by combating centralization and statism in favor of free enterprise and a market economy, they espoused democratic political principles and social justice as supportive of that type of economy. Thus they joined the already extant social currents for liberalization but were more accepting of its controlled nature.[19]

During Figueiredo's *abertura* the national private sector still felt ignored, unconsulted, and pressed between 1) the large role for state enterprises carved out by the military regime and 2) the more powerful international firms attracted by investment incentives. This sector has constantly inveighed against statism and government policies harmful to its interests, but, even with *abertura*, it did not operate cohesively enough as a community of interests to have the ongoing and effective interest-group type of participation that its size would suggest. Narrowly lobbying on an individual basis for special favors for one's firm was more characteristic than representative issue politics on a trade or confederation level. The usual posture was much more reactive or defensive than anticipatory.

The business and trade associations of Rio de Janeiro and São Paulo states are the most important and modern political actors of the sector, but their weight in the national private sector associations is reduced by disproportionate representation of smaller states.[20]

The last several years of *abertura* witnessed a major falling out between business and industry executives and the government, rapidly accelerating during 1983 and into 1984. Although these leaders are conservative capitalists, they increasingly felt that the PDS was not representative of the modern economic sectors of Brazil. Hence, the Partido Popular (PP) emerged briefly as a centrist business-community party. Its merger with the PMDB because of electoral law changes should not obscure the continuing base for such a centrist party now that alignments are more fluid. Business leaders, with bankruptcies all around them, became very critical of the government's ability to manage the economy and, in particular, of Delfim Neto and Treasury Minister Ernane Galvêas. A semi-annual survey of 700 executives by a major business magazine found that those giving the Figueiredo government a "bad" or "very bad" rating went from 17.8 percent in mid-1982 to 42.8 percent in mid-1983 to 77.0 percent in mid-1984; in the economic area, the government was rated the worst of the period of military rule.[21]

In August 1983, under the auspices of a forum sponsored by the *Gazeta Mercantil*, twelve of the nation's top businessmen submitted to the nation (rather than to the government) a dissenting document making clear their dissatisfaction with official policy and suggesting democratic and socially responsible alternatives aimed at consensus and a "viable Brazil."[22] Unsatisfied with the response to this sort of entreaty, business and industry executives cast their political support toward the moderate opposition and, ultimately, to the Liberal Front and the Democratic Alliance.

The Urban Labor Movement

Abertura rules allowed labor meetings, tolerated strikes under some circumstances, and made possible organizing and some collective bargaining. Those urban labor leaders who struggled for an effective political voice for the workers, however, faced heavy disadvantages and were undertaking a long-term project. Workers as a whole were still too repressed, paternalistically controlled, insecure, submissive, and disorganized to be a strong and autonomous political force on an ongoing basis. Government measures placed close limits on wage policy. Little collective consciousness or loyalty existed, there were few daringly independent leaders, and workers still regarded with suspicion the idea of workers' parties and workers as candidates. Labor unions were unable to deliver votes, and no clear national working-class tendencies emerged in the November 1982 elections. Fear of losing what little security one had as an employed person in the 1981-1983 recession in a country with a labor surplus proved a powerful incentive against participation in strikes of any length, especially as there were no strike or unemployment funds. Government and business could hold out much longer. In the much-heralded July 21, 1983, general strike in São Paulo, workers stayed home and no public protests developed.

The political culture has not supported an independent role for labor because politicizing labor to act independently would open up new power relationships that few in the privileged classes have been willing to face. Knowing this, politicians are reluctant to threaten the bureaucratically entrenched, antiunion, and antisocial-conflict domination of labor by government, handed down from the Getúlio Vargas years. In general, the advances of *abertura* went preferentially to middle-class and elite interests.

It is precisely this traditional structure of government control and inattention that the "new syndicalism" based in São Paulo has challenged. This movement took form in São Bernardo (SP) in the late 1970s, after earlier protests, and set out: (1) to replace officially imposed wage policy with direct and free labor-management negotiations, (2) to replace the officially dominated organizational intervention of the Labor Ministry structure with a workplace-based and autonomous union system, (3) to guarantee the unrestricted right to strike,[23] and (4) to improve job security and wage levels after deliberate restraint of real wages by government juggling of cost-of-living and inflation statistics (revealed in 1977). The movement's nucleus consisted of metalworkers, steelworkers, and petroleum and petrochemical workers, later joined in spirit and in strike action by automotive workers, those in services, those from government itself, and, ultimately, day laborers.

Union activism has been most successful in modern industries of the Center-South and South, springing back from the repression of 1980-1981 to become one of the major and more diverse new social forces and ideas developed during *abertura*. The atmosphere of democratic rhetoric, debate, participation, mobilization, and institutional change which characterized the end of the transition, not to mention the growing ineffectiveness of the federal government and the effectiveness of Lula as an articulator, facilitated a broader public acceptance of at least the ideal of full citizenship for laborers, skilled workers, and those in service professions. Yet the response of the Figueiredo government, on balance, was one of some repression and modest reforms seeking to absorb the new movement within the traditional structure of subordination. Minister of Labor Murilo Macedo was relatively liberal, but the Planning Ministry cut or killed his mildly progressive initiatives.

The new labor leaders proved capable of organizing locally, conducting mass demonstrations, and asserting more frequently the disruptive power to strike but were still unable in their more radical and confrontational aims to change the rules of the game by immobilizing the system through social action. Government-placed, rather docile leaders still constituted the majority. Parts of the rhetoric and goals of the new syndicalism permeated labor dialogues nationwide, but outside the metropolitan São Paulo area the degree of activism and success was markedly lower.

Trade, personal, ideology, and regional differences, for example, delayed until August 1983 the creation of the first independent and overarching labor confederation. The Central Unica dos Trabalhadores (CUT) is a militant group under PT auspices organized to parallel and challenge the official structure through worker mobilization. The second and rival interunion organization, Coordenacão Nacional da Classe Trabalhadora (CONCLAT), was founded in November 1983 with both PCB (Brazilian Communist Party) and more moderate PMDB leadership and preferences for negotiation and lobbying rather than social action. Both confederations, illegal in principle, were merely tolerated by the Figueiredo government.[24] It fell, then, to the government of José Sarney, beset by dozens of strikes in many labor sectors in the first half of 1985, to work out a new system of labor relations more in keeping with the spirit of change in the country and broader concepts of political legitimacy.

The Catholic Church

Social activists in the Church were a major force pushing for human rights and democracy during the dictatorship, often taking positions and actions on social questions that were squarely opposed to those of the Médici or Geisel governments. In return, Church activists were subjected to threats and violence. Political liberalization under Figueiredo facilitated greater dialogue with the government, but basic disagreements remained in Church pronouncements on topics such as land tenure, the national security law, and expulsion of activist foreign priests. A "people's church," with explicitly political concerns in its "preferential option for the poor," is emerging from the more activist CEBs, which in São Paulo, for example, supported the unions in the 1979 and 1980 strikes in São Bernardo do Campo and backed the PT in the November 1982 elections.[25] The 1980 visit of Pope John Paul II to Brazil reaffirmed the role of the National Conference of Brazilian Bishops (CNBB) as the authority of the Church in Brazil and sanctioned in very general terms its socially conscious ministry.

The reelection of progressive Bishop Ivo Lorscheiter to another term as CNBB president in its controversy-plagued April 1983 convention demonstrated continued CNBB interest in social matters. About 16 percent of the 257 prelates present were conservatives, while 43 percent were considered progressives.[26] Orthodox clerics strongly resist priority attention to social inequities and the mobilization of the poor to defend their interests. Lately the Vatican has been acting in favor of the orthodox by naming conservative bishops to the hierarchy. The traditionalist cause was further strengthened from above in mid-1985 when the Vatican punished Friar Leonardo Boff with a year's prohibition of public statements as an example for his renowned defense of liberation theology and his book *Church, Charisma, and Power,* which accuses the hierarchy of elitism and weak defense of human rights.

In spite of the current status of the divided hierarchy, the Church will continue to serve, on balance, as a national conscience above parties, in favor of social justice and against violence, and to speak up for and encourage the representation of the unorganized—landless peasants, slum dwellers, urban workers, and Indians. It is possible that if these social sectors now encouraged by the Church gain their own voice in the future, the Church's relative political impact could become more reduced and diffused but still active on the side of evolutionary reform.

The Relinquishment of Executive Control over Succession

By late 1983, the Figueiredo administration was a government without foresight, still reluctantly conceding power by lurches. It was unable to develop policies to smooth political evolution and was too preoccupied with present battles to build cooperative and effective institutions for the longer run. Instead, it continued to avoid wider political options for a broad accord and to rely on quick fixes (*saídas*) for a "way out" by using institutional modifications to favor persons or parties for the short run. Possible solutions, official self-contradictions, and rumors multiplied, adding to the uncertainty and clouding debate as Planalto Palace strategists cast about unsuccessfully for strategems to hold onto power and to thwart Deputy Paulo Maluf's rising presidential prospects.

Schemes considered included parliamentary government, reelection of Figueiredo, direct elections for president (in 1985 or 1986), a two-year transition with Figueiredo followed by direct elections, resignation of Figueiredo, a consensus candidate, a constituent assembly, and a single-member-district electoral system. The common purpose was to push off definitive arrangements and debate over the succession for as long as possible and to come up with a package attractive to enough opposition politicians to encourage or force party realignments in the hope of creating a co-optable center to approve an "acceptable" presidential candidate and a new round of institutional modifications. Success with this strategy was very limited, but palace intrigues and rumors proliferated.

As the government bickered over power relationships and process more than substantive issues, it showed itself incapable of maintaining even the Chamber of Deputies alliance with the PTB and so lost its majority. Government control of the PDS weakened further while within the opposition the idea of a consensus candidate gained ground. Figueiredo slipped from being the controller of presidential succession (presumably on behalf of Interior Minister Mário Andreazza) to coordinator to overseer. In late 1983 Figueiredo announced his decision not to coordinate the PDS succession (contrary to a statement of a year earlier) and said that he really favored direct elections but that the PDS would not yield. The PDS adamantly refused to give up the electoral college process on which it had a supposedly sure grip, with enough supporting votes in Congress to block the constitutional amendment required to institute direct elections. The opposition, in turn, tried to throw obstacles in the way of government plans, to force negotiations for a broadening of the succession process. Within the administration and the PDS, several key policymakers maneuvered to advance their presidential possibilities.

Fear of political-disturbance backlashes caused the government to postpone hard solutions to the economic problems, which therefore kept mounting. Cutting wages and salaries while unemployment was already high after more than three years of recession and erosion of buying power would have been a challenge for even a considerably more popular and effective government. Economic sectors competed to avoid loss of real income in the deepening recession, hindering the implementation of a coherent anti-inflation program against government deficits. Ambitious government economic targets were consistently missed, causing general scepticism. Social unrest, wildcat ("popcorn") strikes, bank robberies, and looting of supermarkets cropped up sporadically in São Paulo, Rio, and the Northeast. The Congress acted increasingly with an eye to these disturbances, which came from what was termed the "social debt," with concern that the economic crisis was creating a social crisis that could cause political instability and thereby endanger *abertura*.

The Rise of Congress

In the first forty-one months of the Figueiredo government, from March 1979 to August 1982, the Congress was unable to turn into law any of the 6,337 bills it originated. The government was able to pass all but one of its 382 bills (the failed bill was the salary law of October 1983), almost exclusively by the provision of *decurso de prazo* (a procedure whereby a bill submitted by the executive becomes law if Congress does not vote on it during a sixty-day period).[27] Congress was kept in check as a mere formalistic legitimizer through severe restrictions placed on it by the executive during the military republic, PDS subservience to the executive to the detriment of congressional power, the merely status/careerist orientation of many of its members, and the lack of a legislative program.

Yet expanding reassertion of congressional influence was one of the most significant political developments of 1983 and a major fact of 1984. It was made possible by a sometimes cohesive opposition majority in the Chamber of Deputies, a weakening of presidential authority, dissidence within the PDS, and a governmental dedication to avoiding exceptional political arrangements. The Congress elected in November 1982 featured 21 senators and 265 deputies who had not served in the previous Congress, a renovation of 52 percent.[28] Congress thus entered

1983 with a fresh and widely accepted electoral legitimacy and faced a discredited technocratic administration needing congressional support to justify its measures. On most issues, the preferences of the federal deputies were moderate, on balance, but in conflict with the executive's, clustering about steps to roll back various restrictive measures implanted by the military republic. Fully 95 percent of a sample of 91.2 percent of deputies were in favor of constitutional reform and 73 percent in favor of direct elections for president.[29]

Whereas in early 1983 the executive was ill disposed to yield anything to Congress and the senators and deputies seemed resigned and conciliatory, by midyear an interparty consensus favoring reestablishment of congressional powers of legislation, investigation, and representation was gaining force. Criticism by legislators of executive misconduct mounted, including criticism by PDS members supporting Maluf and hoping to discredit any official candidate. Congressional investigation of matters such as the national debt embarrassed the executive. By year's end, sessions had become unpredictable and occasionally tumultuous. In late September, for the first time in eighteen years, the Congress voted down an executive decree (No. 2024, on wage and salary calculation) and forced the executive to revise its appraisal of Congress and of political support for its economic program. In succeeding weeks, Congress defeated two government attempts to pass a wage and salary compression package, passed a mitigated third version (thanks to an unusual government-PDS leadership compromise), and approved its first constitutional amendment in twenty years that went against the wishes of the executive.

The Congress became both the center for negotiation on further political liberalization (especially regarding presidential succession) and the effective nationalistic rallying point for those opposing the IMF-sponsored economic measures that the executive branch was developing. Opposition bargaining power grew as more deputies and senators became conscious of the impact of economic policy on social unrest and international creditors expressed preference for economic austerity measures legitimated by congressional consent. Yet, on balance, this early demonstration of congressional power can be attributed more to an indecisive and unpopular executive than to a united and purposeful legislature capable of constructive initiatives.

The Military's Extraction from Power

In contrast to the civilian leaders, the military command showed more unity and stood more committed to President Figueiredo, probably more so than to Médici and Geisel. Figueiredo gradually and quietly isolated and retired the rightist political discontents; the forced retirement (by nonpromotion) of General José Luís Coelho Neto in late 1982 deprived the few remaining hardliners of their chief spokesman. Another hardliner, General Newton de Oliveira e Cruz, former chief of the SNI office in Brasília and then military commander of the Brasília region, received top-level military reprimands for overzealous enforcement of both the brief October 1983 state of emergency in Brasília during congressional debate and voting on a key economic measure and public order measures during April 1984 demonstrations for direct elections. He was transferred to a desk job toward the very end of *abertura*, on November 20, 1984.

Without a national project, a credible subversive threat to internal order, or a political leader to rally around, the majority military moderates strongly preferred a *controlled* disengagement to return to the barracks and to more accepted functions, to professionalize and to reestablish the image of honesty and patriotism above private interests that the military once had. Registry of support for the results of the 1982 elections represented certification for a return to competitive politics. Sufficient social or military support for a coup was then clearly lacking and would have been conceivable only in the case of a serious general breakdown in public order.

Military consensus appeared ultimately to prefer a "trustworthy" civilian and establishment successor to Figueiredo, but sectors of opinion were divided over personal choices. Rumors of a military candidate probably only served the purpose of making the politicians choose a "responsible" civilian more selectively once the possibility of a military candidate was rejected. Obsessed for years with a politically restrictive definition of national security, the military consensus felt more comfortable with a "strong democracy," in which the institution of the state (essentially the established order) can "defend itself," than with a "liberal democracy," which takes free-wheeling chances on open-ended change. Neither unconditional withdrawal from politics nor reassertion of control found full political support in the corps or in society at the end of the transition. Yet by that time the high command was showing evidence of ability to live with the uncertainties, compromises, and inefficiencies intrinsic to democratic resolution of social conflicts, rather than regarding such events as threats to national security. The open question remained the extent to which it would allow itself to be subordinated to civilian control.

The military as an institution lost more than it gained in the exercise of political power, suffering internal divisions and falling in capabilities well behind the general advance of the economy. The armed forces are deficient as a fighting force, a fact brought home by their sober study of Argentina's capabilities and deficiencies in the 1982 Falklands War. The high command did not foresee a threat of war but decided that, with security questions lately more prominent on the continent, it would be advisable for the army to move from the one-year recruit system to develop a larger body of permanent, better-trained, and more combat-ready soldiers. Troops would be outfitted with more modern equipment and would show the flag in more parts of the borderlands (such as in the North).

A change of mission and a refocus of doctrine to incorporate a more externally oriented definition of security is occurring, which will probably set off interservice debates and rivalries. On the other hand, a more internationally focused role and participation in the arms industry to boost self-sufficiency are seen as quite legitimate by most civilian politicians and would preserve a sense of constructive military partic-ipation in national life.

The National Intelligence Service (SNI) and the Intelligence Community

The SNI (created by the military government in 1964) combines domestic and foreign intelligence and counterintelligence functions, gathering data and generating studies and options for the presidency. As a source of ideas, it has for some time replaced the National War College (ESG). The latter generates abstract studies based largely on academic doctrine, but the SNI's "real world" functions of policy analysis and formation, contingency planning, and administrative supervision and control have proved more useful to government officials. The SNI's intelligence school (ESNI) is a very important training ground for the whole intelligence community, including the military sector.[30] Two pres-idents of the military republic—Médici and Figueiredo—were previously directors of the SNI, and its director has been a close presidential adviser with ministerial status. Army influence in the SNI has been marked since 1968, with an unknown number of officers assigned temporary SNI duty, from the director on down. Rivalries have consequently developed between civilian and army intelligence personnel, as well as between the SNI and military intelligence agencies. Toward the end of Figueiredo's term the army began to distance itself from the SNI because of rivalries in state enterprises, scandals, policy differences, and the desire to maintain a lower political profile.

The SNI, which operated under the dictatorship without formal review and with generous funding, was reputed to be a major political actor behind the scenes, a secret government within a government, with influential elements wary of whatever they felt could be unbridled democracy. With its fear of subversion and its autonomy and growth coming from a more repressive period, the intelligence community (or perhaps just certain individuals within it) was more suspicious of democratization toward the end of *abertura* than was the military's high command. It resisted reduction of its power and investigation of its excesses of repression.

Cases such as unpunished official misconduct in financial scandals, the Riocenter bomb blast, alleged 1982 election vote-count interference against Brizola in Rio, the murder of a journalist (Alexandre von Baum-garten) with intelligence community connections, and discovery of microphones planted in Figueiredo's new office raised questions about the range of the SNI's activities and the limits to which the most conservative elements in the executive wanted *abertura* to be taken. Many Brazilian political commentators claimed to see a campaign in 1983 and 1984 to undermine or contain the SNI's political power through revelations of its excesses, which also served to destroy General Medeiros's chances for the presidency. The Figueiredo government began quietly pushing about mid-1983 toward emphasis on intelligence gathering and analysis in the SNI, with curtailment of its covert activities that were out of harmony with the spirit of more open politics. Yet control of the SNI continued to pose a challenge to Figueiredo's successor.

The Presidential Succession

The fast-breaking 1984 politics of the presidential succession that brought *abertura* to a close are sufficiently analyzed from other perspectives in Chapters 3 and 6 to forgo detailed description here. In spite of 85 percent of the public favoring direct election of the president, a strong public opinion mobilization campaign by the opposition, with large demonstrations, failed to convince two-thirds of Congress to pass a constitutional admendment for direct elections because of military opposition and PDS insistence on retention of the electoral college in which it held a majority. Resigned after internal controversy to competing in the weighted electoral college, most of the opposition started to coalesce around Tancredo Neves, governor of Minas Gerais, then PMDB but earlier a founder of the short-lived PP. Neves enjoyed wide public support and a reputation for honesty, moderation, and competence during a long public career. In the political tradition of Minas, he was conciliatory, cautious, and laconic.

The advance of hard-campaigning, glad-handing Deputy Paulo Maluf's well-financed machine badly split the PDS and gave rise to the formation of the crucial centrist Liberal Front caucus (later the PFL—Party of the Liberal Front) by Vice-president Chaves and others as an anti-Maluf group of PDS dissidents. The Front served as a vital bridge between the PDS and PMDB, facilitating the subsequent formation of the Democratic Alliance as a broad-front national consensus movement behind the essentially establishment figure of Neves so rapidly that other PMDB hopefuls fell in to push the bandwagon. With the ground swell of opposition temporarily laying aside old animosities to defeat the PDS nominee, Neves was an easy winner in a veritable coronation at the August 1984 PMDB convention.

The PDS, to the contrary, was rent by governmental indecision and vacillation and went through several presidents. The government was in the minority in the Chamber of Deputies, and public administration took second place to succession politics. Figueiredo, in standing aloof from the candidate selection (unusual for any Brazilian president) and in failing to endorse a party primary, pursued what *appeared* to be a democratic course under existing rules, but did so at the ultimate expense of dissolution of the PDS (with which he was thoroughly disillusioned). Those in government active in the issue were split in preferences but first ignored the general popularity of Chaves (acceptable to many moderates), then irresolutely pushed for Minister of the Interior Mário Andreazza (of the "inner circle"). The contested PDS convention nominated Maluf over Andreazza, picking the PDS candidate whom Figueiredo detested. Neither enjoyed strong support in the nation as a whole, but Maluf was notably unpopular and suffered from a greater image of corruption.

With his direct and brashly "un-Brazilian" style, the otherwise astute Maluf antagonized the PDS state and local power structures (especially in the Northeast) by circumventing them and appealing directly to electoral college delegates. Within weeks of the convention it became apparent that only one Northeast governor (from Paraíba) supported him, and the Northeast was the single most important factor in the PDS electoral college delegation. Clumsy government attempts to use public resources to support him antagonized many delegates. In contrast, Neves, soon called the "Great Conciliator," discreetly used a few mass rallies as a sounding board to demonstrate his public acceptance and establish legitimacy in lieu of direct elections, built agreement as an interparty compromise figure among key politicians nationwide (including PDS governors), and won over the moderate military leadership. Whereas the government rhetoric concentrated on PDS unity, the opposition message was national unity, a "social pact" for a transitional government to establish democratic institutions. Neves thus became a vehicle for a wide range of popular aspirations. Maluf reacted against PDS defections by insisting that the dictatorship's party fidelity law, enforcing party line voting, should apply in the electoral college. The Supreme Electoral Tribunal, in effect, definitively sent his candidacy to defeat by denying his petition.

As had seemed certain for weeks, Tancredo Neves and his running-mate Senator José Sarney were chosen president and vice-president for a six-year term by the January 15, 1985, electoral college, by 70 percent against Maluf's 26.2 percent, with 2.5 percent of the delegates abstaining and 1.3 percent absent. Liberal Front and PDS support were indispensible to their victory. President Figueiredo and the military consensus, despite earlier misgivings, accepted the outcome as the democratic completion of their *abertura*. The centrist cabinet that Neves selected incorporated the many political tendencies that backed him, still with an eye to broad social representation in what came to be called the "New Republic." In the final irony of the contradictory and tormented *abertura* process, seventy-five-year-old Neves was denied the opportunity of ever taking office, not by the military but by an illness that hospitalized him on the eve of the March 15 inauguration and took his life five weeks later. As his condition gradually deteriorated, the entire nation closely followed the conflicting medical reports amid rumors and fears, and government business crept along apprehensively.

Early Prospects for the New Republic

During his five weeks as acting president, Vice-president José Sarney moved circumspectly to avoid appearing to be a usurper of Neves's mandate and to keep intact a mantle of legitimacy and program ideals. After his installation as president, he continued his characteristically cautious and low-key style. Sarney was thrust into a presidency he did not seek, yet achieved early public acceptance. His immediate problem was to build a base in the political class, in part because he lacked the range of relationships and the reputation that Neves had had. Sarney had resigned as PDS president (thereby losing that base), still is not fully accepted as a "convert" by the PMDB, and, being from Maranhão, does not have the political machinery of a major state behind him.

The pro-redemocratization coalition that united rapidly against Paulo Maluf now faced more divisive questions in policy formation and execution, without the articulator who pulled it together. The focus on a particular leader to make up for weak institutions again proved hazardous. A surge of labor demands in the first months of the new government created serious public disagreement between Labor Minister Almir Pazzianotto (PMDB), who favored salary negotiations and mediation in a democratic spirit, and Industry and Commerce Minister Roberto Gusmão (PFL), who favored applying the letter of antistrike laws still on the books from the dictatorship. In the Planning Ministry, progressive former academics presided over holdovers from the time of Delfim Neto. Communications Minister Antônio Carlos Magalhães (PDS) complained publicly about the number of "leftists" in the government: Opposition leftists, to the contrary, were impatient with the conservatism built into the cabinet.

Party realignment and unpopular choices forced by scarcity of resources are straining the heterogeneous coalition upon which President Sarney must depend if legislative support is to go beyond intentions. Congress started early to buck Sarney and will expand its high-spirited assertiveness as the 1986 elections approach and as newly recognized small parties proliferate and create a broader spectrum with influence for more diverse constituencies. Party disintegration and factionalism could be serious threats if politicians fail to forgo short-run gains in order to build long-run confidence in stable coalitions. The PDS stood in regular opposition to the government. The PT and PDT, unlike the PCB, stand as de facto opposition. The PMDB and PFL, chief components of Sarney's Democratic Alliance, are each jealous of presidential policies that might tend to strengthen the other party. Sarney, to the contrary, has striven to remain "above party." Seeking effective leadership consensus for a "national pact" above partisan interests, he met early in his term with a wide variety of social group representatives and convoked all state governors but achieved only ambiguous results.

Wider political participation and greater expectations were being poured into recast political institutions as the provisions of arbitrary

rule were being further dismantled. The celebration over, Brazilians had to go beyond the symbolism of reconciliation and democracy and become accustomed again to the give and take, ambiguities, delays, and dilemmas of working within democratic institutions. Authoritarian attitudes and habits will persist in some political actors. The former opposition will have to adjust to the responsibilities of the national power long denied it, for the civilian government faces most of the same economic strictures that the generals did.

The government and its priorities are being reprofiled during a transitional period to conform the political structure to the socioeconomic changes the nation has undergone and to incorporate into effective citizenship those elements of the population previously excluded. A sense of moment prevails because institutional choices made now, and the reactions to them, will shape Brazil's political evolution for years to come. Particularly crucial will be the balances of power struck between the military and the civilian sector, the president and the Congress, the state enterprises and the private sector, and government and society, as well as among contending civilian factions now expressing themselves more freely. One of the major measures of the quality of democracy in the New Republic will be the extent to which it serves the needs of the poor and destitute majority and provides them with democratic representation, rather than just constituting an intraelite social pact of conciliation to grant a few minimal concessions to the lower classes but postpone or evade the social question.

Issues such as agrarian reform and social services have been long quashed but are now up for discussion and implementation, in rising anticipation of the constituent assembly that is to write a new constitution and reshape the political system. The ideological debate will heat up, reforms will stimulate social divisions, and political conflict will rise. Probable issues in the *constituinte* include modifications of the tax structure, land laws, labor code, and electoral system, with pressure to accommodate demands from the left. Institutionally, power sharing among the three branches of the federal government will be modified toward decentralization, as will the relationship of Brasília to the states and municipalities of the federal system.

The role of the large state enterprises (which generate about 40 percent of the GNP) is coming under careful scrutiny, with pressure to abolish some and to turn others over to private enterprise. The plan is to reduce the state's economic role and expand its role in public services such as education, health, housing, and sanitation. Denunciations of irregularities in public office are becoming more frequent. The electoral system has been partially redesigned to eliminate distortions of representation introduced by former governments to benefit the official party. Illiterates, long denied the vote, have been enfranchised, direct elections for president and mayors of capital cities restored, and the Communist Party (PCB) legalized. The last remaining censorship was removed.

Civilian-military relations are being redefined as the military is rethinking its legitimate mission and its view of national security under democracy, moving from a ruling function toward emphasis on modernization, professionalism, and national defense. Although it is staying behind the scenes, the military will nevertheless retain a keen interest in and try to influence sensitive topics it deems relevant to national security and well-being. These include landholding matters, colonization of the Amazon, Marxist parties, mobilization of labor and the poor, Marxist movements in South American neighbors, border matters, the war materials industry and its exports, and internal military affairs. Investigation of or retribution for past military excesses of repression would touch the most sensitive nerve and so are being discouraged by the civilian government for the sake of stability.[31]

Yet the military is unlikely to be the determinant voice in many issues. It is most probable that during the next several years it will strongly prefer to resume a role as court of last instance for public order, pressuring harder at time of civilian paralysis but intervening directly only if civilian government is grossly incapable or radical and wider disorder threatens social dissolution. For its part, the National Intelligence Service, still strong, is to be reformed to eliminate covert domestic activities and to gather legitimate domestic and foreign information to inform the president and his staff.

The new democracy will create more complications in economic policy because demands for economic change were a powerful force in bringing Sarney to power, in the hope that a representative government would greatly modify the model. Sarney has pledged to stimulate the recent economic recuperation, coming after several years of severe decline in real purchasing power. His government plans for 5 or 6 percent annual economic growth during the next several years and has given notice that it will resist creditor and IMF austerity demands to the contrary, as well as rejecting the right of the IMF to monitor the national economy. Less than that would threaten his political base and perhaps the new democracy as well. Yet he has also given priority to reducing the inflation rate sailing along at about 230 percent yearly in 1985 and to reducing the federal budget deficit.

Looming over all else in the economy is the slightly over $100 billion foreign debt, on which Brazil has been able to pay only the interest since January 1983, at a 1985 rate of around $11 billion a year. The principal of the debt ultimately is unrepayable in its entirety in cash terms. Neither can Brazil afford to be such a large net exporter of capital into the unforeseeable future. The greatest international economic challenge that the government faces in the short run, therefore, is to keep its economy and credit sound by slowing the borrowing rate, continuing to generate a large trade surplus (much of it with the United States), maintaining reserves, and negotiating a longer-term reprofiling of the loan into more realistic terms. During the period of this "breathing space" strategy the government will be subject to internal pressures for more radical action and vulnerable to unfavorable international market conditions and creditor intransigence.

Acknowledgments

I thank Enrique Baloyra, David Fleischer, Scott Mainwaring, Ronald Schneider, Thomas Skidmore, and Amaury de Souza for their comments on earlier versions of this chapter. The responsibility for the final interpretations is, of course, my own.

Notes

1. Secretaria de Planejamento da Presidência da República, Fundacão Instituto Brasileiro de Geografia e Estatística, *Anuário Estatístico do Brasil, 1982* (Rio de Janeiro: IBGE, 1982), p. 706. These 1980 census figures include only those persons economically active and receiving income. The richest 5 percent received 34.9 percent of the national income. The argument that the 1970s saw a substantial reduction in the proportion of the population living in absolute poverty despite little change in unequal income distribution patterns is presented in David Denslow and William Tyler, "Perspectives on Poverty and Income Inequality in Brazil," *World Development* 12, no. 10 (1984): 1019–1028.

2. Richard Sholk, "Comparative Aspects of the Transition from Authoritarian Rule—A Rapporteur's Report," Working Paper Number 114, Latin American Program, Woodrow Wilson International Center for Scholars, Smithsonian Institution, Washington, D.C., 1982, pp. 11–17.

3. Bolivar Lamounier, "Dos Anos 70 aos 80: Estrutura Social, Eleições, e Mudança Política no Brasil," in Enrique Baloyra and Rafael Lopes Pintor (eds.), *Iberoamérica en los anos 80* (Madrid: Centro de Investigaciones Sociológicas/ Centro de Cooperación Iberoamericana, 1982), p. 66.

4. Olavo Brasil de Lima Júnior, "Continuidade e Mudança: Partidos e Eleições no Brasil Contemporâneo," No. 25, Série Estudos (Rio de Janeiro: Instituto Universitário de Pesquisas do Rio de Janeiro, 1984), pp. 4–5. This essay is an excellent analysis of the 1982 elections in perspective. Also see Chapter 3 in this volume.

5. "PMDB Ganha Eleição em 75 das 100 Maiores Cidades," *Jornal do Brasil,* December 6, 1982; "O Mapa Final das Eleições," *Fôlha de São Paulo,* November 27, 1982; and "Oposição Controlará 75% do PIB nos 10 Estados Mais Ricos," *Estado de São Paulo,* December 19, 1982, p. 11.

6. Brasil de Lima Júnior, p. 16, Table 6.

7. Olavo Brasil de Lima Júnior, "Processo Eleitoral e Transicão Política no Brasil," paper presented at the seminar "Oportunidades e Limites da Sociedade Periférica: O Caso do Brasil," sponsored by the Stanford-Berkeley Joint Center for Latin American Studies and the Instituto Universitário de Pesquisas do Rio de Janeiro, Nova Friburgo, RJ, July 18–20, 1983, pp. 13–15 and Table 1. Comparisons with 1978 elections were figured retroactively, based on party affiliations of deputies on March 5, 1982, to control for changes in party affiliations over the period.

8. Bolivar Lamounier, "Opening Through Elections: Will the Brazilian Case Become a Paradigm?," *Government and Opposition* 19, no. 2 (1984): 173–175.

See, for instance, *Isto É,* September 15, 1982, for results of a preelection public opinion survey on party preferences in eight states done by IBOPE for the Globo TV Network, *O Globo,* and *Isto É* magazine. In the sample of 18,000 from these southcentral, southern, and northeastern states (Bahia and Pernambuco) comprising 70.5 percent of the national population, there appeared very little variation in party preference across income levels for the group as a whole. PDS and PTB support increased somewhat with age, while PMDB (particularly), PT, and PDT support decreased somewhat with age.

9. Bolivar Lamounier, "São Paulo: A Geografia do Voto," *Fôlha de São Paulo,* "Folhetim," January 30, 1983.

10. Ronald M. Schneider, "1982 Brazilian Elections Project, Final Report: Results and Ramifications," Brazil Program, Georgetown University Center for Strategic and International Studies, Washington, D.C., December 1982 (mimeographed), pp. 2–13.

11. Gláucio Ary Dillon Soares, *Colégio Eleitoral, Convenções Partidárias, e Eleições Diretas* (Petrópolis: Editôra Vozes, 1984), pp. 46–55. Useful time series data with a radical interpretation is presented in Raimundo Pereira, Álvaro Caropreso, and José Carlos Ruy, *Eleições no Brasil Pós-64* (São Paulo: Global Editôra, 1984). These authors argue that within this trend the 1982 elections, far from establishing a definitive system of middle-of-the-road politics, were only a step toward popular demands for much more progressive structural reforms and the adoption of a socioeconomic model much more beneficial to the masses.

12. Bolivar Lamounier and Rachel Meneguello, "Political Parties and Democratic Consolidation: The Brazilian Case," Working Paper Number 165, Latin American Program, Woodrow Wilson International Center for Scholars, Smithsonian Institution, Washington, D.C., 1985, p. 23.

13. The role of the mass media in politics and *abertura* is analyzed in Joan R. Dassin, "The Brazilian Press and the Politics of *Abertura,*" *Journal of Interamerican Studies and World Affairs* 26, no. 3 (1984): 385–414.

14. The perspective and work of these grassroots movements are described by a participant in Maria Helena Moreira Alves, "Grassroots Organizations, Trade Unions, and the Church: A Challenge to Controlled *Abertura* in Brazil," *Latin American Perspectives* 11, no. 1 (Winter 1984): 73–102. For a critical theoretical interpretation, also see Renato Boschi, "Social Movements and the Institutionalization of a Political Order in Brazil," paper presented at the Conference on Opportunities and Constraints in Peripheral Industrial Society: The Case of Brazil, sponsored by the Stanford-Berkeley Joint Center for Latin American Studies, University of California at Berkeley, January 30-February 2, 1984.

15. Polls surveyed here include those of the Gallup Public Opinion Institute of Brazil in the monthly *Índice Gallup de Opinião Pública* (São Paulo) and occasional surveys by the Brazilian Public Opinion Institute (IBOPE) of Rio de Janeiro, such as the omnibus "Opinião e Imagem" survey published in *Jornal do Brasil,* May 22, 1983.

16. IBOPE survey reported in *Jornal do Brasil,* May 29, 1983.

17. "Popularidade de Figueiredo cai para −44," *O Estado de São Paulo,* August 2, 1984, p. 6. Approval was defined as agreeing that Figueiredo was governing "well" or "very well;" "so-so" and below were considered disapproval. A score of −44 percent results from a summation of all positive (+) and negative (−) evaluations in the sample.

18. This breakup of the partnership is interpreted as the principal force behind decompression and liberalization by Luíz Carlos Bresser Pereira, *Development and Crisis in Brazil, 1930–1983* (Boulder, CO: Westview Press, 1984), pp. 192–204. Also see his insightful class analysis of the liberalization process in "Os Limites da 'Abertura' e a Sociedade Civil," *Revista de Administração de Emprêsas* 23, no. 4 (1983): 5–14.

19. Two of the best analyses of the role of business in the political liberalization are Fernando Henrique Cardoso, "O Papel dos Empresários no Processo da Transição: O Caso Brasileiro," *Dados* 26, no. 1 (1983): 9–27 and Eli Diniz, "Empresariado e Transição Política no Brasil: Problemas e Perspectivas," No. 22, Série Estudos (Rio de Janeiro: Instituto Universitário de Pesquisas do Rio de Janeiro, 1984).

20. Ronald M. Schneider, "Brazilian Elections Study, Analysis No. 5: Business and Politics in an Election Year," Brazil Program, Georgetown University Center for Strategic and International Studies, Washington, D.C., September 29, 1982 (mimeographed), pp. 1–2.

21. "Para o Govêrno, uma Severa Reprovação," *Exame*, August 8, 1984, pp. 30–32.

22. "Os Empresários Abrem o Jôgo," *Senhor*, August 17, 1983, pp. 24–27. The last such unusual document issued by the same staid forum was in late 1978, cast in general but clear terms in favor of democracy, social responsibility, and free enterprise.

23. Maria Hermínia T. de Almeida, "Novas Tendências do Movimento Sindical," in Hélgio Trindade (ed.), *Brasil em Perspectiva: Dilemas da Abertura Política* (Pôrto Alegre: Editôra Sulina, 1982), p. 83.

24. The dynamics of labor relations during *abertura* are analyzed in Margaret E. Keck, "Labor and Politics in the Brazilian Transition," in Alfred Stepan (ed.), *Democratizing Brazil* (forthcoming).

25. The role of the popular church in *abertura* is described in Scott Mainwaring, "The Catholic Church, Popular Education, and Political Change in Brazil," *Journal of Interamerican Studies and World Affairs* 26, no. 1 (1984): 97–124, and his *The Catholic Church and Politics in Brazil, 1916–1985* (Stanford: Stanford University Press, forthcoming). The earlier development of the oppositionist position of the Church in the 1970s is covered in Thomas G. Sanders, "The Catholic Church in Brazil's Political Transition," American University Field Staff Reports, South America, 1980, Number 48.

26. "Discordias Episcopais," *Veja*, April 20, 1983, p. 64.

27. "Quê Congresso foi Esse?," *Visão*, November 8, 1982, p. 30. Another, more detailed survey to the end of 1982 reported that, of the 6,704 bills and proposals for constitutional amendment presented in 1979–1982 by federal deputies and senators, only 131 (1.95 percent) became law. (Nélio Lima, "Congresso: 6700 Projetos; 131 Aprovados," *Jornal da Tarde*, January 1, 1983.)

28. David Fleischer, "Sangue Nôvo no Congresso," *Correio Braziliense*, March 1, 1983, p. 8.

29. "Um Nôvo Poder na Praça," *Veja*, January 5, 1983, pp. 14–21.

30. Alfred Stepan, "Sôbre os Militares, a Sociedade Civil, e a Sociedade Política," paper presented at the Yale University Conference "Democratizing Brazil?," March 1–4, 1983, pp. 9–10.

31. The most complete factual research on the political repression of 1964 to 1979, based on official documents, was published under World Council of Churches sponsorship in *Brasil: Nunca Mais* (Petrópolis: Editôra Vozes, 1985), growing out of a closely guarded project called "Testamunhos Pró-Paz," under the guidance of the Archdiocese of São Paulo.

3

The Brazilian Congress: From *Abertura* to New Republic

David Fleischer

The national legislature has been the Achilles heel of authoritarian regimes in Brazil since Dom Pedro I dismissed the first constituent assembly in 1823. With subsequent critical regime changes, Congress was either closed outright or severely limited in its functions (1889, 1930, 1937, 1964, and 1968/69). Following each of these episodes, Congress was reopened to lend support and legitimacy to the new regime or to elaborate a new constitutional order (1824, 1890, 1933, 1946, and 1970).

This chapter examines the role of the Congress in the process of political liberalization, from the first steps taken by President Ernesto Geisel after 1974 and culminating with the election of Tancredo Neves in January 1985. A final section evaluates performance of the Congress during the critical first four months of the new José Sarney government. My analysis describes the electoral system constituting Congress, backgrounds of those elected, the party system thus represented, and the institutional and representational dynamics linking Congress to the executive and to civil society.

Controlled Liberalization (1974–1979)

The process of *distensão* began in 1974 as the new Geisel government attempted to promote a "slow, gradual, and secure" extrication of the military from government and to return power to a segment of the civilian political class worthy of confidence. As in 1964 when Brazil experienced the first in a wave of military interventions in South America, ten years later the nation again took the lead in the process of political liberalization, which stretched over another eleven traumatic years. In comparison, Ecuador, Peru, Bolivia, Argentina, and Uruguay completed their transitions to elected civilian regimes in much shorter periods. One of the differences evident in the Brazilian authoritarian experience was that the military rulers chose to maintain a functioning congress (although with greatly reduced powers) throughout most of the twenty-one-year period.[1]

In an effort to bolster its declining legitimacy due to faltering performance of the "economic miracle" and a tarnished human rights record in the early 1970s, the Geisel government decided to go for a "quick fix" of political legitimation by holding open, fair, and "unfettered" elections in November 1974. Palace strategists imagined that the opposition party (MDB) might regain its 1967 strength in the Chamber of Deputies (33 percent) and make some modest gains in the Senate. Table 3.1 presents the majority and proportional election results from 1966 through 1982.

Only in 1966 was the government party able to win over 50 percent of the votes cast (and only in the proportional election for the lower house). Because of the well-organized, blank-ballot protest movement in 1970, the government party (ARENA—National Renovating Alliance) had its percentage slightly reduced, but the MDB (Brazilian Democratic Movement) lost proportionately more. In 1974, the MDB was able to co-opt this protest vote, but the results exceeded even these expectations, as the opposition party elected sixteen of the twenty-two Senate seats with just over 50 percent of the votes cast, and 43 percent of the seats in the lower house (Figure 3.1.) In addition, the MDB accumulated majorities in six state legislatures, thus acquiring the right to indirectly elect the next governors in October 1978.[2]

Shaken but not destabilized, the Geisel government embarked on a "pendulum strategy" of "two steps forward, one back," first striking the left and then the right. After reducing the threat from the latter within the military in 1977, Geisel became the only military president since 1964 to impose his will on the presidential succession. To accomplish this feat, Geisel had to manipulate the army high command as well as the electoral system, and thus provide the new Figueiredo government with a secure base from which to further accelerate the liberalization in 1979.[3] However, both the manipulations of the electoral system and the *abertura* transition were destined to return to haunt their creators in 1983–1984.

The 1967 constitution and the massive first amendment of 1969 maintained the concept of constitutional revision by two-thirds majority. With its 43 percent in the Chamber, the MDB held an effective veto power over any changes proposed by the government. The "April package" of 1977 reduced this requirement to an absolute majority and thoroughly gerrymandered the electoral system in favor of the ARENA, which, together with the "Lei Falcão" muzzle on television campaigning, was able to stem the opposition tide in the 1978 elections (Figure 3.2). In these the MDB received majorities in only eight states and one territory, but was able to retain a 44 percent minority in the Chamber.[4]

The tendency of a steadily increasing and politically conscious opposition vote in Brazil's large and even middle-sized urban areas was apparent in the 1974, 1978, and 1982 results. In Table 3.1, we observe that turnout rates climbed slowly (78 percent to 83 percent) over the five elections, but enfranchisement (registered voters as a percentage of the population) increased dramatically, from 26 percent to 48 percent. Most of these new voters were part of the exploding urban population. These demographic tendencies were also occurring on a North-South dimension, favoring the more urbanized and industrialized Southeast and South (Figure 3.3), as detailed in Table 3.2.

Nationwide, the ARENA party began receiving majorities of the vote only in cities below 100,000 population, in an inverse relationship—increasing vote with decreasing *município* size. In the Southeast and South, ARENA fared badly, receiving 38 percent and 51 percent of the vote respectively and majorities only in cities of less than 50,000 population. This inverse relationship was apparent in all regions. The tendency was less pronounced in the two most underdeveloped, rural, and less-urbanized regions, the North and Northeast, where ARENA polled 61 percent and 72 percent, respectively.

Similar data for five selected states from the 1978 and 1982 elections is presented in Table 3.3. With the exception of Rio de Janeiro, the PDS (Democratic Social Party) fared worse in 1982 than the ARENA in 1978. In São Paulo, the most developed and urbanized state, for example, the PDS began accumulating majorities only in *municípios* under 10,000 population. The "city size—opposition vote" tendency was generally reconfirmed in 1982.[5] The state of Rio de Janeiro offers an interesting case, which could be attributed to the "Moreira Franco" factor. This PDS candidate was able to lead his ticket 6.5 points *ahead* of the 1978 ARENA vote in exactly the fifteen *largest* cities in the state. However, the overall trend is apparent in other brackets. As graphically displayed in Figure 3.4, victory was especially sweet for Tancredo Neves in Minas Gerais, where the 1982 vs. 1978 opposition margin was actually larger in the smaller cities.[6] In the state of Ceará (Figure 3.5), the trend is less apparent in cities under 100,000 population, and the results of the two elections were essentially the same due to the strong domination of three ex-military officers as *caciques* (local political bosses).[7]

Abertura (1979–1982)

The *abertura* period impacted heavily upon the Congress and involved further manipulation of the party and electoral systems within a "transformism" strategy aimed at retaining some kind of a workable coalition to support the last two years of the Figueiredo government (1983–1984) and the basis for the election of a "sympathetic" civilian president in the 1984 electoral college (later postponed to January 1985). This period can be divided into four phases culminating with the 1982 elections.

First Phase: 1979

In a rapid series of moves articulated by Justice Minister Petrônio Portela and Chief of the Civilian Staff General Golbery do Couto e

Silva, the new Figueiredo government seized the political initiative from the MDB and began its implosion: amnesty, extinction of the two-party system, direct elections for governors in 1982, release of political prisoners, return of exiles, debureaucratization, complacency regarding a massive wave of strikes, and attempts to improve wage policies—all of which had been demanded by the opposition in Congress over the previous ten years.

Opening the "straight jacket" two-party system from its "yes-no" plebiscitary character into a looser, moderate pluralism of party blocs in the Congress became a prime objective. Survey research conducted among deputies and senators in early 1979 showed 92 percent of the MDB and 85 percent of ARENA in favor of a change to a pluriparty system.[8] Portela's strategy foresaw an implosion of the ARENA as well, so that its successor party would hold but a simple majority in Congress and depend on a coalition with a new center party to be created by ex-ARENA dissidents and ex-MDB moderates.

Second Phase: January 1980–August 1981

The first phase of *abertura* did not survive to see the first party realignments in the Congress take place, due to the untimely death of Portela in January 1980. Ibrahim Abi-Ackel, his replacement from the ex-PSD group in Minas Gerais (who had already aligned himself with the new centrist Popular Party [PP] in formation), was able to reduce the number of desertions from ARENA to only 30. Thus, with 24 converts from the MDB, he maintained an absolute majority for the new government party (PDS) in the lower house, as seen in Table 3.4. The PMDB remained the second largest party, reduced by nearly half from 189 to 94 deputies and from 25 to 16 senators. The new PP was strongest in Minas Gerais and Rio de Janeiro and was organizing to be a strong competitor at the state level in the 1982 elections.

This realignment in Congress and its subsequent delicate process at the local level provided ample rationale for a bargain among party leaders to vote for the postponement until 1982 of municipal elections scheduled for November 1980, which neatly saved the new government from an inconvenient early test at the polls. Within the context of the shock waves of soaring interest rates, repression of the labor movement, and cold relations with an activist Church, right-wing terrorism grew in 1980 and 1981, which culminated with the Riocentro episode on April 30, 1981. By this time, the PDS's majority in the Chamber had dropped to dangerously low levels, a return to the PMDB (Party of the Brazilian Democratic Movement) was underway, and the PTB (Brazilian Labor Party) had been split into two "laborist" parties. Congressional leaders provided crucial support for President Figueiredo following the Riocentro bombing, which was perpetrated by the intelligence community and linked to the First Army command in Rio.

Third Phase: August 1981–February 1982

Following a series of defeats in 1981, General Golbery saw his political maneuvering space reduced and his populist 1982 election strategy vetoed by Planning Minister Antônio Delfim Neto. The latter called for a reedition of the old PSD/PTB alliance, with coalition building in most states, in which the PDS and PP would cover rural areas and use the PP, PTB, or PDT (Democratic Workers Party) in many urban centers to dilute the ever-increasing force of the PMDB. This plan was to be based on heavy doses of "populist" economic policy in 1982. Sensing that SNI Director General Octávio Medeiros, Figueiredo's *in pectore* succession candidate, was gaining the upper hand, Golbery abruptly resigned on August 6, thus to "have better chances to combat the 'continuist' plan from outside of government." Figueiredo immediately replaced Golbery with João Leitão de Abreu, who had held the same position under President Médici (1969–1974).

PDS dissidents joined the opposition on several occasions in the second semester of 1981 to defeat government proposals in the Chamber, most critical of which was the attempt to add the *sublegenda* artifice to the direct election of governors in 1982. (Under the *sublegenda* provision a party would have been credited with all the votes received by all the candidates of that party.) With SNI survey research pointing to opposition victories in most states, upon Figueiredo's return to the presidency in November the government counterattacked with a massive election manipulation package (including straight-ticket voting and no coalitions), which provoked the reincorporation of the PP into the PMDB in February 1982.[9]

Fourth Phase: February–December 1982

With this action, the government was able to reinforce its Chamber majority and inflate the PTB (under Delfim's guidance) as an erstwhile partner. Thus strengthened, the government approved yet another "reform" package, which again raised the constitutional quorum to two-thirds and reworked the composition of the 1984 electoral college in favor of the PDS.[10] These precautionary measures were taken because the government was fearful that it might lose its majorities in Congress (the opposition could then have changed the constitution at will), as well as in the electoral college.

Party Delegations in Congress

Table 3.5 presents the profiles of ARENA and MDB in Congress in early 1979, one year before the party realignments began. Although there are some differences between the two houses, in general, ARENA was more the party of the "producing classes," and MDB more that of the liberal professions. As might be expected, ARENA congressmen had more prior political experience and localism, whereas their MDB colleagues had higher levels of education and younger ages. ARENA had higher return rates and seniority in the Chamber, but, thanks to those elected in 1974, MDB had a higher return rate in the Senate, and seniority there was nearly equal.

Tables 3.6 and 3.7 detail the profiles in 1981 of the six new parties organized in 1980. Comparing the profiles of the ARENA with its successor PDS, we observe that the government party lost educators, lawyers, and other professionals but received more elements from the producing classes (agriculture, business, and industry-transportation). The PDS deputies had slightly less political experience, education, and localism than did ARENA deputies. In terms of the prior pluriparty system (Table 3.7), 42 percent were identified with the two traditional rivals, PSD (Social Democratic Party) and UDN (National Democratic Union), and another 14 percent came from the old PTB and PDC (Christian Democratic Party). General Golbery's strategy of "divide and rule" had reduced the PMDB to half the MDB's strength in the chamber in 1980, but by 1981 the PMDB had regained nineteen deputies. At this point, the profiles of MDB vs. PMDB indicate that the latter had more lawyers, educators, journalists, and other professionals but had lost elements from the health, public servant, and military sectors. This "new" opposition party in the Chamber had more prior political experience and localism but was slightly younger and had less seniority than the MDB in 1979. Some 53 percent of the PMDB had no links with the old pluriparty system (only 32 percent for ARENA); that is, the PMDB was less rent by these cleavages at the state level but more split at the ideological level in Congress. The latter had been somewhat alleviated by the PP exodus in 1980. Still, 34 percent of the PMDB came from the old PSD-PTB alliance, and 9 percent from the progressive wings of the UDN and PDC. Thus, the PMDB should not be considered an "old party with new clothes" but the ex-MDB with "less clothes."

In the press, the PP was nicknamed the "bankers' party," and in fact people involved in commerce-banking and finance made up the largest component of its delegation in 1981, followed by liberal professionals and public servants. Judging from the indicators of prior political careers, the PP was certainly the "politicians' party." Except for the absence of elements from the old PTB and ex-PDC, the exparty profile of the PP was quite similar to that of the PDS. Had it not been for the heavy "electoral engineering" forcing its reincorporation with the PMDB, the PP probably would have emerged as a strong center party in many states after the 1982 elections.

Brizola's PDT delegation of ten deputies was greatly reduced from the twenty-two he commanded within the PTB in 1980 before the split with Ivete Vargas. All ten were tied to the old parties—eight to the old PTB and one each to the PSD and PSB (Brazilian Socialist Party). Nine were returning veterans from the 1975–1979 legislative session— the highest rate of all parties. Composed of lawyers, public servants, and journalists, the PDT bloc had below-average political experience and localism, but was higher on education. With short careers and late entry into politics, the PDT closely resembled the old pre-1965 PTB.[11]

By 1981, Ivete Vargas's PTB had been reduced to only five deputies but by August 1982 had increased to fourteen. Orphaned by Golbery's resignation, the PTB soon acquired Minister Delfim Neto as its new godfather, and ex-president Jânio Quadros as its elder statesman. This small bloc, including two ex-PTB, one ex-PSP (Progressive Social Party), and one ex-PRT (Rural Labor Party), was long on political experience, with higher levels of education and localism than Brizola's PDT. With an average of 8.42 years of Chamber experience, the PTB had the most seniority.

Only reluctantly did PT (Workers Party) organizers in São Paulo accept a small bloc of five deputies and one senator into their party in 1980 because of the latter's incompatibility with the other new parties being organized in Congress. In 1981, only two of the six PT deputies had affinities with the old parties (PSD and PSB). Two-thirds were lawyers or professionals and one was an industrial worker. As might be expected, the new party was short on political experience and the youngest of all delegations. During the repression of PT labor leaders in 1981 and 1982, the congressional delegation served the party well in generating access to public opinion.

The 1982 Elections

General Results

Having again synchronized municipal elections with state and federal elections (for the first time since 1970) and established mandatory straight-ticket voting, the government hoped to "localize" the elections and provoke a "reverse coattails" effect. Because the PDS controlled an overwhelming majority of local elected offices (mayor and city council) in all states except Rio de Janeiro, the government expected that voters would support local PDS candidates and consequently the "top of the ticket" (governor and senator) as well, at the risk of invalidating their ballots.

This proved to be the case in the "solid Northeast" (Figure 3.6) where these artifices helped the PDS to victory.[12] As has been the case with Brazil's long history of electoral law manipulations, the "witchcraft returned to plague the witch" in the Central-South and Northern regions, where the opposition won ten of the twenty-three states—an area accounting for nearly 70 percent of Brazil's population, GNP, and tax base. The PP-PMDB fusion had greatly strengthened the latter, and the election turned into a "straight coattails" effect in the Central-South in favor of the PMDB, which decimated the PDS at the municipal level.

After the "Maluf miracle" in the first semester of 1980,[13] the PMDB had been reduced to only 38 mayors in São Paulo state, but in 1983 jumped to 307 (vs. 253 for the PDS). In Goiás, the PMDB grew from 60 cities to 185, and in Paraná from 14 to 183. Because these PMDB mayors hold mandates until 1989, they constitute a formidable machine for the 1986 elections.

Despite the desperate manipulations, the PDS was reduced to a simple majority in the Chamber but retained an absolute majority in the electoral college and a two-thirds majority in the Senate, as detailed in Table 3.8. The Senate margin was based on the PDS's eighteen "bionic" senators elected in 1978, a Geisel administration contrivance. By setting the electoral college delegates at an equal six per state (winner-take-all), instead of proportionate to the state's population (as was the case in 1978), the PDS accumulated a seventeen vote margin in the indirect presidential election scheduled for January 1985. Had the 1978 rules remained in force (a hypothesis detailed in Table 3.8), the combined opposition parties would have held a five-vote margin. Table 3.8 also depicts the inequalities of representation in Brazil's lower house. With its 43.2 percent of the party vote, the PDS received 49 percent of the seats. On a one-man-one-vote basis, instead of its eight deputies, the PT should have elected seventeen.

Tables 3.9 and 3.10 analyze the regional basis of these inequalities.[14] With only 29.3 percent of the population and 23.8 percent of voters in 1982, the Northeast commanded 39.2 percent of the Senate, 31.1 percent of the Chamber, and one-third of the 1985 electoral college. Within the PDS, the inequalities are even more striking, due to the party's hegemony in the Northeast region. With 35.6 percent of the PDS vote in 1982, the Northeast delegation held a 53.3 percent absolute majority within the government party bloc in the Senate and a simple majority of 42.1 percent in the Chamber, as well as 43.2 percent of the party's August 1984 national nominating convention, and 49 percent of the PDS's votes in the January 1985 electoral college. As we shall see below, these inequalities assisted Maluf's convention victory, but were an important part of his defeat in the electoral college.

In contrast, the more populous Southeast region, with 43.4 percent of the population and 48.9 percent of the 1982 voters, had but 17.4 percent representation in the Senate, 35.3 percent in the Chamber, and only 29.9 percent in the electoral college. Still worse, these four states gave the PDS its largest number of voters (37.2 percent) in 1982, but accounted for only 11.1 percent of the PDS Senate delegation, 25.5 percent in the Chamber, and a mere 18 percent of the PDS's votes in the electoral college.

Party Profiles

As compared to the Chamber elected in 1978 (Table 3.6), in 1983 we find more deputies from the sectors of agriculture, business, and public service, and fewer lawyers and military officers (Table 3.11). Research conducted by *Veja* newsmagazine in December 1982 among

437 deputies-elect identified 163 (37.3 percent) as "farmers," and 42 percent declared "agriculture, cattle production, or agricultural industry" to be one of their sources of income.[15] The probable reasons for this "great influx of farmers" in the 1983 legislature are: (1) *Veja's* analysis computed "multiple professions" (up to five) instead of principle occupation as in Table 3.11; and (2) over the past ten years, many liberal professionals have invested in agricultural ventures, as was the case with the stockmarket in the early 1970s.

During the heat of initial discussions of the Sarney government's land reform proposals in early June 1985, the *Jornal do Brasil* published a list of sixty-three deputies (13 percent) and twelve senators (17 percent) identified as "large landowners."[16] Senator Altevir Leal (PDS-AC) holds 2 million hectares (13 percent of the state of Acre); Deputy Augusto Franco (PDS-SE) holds 10,000 hectares (5 percent of Sergipe); and Senator Saldanha Derzi (PMDB-MS) owns 200,000 hectares in Mato Grosso do Sul. The landholding deputies were fairly evenly distributed (proportionate to delegation size) among the three largest parties, with a slight advantage for the PDS: PDS, twenty-four (18 percent); PMDB, twenty-six (13 percent); and PFL (Party of the Liberal Front), thirteen (13 percent).[17]

In this regard, the PDS had fewer farmers, lawyers, professionals, and military officers, but more businesspeople and public servants in 1983 than the ARENA had in 1979. On this same trend, the combined opposition parties in 1983 had even more farmers proportionately than the MDB in 1979, with the PMDB very close to the PDS in this regard. Regarding links with the pre-1966 party system, the PDS had fewer elements from the ex-PSD and ex-UDN in 1983 than the ARENA in 1979, whereas the PMDB gained more ex-PTB and ex-UDN deputies because of the PP fusion with the PMDB in 1982. (Compare Table 3.12 with Table 3.7.) The PDT continued to recruit heavily among lawyers and journalists. The PTB's occupational composition was more diversified than in 1981, whereas the PT increased its contingent of educators.

In general, the "class of 1983" brought more prior political experience to the Chamber, especially in administrative positions, with slightly more university education but less localism. In 1983, the PDT, PTB, and PT elected more candidates born out-of-state than in 1981. Of the fifty-nine new seats available in the Chamber in 1983, the PDS captured only eleven, versus thirty-two for the PMDB. Thus, the latter had a larger turnover rate (49 percent) than the former (only 41 percent new deputies). The smaller parties had turnover rates inversely proportional to their size in 1983. The average age of the Chamber in 1983 was only half a year younger than in 1979. The ages of the PDS deputies were nearly the same as their ARENA counterparts, but the PMDB was over a year older than the MDB in 1979 (one of the results of the PP-PMDB fusion). The three smaller parties were all over a year younger in 1983 than in 1981.

Transition (1983–1984)

Presidential Succession Politics

True to the traditional Brazilian theme of *"ganhou mas não levou"* (you won, but you didn't get the prize), the government and the PDS began an inglorious descent into defeat in early 1983. During this period, the PDS declined from its 361 electoral college votes "won" in 1982, to 248 by November 1984, to a final 180 votes cast on January 15, 1985.

Early in 1983, President Figueiredo lost a good opportunity to reassert political command of the PDS and the succession process when his apparent candidate (Medeiros) was eliminated during the "star wars" corruption and violence scandals in January, which included the misuse of government funds and the alleged assassination of a journalist. Had he reorganized his cabinet to include the diverse PDS factions; eliminated the "tainted," unpopular, and ineffective ministers; and chosen to favor a "clean" politician of the center as his successor, such as Vice-president Aureliano Chaves or Social Security Minister Hélio Beltrão, the PDS would have had better chances of maintaining a majority in the electoral college.

The disintegration of the PDS began in June and July 1983, when the president suffered two humiliating defeats that, given the state of his coronary arteries, could have cost him his life: (1) the total defeat of the Paulo Egídio faction by Maluf in the São Paulo state PDS convention and (2) the dissident *Participação* faction's ability to elect 35 percent of the PDS national party directorate during the party's July convention in Brasília.

After his July 1983 coronary bypass operation in the United States in Cleveland, Ohio, and two months of convalescence, President Figueiredo returned in time for the first defeats of military government decree-laws by the Congress in October. Forced to operate with a simple majority in the Chamber, PDS leaders tried to strike a coalition bargain with the PTB president, Deputy Ivete Vargas, so that they would be able to pass critical legislation. The PTB received some minor federal appointments, but was not included in the cabinet. In October, the PTB and several PDS dissidents bolted the coalition because they were against the repressive salary decrees, and the government never recovered a majority.

During a trip to Africa in November, Figueiredo tried to demoralize the PDS further by stating that "I personally would like direct elections for president in 1984, but I am impeded by the PDS." Many observers were reminded of the 1937 presidential campaign, when President Vargas supposedly encouraged the "semi-official" candidate, José Américo, but never gave his public blessing, all the time plotting a *continuísmo* strategy (a strategy to prolong his stay in office). Interior Minister Mário Andreazza seemed to be playing the role of José Américo, while Chief of Staff

Leitão de Abreu and Mines and Energy Minister César Cals tried to broker a *mandato-tampão* (an extended term in exchange for a government concession to the opposition) for Figueiredo himself, in return for direct elections in 1986. Survey research conducted in early November 1983 showed that Congress was close to a two-thirds majority on direct elections but, except for Brizola's PDT, very negative on the issue of *continuísmo*.[18]

January 1984 marked the start of a three-month popular campaign to pressure Congress, especially PDS deputies, in favor of the Dante de Oliveira amendment calling for "Direct Elections Now." Public rallies under this slogan mobilized millions of people in hundreds of cities to pressure Congress. Sensing a last minute ground swell in favor of the amendment, the government hastily introduced its own massive package two days before the crucial vote and pulled out all the authoritarian stops: (1) Brasília and the surrounding region were placed under emergency military rule, (2) PDS mayors and city council members were impeded from traveling to Brasília to pressure "their" deputies, (3) live television and radio coverage was muzzled, and (4) Planning Minister Delfim Neto applied severe economic pressure on wavering PDS deputies.[19]

The amendment failed the two-thirds quorum in the Chamber by fifty-two votes on April 25, 1984, and the government's miniconstitutional reform package (establishing direct elections in 1988) suffered a similar fate two months later. Because of "bad faith" drafting, a simple majority item vote would have approved direct elections in 1984; when the opposition and the *pró-diretas* faction of the PDS moved to take advantage of this loophole, the government was "forced" to withdraw its entire package.

During this same period, Senator Marco Maciel and Vice-president Aureliano Chaves, together with ex-PDS president Senator José Sarney, formed the Liberal Front as a dissident bloc from the PDS and in August formalized the Democratic Alliance with the PMDB and the Tancredo Neves-José Sarney ticket. Because most of the Liberal Front delegates still voted in the PDS national nominating convention, they were instructed to vote for Deputy Paulo Maluf because he was seen as easier to defeat than Minister Andreazza, who would have better reunited the PDS. In addition, some two-thirds of the convention delegates were local party "hacks" holding no elected office and thus very vulnerable to Maluf's campaign tactics.

Neves had sealed a "*mineiros'* pact" with Chaves in 1983; whoever waxed strong in his respective party and got the nomination would receive the total support of the other. Deputy Ulysses Guimarães— PMDB elder statesman, national party president, and "anti-candidate" in 1973—was forced by a coalition of PMDB governors to withdraw his candidacy in support of Neves. Thus, with the PMDB and Minas Gerais united, and with a dissident PDS running mate from the Northeast,

Neves needed only to maintain popular mobilization and secretly strike a bargain with more moderate members of the army high command with authority over troop commands.

The more heavyhanded the tactics used by Maluf campaigners, their allies within the Figueiredo government, and military hardliners, the more electoral college members aligned themselves with Neves and the more support he gained with the high command. Thus, Maluf lost forty of the eighty-one PDS delegates, and Neves gained the discreet support of Generals Ivan Souza Mendes and Leônidas Pires Gonçalves (appointed as minister-director of the SNI and minister of the army, respectively, by Neves in March 1985).[20]

Ceará Vice-governor Adauto Bezerra subsequently revealed what went wrong with Maluf's strategy in the Northeast, the traditional government party stronghold that had helped Maluf win the PDS nomination in the August 1984 party convention. The region's real political leaders (governors, senators, and deputies) were passed over, forgotten, and alienated during the "full court press" applied to the "hack" convention delegates and their families. Those "legitimate" leaders reacted with a vengeance in October and November by mobilizing their elected majorities in the state legislatures in favor of Neves, out of fear that once in office Maluf would continue his "grassroots" tactics so that in the next state party conventions and executive committee sessions these political leaders would be replaced by loyal *malufistas*. The "coup de grace" was delivered to Maluf by the Superior Electoral Court in November in a ruling stating that the party fidelity sanctions of the Organic Party Law applied to legislative proceedings in the Congress, and not to the electoral college.

The Electoral College

Meeting as scheduled, in a climate of complete liberty with abundant national and international news coverage, the electoral college chose Tancredo Neves with 480 votes against Maluf's 180, with 26 abstentions, as detailed in Table 3.13 and illustrated in Figure 3.7. The Neves-Sarney slate received 309 votes from the four opposition parties combined (35 short of the absolute majority) and another 171 from the PDS. A total of 113 of the latter came from the Partido da Frente Liberal (PFL). Obviously, without the support of these PDS dissidents, Neves's victory would have been impossible. Table 3.14 demonstrates the importance of the Northeast (155 votes) for the Alliance victory, many votes of which were PDS dissidents. This was Maluf's "Waterloo" and became President Sarney's problem, as he attempted to conciliate the PFL and PMDB in this region in the distribution of federal appointments and other "political goods."

In early November, eleven of the PTB's fourteen votes were pledged to Maluf (on instructions from the party's benefactor, Minister Delfim Neto),[21] but by January the latter had changed his mind and Maluf received only three PTB votes. Brizola's PDT remained firm for Neves, although not formally joining the Alliance. Only Deputy Aguinaldo Timóteo (PDT-RJ) voted with Maluf, and he was expelled from the party. The PT national directorate had decided not to join the Alliance when it was formed in August 1984 and continued firm in its principles against any form of indirect election. Its three dissident deputies who voted for Neves were expelled from the PT, but their mandates could not be canceled because of the Superior Electoral Court (TSE) decision. The Neves-Sarney slate received fifty-five votes from the independent PDS bloc not affiliated with the PFL, some members of which have since gravitated to the latter. Twelve of the PDS's sixteen abstentions came from the South (Rio Grande do Sul and Santa Catarina) where grassroots party loyalty sentiments were strong.

The Democratic Alliance (1985)

Congressional Reorganization

With the formal constitution of the PFL as a party bloc within the Senate and Chamber in February 1985, the PMDB achieved a simple majority in the Chamber and the PMDB-PFL alliance an absolute majority in the Senate. Prior to the start of the 1985 legislative session on March 1, the parties caucused and bargained in late February to distribute the leadership positions for the 1985–1987 term. In the Chamber, the PDS accepted the PMDB's majority status and quickly agreed to a proportional division of the seven-member governing board, with the PMDB holding the presidency, second vice-presidency, and third secretariat; the PFL received the first vice-presidency; the PDS the first and second secretariats; and the PDT the fourth secretariat. The smaller PTB and PT received positions as alternates.

Within the PMDB caucus, Deputy Ulysses Guimarães handily defeated "authentic" Deputy Alencar Furtado (PMDB-PR) by a 121–56 vote. However, the latter did not withdraw his candidacy during the full floor vote and received 210 votes (*malufistas*, discontent PMDB deputies, and 5 from the PT). Guimarães's 245 votes were only 5 above the majority figure and dangerously close to forcing an embarrassing second round of balloting. Although Guimarães (a national symbol in the *"Diretas Já"* campaigns) was recognized by many as the most revered and prestigious PMDB member in the Chamber, many "authentic" deputies gravitating toward the "independent left" bloc of the party believed he was the personal choice of the president-elect and that this constituted an unacceptable continuation of executive branch tutelage of the Chamber's internal decisionmaking. Thus, Guimarães began his term on the political defensive.

The Senate played out a somewhat different scenario. The PDS stubbornly argued that it had accepted the majority criteria in the Chamber and demanded that the Democratic Alliance accept the PDS's simple majority position in the Senate—thus, in the proportional distribution, the presidency of the Senate would go to the PDS. Of course, this was totally unacceptable to the Alliance and the president-elect, because the Senate president is also the president of the Congress and presides over joint sessions, in addition to making critical decisions on behalf of the legislature as a whole.

The Alliance argued that the PMDB-PFL coalition held an absolute majority in the Senate, and so if the PDS would not strike a bargain similar to that in the Chamber, the Alliance would vote it down and elect all seven positions with a PMDB-PFL slate. With one exception, the latter was the final result. Senator Passos Porto (PDS-SE) was able on his own personal prestige to collect enough votes to be elected second vice-president. To accommodate its coalition partner in the Senate, the PMDB ceded five of the seven positions to the PFL, with the PMDB holding the presidency and first secretariat. With the loss of the second vice-presidency, the PFL was reduced to four slots but still retained a majority on this presiding executive board.

Neves had discreetly indicated his preference within the PMDB in favor of Floor Leader Humberto Lucena (PMDB-PB) as president, as they had been close colleagues in the ex-PSD in the Chamber of Deputies. However, Lucena was defeated in the PMDB caucus by a "young Turk" insurgency led by Neves's own alternate, Senator Alfredo Campos (PMDB-MG), which selected Senator José Fragelli (PMDB-MS) on a tight 12-11 vote. Had Senators Itamar Franco and José Sarney not been absent, Lucena might have won.

The election of Fragelli created an unexpected problem for Neves, in that it was assumed that once Lucena was elected Senate president, Senator Fernando Henrique Cardoso (PMDB-SP) would become the floor leader. The latter had turned down invitations for several cabinet positions in favor of remaining in the Senate and was left without a leadership position. Thus, when Neves finally announced his cabinet formally on March 12, Cardoso was named to a new position created especially for him—leader of the government in Congress.

The new Alliance leadership in the Senate moved quickly to reorganize top staff positions, in an effort to reform administrative procedures, both to improve the Senate's public image and its internal operations. During the years of ARENA/PDS domination, the Senate had been turned into "job factory." In December 1984, the twilight of the "ancien regime," some 2,000 relatives, hacks, and other hangers-on had been appointed without competitive examination, whereas some 150 highly qualified persons selected from a pool of 3,000 candidates by public examination were passed over. In the Chamber, the Alliance leaders lacked the courage and political base to effect such administrative reforms, and the staff power structure remained intact.

The Sarney Presidency

Because of Tancredo Neves's sudden infirmity, the Congress was forced to occupy rapidly the power vacuum thus created and to assume an advanced institutional role beyond what it would have had with Neves firmly in power. Acting President José Sarney was very constrained in exercizing the presidency so as not to appear the "crass usurper" of Neves's presidency and therefore sought support and legitimation from legislative leaders. The latter took the initiative during the wee hours of March 15, 1985, even before Sarney was sworn in and negotiated the transfer of power to the vice-president-elect, which was an acceptable transfer to the outgoing regime.

During its first sixty days, the new government functioned as an informal semiparliamentary system, with Senator Fernando H. Cardoso and Deputy Ulysses Guimarães as "co-prime ministers." The Democratic Alliance leadership (PFL and PMDB) took over the coordination of the remaining (and hotly contested) subministerial appointments. Important political and financial decisions, which had been quickly resolved by previous military governments through presidential decree-laws or simple administrative fiat, were thrust upon the Congress or became the initiative of the latter.

Instead of simply declaring the extrajudicial liquidation of the failed Banco Sul Brasileiro or opting for an injection of 900 billion cruzeiros, the government decided that a political solution negotiated within the Congress was a better alternative. Under lobby pressure from hundreds of bank employees camped out on the lawn in front of Congress, the latter finally decided to turn the failed bank into a federal enterprise and Deputy Sinval Guazelli (PMDB-RS) was appointed its new president by Sarney. Northeastern legislators complained of an "easy bailout" accorded to Southern states, while their region's terrible problems of drought and floods were neglected.

Congress also took the initiative in modifying legislation governing party organization and elections, which in the past would have been handled by yet another "package of reforms" devised by government "political engineers." These modifications, approved in May and June, abolished the *sublegenda*, party fidelity, and *Lei Falcão* regulations; unfettered procedures for organizing new parties; liberated 202 *municípios* (including 25 capital cities) from national security legislation and regulated the direct elections of their mayors that took place on November 15, 1985; and established direct elections for the next president.

Regarding the latter change, as the May 8–9, 1985, vote on election law modifications approached, pressures mounted in Congress to include provisions dealing with the next presidential election and even to shorten Sarney's mandate. To head off such efforts, and at the same time gain legitimacy and initiative lost during his opposition to the direct elections amendment in April 1984, President Sarney submitted his own proposal to Congress on May 6 to restore direct presidential elections without specifying the next date and thus without shortening his mandate. Sarney's proposal was passed in toto two days later and provided for the election of the next president by an absolute majority, with a runoff (if necessary) to be held thirty days later between the top two candidates— essentially the system used in France. The president's rapid success enhanced his leadership within the Democratic Alliance and among the population and left the question of length of mandate and election date to the constituent assembly scheduled to meet in early 1987, thus precluding a direct presidential election in 1986—an election which was much desired by Governor Leonel Brizola and the PT.

However, even as acting president, Sarney did not relinquish all autonomy of his office in relations with the legislature. The president vetoed the creation of the new state of Tocantins to be carved out of the northern half of Goiás, which had passed both houses of Congress, alleging an additional financial burden on a government pledged to austerity. When required to rapidly replace the governor of the Federal District (Brasília) with a temporary 30-day interim appointment, he bypassed confirmation procedures with the Senate as dictated by the constitution, claiming the non-applicability of these procedures in the case of a short-term appointment. Following an outcry in Congress over a "secret" decree law (concerning the SNI) published in the daily record, Sarney promised not to use decree-laws, decurso de prazo, and other authoritarian powers inherited from the military regimes.[22]

During the interim period, with the new government functioning at less than half steam, the political class felt compelled to display an image of normalcy or business as usual in Brasília to show that a power vacuum did not exist. Congress was the logical candidate for this role. When Neves died on April 21, Sarney fully assumed the presidency and totally activated the executive branch so that during his second two months in office relations with the legislature became more balanced as the latter retreated to its traditional legislative and oversight functions.

On May 8, Finance Minister Francisco Dornelles made a historical presentation before Congress regarding the nation's domestic financial situation and the impending renegotiation of the foreign debt—the first such performance by a cabinet minister in twenty-one years. However, members of Congress were handicapped by constrictive internal rules imposed by the military in 1969 that limited their action to one-shot questions with no rebuttals. On May 15, in response to increased oversight debate in the Chamber regarding foreign policy (a resolution calling for renewing diplomatic relations with Cuba had been passed), Foreign Minister Olavo Setúbal gave a long presentation of Brazil's foreign policy objectives and answered many questions before the Chamber Foreign Relations Committee.

Of the twenty-one non-military cabinet ministers appointed by Tancredo Neves, fourteen were current or ex-legislators (five federal deputies, three senators, and six ex-deputies—three of the latter *cassados*—individuals who had had their political rights suspended by the military regime). With the exception of nephew Dornelles and Antônio Carlos Magalhães, all cabinet positions were filled with nominees from the PMDB or PFL in an effort to cement the Democratic Alliance in power. This brought legislators and the parties into government even more than during the João Goulart presidency, and rivaled the Jânio Quadros and parliamentary periods of the early 1960s.

Still, many PMDB deputies, especially among the "Independent Left," retained their knee-jerk reaction against any actions by "the government"—a conditioned reflex after twenty-one years. President Sarney had to cancel a trip to Peru and postpone a trip to Uruguay because a quorum could not be mustered in the Senate to approve his leave of absence. In August, however, the Senate approved Sarney's September trip to the UN in New York with no problems. To avoid debate, Sarney waited until June 27 (the day before mid-term adjournment) to send to Congress his message convoking the constituent assembly for 1987. In a similar action, the president chose July 5 to announce severe budget cuts for state enterprises and other deficit-reducing measures aimed at placating the IMF and hoped that foreign debt negotiations would be near completion before the recess period ended on August 1. The last act of Finance Minister Francisco Dornelles (Tancredo's nephew) before being dismissed in August was to conclude a 140-day postponement of the deadline for renegotiation of Brazil's interbank credit lines that would have fallen due on August 31. Thus, the final stage of renegotiation of the foreign debt occurred in December and early January—exactly when the Congress is in recess. Many felt that this was done to exclude Congress from the process of renegotiation and that Congress might try to call itself into special session.

On this sensitive issue of the foreign debt, Congress threatened to demand access to information on the letter of intent negotiated with the IMF and the agreements made with the creditor banks. Some legislators would like both to be submitted to Congress for approval, as any foreign treaty or agreement must be in accordance with the constitution. Until 1985, only Latin American foreign and finance ministers had met in the Cartagena forums to discuss the debt issue. In June 1985, however, the issue was on the agenda of the Latin American Parliament meeting in Brasília. A special meeting of this body was convened for October in Punta del Este to discuss the debt question exclusively.

In mid-July the legislative relations office of the president's staff compiled figures for the 943 speeches made on the floor of the Chamber of Deputies during the first semester, which are separated by party in Table 3.15. As might be expected, the PMDB and PFL were the most favorable to "their" government, with the PFL ahead by 5 percent. The PDS, however, was not the most negative, being surpassed by the PT and the PTB, with the PDT being slightly less negative than the PDS, which reflects the government's potential allies within the latter.

In June 1985, it was the Chamber's turn to project a tarnished image to the public. On a crucial roll-call vote on the municipal elections, eight deputies were photographed from the galleries using the electronic voting system to vote twice. The public recrimination was tremendous, and Chamber President Guimarães was forced to initiate censure proceedings against the offenders, which resulted in his issuing a formal censure in writing.[23] For Guimarães, the situation was especially delicate, because a majority of those involved was from the PMDB.

On January 15 and March 15, the Congress received a concentration of lobbyists not seen since the early 1960s. These representatives of national and international interests had concentrated their efforts within the executive branch over the past twenty-one years, but in 1985, sensing a resurgence of the legislature, they shifted their efforts to Congress. One example was the public debate of a business-class proposal to mobilize a war chest of some 5 trillion cruzeiros (US$600 million) to help elect in 1986 at least 300 members of the constituent assembly "favorable to private enterprise." Newspapers were quick to identify nearly 300 members of the current Congress as "members of the propertied classes."

During the debates on legislation regulating party access to television and radio time during the two months prior to the November 15, 1985, municipal elections, the pressures from the television industry association (ABERT) were too strong, and the PMDB leadership finally decided to sponsor ABERT's draft bill. Chamber leaders working against the bill simply "disappeared" from national television news coverage. The bill eventually was defeated on a floor vote, but a leadership bargain struck in the Senate provided for reconsideration by the Chamber in August. The ABERT association is one of the most powerful interest groups and the most feared by politicians.

In August and September, the press mounted a formidable campaign to discredit the Congress regarding the payment of per diems to absent members and other indicators of "inactivity" in the legislature. Following a national address by Senator José Fragelli and Deputy Ulysses Guimarães on September 13, 1985, and the increased intensity of the municipal campaigns, these attacks subsided.

The 1985 municipal elections were a "test by fire" for the Democratic Alliance and resulted in expanded party factionalism in the congress. Table 3.16 describes the party delegations in both houses as of the close of the session at the end of June. In the second semester, dissident PMDB candidates drew some deputies to new party labels, and more "erosion" of the PDS occurred. It was possible that the eighty-some members of the PMDB "independent left" might break away to form a socialist party. The Sarney government avoided such a split with the adroit adoption of the cruzado zero-inflation plan on February 28, 1986.

However, after the November 1986 election, Sarney may construct a large party of the center, aggregating the PFL, PMDB moderates, and PDS "independents," which could reach a 250-deputy absolute majority in the constituent assembly.

Despite the many liberalizing measures adopted during the first half of 1985, the executive still retains strong powers inherited from the authoritarian military period: full powers over all financial, taxation, and civil service questions; control over the contents of the national budget (the Congress may only approve or disapprove the budget); the *decurso de prazo* mechanism; and Congress' own crippling internal rules that curtail its oversight and investigative capacity. Furthermore, even if the Congress rapidly recuperates most of its prerogatives of the pre-1964 era, it does not have qualified staff in sufficient numbers nor an agile enough bureaucratic structure to adequately perform these "new" functions.

This agenda will only be addressed during and after the 1987 constituent assembly. The latter has opened yet another front of conflict between the executive and legislative branches. First, many legislators believe that it is the prerogative of the Congress to convoke a constituent assembly, not the president's. Still worse, the idea of the executive constituting a fifty-member "blue ribbon" commission of notables to draft a "working document" for the 1987 assembly during 1985 and 1986 is repugnant to many legislators, who compare this idea to the commission organized by Vargas in 1932 in preparation for the 1934 constituent assembly.[24] Neves had envisioned a thirty-three-member commission of notables, but Sarney expanded this body to include more representatives from civil society, which would necessitate organization by subcommittees. Some legislative leaders, notably the "independent left bloc" in the PMDB, have constituted an alternative commission within Congress so that the assembly will not be presented with a fait accompli in 1987. Sensitive to this potential institutional conflict, Sarney held back the decree organizing the commission as long as possible.

During the second semester of 1985, the Sarney government suffered some reverses in its relations with Congress. First, the government's efforts to draft an "emergency" tax reform package to save local governments from bankruptcy were demolished by a more comprehensive bill presented by Deputy Airton Sandoval (PMDB-SP) and supported by the National Municipal Front, which forced the Alliance leadership into compromise negotiations. Second, Sarney's bill calling for the election of the constituent assembly in 1986 ran into difficulties and had to be negotiated. Third, the impatient Congress decided not to wait until 1987 to get its institutional prerogatives back and constituted a joint committee to draft such proposals for 1986. Fourth, proposed legislation to grant full amnesty and reintegration of all military personnel deprived of their political rights and positions since 1964 put the government in a delicate position vis-à-vis the current military leadership. Finally, the consideration and approval of the 1986 budget by Congress encountered difficulties, in spite of the authoritarian norms still in place that supposedly inhibit such prerogatives by Congress.

Sensing his delicate position as "permanent acting president" and having served twenty-four years in Congress, Sarney has tried to maintain good relations with that body. The political council of legislative leaders meets weekly (and more often if necessary) with the president and his advisors to coordinate strategies. In 1986 this relationship became more strained following the conservative cabinet reshuffle of February 15 and tension on the agrarian reform issue, but it will reach an equilibrium position following the general elections, during the deliberations of the national constituent assembly.

Notes

1. Robert Wesson and David Fleischer, *Brazil in Transition* (New York: Praeger, 1983) and Walder de Góes and Aspásia Camargo, *O Drama da Sucessão e a Crise do Regime* (Rio de Janeiro: Nova Fronteira, 1984).

2. For an analysis of the 1974 elections, see Fernando H. Cardoso and Bolivar Lamounier (eds.), *Os Partidos e as Eleições* (Rio de Janeiro: Paz & Terra, 1975) and Sebastião Nery, *As 16 Derrotas que Abalaram o Brasil* (Rio de Janeiro: Francisco Alves, 1975). The MDB's "right" to elect four "bionic" governors in 1978 was eliminated by the April package in 1977.

3. For a review of the Geisel government, see Walder de Góes, *O Brasil de General Geisel* (Rio de Janeiro: Nova Fronteira, 1978). For a review of the *casuísmos* since 1964, see David Fleischer, "Constitutional and Electoral Engineering in Brazil: A Double-Edged Sword (1964–1982)," *Inter-American Economic Affairs* 37: 4 (1984): 3–36. More specifically on the "April package," see David Fleischer, "Renovação Política—Brasil 1978: Eleições Parlamentares sob a Égide do 'Pacote de Abril,'" *Revista de Ciência Política* 23:2 (1980): 57–82.

4. For analyses of the 1978 elections, see Bolivar Lamounier (ed.), *Voto de Desconfiança* (Petrópolis: Vozes, 1980) and Fundação Milton Campos (ed.), *As Eleições Nacionais de 1978*, 2 vols., (Brasília: Fundação Milton Campos, 1979).

5. The association between levels of urbanization and the increasing opposition vote in Brazil has been noted by many authors, among them Gláucio Soares, *Colégio Eleitoral, Convenções Partidárias e Eleições Diretas* (Petrópolis: Vozes, 1984), pp. 22–26 and Fábio W. Reis, "O Eleitorado, os Partidos e o Regime Autoritário Brasileiro," in Bernardo Sorj and Maria Hermínia T. Almeida (eds.), *Sociedade e Política no Brasil Pós-1964* (São Paulo: Brasiliense, 1983), pp. 70–83.

6. Data compiled from David Fleischer, "Uma Análise das Eleições de 1982 em Minas Gerais," paper presented at the Eighth Annual Meeting of ANPOCS, Águas de São Pedro, SP, October 23–26, 1984.

7. In 1978, the three *caciques* of Ceará (Távora, Bezerra, and Cals) were somewhat divided, whereas in 1982, by adroit distribution of political positions and the selection of a "neutral academic" as governor, the three factions were temporarily united. When Vice-governor Adauto Bezerra joined Governor Gonzaga Motta in support of the Democratic Alliance, Ceará's six delegates and a majority of its electoral college votes went to Tancredo Neves. Had Motta been appointed to Neves's cabinet, Bezerra would have assumed the governorship,

which was one of the latter's reasons for joining forces with the Alliance in November 1984.

8. Luiz H. Bahia, Olavo Brasil de Lima Jr., and César Guimarães, "O Perfil Social e Político da Nona Legislatura," *Jornal do Brasil*, April 22–24, 1979.

9. See Fleischer, "Constitutional and Electoral Engineering in Brazil," op. cit. The November 1981 package was passed by *decurso de prazo*.

10. For a description of the changes made by the May package, see *Jornal do Brasil*, June 24, 1982, p. 4.

11. For an analysis of the recruitment profile of the old PTB, see David Fleischer, "O Pluripartidarismo no Brasil: Dimensões Sócio-Econômicas e Regionais do Recrutamento Legislativo, 1946–1967," *Revista de Ciência Política* 24 (1981): 49–75.

12. In contrast, without these artifices and with unfettered access to television campaining, in 1974 the MDB won five of these nine states. (Figure 3.1.)

13. For similar analyses of the consequences of the "Maluf miracle" in the 1982 elections, see Gláucio Soares, "O Maluf não Compensa," *Fôlha de São Paulo*, June 17, 1984, p. 3 and David Fleischer, "Memória do Eleitor não Assusta," *Correio Braziliense*, June 17, 1984, p. 4.

14. For a general treatment of "electoral inequality," see Gláucio Soares, "Desigualidades Eleitorais no Brasil," *Revista de Ciência Política* 7 (1973): 25–48. For a more recent analysis of benefits accruing to the Northeast, see David Fleischer, "O Regionalismo na Política Brasileira: As Bancadas Nordestinas na Câmara Federal (1983)," in Joaquim Falcão and Constança Sá (eds.), *Nordeste: Eleições 1982* (Recife: Editôra Massagana/FUNDAJ, 1985), pp. 17–37.

15. "Um Nôvo Poder na Praça," *Veja*, January 15, 1983, pp. 14–21.

16. "Latifundiários do Congresso Atacam Plano de Sarney," *Jornal do Brasil*, June 9, 1985.

17. By June 1985, the PDS had lost 100 deputies from its 1983 total, mostly to the PFL.

18. Survey research conducted by the *Correio Braziliense* on November 8, 1983, and analyzed in David Fleischer, "Partidos e Mudanças Institucionais: Congresso Nacional, Novembro de 1983," paper presented at the Eighth Annual Meeting of ANPOCS, Águas de São Pedro, SP, October 23–26, 1984. Brizola supported the two-year *continuísmo* mandate (*mandato-tampão*) to have a shot at direct elections for the presidency in 1986.

19. This fourth measure, withholding or increasing disbursements for local projects, was very effective, a sort of local "pork barrel" or carrot and stick.

20. "Cem Dias de Mêdo," *Veja*, January 16, 1985, pp. 40–45 and Gilberto Dimenstein, et al., *O Complô que Elegeu Tancredo* (Rio de Janeiro: Edições JB, 1985).

21. *Estado de São Paulo*, November 7, 1984, pp. 32–33.

22. The *decurso de prazo* artifice is similar to a "pocket approval." Legislation is sent to Congress by the president and designated with a 60-day limit; if it is not acted on within this limit, it automatically becomes law.

23. Chamber rules provided two harsher alternatives: (1) suspension for fifteen days and (2) outright suspension of mandate.

24. Afrânio de Melo Franco chaired the 1932-1933 commission. His son, Affonso Arinos de Melo Franco, was Tancredo Neves's choice to chair the similar commission in 1985.

TABLE 3.1
Majority and Proportional Elections in Brazil by Party, 1966-1982
(in percents)

PARTY	ELECTION				
	1966[a]	1970[a]	1974[a]	1978[a]	1982[b]
ARENA/PDS					
Majority	44.7	43.7	34.8	35.2	37.3
Proportional	50.5	48.4	40.9	40.0	36.7
MDB/Opposition					
Majority	34.2	28.6	50.1	46.6	52.2
Proportional	28.4	21.3	37.8	39.3	48.2
BLANK VOTES					
Majority	11.7	21.7	9.2	10.1	7.5
Proportional	14.3	20.9	14.2	13.5	10.9
NULL VOTES					
Majority	9.4	6.0	5.9	8.1	2.7
Proportional	6.8	9.4	7.1	7.2	4.2
TOTAL[d]					
Majority	(17,260)	(23,493)[c]	(28,981)	(37,602)	(48,214)
Proportional	(17,286)	(22,436)	(28,981)	(37,554)	(48,481)
ELECTORATE	(22,335)	(28,966)	(35,811)	(46,030)	(58,616)
% Voters/ Electorate	77.4%	81.1%	80.9%	81.7%	82.7%
POPULATION	(84,996)	(94,865)	(104,548)	(113,894)	(123,192)
% Electorate/ Population	26.3%	30.5%	34.3%	40.4%	47.6%

[a]Election for senator and federal deputy.
[b]Election for governor and federal deputy.
[c]Election of two Senate seats.
[d]In thousands.

FIGURE 3.1   MDB Victories in Majority
Elections (Senate) in 1974

FIGURE 3.2   MDB Victories in Majority
Elections (Senate) in 1978

FIGURE 3.3   Geographic Regions of Brazil as Defined by the IBGE

TABLE 3.2
Distribution of ARENA Vote in 1978 for Chamber of Deputies, by Population of Município, Five Regions (Excludes Brasília Precincts)

Municípios by Population	North[a]		Northeast[b]		Southeast		South		Central-West		BRAZIL[c]	
	No. of Munc.	% ARENA	No. of Munc.	% ARENA	No. of Munc.	% ARENA	No. of Munc.	% ARENA	No. of Munc.	% ARENA	No. of Munc.	% ARENA
Over 500,000	02	41.2	03	42.7	09	22.2	02	37.6	01	34.8	17	26.8
100,000-500,000	03	57.3	32	57.7	58	35.5	24	45.3	04	50.5	121	42.1
50,000-100,000	15	71.8	70	76.1	90	45.0	50	47.6	11	55.2	236	54.3
20,000-50,000	44	77.5	359	82.6	235	55.6	164	55.7	66	61.2	868	66.0
10,000-20,000	45	81.2	429	83.1	321	66.9	213	59.1	103	63.6	1,111	71.6
5,000-10,000	19	79.6	327	83.6	339	70.1	186	62.2	82	64.8	953	73.9
2,000-5,000	06	90.9	138	81.9	331	70.6	76	67.3	50	69.0	610	74.3
Under 2,000	00	--	16	78.0	27	84.7	04	81.5	00	--	38	82.3
TOTAL	134	61.0	1,374	72.4	1,410	38.3	719	51.3	317	57.5	3,954	50.4
No. Votes[d]	818,962		6,907,626		14,464,693		6,031,381		1,461,103		29,683,765	

Source: PRODASEN data base, Brazilian National Senate.

[a] Excludes Acre & Rondônia.

[b] Excludes Fernando de Noronha.

[c] Excludes Acre, Rondônia & Fernando de Noronha.

[d] Excludes blank and void ballots.

(Munc. = Município)

TABLE 3.3

Distribution of ARENA vs. PDS Vote in 1978 and 1982 for the Chamber of Deputies, by Population of Município: Selected States (Excludes Brasília Precincts)

Municípios by Population	Ceará[a]			Bahia[a]			Minas Gerais[b]			Rio de Janeiro[c]			São Paulo[c]		
	No. of Munc.	%[d] ARENA 1978	%[e] PDS 1982	No. of Munc.	%[d] ARENA 1978	%[e] PDS 1982	No. of Munc.	%[d] ARENA 1978	%[e] PDS 1982	No. of Munc.	%[d] ARENA 1978	%[e] PDS 1982	No. of Munc.	%[d] ARENA 1978	%[e] PDS 1982
Over 100,000	05	55.8	49.4	09	48.0	33.5	12	34.5	29.8	15	22.8	28.3	34	26.2	19.7
50,000–100,000	13	78.1	84.0	17	86.6	66.7	33	50.0	40.4	11	39.3	35.8	43	38.9	31.1
20,000–50,000	59	86.6	85.5	110	85.0	75.6	98	68.4	54.2	18	44.4	43.9	99	45.8	38.5
10,000–20,000	33	86.8	90.6	126	87.5	81.2	172	77.0	60.0	16	49.0	40.9	122	54.4	48.1
5,000–10,000	26	89.9	89.4	67	88.2	82.6	204	78.6	64.5	14	59.0	48.0	121	58.3	50.0
Under 5,000	05	91.8	91.3	07	91.0	78.2	203	77.1	65.4	00	--	--	152	64.9	60.5
TOTAL	141	75.5	74.1	336	74.8	63.4	722	58.0	47.4	64	25.3	29.9	571	33.1	26.7
No. of Votes[f]	1,276	1,695		1,742	2,570		3,497	4,876		3,479	4,680		7,019	9,769	

Source: PRODASEN data base, Brazilian National Senate.

[a] Two parties elected deputies in 1982.
[b] Three parties elected deputies in 1982.
[c] Five parties elected deputies in 1982.
[d] "Crossover" & party label votes permitted.
[e] "Crossover" & party label votes prohibited.
[f] In thousands. Excludes blank and void ballots.

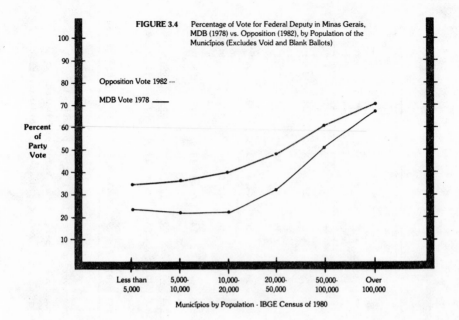

FIGURE 3.4 Percentage of Vote for Federal Deputy in Minas Gerais, MDB (1978) vs. Opposition (1982), by Population of the Municípios (Excludes Void and Blank Ballots)

Opposition Vote 1982 ···

MDB Vote 1978 ──

Percent of Party Vote

Municípios by Population - IBGE Census of 1980

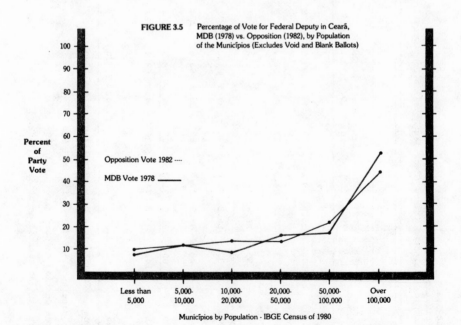

FIGURE 3.5 Percentage of Vote for Federal Deputy in Ceará, MDB (1978) vs. Opposition (1982), by Population of the Municípios (Excludes Void and Blank Ballots)

Opposition Vote 1982 ····

MDB Vote 1978 ──

Percent of Party Vote

Municípios by Population - IBGE Census of 1980

TABLE 3.4
Party Realignments in the National Congress, 1980–1982, by Prior
Identification with ARENA or MDB

	Chamber of Deputies[a]			Federal Senate[a]		
	ARENA	MDB	TOTAL	ARENA	MDB	TOTAL
March 1980						
PDS	201	24	225	36	01	37
PMDB	03	91	94	01	16	17
PP	25	43	68	04	03	07
PTB[b]	01	22	23	00	01	01
PT	00	05	05	00	01	01
Undecided	01	04	05	01	03	04
March 1981						
PDS	191	21	212	34	02	36
PMDB	05	108	113	01	19	20
PP	26	40	66	07	03	10
PDT	00	10	10	00	00	00
PTB	03	02	05	00	00	00
PT	00	06	06	00	00	00
Undecided	06	02	08	00	01	01
December 1981						
PDS	192	22	214	35	02	37
PMDB	10	111	121	01	19	20
PP	26	41	67	06	04	10
PDT	00	09	09	00	00	00
PTB	03	01	04	00	00	00
PT	00	05	05	00	00	00
August 1982						
PDS	196	28	224	35	01	36
PMDB[c]	32	136	168	07	20	27
PTB	03	11	14	00	02	02
PDT	00	09	09	00	01	01
PT	00	05	05	00	01	01
TOTAL for August 1982	231	189	420	42	25	67

Source: Compiled by the author.

[a]Data for ARENA and MDB are from February 1, 1979, before any realignments
began. Includes results from November 15, 1978, election.
[b]Before the break between the Ivete Vargas and Leonel Brizola factions caused
the PTB/PDT split in May 1980.
[c]After the reincorporation of the PP into the PMDB, which was ratified by the
latter's national party convention in February 1982.

TABLE 3.5
Recruitment Profile by Party, Senate and Chamber of Deputies, 1979

	Federal Senate			Chamber of Deputies		
	ARENA	MDB	TOTAL	ARENA	MDB	TOTAL
PRINCIPAL OCCUPATION						
Agriculture	14.3	12.0	13.4	14.7	3.2	9.5
Comm.-Banks-Finance	19.0	8.0	14.9	11.7	13.2	12.4
Industry-Transportation	2.4	4.0	3.0	6.1	3.7	5.0
Lawyer-Judge	7.1	12.0	9.0	12.6	23.3	17.4
Health Professions	11.9	16.0	13.4	9.5	10.1	9.8
Education	7.1	16.0	10.4	9.5	16.9	12.9
Journalism	11.9	12.0	11.9	4.8	10.6	7.4
Other Professions	7.1	8.0	7.5	14.3	7.4	11.2
Public Employees	11.9	8.0	10.4	12.1	9.0	10.7
Military	7.1	4.0	6.0	4.8	2.6	3.8
TOTAL %	100.0	100.0	100.0	100.0	100.0	100.0
(N)	(42)	(25)	(67)	(231)	(189)	(420)
ADMINISTRATIVE POSITIONS	61.9	68.0	64.2	51.1	36.5	44.5
Federal	31.0	24.0	28.4	7.8	6.9	7.4
State	50.0	44.0	47.8	45.0	23.8	35.5
Municipal	4.8	16.0	9.0	11.3	10.6	11.0
ELECTIVE POSITIONS	95.2	84.0	91.0	62.8	57.1	60.2
Federal	71.4	48.0	62.7	0.4	0.0	0.2
State	69.0	56.0	64.2	48.5	41.3	45.2
Municipal	38.1	56.0	44.8	36.4	36.0	36.2
% Born in State Rep.	83.3	72.0	79.1	92.6	84.1	88.8
% with Univ. Education	88.1	92.0	89.6	83.5	88.9	85.9
% Univ. Educ. in State Rep.	43.2	50.0	45.8	61.1	71.3	65.9
Pre.-C.D. Pol. Career (Years)	22.16	20.82	21.66	10.27	7.97	9.24
No. of Pol. Positions Pre-C.D.	4.26	3.88	4.12	2.19	1.55	1.90
Age First Pol. Position	30.36	29.02	29.86	33.21	33.24	33.22
Current Age (Feb. 1, 1979)	57.28	53.61	55.91	48.90	45.77	47.49
Seniority (Years)	4.19	3.92	4.10	5.48	4.52	5.05
% Returning Veterans	50.0	68.0	56.7	56.7	54.0	55.5

Source: Compiled by author.

TABLE 3.6
Recruitment Profile by Party Affiliation, Federal Deputies, 1981

	Current Party Affiliation—1981							
	PDS	PMDB	PP	PDT	PTB	PT	None	TOTAL
PRINCIPAL OCCUPATION								
Agriculture	16.5	3.6	6.0	10.0	0.0	0.0	0.0	10.5
Comm.-Banks-Finance	12.3	13.3	16.7	0.0	0.0	0.0	12.5	12.6
Industry-Transportation	6.6	4.4	1.5	0.0	0.0	16.7	12.5	5.2
Lawyer/Judge	9.9	27.4	12.1	40.0	20.0	33.3	12.5	16.2
Health Professions	8.9	6.2	15.2	0.0	0.0	0.0	12.5	8.8
Education	12.3	15.9	15.2	0.0	20.0	16.7	12.5	13.6
Journalism	4.2	10.6	9.1	20.0	0.0	0.0	12.5	7.1
Other Professions	12.3	9.7	7.6	0.0	20.0	33.3	0.0	10.5
Public Employees	12.3	7.1	13.6	30.3	40.0	0.0	0.0	11.4
Military	4.7	1.8	3.0	0.0	0.0	0.0	25.0	4.1
TOTAL %	100.0	100.0	100.0	100.0	100.0	100.0	100.0	100.0
(N)	(212)	(113)	(66)	(10)	(05)	(06)	(08)	(420)
ADMINISTRATIVE POSITIONS	44.3	36.9	53.7	20.0	40.0	16.7	62.5	43.8
Federal	7.5	5.3	14.9	20.0	0.0	0.0	12.5	8.3
State	38.2	25.7	40.3	0.0	40.0	16.7	62.5	34.5
Municipal	8.5	14.2	10.5	0.0	20.0	0.0	37.5	10.2
ELECTIVE POSITIONS	59.4	58.4	55.8	50.0	60.0	16.7	50.0	57.4
State	44.8	45.1	40.3	20.0	40.0	0.0	50.0	42.9
Municipal	35.4	38.1	31.3	30.0	20.0	16.7	37.5	34.8
% Born in State Rep.	89.6	90.3	83.4	80.0	100.0	100.0	87.5	88.8
% with Univ. Education	78.7	88.5	95.5	90.0	100.0	83.3	75.0	84.5
% Univ. Educ. in State Rep.	59.4	77.9	60.6	88.9	50.0	60.0	66.7	65.7
Pre-C.D. Pol. Career (Years)	9.76	8.06	10.20	6.91	11.76	3.60	6.50	9.19
No. of Pre-C.D. Pol. Positions	2.02	1.69	2.09	0.07	1.80	0.67	2.13	1.88
Age in First Pol. Position	34.10	32.76	32.54	36.02	31.41	29.78	33.97	33.47
Current Age (Apr. 1, 1981)	51.48	46.81	49.99	50.29	51.60	39.53	47.62	49.72
% Returning Veterans	56.1	45.1	53.7	90.0	80.0	66.7	75.0	54.3
Seniority (Years)	7.49	5.87	7.15	7.35	8.42	6.15	7.15	6.98

Source: Compiled by author.

TABLE 3.7
Federal Deputies and Senators, Affinities with Ex-Parties (1945-1965) by
Current Party Identification in 1981

Ex-Party	Party Identification on April 1, 1981							
1945-1965	PDS	PMDB	PP	PDT	PTB	PT	NONE	TOTAL
DEPUTIES								
PTB	15	15	02	8	2	0	0	42
PSD	41	23	14	1	0	1	1	81
UDN	47	06	16	0	0	0	0	69
PSP	06	01	07	0	1	0	0	15
PDC	15	04	01	0	0	0	0	20
PTN	02	01	01	0	0	0	0	04
PST	02	00	00	0	0	0	1	03
PR	10	01	02	0	0	0	0	13
PRP	04	00	00	0	0	0	0	04
PSB	01	01	01	1	0	1	0	05
PRT	01	01	00	0	1	0	1	04
TOTAL KNOWN	144	53	44	10	4	2	3	260
NOT KNOWN	68	60	22	0	1	4	5	160
GRAND TOTAL	212	113	66	10	5	6	8	420
SENATORS								
PTB	03	04	00				0	07
PSD	15	04	05				1	25
UDN	15	02	02				0	19
PDC	01	02	01				0	04
PST	00	01	00				0	01
PL	01	01	00				0	02
PSB	00	01	00				0	01
TOTAL KNOWN	35	15	08				1	59
NOT KNOWN	01	05	02				0	08
GRAND TOTAL	36	20	10				1	67

Source: Compiled by author.

FIGURE 3.6   Opposition (PMDB & PDT) Victories
in Majority Elections (Governor)
in 1982

TABLE 3.8
Results of the November 15, 1982, Elections and Composition of the
January 15, 1985, Electoral College, by Political Party

	PDS	PMDB[a]	PDT	PTB	PT	TOTAL
Votes						
No.[b]	17,780	17,674	2,393	1,829	1,449	41,136
%	43.2	43.0	5.8	4.5	3.5	100.0
Governors[c]	13	9	1	0	0	23
Senators[d]	45	22	1	1	0	69(35)[e]
Federal Deputies						
No.	235	200	23	13	8	479(240)[e]
%	49.0	41.8	4.8	2.7	1.7	100.0
Delegates						
Electoral College[f]	81	51	6	0	0	138
Electoral College Composition[g]	361	273	30	14	8	686(344)[e]

Hypothesis: Electoral college if 1978 norms were in force.

Delegates[h]	90	89	16	0	0	195
Composition[i]	367	314	40	14	8	743(372)[e]

Source: Compiled from preliminary election statistics reported by the
Superior Electoral Court (TSE), *Diário da Justiça*, November 28, 1983, pp.
18,630–18,686.

[a] The PP entered a fusion with the PMDB in February 1982.
[b] Election for federal deputy. (Excludes 5,286,684 blank and 2,058,459 void ballots. In thousands.
[c] Only twelve PDS governors were elected directly; Rondônia appointed thru 1987.
[d] Includes forty-four senators elected in 1978 (twenty-two "bionics") and three new seats elected from Rondônia. With the death of Sen. Nilo Coelho (PDS-PE) at the end of 1983, the PMDB acquired its twenty-second seat because the alternate elected in 1978 had since left ARENA for PP and then PMDB. Thus, the PDS lost its two-thirds majority.
[e] Numbers in parentheses indicate the absolute majority.
[f] Six delegates representing the majority party in each of the twenty-two State Assemblies. Due to a tie in Mato Grosso do Sul, the PDS and PMDB each got three delegates.
[g] Met on January 15, 1985. Included senators, federal deputies, and delegates.
[h] Minimum of three per state, plus one for every million in population.
[i] Would have met in October 1984.

TABLE 3.9
Regional Political Representation in Brazil; 1982 Elections, Congress in 1984, and 1985 Electoral College (in percents)

Region	Population[a] 1980	Electorate[b] 1982	Voters[b] 1982	Congress 1984[b] Senate	Chamber	Electoral College 1985-A[c]	1985-B[d]
North	5.0	4.2	3.8	17.4	9.8	12.1	10.4
Northeast	29.3	25.8	23.8	39.2	31.1	33.5	32.0
Southeast	43.4	46.2	48.9	17.4	35.3	29.9	33.9
South	16.0	18.0	18.2	13.0	17.1	15.9	16.1
Central-West	6.3	5.8	5.3	13.0	6.7	8.6	7.6
Total %	100.0	100.0	100.0	100.0	100.0	100.0	100.0
TOTAL N	119,071,000	58,616,588	48,481,170	69	479	686	743

Source: Compiled by author.

[a] IBGE census, September 1980.
[b] Diário da Justiça, November 28, 1983.
[c] Included 69 senators, 479 federal deputies, and 138 state delegates.
[d] Would have included 69 senators, 479 federal deputies, and 195 state delegates.

TABLE 3.10
Regional Political Representation of the PDS; 1982 Elections, Congress in 1984, PDS Convention, and 1985 Electoral College (in percents)

Region	Voters[a] 1982	Congress 1984[a] Senate	Chamber	1984[b] PDS Convention	Electoral College 1985-A[c]	1985-B[d]
North	4.3	20.0	11.9	13.1	11.9	11.2
Northeast	35.6	53.3	42.1	43.2	49.0	50.1
Southeast	37.2	11.1	25.5	24.4	18.0	17.7
South	18.0	8.9	14.9	13.8	14.2	15.5
Central-West	4.9	6.7	5.6	5.5	6.9	5.5
Total %	100.0	100.0	100.0	100.0	100.0	100.0
TOTAL N	17,779,849	45	235	961	361	367

Source: Compiled by author.

[a] Diário da Justiça, November 28, 1983.
[b] Included 45 senators, 235 federal deputies, 560 state delegates, and 121 members of PDS National Directorate.
[c] Included 280 senators and federal deputies and 81 state delegates.
[d] Would have included 280 senators and federal deputies and 87 state delegat

TABLE 3.11
Chamber of Deputies: Recruitment Profile by Party, 1983

	PDS	PMDB	PDT	PTB	PT	TOTAL
PRINCIPAL OCCUPATION						
Agriculture	11.9	11.5	8.7	7.7	0.0	11.3
Comm.-Banks-Finance	15.3	17.5	8.7	15.4	12.5	15.9
Industry-Transportation	7.2	2.5	4.3	0.0	12.5	5.0
Lawyer-Judge	11.1	16.5	26.1	15.4	12.5	14.2
Health Professions	10.2	6.5	4.3	0.0	0.0	7.9
Education	9.8	15.5	8.7	15.4	37.5	12.7
Journalism	5.1	9.0	17.4	23.1	0.0	7.7
Other Professions	12.8	9.0	4.3	15.4	25.0	11.1
Public Employees	14.9	11.5	8.7	7.7	0.0	12.7
Military	1.7	0.5	8.7	0.0	0.0	1.5
TOTAL %	100.0	100.0	100.0	100.0	100.0	100.0
(N)	(235)	(200)	(23)	(13)	(08)	(479)
ADMINISTRATIVE POSITIONS	58.3	46.0	17.4	23.1	0.0	49.3
Federal	14.5	9.5	13.0	7.7	0.0	11.9
State	49.4	32.5	4.3	7.7	0.0	38.2
Municipal	10.2	13.5	0.0	7.7	0.0	10.9
ELECTIVE POSITIONS	60.0	62.5	30.4	46.2	37.5	58.9
State	44.3	50.5	13.0	23.1	37.5	44.7
Municipal	34.0	35.0	17.4	38.5	0.0	33.2
% Born in State Rep.	83.0	88.0	56.5	53.8	50.0	82.5
% with Univ. Education	84.7	88.8	82.6	76.9	75.0	85.6
% Univ. Educ. in State Rep.	62.1	73.3	72.2	70.0	100.0	68.2
Pre-C.D. Pol. Career (Years)	10.94	10.02	5.06	8.62	0.50	10.04
No. Pre-C.D. Pol. Positions	2.24	1.88	0.52	10.8	0.38	1.95
Age First Pol. Position	32.22	31.68	37.45	32.85	35.84	32.33
Current Age (Feb. 1, 1983)	49.17	47.15	48.59	50.04	38.34	48.14
% "Freshmen" Deputies	40.9	49.0	56.5	61.5	87.5	46.3

Source: Compiled by author.

TABLE 3.12
Affinities with Ex-Parties (1945-1965 and 1966-1979), by Current Party
Identification in 1983, Federal Deputies

Ex-Party	Current Party, 1983					
	PDS	PMDB	PDT	PTB	PT	TOTAL
1945-1965						
PTB	13	35	10	04	00	62
PSD	52	34	01	01	00	88
UDN	65	24	00	00	01	90
PSP	06	05	00	00	00	11
PDC	11	12	00	00	00	23
PTN	02	02	00	00	00	04
PST	02	02	00	01	00	05
PR	11	02	00	00	00	13
PL	00	00	00	01	00	01
PRP	03	02	00	00	00	05
PSB	01	04	03	00	00	08
PRT	00	01	00	00	00	01
PCB	00	07	00	00	01	08
TOTAL KNOWN	166	130	17	07	02	319
NOT DETERMINED	69	70	09	06	06	160
GRAND TOTAL	235	200	23	13	08	479
1966-1979						
ARENA	195	31	00	01	00	227
MDB	15	143	16	07	04	185
TOTAL KNOWN	210	174	16	08	04	412
NOT DETERMINED	25	20	07	05	04	67
GRAND TOTAL	235	200	23	13	08	479

Source: Compiled by author.

TABLE 3.13
Electoral College Vote, January 15, 1985, by Party

PARTY	Paulo Maluf	Tancredo Neves	Abstain	Not Present	TOTAL
CHAMBER					
PDS	125	39	07	01	172
PFL	00	63	00	00	63
PMDB	02	196	01	01	200
PDT	01	20	01	01	23
PTB	03	10	00	00	13
PT	00	03	00	05	08
TOTAL	131	331	09	08	479
SENATE					
PDS	26	05	00	01	32
PFL	00	10	00	00	10
PMDB	00	24	01	00	25
PDT	00	01	00	00	01
PTB	00	01	00	00	01
TOTAL	26	41	01	01	69
DELEGATES					
PDS	23	11	07	00	41
PFL	00	40	00	00	40
PMDB	00	51	00	00	51
PDT	00	06	00	00	06
TOTAL	23	108	07	00	138
GRAND TOTAL	180	480	17	09	686

Source: O Estado de São Paulo, January 16, 1985, pp. 22-23.

FIGURE 3.7   States where the Democratic Alliance
held a Majority of Representatives to
the January 15, 1985 Electoral College

TABLE 3.14
Electoral College Vote, January 15, 1985, by State and Region

STATE/REGION	Paulo Maluf	Tancredo Neves	Abstain	Not Present	TOTAL
Acre	06	11	00	00	17
Rondônia	06	11	00	00	17
Roraima	01	03	00	00	04
Amapá	03	01	00	00	04
Amazonas	04	13	00	00	17
Pará	10	14	00	00	24
North Totals	30	53	00	00	83
Maranhão	10	16	00	00	26
Piauí	04	14	00	00	18
Ceará	14	17	00	00	31
R. G. Norte	06	11	00	00	17
Paraíba	09	11	01	00	21
Pernambuco	05	28	00	02	35
Alagôas	03	14	00	00	17
Sergipe	07	09	01	00	17
Bahia	13	35	00	00	48
Northeast Totals	71	155	02	02	230
E. Santo	04	14	00	00	18
Rio de Janeiro	09	42	02	02	55
Minas Gerais	05	57	00	01	63
São Paulo	15	50	00	04	69
Southeast Totals	33	163	02	07	205
Paraná	06	37	00	00	43
S. Catarina	09	12	04	00	25
R. G. do Sul	11	22	08	00	41
South Totals	26	71	12	00	109
Goiás	04	21	00	00	25
Mato Grosso	11	06	00	00	17
Mato Grosso do Sul	05	11	01	00	1
Central-West Totals	20	38	01	00	59
BRAZIL TOTALS	180	480	17	09	686

Source: Jornal do Brasil, January 16, 1985, p. 1.

TABLE 3.15
Speeches Made by Federal Deputies, First Semester of 1985 (in percents)

Content Regarding Government	PMDB	PFL	PDS	PDT	PTB	PT	TOTAL
Favorable	70.2	75.7	33.7	37.4	27.3	16.9	52.5
Unfavorable	23.6	22.5	61.1	50.4	66.7	72.3	40.9
Neutral	6.2	1.8	5.2	12.2	6.0	10.8	6.6
Total %	100.0	100.0	100.0	100.0	100.0	100.0	100.0
(N)	(390)	(111)	(211)	(115)	(33)	(83)	(943)

Source: "Pesquisa Mostra como Partidos vêem Govêrno," Correio Braziliense, July 19, 1985, p. 3.

TABLE 3.16
Party Composition of the National Congress, June 1985

Party	Senate	Chamber
PMDB	25	199
PDS	25	135
PFL	17	100
PDT	01	25
PTB	01	10
PT	00	05
PCB	00	03
PC do B	00	02
TOTAL	69	479

NOTE: In August 1985, 20 other parties were provisionally recognized by the TSE.

4

The Changing Political Discourse in Brazil, 1964–1985

Robert A. Packenham

A hell for liberals
A purgatory for Marxists
A paradise for conservatives

With apologies to historian J. A. Antonil, this was the old order—Brazilian intellectuals' interpretations of Brazilian politics through the 1940s or 1950s.[1] There was a change in the sixties and early seventies, however; Marxist approaches, which were already important, became even stronger and came to dominate the discourse. And still more recently, in the last decade or so, there has been another major shift. Theory and practice have come together to produce a more pluralistic climate that has challenged the earlier Marxist hegemony.

In this chapter the major trends in the substance and terms of theoretical discourse about Brazilian politics since 1964 are described. I seek to demonstrate that a major shift in the intellectual culture has occurred during this twenty-year period—from the Marxist hegemony of the first decade to a more pluralistic discourse in the second decade. In addition, I try to identify some of the social science and political issues that this shift raises, analyze some of its social scientific and political meanings, and assess its prospects for the future. Contrary to many observers, I do not believe that the recent changes are necessarily permanent. I do believe, however, that they are deep, widespread, and of the greatest significance. They are important not only for their own sake, but also because their fate is closely related to the fate of democratic political institutions in Brazil.

A few comments about the scope and method of the chapter are necessary at the outset. The focus here is entirely on Brazilian social scientists and intellectuals; no attempt is made to include interpretations by foreigners. In dealing with the different trends in the different periods,

---

I recognize, of course, that there were different kinds of thinkers in both periods. The argument is about central tendencies, not each and every case. Nor do I suggest that all authors within any category think the same. Obviously there is great variety within both major categories as well as within each of the subcategories to be developed. Throughout the essay, I cite and analyze specific trends, authors, and studies in order to give both illustrative support to the general argument and concrete examples of the variety and exceptions.

Marxist Interpretations

Four Variations on a Marxist Theme

In the late 1960s and the first half of the 1970s, and perhaps even longer, the dominant perspectives for analyzing Brazilian politics and foreign relations were Marxist interpretations of one sort or another. This point is well documented in an important recent survey by Luíz Carlos Bresser Pereira of major "interpretations of Brazilian social formations" from the 1920s through the 1970s.[2] According to him, there were three major interpretations of Brazilian society, economy, and polity in the 1960s and 1970s.

First, there was the "functional-capitalist" interpretation. This perspective originated as a critique of the "national-bourgeoisie" interpretation that had been influential before and was discredited by the revolution of 1964. The basic postulate of the functional-capitalist interpretation is that Brazil was always a capitalist country and that even its pre-capitalist elements were "functional for capitalist accumulation." Caio Prado Junior, Fernando Novaes, João Manoel Cardoso de Mello, Boris Fausto, Francisco de Oliveira, Lúcio Kowarick, Manoel Berlinck, and Luciano Martins are some of those cited by Bresser Pereira as examples of authors working in this perspective.[3]

Second, there was the "imperialist superexploitation" interpretation. This perspective also began as a critical response to the 1964 revolution and also criticized imperialism as "the major cause of underdevelopment." However, according to Bresser Pereira it was "much more radical" than the functional-capitalist interpretation because it dealt not only with Brazil but with all of Latin America, not only with the exploitation of workers but with their "superexploitation," not only with the need for socialism but also with the need to choose between violent revolution and fascism. André Gunder Frank, Ruy Mauro Marini, Theotônio dos Santos, and Florestan Fernandes are the four authors cited by Bresser Pereira as examples of this interpretation.[4]

Third, there was the "new dependency," or *dependência*, interpretation. This perspective shares much with the first two interpretations, although it is "less radical." According to Bresser Pereira, the essential points about this interpretation are not only its theoretical concept of dependency—the idea of the linkage between external imperialism and internal class structures—but also its recognition of the "new fact" of the massive entry of multinational industrial enterprises into Latin America, especially Brazil, and its analysis of the "new form of dependency, developmentalist . . . but exclusionary" that is thereby generated. The most important author in this group, says Bresser Pereira, is Fernando Henrique Cardoso, but he also lists many others in it, including José Serra, Maria da Conceição Tavares, Antônio Barros de Castro, Paul Singer, Celso Furtado, and himself.[5]

Bresser Pereira also discusses briefly a fourth approach, the "hegemony of industrial capital" interpretation, which began to take form in the 1970s, is still embryonic in its development, and is found mainly in some recent work by himself and Luciano Martins.[6]

Bresser Pereira argues that the three principal interpretations are all "leftist" (*interpretações de esquerda*). He regards the imperialist super-exploitation interpretation as the "most radical and the least plausible"; the functional capitalist interpretation as in the middle of the group ideologically; and the new dependency interpretation as the "most realistic" of the three. "The first two interpretations," he wrote, "are basically Marxist. The third has strong Marxist influences but includes non-Marxist authors like Celso Furtado." The fourth, embryonic interpretation, regarding the hegemony of industrial capital in the seventies, is also, says Bresser Pereira, basically a Marxist interpretation. For him, therefore, all the major theoretical interpretations of the two decades since 1964 that he deals with in his essay are wholly or mainly Marxist, although one of them, the new dependency interpretation, also "includes some non-Marxist authors such as Celso Furtado."[7]

Bresser Pereira's article is a valuable contribution to the analysis of development theory and ideology in Brazil. It surveys and analyzes the writings of some eighty-five authors and about two hundred books and articles over a fifty-year period. His categories of interpretations are interesting and useful. For the sixties and at least the first half of the seventies, his portrait of a Brazilian intellectual world dominated by various Marxist perspectives is, on the whole, accurate and useful.

For several reasons, however, it is necessary to supplement and modify the picture painted by Bresser Pereira.[8] First, as an economist, he is understandably more concerned with the economic and social aspects of development treated in these writings than with political aspects. Second, because his survey is so broad, he could not go into depth about the writings of any single author. Third, he omits or minimizes certain intellectual currents that deserve attention. For instance, he underestimates the degree to which even sophisticated and "moderate" authors were gripped by sweeping Marxism in the first post-1964 decade, and he also seriously underestimates the diversity of currents in the period after 1974.

Therefore in the rest of this section I shall discuss more fully the political aspects of interpretations of Brazil in the period from 1964 to

about 1974. (In the next section I do the same for the period 1974–
1984.) To give greater specificity and depth to the analysis, and also to
illustrate how powerful the Marxist influences noted by Bresser Pereira
were in Brazil in the sixties and early seventies, in the course of the
survey I shall refer frequently to the new dependency interpretation in
general and to the writings of the distinguished political sociologist
Fernando Henrique Cardoso in particular.

The "New Dependency" Interpretation and the
Political Thought of Fernando Henrique Cardoso

Reference to Cardoso is particularly suitable in this context for several
reasons. First, he is indisputably a major figure whom few (if any)
responsible persons would characterize as a "vulgar Marxist." If powerful
and sweeping Marxist claims are made in his work, they were present
in the writings not only of vulgar Marxists but also of many other
sophisticated and influential Brazilian political analysts. Second, in
contrast to many of the other authors Bresser Pereira writes about,
Cardoso's works are intensely concerned with *politics*—with the interaction between the economic and political systems and with the nature
of the political system. Third, the case of Cardoso illuminates in a
uniquely vivid and important way the changes that occurred in the
Brazilian political discourse in the late seventies and the early eighties:
the shift from Marxism to other tendencies, the ambivalencies and
ambiguities of the shift, and the interrelationships between the intellectual
changes and the political and economic contexts.

With regard to thinking about internal political developments, a number
of theoretical perspectives that had been prominent before 1964—such
as modernization theory, political-development theory, ECLA theories,
and nationalist theories of indigenous capitalism—were all largely discredited by the 1964 coup-revolution and its aftermath. They were
replaced by neo-Marxist *dependência* ideas, ideas about bureaucratic
authoritarianism, and the other approaches mentioned by Bresser Pereira.
In these formulations, liberal democratic political institutions were "formal," capitalist states were by definition expressions of the "pact of
class domination," and political and economic elites in Brazil were "the
anti-nation inside the nation."[9] The only real solution to Brazil's internal
political troubles had to be seen in the context of a change in the
economic system from capitalism to socialism.[10]

These were not the views of "vulgar Marxists" but rather of some
of the most sophisticated intellectuals and social scientists in Brazil.
They were not Leninists. They favored democracy (though not liberal
democracy) and they opposed the Leninist idea of a dictatorship of the
proletariat. They believed that a certain kind of development—an associated, dependent, distorted development—was possible under capitalism and they rejected the ideas associated with the writings of André
Gunder Frank regarding the "development of underdevelopment." They

rejected the view, advanced by Marini and others, that capitalism was necessarily "superexploitative."

In rejecting "vulgar Marxism," however, they did not reject Marxism; quite the contrary. They rejected the idea of capitalism as superexploitative but affirmed and assumed the Marxist premise that capitalism is exploitative by definition. They accepted and affirmed the Marxist notions of class struggle; of class domination and subordination; and of class interests that are conflicting, dichotomous, and irreconcilable. Bargaining, negotiation, and compromise among these interests made no sense in these theoretical perspectives, and those few intellectuals who challenged these prevailing perspectives were bitterly criticized.

Moreover, in these arguments democratic political institutions were merely "formal" if not accompanied by social and economic democracy; economic and social democracy were inconceivable under capitalism and could be achieved only under socialism. Hence any "democracy" under capitalism was really not democratic, and genuine democracy could only be achieved under socialism. Class and nation were not concepts of parallel status; class was a more basic category, and therefore national autonomy under capitalism without a change to socialism was merely national capitalism.[11] In this perspective, the Weberian concept of a social science enterprise or "vocation" separable from the political enterprise or vocation made no sense. To the contrary, social science was and needed to be subordinated to the class struggle.[12]

During this period, and afterward as well, analogous arguments were made about Brazil's role in the world. The ECLA thesis that industrialization led to less dependency was challenged and rejected. So were nationalist arguments that strengthening the domestic bourgeoisie would reduce dependency; the dominant view was that even if the domestic bourgeoisie were strong (and it was not), it was still only an internal manifestation or "expression" of external dependency.[13] Analyses suggesting that in some respects Brazil was reducing its dependency through internal and external diversification, state control of vital sectors and infrastructure, small increments in technological autonomy, and the like, were ridiculed as positivistic, formal, and antinational.[14] The answer, the dominant view of the time maintained, was not to be found in small changes within the capitalist system; such incremental changes in degree of dependency were said to be analogous to decreases in the degree of slavery, and thus to be meaningless or worse.[15]

Many otherwise informed scholars in the United States and in Brazil are unaware how powerful these Marxist influences have been, and are, in Brazil. For example, it is widely believed that the propositions just presented are the arguments not of a sophisticated and subtle thinker like Cardoso but rather the views of some vulgar, extremist Marxist. In fact, however, every passage in those paragraphs is drawn specifically from Cardoso's work and represents the dominant themes in his scholarly writings throughout the entire period from 1965 to 1980. It is also widely assumed (by both admirers and critics) that Cardoso's writings are more influenced by Weberian than by Marxist perspectives. That assumption also is false. Nor has Cardoso himself ever made such a claim; indeed, he has repeatedly stated just the opposite.[16]

Joseph Kahl, who has studied Cardoso's work intensively and sympathetically, states that his main models have been Marx and Max Weber.[17] Cardoso himself has declared, according to Kahl, that, "I insist on the necessity of linking theories with facts, because behind my thought lies the shadow of Marx. Or better, the force of Marx; the link between them is practice."[18] Whereas Cardoso is ambivalent and tentative in his willingness to be associated with liberalism, he has repeatedly affirmed that his basic approach methodologically, epistemologically, and theoretically is Marxist, and he has been indignant when, as frequently happens, this point has been challenged or omitted.[19]

In the late sixties and the seventies Cardoso wrote a great deal in a scholarly vein about *dependência*. *Dependência* ideas attempt to wed Marxism and nationalism in a marriage in which Marxism is clearly the dominant element. About the dependency approach Cardoso has written:

> The idea of dependency is defined in the theoretical field of the Marxist theory of capitalism. Once this is established, there is no need to deny the existence of a theoretical field for dependency itself; but this latter theoretical field is one limited by and subordinated to the Marxist theory of capitalism, into which dependency analyses are inserted.[20]

This means that the basic conceptual, methodological, and theoretical apparatus of the dependency perspective is Marxist. This is why, for example, Cardoso and Enzo Faletto affirm that their "methodological approach" is one "which found its highest expression in Marx" and that "without the concept of capital as the result of exploitation of one class by another it is not possible to explain the movement of capitalist society."[21] From Marx, Cardoso derives—well or badly, for good or ill—most of his fundamental methodological, conceptual, and theoretical tools, including the notion of material forces of production as primary categories, social relations of production, dialectical reasoning, surplus value, exploitation, accumulation, subjective and objective interests, class struggle, and so on. These concepts, and the overall Marxist framework of which they are a part, are the essential starting points in his dependency writings and in most of his other scholarly work. It is from these concepts that he has always begun, and it is to them that he has always returned.

In most of Cardoso's scholarly writings, not just those on dependency, there is a fundamental division of the world, despite numerous variations and subtleties, along Marxist lines into "the two great contemporary socio-economic systems, capitalism and socialism."[22] For Cardoso, the only genuine solution to the problems of development is socialism, by which he means not "social democracy"—an epithet for many within the Marxist tradition—or Fabian socialism, but Marxist socialism. Cardoso has said little regarding the specific context of socialism. He has referred occasionally to abstractions like "freedom" and "justice,"[23] but he has seldom been concrete. On the few occasions when he has been specific, the countries he has cited most frequently as examples of socialism are Cuba[24] and China.[25] To the best of my knowledge, Cardoso has nowhere discussed the apparent contradiction between such citations, on the one hand, and his clear and repeated rejection of Leninism as a political tactic, on the other.

One of the most important manifestations of Cardoso's Marxism is his recent discussion of the state. Cardoso defines the state as "the basic pact of domination that exists among social classes or fractions of dominant classes and the norms which guarantee their dominance over the subordinate strata."[26] Notice that this is a *definition*. It is not amenable to alteration in light of evidence; it is taken to be true axiomatically. And it is flatly contradictory to the notion of the state as a social contract. Having made this definition, Cardoso then makes a distinction between the state and "regime," which he defines as:

> the formal rules that link the main political institutions (legislature to the executive, executive to the judiciary, and party system to them all), as well as the issue of the political nature of the ties between citizens and rulers (democratic, oligarchic, totalitarian, or whatever).[27]

This distinction and these definitions are very important. By making the distinction between state and regime primary and the distinction among "democratic, oligarchic, totalitarian, or whatever" regimes secondary, Cardoso is saying that any capitalist state is a pact of domination of one class over another, so no matter whether it is a relatively good capitalist state or a relatively bad one it must be replaced by a socialist state. In this view, any socialist state—which by definition is not a pact of class domination since there are no classes in socialism—in this critical respect is by definition superior to any capitalist state. And by lumping "democratic, oligarchic, totalitarian, or whatever" regimes together under one heading, this approach minimizes the significance of differences between such regimes. In this view, "democratic" England might have better "formal rules" than bureaucratic-authoritarian regimes in Latin America, or Mussolini's Italy, or Franco's Spain, or Nazi Germany for that matter, but still they are all capitalist states in which one class dominates another, and that is the more important distinction.

Cardoso makes a great deal of this distinction between state and regime, and so do a number of commentators on his work. Thus in the new postscriptum to his classic work with Faletto, Cardoso stresses that even in formal democracies in Latin America such as Venezuela, Colombia, or Costa Rica, the state is still a pact of domination and the only acceptable solution is socialism.[28] By this line of reasoning, even if Brazil were to continue its processes of liberalization and democratization to the point where a multiparty system or a two-party system with regular competitive elections were firmly established, civil liberties were widely respected, and other features of a political democracy were in place, as long as capitalism persisted the state would still represent a pact of class domination, the democracy would still be only formal, and socialism would still be the only acceptable solution. Although progress of a second order may have been achieved, first-order progress would await a transformation to socialism.

Cardoso's answers to the questions of what this socialism would look like and how one would get there are ambiguous. Bloody revolutions are not necessarily required, but the possibility that they may be one acceptable route is not excluded. Leninism and Stalinism are opposed, but Mao's cultural revolution, the Chinese case generally, and Fidel's Cuba are repeatedly used as examples of participatory democracy, substantive democracy, and authentic socialism. A dictatorship of the proletariat is rejected, but the idea that socialism has no room in the long run for the bourgeoisie is maintained. Although socialism is always preferred to capitalism, concrete cases of socialism are never compared systematically to concrete cases of capitalism. Rather, concrete cases of capitalism (which have flaws) are compared to idealized versions of socialism (which are flawless). Thus the superiority of socialism is assumed. It is not a debatable subject.

The foregoing survey of the ideas of the new dependency interpretation in general, and Cardoso's views in particular, supports and extends Bresser Pereira's hypotheses about the dominance of Marxist perspectives in Brazil. It demonstrates that these perspectives pervaded not only the functional-capitalist and imperialist superexploitation interpretations but also the new dependency perspective. It shows that Marxist views infused interpretations not only of economic and social systems but also of political systems. Because Cardoso is by common consent the most subtle, moderate, and sophisticated of the new dependency authors, it follows that most other authors were even more extreme and sweeping in their Marxism than he was. This shows how extraordinarily powerful Marxism was in Brazilian intellectual culture. It also makes the changes that occurred in Brazilian political discourse in the late seventies and early eighties—in which Cardoso again played a prominent and illuminating role—even more notable.

New Tendencies

In the political and intellectual atmosphere of the late sixties and early seventies in Brazil, the Marxist arguments were widely accepted. Relatively few intellectuals were able to mount effective challenges to them.

In the middle and late seventies and early eighties, however, the hegemony of the Marxist ideas lessened. Some Marxists modified their earlier views. Some non-Marxists now found their ideas gaining wider acceptance. New types of analysts who fit poorly into Bresser Pereira's categories appeared and occupied important intellectual space. These authors disagreed about many questions, including how to characterize the changes in Brazil. Some of them rejected all labels or categories or at least said they did. (However, they did not specify how communication can occur without *any* labels or categories.)[29] Those who moved away from or broke with Marxism did not necessarily do it directly or explicitly; their moves were usually more subtle or implicit than that. But almost all Brazilian intellectuals agreed that major changes occurred and that they were important. The first group to examine is Marxists who amplified and modified their views.

"Marxist Liberals" and Social Democrats

In the middle and late seventies some of the very Marxists or neo-Marxists who had earlier denounced "bourgeois" institutions and processes began to tolerate and even support them—not only theoretically but also in their own political actions. This was a very significant change in which most of the Brazilian intellectual left participated. This is not to say that they rejected entirely their earlier views or agreed entirely with each other. They did neither. But important changes did occur in the thought (and action) of most Brazilian Marxists.[30]

One expression of this change came from former members of the revolutionary left. By the mid-1970s the military government had more or less decimated the guerrilla left as a political and military force. Most of its members were dead, in prison, or (the largest number) in exile. The demonstrated capacity of the military government to deal effectively with armed insurrection led most of the survivors to question the feasibility of that approach. Their reflections on the ethical content of their revolutionary activities, their years of exile, and the context of *abertura* after 1974 were among the factors that led them also to question the desirability of revolution and to view more hopefully the possibilities for democratic change. They emerged from their experiences and reflections highly critical of Marxism-Leninism as a dogmatic religion and of the bureaucratic, totalitarian character of vanguard political parties.[31]

A second expression of the change in Marxist thought came from a group that might be called Brazilian-style Eurocommunists. The authors in this camp were not altogether happy about this label, but it was and is widely applied to them by other Brazilian intellectuals. In their view, socialism was to be achieved democratically, peacefully, and on the basis of the national experience, not foreign intervention. Party activity should include appeals to the middle sectors as well as to the working class, and alliances with other parties were not prohibited. Internal party democracy, criticism, and dissent were also preferred over democratic centralism and the idea of party doctrine as infallible dogma. The authors in this camp were still critics of liberalism and even of social democracy as theoretical and political positions, and they still held that the only true democracy was Marxist socialism. But they were willing to work with the other political groups and insisted that Marxist socialism be democratic.[32]

A third manifestation of change in leftist thinking occurred among what might be called Brazilian social democrats or democratic socialists. These terms do not readily lend themselves to precise definition. However, the general idea is "a synthesis of socialism and democracy." What is implied is a political regime based on the rule of law, freedom of groups and individuals, peaceful cooperation among groups and political parties, nationalism, and a variety of reforms and state actions designed to address in an evolutionary, peaceful fashion the social and economic problems of capitalist society.[33]

In Brazil as in Europe social democrats tend to divide into two main subgroups. Both subgroups agree on the main outlines of social democracy as just described, and they agree also that attention must be placed both on civil society and on political institutions. However, their emphases differ. In Brazil the subgroup giving somewhat greater emphasis to the processes and institutions of civil society, particularly social movements, trade unions, and the like, includes such thinkers as Francisco Weffort, Marilena Chauí, José Álvaro Moisés, Lúcio Kowarick, and Eder Sader. In this subgroup one of the main theoretical and practical questions is how to respect the autonomy of social movements and at the same time get them involved in politics so they can protect their interests. This subgroup of social democrats—who also accept the term "democratic socialists"—includes some of the main thinkers (Francisco Weffort, Marilena Chauí) of the Partido dos Trabalhadores (PT) and is found largely, though not exclusively, in São Paulo, especially at the Centro de Estudos de Cultura Contemporânea (CEDEC).[34] For some of the members of this subgroup, these ideas were the elaboration and expansion of an earlier tradition, but for others (e.g., Weffort) they represented a considerable change from the earlier form of Marxism that was much more economicist and harsh in its criticisms of bourgeois political institutions.

The second subgroup tends to give greater emphasis than the first subgroup does to the state and political institutions. In this subgroup the most important proponent by far is Fernando Henrique Cardoso. In his academic writings in the late sixties and throughout the decade of the seventies Cardoso had regarded elections, legislatures, political parties, and many other features of politics in bourgeois societies as "formal" expressions of the "pact of class domination" of the capitalist state. In the eighties he published sober scholarly studies of elections, became a party official, was elected a federal senator, and in 1985 became a national political and legislative leader in the Sarney government. In the 1970s he employed the infinitely elastic Marxist concept of "interest" to single out any group, individual, or institution in Brazilian society that he happened to disapprove of or disagree with at the moment as "the anti-nation inside the nation" and an "internal manifestation of external capitalism." In the 1980s he defended the idea of the legitimacy of divergent interests, and, in consequence, of bargaining and negotiation.

No Brazilian intellectual exemplified the change in Marxist thinking more vividly, articulated it more explicitly and comprehensively, or had more political impact than Cardoso. For these reasons, and because of his important role in the Brazilian Marxist tradition as discussed earlier, his new "liberal" ideas were bound to be criticized by some Marxists. For example, Carlos Nelson Coutinho charged that Cardoso's acceptance of the legitimacy of negotiated resolutions of conflicts within capitalist society constituted an acceptance of capitalist hegemony. For Coutinho this was an example of the "assimilation by contemporary social democracy of liberal thought," and he was very critical of it.[35] Non-Marxists also noticed the changes. Some skeptics referred to "Marxist liberals"—a contradictory label for a contradictory phenomenon they compared to *"sorvete fervido,"* boiled ice cream.[36]

Were the new "liberal" elements in Cardoso's political thought, and in Marxist thought more generally, inconsistent with Marxism, as Coutinho and others maintain, or were they merely an evolution within Marxism, as many theorists and activists in Brazil, Western Europe, the United States, and other parts of Latin America contend? There seems little doubt that Marxist categories are able to expand enough to absorb liberal notions. However, they can also contract in ways that make liberal political institutions, protections, and processes inconsistent with them and thus illegitimate from a Marxist viewpoint. This is one reason the new social democratic thought is controversial among both Marxists and non-Marxists. It is also one of the reasons Cardoso is not particularly pleased to have the term liberal applied to his politics, although he has occasionally done this himself: "You know, *we liberals* easily sign petitions, protest torture, and so on, but we must learn to influence the regime from the bottom, not from the top."[37] Like other social democrats, he is uneasy with the term because of its historic associations (see below) and its inconsistencies with Marxist categories, among other reasons. But the evidence is very strong that during recent years he has embraced numerous elements of political liberalism as that term is defined here.[38]

To be sure, liberal, Weberian, and other non-Marxist categories and ideas were not totally new in Cardoso's thought. He has always been an eclectic thinker drawing heavily on many non-Marxist as well as Marxist authors and concepts in his scholarly work. Moreover, throughout his career he has consistently opposed authoritarian regimes of the right. He has consistently argued that economic development does not require political authoritarianism but can be accomplished democratically. He has opposed the idea that socialism necessarily requires either a bloody revolution or a Stalinist dictatorship of the proletariat. He has repeatedly declared himself in favor of such liberal democratic concepts as popular participation, multiparty elections, the rule of law, civil liberties, diversity of political parties and interest associations, and the autonomy of political parties and interest associations from the state.

Nevertheless, these non-Marxist influences and themes became much stronger in the middle and late seventies and the eighties, especially when Cardoso ran for the Federal Senate, was elected, and became a very important national political leader in Brazil. Political writing and activity were by no means new for Cardoso but they became larger parts of his professional life. During the seventies, the non-Marxist themes became stronger in his popular and political writings and declarations at the same time that his academic, social-scientific work maintained and in many respects intensified and sharpened its Marxist character. It is not true, as many people assume or argue casually without citations, that Cardoso's academic writings became less radical during the decade of the seventies. To the contrary, to the extent that there were changes his academic writings clearly became more radical.[39] However, during the early eighties, when Cardoso's political involvements deepened, his academic productivity declined and so also did visible Marxist elements in his thought.

Cardoso's political declarations are significantly different from his academic writings. The latter are full of discussions of capitalism, socialism, class structures, class exploitation, dialectics, modes of production, historical materialism, formalism, dependency, imperialism, and so on. These topics are far less prominent in his political works.[40] In these works the focus is on such topics as democracy, elections, parties, participation, economy, economic policy, the people, mass party, and the social question. The latter three terms are the closest one gets as organizing themes to anything resembling classes, to say nothing of exploitation, capitalism, socialism, imperialism, or dependency.

In the body of these political writings as well as in their topical headings, the same dedication to liberal notions of democracy and opposition to radical, Marxist notions of democracy are again in evidence. Thus, Cardoso sounds very much like T. H. Marshall when he states "the people is the totality of its citizens, and therefore the democratic way can only be found when all citizens participate together."[41] No class struggle there. When he says that the expansion of political democracy will reduce social and economic inequalities even though it cannot and will not eliminate them entirely,[42] Cardoso again reads very much like Marshall. There are repeated references to "social pacts" and "democratic pacts"; referring to his own political party, the PMDB (the Party of the Brazilian Democratic Movement), Cardoso says:

> we are the only party able to compose the new social pact, in which workers, salaried middle classes, liberal professions, and plundered national enterpreneurs [!] may enter along with the enormous mass of unemployed. We are the only party that can compose this social pact, govern in accord

with it, and present programs and projects which represent the combined interests of these layers of the population. . . .[43]

Nothing there about the state as the pact of domination or the conflicting and irreconcilable interests of social groups, classes, and class fractions in situations of dependent capitalist development. Asked his views on socialism in the Soviet Union, China, and Cuba, Cardoso ignores Cuba but says that socialism "of the sort that is in power . . . in the USSR or even in China" reflects an "abyss between the nineteenth century ideal and the twentieth century reality."[44]

The political writings, in short, stress the liberal Weberian side of Cardoso's Marxist/liberal-Weberian approach substantially more than the academic social science writings do. The differences may reflect at least in part the difference between dealing as a sociologist mainly with intellectuals and students from the elite and dealing as a political activist with broader strata in Brazilian society. Thus, explaining why he does not favor a Socialist party in Brazil at this time Cardoso says, "I am not in favor of a Socialist Party of intellectuals, of the elite. What good is there in people running around saying, 'I am a socialist.', 'I understand Marxism-Leninism.', and 'bla-bla-bla'? This doesn't change anything."[45] Referring to the style of his meetings with factory workers and labor leaders during his Senate campaign, Cardoso says, "They gave us a fantastic reception. It was a lot easier dealing with them, they were more open than if one went to speak to students."[46]

Political Liberals

A second type of interpretation that gained increased prominence in the middle and late 1970s and the 1980s may be called, for lack of a better term, the political liberal interpretation. In order to understand the significance of this development, and before defining and describing it more specifically, it is necessary to say a bit about the traditional place of liberalism in Brazil and, indeed, in most of the rest of Latin America.

Liberal ideas have suffered a double blow in Brazil. On the one hand, they are associated historically with elitism and capitalist exploitation. On the other hand, they are also associated with the "development" and "modernization" theories of the fifties and sixties that were discredited by the 1964 coup and other events. As a result the very term "liberal" is an ambiguous, tainted symbol in Brazilian political discourse, as indeed it is throughout Latin America and most of Western Europe. Historically, liberal political parties have usually been conservative and sometimes reactionary. Political liberalism is often thought to be insep-arable from economic and social liberalism and therefore, in this view, from elitism and capitalist exploitation, Chicago-school economics and the International Monetary Fund (IMF), and U.S. culture and foreign policy. In short, liberalism is seen as both antidemocratic and antinationalist.

Students of Brazilian intellectual history with varying perspectives have thus concurred in minimizing the impact of liberal ideas on Brazilian society and intellectual traditions. For example, Bresser Pereira states flatly that "a liberal interpretation does not exist in Brazil." He attributes this lack to the "theoretical poverty" of the interpretation and to the "lack of intellectuals with the ability to formulate it."[47] Wanderly Guilherme dos Santos offers a rather different set of reasons to explain why political liberalism has not taken root in Brazilian society.[48]

Regardless of which interpretation best explains the fact, it is true that neither political liberalism nor Marxism has deep roots in Brazilian society. The Marxist hegemony of which Bresser Pereira and others speak is exercised within intellectual circles, not the society at large. But with respect to those intellectual circles, is it really accurate to say that there is no liberal interpretation? Or that no liberals have had the capacity to formulate such an interpretation? I suggest that there have been a number of types of investigation, cogitation, and theorizing that call into question the idea that there is no significant liberal or neoliberal interpretation of Brazilian *politics*. The authors writing in this category have differed among themselves on many things but not on their commitment to *political* liberalism.[49]

Influential and sophisticated political liberals may be found not only in the academy but also in law, journalism, and diplomacy. Jurist-scholars Raymundo Faoro and Victor Nunes Leal and the historian Sérgio Buarque de Holanda were innovators in Brazilian political analysis and staunch defenders of democratic political values against authoritarianisms and totalitarianisms of either the right or the left.[50] More recently, academic social scientists such as Bolivar Lamounier and Wanderley Guilherme dos Santos have also worked in this broad tradition. For example, Lamounier has stressed that certain "liberal" mechanisms, such as competitive elections, are not merely "formalisms" but genuine, vital institutional protections. He has also argued that "it is legitimate, within certain limits, to speak of degrees of democracy."[51] Dos Santos, who was a Marxist in the late fifties and the early sixties, has been trying for more than two decades to work out a theoretical position that simultaneously honors liberal political values, principles of social justice, and the specificities of "the Brazilian reality," while avoiding the errors and abuses committed by Brazilian liberals in the past.[52]

Another manifestation of political liberalism has been the writings of exceptionally able journalists such as Fernando Pedreira or Carlos Castello Branco. Consider Pedreira: Some of his books have been extended essays on a single political theme, for example, *Março 31: Civis e Militares no Processo da Crise Brasileira* (1964). Others have been collections of shorter journalistic essays, such as *Brasil Política, 1964–1975* (1975), *A Liberdade e a Ostra* (1976), and *Impávido Colosso* (1982).[53] All of them have, in a style unmatched for clean, simple elegance, gone well beyond punditry to serious, subtle political analysis. (According to the late Tristão de Athayde, Pedreira is "the most brilliant, the most cultivated, and the most openminded of our political commentators.")[54] Pedreira's themes have included a constant defense of political democracy, aversion to dogma of all kinds, and a relentless attack on the corrupting and stultifying effects of bureaucracy.[55]

Still another author in this category, although he is different in certain ways from those previously mentioned (who also differ among themselves), is José Guilherme Merquior. Merquior has written fifteen books in a variety of fields ranging from literary criticism to structural anthropology to political theory. For my purposes the most relevant are perhaps *A Natureza do Processo* (1982) and *O Argumento Liberal* (1983).[56] For Merquior, "Modern liberalism is a social liberalism, a liberalism which avoids the ingenuousness and innocence regarding the complexity of social phenomena that characterized classical liberalism. Modern liberalism does not have the kinds of anxieties or complexes regarding social questions which classical liberalism had. And it is this modern version of liberalism to which I link my own thinking."[57] Merquior names Celso Lafer, Cândido Mendes de Almeida, Marcílio Marques Moreira, Luiz Navarro de Brito, Francisco de Araújo Santos, Sérgio Paulo Rouanet, and Vamireh Chacon as "other essayists" with whom he has been trying to "define an area of national reflection about the psychological, ethical, and historical meaning of freedom, in a line of thought that is seen not as the superseding of the great tradition of liberal thought but rather as its unfolding."[58]

Another, and final, manifestation of the recent prominence of liberal political ideas (again, of greatly varied shades) may be seen in the debates that were part of the process of political *abertura* in Brazil. Consider, for example, a series of articles published in the *Caderno de Leituras* of the *Jornal da Tarde* in São Paulo between 1977 and 1981, many of which appeared in a collection entitled *A Conquista do Espaço Político* (1983).[59] The purpose of the series was to debate political themes related to the *abertura*. Among the participants were Raimundo Faoro, Tércio Sampaio Jr., Evaldo Amaro Vieira, Oliveiros S. Ferreira, José Eduardo Faria, Roque Spencer Maciel de Barros, Lenildo Táboa Pessoa, Eduardo Seabra Fagundes, Fernando Pedreira, Wanderley Guilherme dos Santos, Gerard Lebrun, Marçal Versiani, Leôncio Martins Rodrigues, and Fábio Konder Comparato. This is a very diverse group. Some of them would reject the label "political liberal." Yet on the whole they were able to agree on the notion of democratization as "an apprenticeship and application of a method of living together with conflicts."[60]

Whatever else one may say about this notion of democratization, it is not one that would have had the same support among intellectuals in the late sixties and the early seventies that it has had in the last decade. As Fernando Pedreira put it, "After fourteen years of a military regime even the infantile left, even our sub-Marxists (who are so numerous) seem reconciled with the value of liberalism and bourgeois freedoms. Let us hope that the return of full democracy (if it comes) does not make us quickly unlearn what we learned at such cost during those painful years."[61]

In the earlier period, the focus of discussion about the Brazilian political model was the question of legitimacy. In the late seventies and eighties, the focus began to be on the question of how to submit *any* power, whatever its basis of legitimacy, to societal control.[62] In addressing this theme, the authors were not necessarily optimistic about prospects for installing a representative democracy on liberal foundations, but they tended strongly to agree on the need to preserve political liberalism in some form as a way for society to check state power. As Wanderley Guilherme dos Santos put it, political liberalism was not a sufficient condition for the democratization of power, but it was a necessary condition.[63]

In sum, ideas of the kind propounded by these and other authors about political liberalism are now very important in the Brazilian intellectual community and also among political, media, and other elites. These ideas were much less important before the mid-seventies. They need to be included in any survey of recent trends, and they challenge Bresser Pereira's thesis that no liberal interpretation exists in Brazil.

The New Academic Social Scientists

A third diverse manifestation largely outside the earlier Marxist patterns derived from the explosion in the number of Brazilians with advanced training in political science, anthropology, sociology, economics, and other social science disciplines in the sixties and early seventies. In 1964 Fernando Pedreira could still write that "the only advanced training institute in the social sciences that Brazil has had during the past three decades has been the Communist Party."[64] Possibly (although it is not entirely clear) Pedreira was speaking metaphorically; even at the metaphorical level the statement was debatable in 1964. But at that time it was a legitimate, serious, plausible argument. It would be impossible to make that kind of argument today.

Today, according to Hélgio Trindade, there is a growing tendency among social scientists of various methodological and theoretical tendencies "to approach concrete manifestations of social reality, whether political or economic, with more humility and without the comfortable protection of the universalizing generalizations of classical theories or of other forms of ethnocentrism."[65] Trindade even cites the *autocríticas* (self-critiques) of "renowned" figures such as Fernando Henrique Cardoso and Celso Furtado as evidence of this growing resistance to the attractions of sweeping theoretical generalizations. And what are the origins of this process? For him, aside from the complexity of social reality itself, the roots lie in the substantial and rapid development of the social sciences from the mid-sixties to the mid-eighties.[66]

Perhaps nowhere in Latin America, or indeed the entire Third World, has the growth in quantity and quality of the social sciences been so dramatic as in Brazil. Bolivar Lamounier has recently noted that almost the entire structure of postgraduate social science education now in place in Brazil was erected after 1965. Until that date in the areas of sociology, political science, and history, only the University of São Paulo (USP) maintained regular masters and doctoral programs. Even so, a recent study of the fields of anthropology, sociology, and political science shows that between 1945 and 1965 (inclusive) only 41 masters, doctoral, and livre docência theses were defended—that is, an average of 2 per year. In the same institution from 1966 to 1977, by contrast, 158 theses were defended—that is, an average of 13 per year. If one looks at the current production of advanced degrees at all postgraduate levels through-out Brazil in these same three fields, one finds that the *annual* production is equal to at least half the total production at USP from 1945 to 1977.[67]

Moreover, the quantitative change has been accompanied by qualitative changes. One such qualitative change, according to Bolivar Lamounier, is away from what he calls a "bureaucratic-mandarin model" toward what he calls a "pluralist and flexible model" of the social science enterprise that reflects a "coming of age" of a new generation of professional social scientists in Brazil.[68] Taking these ideas and other analyses and data as points of departure, the anthropologist Otávio Velho has elaborated a detailed profile of some social processes involved in the evolution of the advanced social sciences in Brazil since the 1960s. Among the features he finds to be associated with this process are a stress on professionalization in contrast to the traditional creation of a class of intelligentsia, institutionalization rather than creative individ-ualism, "training" rather than "education in the classical sense," spe-cialization rather than a totalizing or global vision, "research" rather than integrated general interpretations, operational concepts rather than intuitive concepts, internal democracy rather than hierarchical decision-making in social science organizations, and mass-oriented rather than elite-oriented scholars.[69]

This is not the place to document the degree to which all these changes actually did occur, how they all played themselves out in concrete terms, where they are going next, and so forth. It can be suggested, however, that some such changes of the sort analyzed by Velho did occur and have had significant implications for the kinds of interpretations that are made of Brazilian politics. Take the point about increased pluralism. Increases in diversity are manifest not only in the greater number of centers of advanced social science training and research but also in the increasing variety of types of education and training of the faculty who teach and do research in these organizations. In political science, for example, all of the permanent faculty at the oldest facility

TABLE 4.1
Unity/Diversity of Training of Permanent Faculty in Four Masters and Ph.D.
Programs in Political Science, 1979-1980

Program	(1) Total Number of Permanent Faculty	(2) Number of Universities Involved in in Highest Degrees of Permanent Faculty	(3) Highest Number of Faculty Trained in Any Single University	Unity of Training Index (3)/(1) (Maximum Unity = 1.00)	Diversity of Training Index (2)/(1) (Maximum Diversity = 1.00)
University Research Institute of Rio de Janeiro (IUPERJ)	12	8	3 (U. of Chicago)	.25	.67
Federal University of Minas Gerais (UFMG)	14	8	4 (UFMG)	.29	.57
University of São Paulo (USP)	13	1	13 (USP)	1.00	.08
UNICAMP	6	4	3 (USP)	.50	.67

Source: Calculated from data in CAPES, Pós-Graduação: Catálogo de Cursos, 1980, Vol. 4, Ciências Sociais (Brasília: CAPES, 1982), pp. 73-84.

for graduate training in Brazil, the University of São Paulo (USP), also received their highest graduate degrees from USP. At the three newer centers for graduate training in political science, the percentages of the permanent faculty receiving their highest graduate degrees from the institutions at which they were teaching were 25 percent, 29 percent, and 50 percent, respectively (See Table 4.1). Similar patterns obtain in other areas in the social sciences such as sociology and anthropology.[70]

No social science discipline was more affected by these quantitative and qualitative changes in graduate training than political science. The new political scientists studied almost everything: interest groups, bureaucracies, the military, legislatures, elections, political parties, political machines, public policy, science and government, urban politics, rural politics, neighborhood movements, unions and politics, business and politics, technocracy and politics, political thought in Brazil, Brazilian ideologies, political clientelism, and so on.[71] The scholars doing these studies varied greatly in the kinds of theoretical, methodological, epistemological, and ideological tools they used in their work. The expansion of the number and diversity of educational and training paths made for greater variety in these respects than had obtained before.

The practitioners of these new approaches were different from those who used earlier approaches in other ways as well. First, as Trindade, Lamounier, Velho, and others have also argued, they stressed "systematic empirical research"[72] more than general and abstract theorizing. Second, they were political scientists who regarded political institutions and processes as subjects worthy of scholarly investigation. This contrasted with the earlier approaches in which political institutions and processes were mainly interpreted by sociologists or economists as derivative from or expressions of vast social and economic forces and therefore not really worthy of intensive study or emphasis in their own right. Third, as we shall see below, the new social scientists tended to take a somewhat different posture than their predecessors with regard to classic dilemmas of balancing "detached" scholarship and "committed" scholarship.

Because the new political scientists took political institutions and processes—both informal and "formal" in the Marxist sense—seriously, and because they did concrete and systematic empirical research on them, they tended to do research and writing that differed in certain substantive as well as methodological and epistemological respects from the Marxist interpretations that had been more dominant in the earlier period. In other words, although, as previously indicated, individual new political scientists varied greatly in their theoretical, epistemological, methodological, and ideological perspectives, nevertheless the nature of their discipline, political science, was such that as a group they examined political institutions and processes differently from the way they had been examined before. In some cases this was so even for those new political scientists who continued to work within the Marxist tradition.

On the whole, these changes have been positive in their consequences. Serious political studies in Brazil today are more numerous, more varied, more empirical, more systematic, and more respectful of the possible autonomy and integrity of the political sphere than they were twenty or even ten years ago. In consequence they also open up possibilities not only for still more and better empirical research but also for types of creative theoretical, normative, and policy analysis that were not possible before. In a country like Brazil, where the political present is clearly better than the recent past but still far from what it might be; where democratic political values, processes, and institutions remain precarious; and where the political future remains open, fluid, and at least in part amenable to skillful, wise political innovation and invention—in circumstances such as these, opening up such possibilities is a development of no small importance.

Finally, but by no means least important, the new political science opens up the possibility, though unfortunately not the guarantee, of transcending an over-muscular sociology of knowledge that had imprisoned and poisoned much social science in Brazil in the past. Inherent in the Marxist approaches is the notion that social science and class struggles are not only intertwined but that the former is and should be subordinated to the latter—the idea that social science is a "tool" or "instrument" of the class struggle, to whose logic and imperatives it is and must be subordinated.[73] This notion makes a huge, unwarranted leap from the daily reality with which every social scientist must live, like the certainty of death and taxes, to a self-destructive rationale for obliterating the differences between the scientific and the political vocations. Some of the new social scientists have another view. Velho puts it this way:

> Surely today it is obvious, even banal, to note that all thought is compromised. The liberal idea of purely neutral thought explains little; it only describes the appearance of an eventual field of forces which occasionally can be crystalized. However, it is not necessary to make an abstract virtue out of an inescapable necessity. One can imagine a kind of thinking whose "interest" is precisely the *search* for objectivity, whose commitment and potential are precisely in the affirmation of that search. Probably this is the kind of "person" in the scientific community that ought to be developed. Perhaps this is the best reading of Mannheim's intuition . . .[74]

So these changes have had several positive aspects. On the other hand, it should not be supposed that they necessarily come without costs. The new political science, no less than earlier modes of analysis, has its irrational totems and taboos.[75] The stress on information, training, and operational concepts means less stress on interpretation, classical education, and creative innovation. The new emphasis on disaggregated parts may make it harder for some to see the aggregated whole. In sum, the capacity to be creative and to theorize broadly may diminish in some ways in the new political science.[76]

These costs are real but not crippling. Under the best of circumstances and with the most careful mechanisms of quality control, all scientific institutions still certify and reward some people who are dull, or foolish, or afraid. That is true everywhere. It is true in the United States, and it is true in Brazil in the ranks of its new (and old) political scientists. But this does not mean the end of creative political science. Far from it. A political science that can claim such works as Bolivar Lamounier's "Representação Política: A Importância de Certos Formalismos," José Murilo de Carvalho's *A Construção da Ordem*, Simon Schwartzman's *As Bases do Autoritarismo Brasileiro*, or Wanderley Guilherme dos Santos's *Kantianas Brasileiras*, just to name a few examples, does not have to worry that its scholars are unable to address challenging theoretical questions in a creative way.[77]

Interpretations of Brazil's International Political Economy

Other categories of interpretations of Brazilian domestic politics beyond the ones treated here might also be discussed—for example, "popular culture" interpretations,[78] interpretations by Catholic-left intellectuals,[79] and others, but I shall not go into them here. Before concluding this section, however, it is appropriate to say a brief word about the study of Brazil's international political economy in recent years.

All three of Bresser Pereira's interpretations of the sixties and seventies (the functional-capitalist, imperialist-superexploitation, and the new-dependency interpretations) related Brazil to the international capitalist system mainly in terms of Marxist theoretical, methodological, and conceptual approaches. Since the early seventies there have been several lines of investigation and interpretation that have not been linked so heavily to that tradition. Thus, there has been an increase during that time in the appearance of concrete, empirical studies of different aspects of Brazil's foreign policy and its place in the international system. This trend regarding Brazilian foreign relations studies is roughly analogous to the one just noted regarding the new political science in the domestic sphere, although it has occurred on a smaller scale and began from a smaller base. The study of foreign policy and international relations does not have a strong academic tradition in Brazil. Traditionally such work has been legalistic, essayistic, and sometimes polemical, and often the line between academic and non-academic work has been blurred.[80]

The more recent studies have been varied in their topics and approaches, but several have been more academic, more focused thematically, and less theoretically ambitious than older studies. The authors of the more recent studies also tend to be relatively young. These authors have varied considerably in their methodological, epistemological, and ideological orientations and in their substantive emphases. Most of them do not challenge Marxist interpretations directly, systematically, and explicitly. Indeed, some of these authors are Marxists of one sort or another themselves. But most of them differ from the earlier Marxist authors in the sense that their works tend to be more systematically empirical and more precisely focused in substantive terms.[81]

There have also been various small groups of somewhat more established authors who have more directly and explicitly challenged some of the Marxist arguments. These groups have been extremely different from each other in a number of dimensions, including the right-left ideological dimension. On the one hand, they include geopolitical and psychodynamic interpretations of Brazil's international role.[82] On the other hand, they include interpretations of Brazilian dependency by such authors as Hélio Jaguaribe and Celso Furtado.[83] For example, in 1982 Furtado published a remarkable article directly and fundamentally challenging the premises of both the functional-capitalist and the new-dependency interpretations. The latter question the suitability of the present model of industrialization for Third World countries because,

among other reasons, dependence on the industrialized countries is built
into such a model. Furtado does not deny that dependency accompanies
industrialization. However, he argues that dependency is neither an
inevitable nor a permanent feature and that it is futile to resist the
cultural unification of the world being brought about by the modern
system of communication and by the force of example of a high standard
of living in industrialized countries. The better strategy, in his view, is
to use such elements of economic power as the Third World countries
have to gradually reduce and eventually end dependency.[84]

In other words, Furtado conceptualizes dependency relations in terms
of power disparities either in capitalist or socialist systems and regards
the issue of the relationship between such power disparities and exploitation under either capitalism or socialism as a question to be
addressed empirically, case by case, rather than as a matter to be settled
by definition and theoretical fiat. In this formulation, the issue of
dependency becomes interesting and meaningful rather than, as in the
new dependency view, analogous to "degrees of slavery" and analytically
meaningless. Furtado's statement is thus a direct, explicit challenge to
the fundamental premises of the Marxist perspectives. He and Jaguaribe
have advanced similar ideas before but this essay goes beyond Furtado's
earlier statements.

Why the New Tendencies May Continue

> FHC: "We want the return of liberalism."
> AA: "We have already had liberalism, and I insist that the PDS [the
> government party] is the party that wants to achieve justice through
> liberty."
> FHC: "But I want to achieve liberalism without the PDS."
> —Exchange between Fernando Henrique Cardoso
> and Afonso Arinos de Melo Franco, 1982.[85]

> For us the concept democracy implies the possibility of alternation in
> power; divergency and heterogeneity of interest and activities as good
> and necessary features, not as evils to exorcize; the idea that the majority
> should not suppress the minority because no one monopolizes truth;
> participation in decisions that affect our lives; the legitimacy of different
> interests and consequently of negotiation; and civility in political discourse,
> without which democratic politics cannot exist.
> —PMDB policy statement, 1981.[86]

How stable are the new types of interpretations of Brazilian politics?
Or, to put the question the other way around, how precarious are they?
Nobody knows for sure, because the answer lies in the future. Agreement
is widespread among informed observers that both the political and
economic situations inside Brazil, and various external factors, will affect
whether or not the new tendencies continue. Judgments and opinions

vary, however, regarding the ways these political and economic factors will interact with past and present intellectual interpretations in shaping future tendencies.

On the one hand, there is the view that the change away from Marxism among Brazilian intellectuals is not superficial but deep and widespread. According to this view, it is wrong to suppose that those Marxist ideas that were dominant in the past are dominant any longer or will necessarily exert such powerful influences in the future. In this view, it is a mistake to suppose that past intellectual patterns determine future trends.[87]

The campaign and election of 1982, their aftermath through mid-1985, and indeed many other elements of the "slow and gradual" processes of *distensão* and *abertura* during the last decade, lend support to these assessments. Perhaps the most dramatic example is the case of Leonel Brizola, elected oppositionist governor of the state of Rio de Janeiro in 1982. Before 1964 Brizola was a militant who organized armed cells, urged enlisted men to imprison their officers, and generally sought to radicalize the nation. By 1985, after fifteen years of exile, he seemed to be firmly committed to democratic and orderly procedures as well as to social justice. He has remained in favor of reducing the influence of multinationals in Brazil, but he was cooperative and pragmatic in his relations with President Figueiredo, the local PDS (government) party, and even with the military hierarchy.[88] And the *socialismo moreno* (dusky socialism) he has in mind for Brazil "questions" capitalism but does not reject capitalism; it is "fascinated" by the Cuban revolution but rejects the Cuban path for Brazil: "I remember once going to Miami and seeing the Cuban bourgeoisie there. I thought to myself, our bourgeoisie is too big to fit in Miami. We'll have to find the alternative path that doesn't exclude anybody."[89]

"The path that doesn't exclude anybody" sums up one of the key theoretical principles that distinguishes the new tendencies from the previous Marxist interpretations in which many groups and class fractions must be excluded. Those excluded include the dominant class that exploits the popular classes, "the anti-nation inside the nation," internal expressions of foreign interests, and so forth. If one is working within neo-Marxist premises, the idea of including these sectors—of supporting, or even tolerating the inclusion of "nonpopular" groups, classes, and class fractions within the opposition coalition—is impossible. It is heresy.

Yet this is precisely what happened in Brazil in the campaign of 1982. The Party of the Brazilian Democratic Movement (PMDB) explicitly opted for a heterodox coalition that included both popular classes and elements of the bourgeoisie. In a remarkable major policy statement in 1981, the PMDB explicitly repudiated the exclusionary view inherent in the traditional Marxist approaches.[90] Not surprisingly, this intellectual decision and political strategy were controversial on the left. The Workers Party (PT) in particular criticized the PMDB very sharply on this point.

The PT opted strongly for the more traditional Marxist view aptly summarized in its title—a workers' party should represent the workers and the workers only, and should reject appeals to and coalitions with the bourgeoisie. Intellectuals as well as politicians divided over the issue. When the results were in, however, the voters, including most workers, strongly supported the PMDB and gave relatively little support to the PT. At least in electoral terms, therefore, and arguably in other terms as well, the strategy of the PMDB and of those intellectuals who supported it was vindicated. And to date the PMDB and other oppositionist governors and legislators have continued to operate on these premises after taking office.

This is not to say that all elements in the PMDB necessarily accepted the new interpretations. The PMDB coalition was so broad it included not only popular and working-class groups, and elements of the bourgeoisie, but also a number of groups, parties, and party factions from the revolutionary left. These latter included parts of the Brazilian Communist Party (PCB), of the Communist Party of Brazil (PC do B), and even of the October 8 Revolutionary Movement (MR-8).[91] In varying degrees, these elements fit uneasily with most of the PMDB coalition and with its new rules for the game. Nevertheless, they have participated in the coalition, and to date they have behaved by those rules.

Nor is it suggested that all the elements supporting the PT were traditional Marxists or that they all rejected the newer interpretations. There was some intellectual and political heterodoxy within the PT as well, extending in various directions.[92] Nevertheless, it remains the case that the PMDB expressed the new tendencies away from traditional Marxism substantially more than the PT. This fact, coupled with the PMDB's much greater electoral success contrasted to that of the PT, lends support to the view that the new ways of understanding Brazilian politics described in this paper may continue.

Besides these internal reasons for thinking the new tendencies may continue, there are also some external reasons. Throughout the world in the sixties and the early seventies, political and intellectual trends had tended to discredit the earlier liberal-pluralist perspectives on development and to replace them with various kinds of Marxist, dependency, and corporatist perspectives. But history kept moving. In the last half of the seventies and the first half of the eighties, these trends began to reverse themselves. Marxist regimes started to look worse than before, and pluralist democracies started to look better. Thus, in the seventies the fall of the Gang of Four in China, the rise and fall of the Pol Pot regime in Cambodia, the rise and decline of Eurocommunism, the fading (though not the death) of the appeal of the Cuban revolution, the Soviet invasion of Afghanistan, the fate of Solidarity in Poland, and other events in Latin America, Africa, and elsewhere have in their turn raised new doubts about the Marxist approaches. Marxism as a compelling intellectual orientation declined even in France—*especially* in France—

where it once had been dominant. This last example was particularly significant for Brazilian Marxist intellectuals, so sensitive to French influences.

Corporatism has not been seized upon in many places in Latin America as a development model attractive to intellectuals, nor have various other forms of traditional conservatism. Despite the manifest conservatism of Brazilian society, and notwithstanding the pervasive influence of corporatist, organic-statist institutional forms in its political history, these theoretical traditions have weakened rather than strengthened as prescriptive models among Brazilian intellectuals and scholars.[93]

What has happened instead is that the previously discredited pluralist democracy, so badly battered both as an empirical model and as a prescriptive model in the sixties and early seventies, began to make a comeback, as it were, albeit in slightly different form in some cases. Political democracy began to look more attractive and feasible again, not only in Brazil but also in Spain, Portugal, Peru, Ecuador, and Uruguay—to say nothing of Costa Rica, Venezuela, and Colombia, where political democracies had been in place for decades. In Argentina, the emergence of political democracy with the election in 1983 of Raúl Alfonsín seemed a near-miracle after seven years of harsh military rule and, more broadly, more than fifty years of political pain. Few observers viewed that development with anything but satisfaction; cavils about the imperfections of bourgeois democracy were scarce. And in countries as diverse as Chile, Paraguay, and much of Central America, stable pluralist democracy, for all its faults, began to look attractive indeed contrasted to what was in place or appeared likely to be in place in the near future. These events abroad reinforced, and continue to reinforce, the trends of thought in Brazil, even though they were far from being the most important influences on those trends.

Why the New Tendencies Are Precarious

"I doubt that liberal democracy can function well in Brazil because the social classes do not have organizations to represent their interests, therefore a formal liberal democracy would not be a genuine opening to the people."
—Fernando Henrique Cardoso, about 1974[94]

"a liberal interpretation does not exist in Brazil."
—Luíz Carlos Bresser Pereira, 1982.[95]

"The declaration of principles of many Brazilian democrats may be defined as follows: Before democracy is established, we will all be in favor of freedom to organize political parties (as long as it is for our party); in favor of freedom of opinions (as long as it is against our enemies); in favor of the freedom to come and go (as long as, coming or going, it favors our side). From this I deduce three antinomies of Brazilian political reasoning: (1) the majority of Brazilian democrats is made up of out-of-power authoritarians; (2) the majority of Brazilian democrats is like the majority of its Catholics, that is, not practicing; and, finally (3) a democrat is everyone who thinks and acts the way I do. Obviously, there is a *dialectical* justification for all of this. After all, what is it that the dialectic does not justify?"

—Wanderley Guilherme dos Santos[96]

External economic factors affect Brazilian politics and interpretations of Brazilian politics in complex ways. The oil shocks of 1973 and 1979, the debt crisis since 1982, and the combination of high interest rates and sluggish growth rates in the industrial economies have had major repercussions in Brazil. Brazil's debt exceeds $100 billion. In order to get IMF support to cope with the debt, the Brazilian government has taken austerity measures (limits on wage increases, food subsidies, business credit), which in turn are associated with increases in popular discontent and violence. Unemployment, underemployment, and inflation have never been higher in recent decades. These economic and social phenomena interact with each other and with the political process in Brazil in ways that put severe strains on the processes of liberalization and democratization and thus on the theoretical perspectives that are emerging to understand, cope with, and foster those processes.

Internal Brazilian politics not only reinforces the new tendencies; it also makes them precarious, beginning with the fact that the *abertura* itself is precarious. Although Brazil's political liberalization has had widespread popular support, and the military government's legitimacy sank to very low levels in its last years, still the *abertura* was largely controlled from the top. If the processes of liberalization and democratization should be reversed, and especially if the military were to return to power, then the arguments of those intellectuals who have supported liberalization and democratization would weaken and the arguments of those intellectuals opposed to the new theoretical tendencies would gain strength. This has happened in the past. For instance, one could certainly argue that the dominance of strident Marxism among intellectuals in the late sixties and early seventies was powerfully sustained by the harshness of the political authoritarianism of the time, and that the rise of the new tendencies has benefited from, as well as helped to nurture, the less authoritarian political climate of the late seventies and the eighties.[97]

If one major threat to the new intellectual tendencies is the possibility of the return of a military regime, other threats come from various aspects of the old opposition (now government) and the civil society. With respect to the civil society, there is the possibility that liberalization and democratization will be long, difficult tasks because they have to confront an authoritarian, centralist tradition that has profound historical roots in Brazil and that extends deep into the fabric of daily personal life (family, workplace, private social relations, and so forth) as well as the political system in the more overt, explicit sense. Only a few years ago such ideas of an authoritarian, centralist tradition in Brazil were ridiculed as "folklorism" by the dominant Marxism of the time, but today they are taken seriously and supported by sophisticated and influential scholarly works. The authors of these works are not cynics. They do not believe that the authoritarian customs and traditions in Brazil that they describe are immutable. To the contrary, they think changes are both feasible and desirable. But they insist that these customs and traditions have to be dealt with if a more democratic society and polity are to be achieved.[98]

With respect to the former opposition (now government), consider again the case of Leonel Brizola but this time from a different point of view. Earlier I noted the evidence that he supports democracy, and it is notable. At the same time, not everyone in Brazil is sure he has changed or that his democratic propensities would continue under different circumstances. The fear among some observers is that he would betray democratic principles while asserting that such action was necessary in order to "save democracy"—a practice that is an important reason for the breakdown of democracies.[99] Stated differently, the fear is that Brizola and perhaps other current democrats in Brazil would act in line with the thought of the nineteenth-century Frenchman, Louis Veuillot: "When I am weaker than you, I ask for freedom because that is according to your principles; when I am stronger than you, I take your freedom away, because that is according to my principles."[100] Here as before, the link between practice and theory is complex and uncertain but includes the proposition that at least in some respects blows to democratic practice would hurt the emerging intellectual tendencies, whereas the success of democratic practice in some ways encourages them.

Prospects for the new tendencies are also affected, more directly and more clearly, by features of the intellectual community itself. In the political sphere the threats to the new tendencies come mainly from the right, especially from the continuing possibility of a return to military rule. (That does not seem at all likely at this writing, but it is possible.) In the intellectual community, by contrast, the main threats to the new tendencies come from the left. In the academy, conservative thought and right-wing ideology have practically died out. As Schwartzman has well stated:

> One of the most significant, and least analyzed, characteristics of Brazil in the last few years has been the failure of ideologies of the right and the success of ideologies of the left. This proposition may seem absurd, but in fact it is quite true. It was simply not possible, even though it was often tried, to form an articulated conservative ideology that would be accepted by significant sectors of the population. The attempt to do this through the government program of 'moral and civic education' was a failure. The ideologies of national security never took hold outside the narrow limits of those groups and institutions that created them. The most traditional and conservative forms of Catholic thought, and of right-wing

nationalism, never gained real support. And thus it went. On the other hand, in spite of the repression—and often because of it—leftist ideologies flourished in the most educated strata of society.[101]

Thus conservative thought and ideology do not presently constitute a significant threat to the new intellectual tendencies. The major threats to them within the intellectual community have two facets. One is the fragility and vulnerability of the liberal tradition in Brazil, which was alluded to earlier. These features affect intellectuals as well as the rest of society. They are part of the intellectual tradition in Brazil. The historical connotations of liberalism (elitism, exploitative capitalism, and so forth) produce in intellectuals a certain ambivalence toward not only liberalism as a symbol but also, and more significantly, toward liberal political ideas and practices. On the one hand, Brazilian intellectuals often make more or less casual statements such as, "We are all liberals" or "We want a liberal society." And there are all the indications of and factors favoring liberal political principles that were noted above. On the other hand, however, there is widespread reluctance or at least uneasiness to be identified as a "liberal" or even a "neo-liberal." "Democracy" is an acceptable term, but "liberalism" is a term with mixed messages.

And yet use of the term "democracy" rather than "liberalism" does not solve the problem, either. If one now says, for example, that there are new tendencies in practice and theory in the direction of democracy, then one might be implying that the previous tendencies were undemocratic. In fact, sometimes they were. However, it must be recalled that the proponents of the Marxism that was dominant in the late sixties and early seventies also claimed to be democratic—and still do in most cases. They say, in fact, that the ideas they championed more genuinely express democratic values than the current tendencies do.

The term and symbol "democratic," in short, is claimed by many. Referring to the new tendencies as trends toward democratic thought rather than as trends toward a new political liberalism or neo-liberalism is therefore a solution that raises as many issues as it resolves. When people say the new tendencies are more democratic than the old ones, what they are really saying is that they defend principles that earlier were not so strongly defended, such as alternation in power, heterogeneity of groups, the legitimacy of divergent interests, protected minorities, bargaining and negotiation among interests, and political civility. In other words, liberal principles. Yet the fragility and taintedness of liberalism as a symbol in Brazil prevent many members of the intellectual community from acknowledging that they support liberal principles.

One hastens to add that in its broad outlines this pattern is by no means confined to Brazil. In varying forms and degrees it obtains in most of Latin America and much of Western Europe, among other places. In some of these other places, however, liberal democratic political institutions, processes, and political theory are more firmly established than they are in Brazil. And in all these other places the same contradictions identified in Brazil between simultaneously claiming and rejecting political liberalism also obtain.

If the fragility and ambivalence of the public, admissible commitment to democratic liberalism is one side of the threats within the intellectual community to the new tendencies, then the continuing strength of Brazilian Marxism is the other. Despite the growing influence of the new tendencies, the Marxist tradition remains strong. Pedreira, Cardoso, and others have argued persuasively that neo-Marxism comes in surges or cycles in Latin America in general and Brazil in particular.[102] For example, dependency ideas were not entirely new but rather the most recent in a series of Marxist impulses.[103] Marxism may be in a relatively low point in the cycle now, but the wheel could turn again and probably will. At that point any present-day liberal or neo-liberal could become as ideologically and politically vulnerable to leftist attacks as others have been in the past. These considerations, moreover, affect political scholarship as well as politics. Scholarship about politics is, for better or for worse, not only a search for truth but also expressive behavior with political roots and branches that are vulnerable.

It may be, as many social scientists in Brazil argue, that the present new social science trends are irreversible and that a reversion to the earlier forms of Marxist dominance is impossible.[104] On the other hand, a unilinear view of the growth of the social sciences is erroneous. So is the idea that the end of ideology has arrived among systematic interpreters of Brazilian politics. The liberal principles that are today so widely shared and respected were only a few short years ago savaged by Marxist critics as bourgeois mystifications and formalisms. Such criticism found eager listeners then, and could again. Marxism is endlessly recuperative, especially among intellectuals in capitalist countries. Its key concepts expand and contract to meet any contingency. The dialectic justifies just about anything. It can include almost everybody, but it can also exclude almost anybody. Yesterday Brazilians were told that the only solution to the country's ills was Marxist socialism and that "socialism within the framework of capitalism is not socialism."[105] Today the platform is "more democracy and less socialism."[106]

It is an extraordinary turnaround. If the wheel can turn that far that fast in one direction, one should not rule out completely either the possibility that it might keep turning or the possibility that it might turn equally far and fast in the opposite direction. The latter does not seem likely, but it is certainly not impossible. In Cardoso's words, "As much as social scientists strive to enclose the structural possibilities of history in their own constructs, history continually makes us *dupes de nous-mêmes*, and astonishes us with unexpected revelations."[107] In a sense this is banal. No sensible person doubts that history is full of surprises. Yet, if this principle is worth noting in other contexts, then it is equally worth noting in this context. Of course, it can work in favor of the new tendencies as well as against them.

Conclusion

It is important to comment on two themes: the interrelations between ideas and politics and the dangers associated with the use of labels when one analyzes intellectual currents.

As to the first theme, the topics addressed in this chapter gain a special urgency from the historical moment through which Brazil is now passing. After twenty-one years of military rule, and a complex process of political *abertura* since 1974, Brazil returned in March 1985 to a civilian political regime that has many liberal features and incomplete but significant democratic features as well.

Clearly Brazil's gradual political transformation during the last decade helped to make possible the new political discourse among intellectuals that has been discussed in this chapter. It was by no means the only reason for that change. As we have seen, various factors—endogenous changes in the institutional structure of Brazilian intellectual life, changes in the personal and professional situations of leading individuals in the intellectual community, and shifts in international intellectual and political trends, among others—also helped to shape the new modes of analysis. Nevertheless, events in the political system were among these causal elements. In this sense the changing political discourse has been the object of study—if you will, the dependent variable that I have been describing and explaining.

Important as this causal relationship is, it is not the only one that deserves mention. In addition, it is important to stress that the causal arrow also runs in the opposite direction. Not only has politics influenced the discourse; the discourse also influences politics. The ways in which intellectuals think about politics is an independent variable as well as a dependent variable.

If Brazilian intellectuals, whose influence in Brazilian politics is significantly greater than that of their U.S. counterparts in U.S. politics, refer to elections, political parties, and legislatures as mere "formalisms" that are irrelevant or even damaging to "substantive democracy," then those institutions are diminished as mechanisms for dealing with political issues in Brazil. If any capitalist state, even a "formally" democratic one, is disparaged as merely a device by which elites dominate and exploit popular classes, then the new Brazilian political regime will have even greater problems of legitimacy than it already has. If any group, individual, or class fraction within Brazil that has ties with capitalism can at any time be arbitrarily called an internal "expression" of external (capitalist) interests, or stigmatized as the "anti-nation inside the nation," then it will be impossible to recognize the legitimacy of divergent, conflicting interests or to bargain about, negotiate about, and reconcile them in a democratic fashion.

If, on the other hand, the intellectuals use different kinds of discourse, such as the ones that became prominent in the last ten years, then the prospects for the new civilian regime are improved. During this period many Brazilian Marxists who were used to seeing the capitalist state and its bourgeois accoutrements of elections and other appurtenances as the means of class oppression also came to see them as arenas within which goals of justice and human dignity could be pursued. As a result, many Marxists could and did work intellectually and politically within the electoral and legislative frameworks, and their influence was felt outside Marxist circles as well. In parallel fashion the writings of political liberals and of many of the new academic social scientists of greatly varied ideological and theoretical hues also reinforced the new tendencies in the society at large to legitimate electoral and other democratic political mechanisms, respect minority rights, honor divergent interests, and maintain civility and mutual tolerance in political interactions.

The concepts, categories, and theoretical perspectives of intellectuals are, of course, only one influence on Brazilian politics, and far from the most important one. Brazil today faces awesome economic, social, political, and international problems. These problems put enormous strains on the new political regime. The untimely passing of Tancredo Neves added even further to these strains. Will the new regime be able to hold? No one can say. What can be said, however, is that the way people think, talk, and write about politics will be one factor affecting its ultimate fate, and that Brazilian intellectuals will continue to play an important role in shaping that factor.

Now to the second theme. One of the issues that is raised by the sort of exercise undertaken in this chapter, or in Bresser Pereira's survey of "interpretations of Brazilian social formations,"[108] is that of labels or categories. Writing about the ideas of Brazilian intellectuals who interpret politics makes one particularly sensitive to the dangers of using labels. If one forgets to be sensitive about it, they soon remind one. On the other hand, one also finds that for Brazilian intellectuals no less than for others, it is impossible to avoid using labels. For example, Bresser Pereira has six categories to classify all major interpretations of Brazilian social formations during the last sixty years; of the interpretations during the last twenty years, he says that all are Marxist or have strong Marxist influences; and he says that a liberal interpretation does not exist in Brazil. The categories "functional-capitalist," "imperalist superexploitation," "new dependency," "Marxist," and "liberal" used by Bresser Pereira are labels no less than the categories "Marxist," "Marxist liberal," "political liberal," and "new academic social scientists" that are used in this chapter.

It is not hard to see why people react negatively to labels. We live in an age in which none of the theoretical and ideological perspectives passed down from previous centuries is adequate to deal with the complex problems we face today. (The most recent of the three great "isms" is more than a century old.) And there are also specific reasons why Brazilians are particularly averse to such labels. The labels are imported and in this area Brazilians, like others, prefer domestic production. Beyond this, Brazilians are world-renowned as improvisers (as witness the institution of *jeito*, a knack for circumventing formal procedure), and they are very good at it. (Alas, not only democrats but also non-democrats are good at improvisation.) If Roberto da Matta is right, and I think he is, Brazilians also prefer implicitness to explicitness and indirection and ambiguity to directness and clarity.[109] They are very good at that, too. Finally, like others, Brazilians want to keep the future open-ended and to use new concepts, theories, ideologies, and labels to deal with it.

There is no disagreeing with the foregoing, but it is only half the story. If one cannot live with labels, it is equally the case that one cannot live without them. Even geniuses at improvisation and ambiguity cannot escape this law. To begin with, language, and thus communication, are impossible without labels. This is an obvious but not a banal fact. It is a critical constraint on the objections to labels. Moreover, one needs the theoretical insights and conceptual tools that the great ideologies, despite their manifold, manifest flaws, provide. As Brazilian intellectuals have long recognized, some insights from Marx are useful. And as they have come increasingly to argue in recent years, some of the concepts and theoretical perspectives of political liberalism, whether or not the explicit terminology is used, are also useful.

In the foregoing spirit, then, I suggest—again with apologies to Antonil—that whereas in the very recent past the Brazilian intellectual community was a paradise for Marxists and a hell for liberals, today it is a purgatory for both.[110] Today one might characterize the situation as follows:

A purgatory for liberals
A purgatory for Marxists
A hell for conservatives
A paradise for nobody.

This pattern is very different from the ones that prevailed in the period from the 1940s to the 1970s. How long it will persist, and what patterns will follow it in their turn, remain to be seen.

For Marxists, the recent trends are a demotion; for liberals, a promotion. Perhaps both developments are salutory. Marxism seems to have been overvalued and political liberalism seems to have been undervalued. Yet it could be a mistake to extend either trend any further. All of Marxism should not go to Hell and all of political liberalism does not deserve to enter Heaven. All of the current "big" theoretical perspectives are flawed as comprehensive guides for analyzing and guiding political processes, although some are less flawed than others, and each has something to offer.

This awareness of the limited intellectual and political utility of all the major theoretical perspectives brings to mind this final thought. In the nineteenth century the ostensible issue in the West was the conflict between monarchy and republicanism, but the real issue was capitalism versus the proletariat. Now in the twentieth century the ostensible issue is capitalism versus the proletariat, but what is the real issue?[111] And will Brazil, an industrializing country, seek a variant of its own? These are good questions. How Brazil's citizens and intellectuals—Marxists, social democrats, liberals, unclassifiables, and others—will address them in the future remains unclear. That they can do so creatively, however, and that the task is fundamentally theirs alone, is not.

Acknowledgments

Earlier versions of this paper were presented to meetings of the Conference on Opportunities and Constraints in Peripheral Industrial Society: The Case of Brazil, sponsored by the Stanford-Berkeley Joint Center for Latin American Studies and the Instituto Universitário de Pesquisas do Rio de Janeiro (IUPERJ), in Nova Friburgo, Brazil, July 18–20, 1983, and in Berkeley, January 30–February 2, 1984. Grants for research, travel, and maintenance from the Inter-American Foundation, the Andrew W. Mellon Foundation, and the Tinker Foundation, administered through the Stanford-Berkeley Joint Center, supported this work and enabled me to spend July and August 1983 in Brazil. I am grateful to the following friends and colleagues who made helpful comments and criticisms on earlier versions of this paper: Wanderley Guilherme dos Santos, Gláucio Soares, John D. Wirth, Wayne Selcher, Thomas Skidmore, Barry Ames, Michael Barzelay, Maria Regina Soares de Lima, Olavo Brasil de Lima Júnior, Fábio Wanderley Reis, Walder de Góes, and David Fleischer. None of these organizations and individuals, however, necessarily agree with the ideas presented in the paper or is responsible for any errors of fact or interpretation in it.

Notes

1. In his book *Cultura e Opulência do Brasil* (1711), the Jesuit scholar J. A. Antonil declared Brazil to be "A hell for negroes, a purgatory for whites, and a paradise for mulattoes." This well-known aphorism is the basis for the opening lines, which were suggested to me by my colleague Professor John Wirth. For a survey of six major interpretations of Brazil from the 1920s through the 1970s, see Luíz Carlos Bresser Pereira, "Seis Interpretações sôbre o Brasil," *Dados* 25, no. 3 (1982): 269–306. Bresser Pereira's survey supports the proposition that during most of this century the Brazilian intellectual community was indeed "a paradise for conservatives." The issues involved in the use of categories such as liberal, Marxist, and conservative in the Brazilian context are discussed at several points in this article, especially in the sections on new tendencies and the conclusion.

2. Bresser Pereira, ibid. Bresser Pereira's article has now been published in English translation as "Six Interpretations of the Brazilian Social Formation," *Latin American Perspectives* 11, no. 1 (Winter 1984): 35–72. In the present article,

however, all the citations are to the original article published in *Dados* and all translations into English are my own.

3. Ibid., pp. 278–284.

4. Ibid., pp. 284–287.

5. Ibid., pp. 287–294.

6. Ibid., pp. 294–298.

7. Ibid., p. 298.

8. Although the scope and depth of his article are formidable, Bresser Pereira himself (p. 298) explicitly disavows the idea that his coverage is comprehensive. I seek among other things to address some interpretations he has omitted or emphasized less than others.

9. Fernando Henrique Cardoso, *O Modêlo Político Brasileiro e Outros Ensaios* (São Paulo: Difel, 1972), p. 200.

10. Fernando Henrique Cardoso and Enzo Faletto, *Dependency and Development in Latin America* (Berkeley and Los Angeles: University of California Press, 1979), p. xxiv.

11. Fernando Henrique Cardoso, "'Teoria da Dependência' ou Análises Concretas de Situações de Dependência?," *Estudos I*, CEBRAP, São Paulo, 1971.

12. Fernando Henrique Cardoso, *As Idéias e seu Lugar: Ensaios sôbre as Teorias do Desenvolvimento* (Petrópolis: Vozes, 1980), pp. 100–101.

13. Cardoso and Faletto, *Dependency and Development in Latin America*, passim.

14. Fernando Henrique Cardoso, "Um Cientista do Ar," *Fôlha de São Paulo*, January 7, 1977, p. 3.

15. Ibid.; also Cardoso and Faletto, *Dependency and Development*, p. xii.

16. See note 19 below.

17. Joseph Kahl, *Modernization, Exploitation, and Dependency in Latin America* (New Brunswick, N.J.: Transaction Books, 1976), p. 129.

18. Quoted in Ibid., p. 188.

19. See, for example, Cardoso, "Notas sobre el estado actual de los estudios sobre la dependencia," *Revista latinoamericana de ciencias sociales* (FLACSO), Santiago de Chile, no. 4 (December 1972): 3–31; idem, "O Inimigo de Papel (The Paper Enemy)," *Latin American Perspectives* 1, no. 1 (Spring 1974): 64–74; idem, "The Consumption of Dependency Theory," *Latin American Research Review* 12, no. 3 (1977): 7–24, reprinted in *Idéias e seu Lugar* (1980); Cardoso and Faletto, *Dependency and Development*, esp. pp. vii–xxv and pp. 199–216.

20. Cardoso, "Notas sobre el estado actual de los estudios sobre la dependencia," p. 17; also Cardoso and Faletto, *Dependency and Development*, pp. ix–xxiv.

21. Cardoso and Faletto, *Dependency and Development*, pp. ix, xiii.

22. Ibid., p. 178.

23. Ibid., pp. xxiii–xxiv.

24. For example, in Ibid., pp. 178, 195.

25. For example, in Cardoso, *As Idéias e seu Lugar*, p. 118.

26. Fernando Henrique Cardoso, "On the Characterization of Authoritarian Regimes in Latin America," in David Collier (ed.), *The New Authoritarianism in Latin America* (Princeton: Princeton University Press, 1979), p. 38.

27. Ibid.

28. Cardoso and Faletto, *Dependency and Development*, pp. 199–216.

29. For more on this point, see the conclusion.

30. I am grateful to Edgar Magalhães and, especially, Marilena Chauí for informative conversations which helped me to understand these changes. The

discussion of the first type of Brazilian social democracy draws heavily on my conversations with Professor Chauí. Neither of them, however, is responsible for the interpretations and factual account rendered here.

31. Various memoirs of these experiences have been written. See, for example, Fernando Gabeira, *O Quê é Isso, Companheiro?* (Rio de Janeiro: Condecri, 1979).

32. See Carlos Nelson Coutinho, *A Democracia como Valor Universal: Notas sôbre a Questão Democrática no Brasil* (São Paulo: Ciências Humanas, 1980). Coutinho's reservations about the term "Eurocommunism" are expressed on pp. 13–16. See also Leandro Konder, *A Democracia e os Communistas no Brasil* (Rio de Janeiro: Graal, 1980), and Luís Werneck Viana, "Comentários," in Bolivar Lamounier, et al (eds.), *Direito, Cidadania e Participação* (São Paulo: Queiroz, 1981), pp. 258–264.

33. Marilena Chauí, *Cultura e Democracia: O Discurso Competente e Outras Falas*, 3d edition (São Paulo: Moderna, 1984), pp. 179–180.

34. See, for example, Francisco Weffort, *Por Quê Democracia?*, 2d edition, (São Paulo, 1984); Marilena Chauí, *Cultura e Democracia*, op. cit.

35. Coutinho, *A Democracia como Valor Universal*, p. 40. Coutinho tempers his criticism by adding, "At several other points in his rich reflection, however, Cardoso overcomes the limits of liberalism."

36. See "Não Encontramos um só Liberalismo, mas Vários," in Maria Lúcia de Oliveira (ed.), *A Conquista do Espaço Político* (São Paulo: Jornal da Tarde, 1983), p. 102.

37. As quoted in Kahl, *Modernization, Exploitation, Dependency*, p. 179, emphasis added. See also note 85 below.

38. See note 49 below.

39. The best indicator of this, although by no means the only one, is the change from the 1969 edition of Cardoso and Faletto, *Dependencia y desarrollo en America Latina* (Mexico: Siglo Veintiuno, 1969) to the 1979 English edition, *Dependency and Development in Latin America*. For an analysis of continuity and change in the two editions see the review essay by Robert Packenham, "Plus Ça Change . . . ," *Latin American Research Review* 17, no. 1 (1982): 131–151.

40. As sources here I rely upon Fernando Henrique Cardoso, *Democracia para Mudar: 30 Horas de Entrevistas*, Coleção Documentos da Democracia Brasileira, volume 4 (Rio de Janeiro: Paz e Terra, 1978), an edited collection of 30 hours of Cardoso's press interviews between 1974 and 1978; statements by Cardoso in *Revista do PMDB*, Ano 1, Numero 1 (July 1981); and the Brazilian press.

41. Cardoso, *Democracia para Mudar*, p. 33.

42. Cardoso in *Revista do PMDB*, p. 37.

43. Ibid., p. 36; also Cardoso, *Democracia para Mudar*, pp. 32–33.

44. Cardoso, *Democracia para Mudar*, p. 59.

45. Ibid., p. 84.

46. Ibid., p. 105.

47. Bresser Pereira, "Seis Interpretações sôbre o Brasil," p. 298.

48. dos Santos, *Ordem Burguesa e Liberalismo Político* (São Paulo: Duas Cidades, 1978).

49. In order to develop this point, I wish at the outset to define my terms. By liberalism, I mean political liberalism, not economic and social liberalism. In this sense political liberalism is not logically or definitionally associated with any particular type of economic or social system. Political liberalism involves political liberty or freedom—freedom of association; freedom of thought and speech; freedom of religion, assembly and the press; and so on. It may logically

occur in various kinds of cultural and economic systems. Political liberalism in this sense of an "assemblage of basic freedoms" is part of "the heritage of civilized life" that cannot be located exclusively in any particular political, economic, social, or religious creed. See Ibid., p. 67. In this sense there are, I believe, a number of liberal interpretations of Brazilian politics that have manifested themselves in a variety of ways and at different moments during recent decades. Like Marxist liberals, political liberals are uneasy with the term "liberal" because of its historic and recent associations and connotations. Political liberals, however, are less likely than Marxist liberals to seek to combine their liberal political categories and principles with Marxist premises and categories that are probably incompatible.

50. See Sérgio Buarque de Holanda, *Raizes do Brasil* (Rio de Janeiro: José Olympio, 1956); Raymundo Faoro, *Os Donos do Poder* (Rio de Janeiro: Globo, 1958); Víctor Nunes Leal, *O Município e o Regime Representativo no Brasil: Contribuição ao Estudo do 'Coronelismo'* (Rio de Janeiro: Revista Forense, 1948).

51. Bolivar Lamounier, "Representação Política: A Importância de Certos Formalismos," in Bolivar Lamounier, Francisco Weffort, and Maria Victória Benevides (eds.), *Direito, Cidadania e Participação* (São Paulo: T. A. Queiroz, 1981), pp. 230–257; idem, "Opening Through Elections," *Government and Opposition* 19, no. 2 (Spring 1984): 167–177. The passage quoted is from the latter article at p. 168. Two other important papers by Lamounier are "O Discurso e o Processo," (São Paulo, mimeographed, about 1978), and "Apontamentos sôbre a Questão Democrática Brasileira," (São Paulo, mimeographed, about 1983).

52. See especially Wanderley Guilherme dos Santos, *Ordem Burguesa e Liberalismo Político;* idem, *Poder e Política: Crônica do Autoritarismo Brasileiro* (Rio de Janeiro: Forense-Universitário, 1978); idem, *Cidadania e Justiça: A Política Social na Ordem Brasileira* (Rio de Janeiro: Campus, 1979); idem, "Reflexões sobre a Questão do Liberalismo," in Bolivar Lamounier, et al (eds.), *Direito, Cidadania e Participação,* pp. 155–188; idem, *Kantianas Brasileiras: A Dual-Ética da Razão Política Nacional* (Rio de Janeiro: Paz e Terra, 1984).

53. Fernando Pedreira, *Março 31: Civís e Militares no Processo da Crise Brasiliera* (Rio de Janeiro: José Álvaro, 1964); idem, *Brasil Política, 1964–1975* (São Paulo: Difel, 1975); idem, *A Liberdade e a Ostra* (Rio de Janeiro: Nova Fronteira, 1976); idem, *Impávido Colosso* (Rio de Janeiro: Nova Fronteira, 1982).

54. From the dust jacket of Pedreira, *Impávido Colosso.*

55. As a reviewer of Pedreira's book *Impávido Colosso* put it, "The threads which tie these essays together are antidogmatism, liberalism, and the conviction that despite all its flaws democracy is still the best way to solve human problems." "A Política com Humor," *Jornal do Brasil,* March 28, 1982, "Caderno Especial," p. 4.

56. José Guilherme Merquior, *A Natureza do Processo* (Rio de Janeiro: Nova Fronteira, 1982); idem, *O Argumento Liberal* (Rio de Janeiro: Nova Fronteira, 1983); idem, "Power and Identity: Politics and Ideology in Latin America," *Government and Opposition* 19, no. 2 (Spring 1984); 239–249.

57. Merquior, *O Argumento Liberal,* back cover.

58. Ibid., p. 12.

59. See Maria Lúcia de Oliveira (ed.), *A Conquista do Espaço Político* (São Paulo: Jornal da Tarde, 1983).

60. Maria Lúcia de Oliveira, "Introdução" in ibid., p. 14.

61. Fernando Pedreira, "Dois Grandes Desafios: Um vem do Socialismo," in ibid., p. 117.

62. Maria Lúcia de Oliveira, "Introdução" in ibid., pp. 15–16.

63. Wanderly Guilherme dos Santos, "A Quem Sirvirão as Instituições Liberais?," in ibid., pp. 117–120. See also Lamounier, "Representação Política."

64. Pedreira, *Março 31*, p. 177.

65. Hélgio Trindade, "Paradoxos da Conjuntura Política: A Sociedade Civil sob Pressão," in *Brasil em Perspectiva: Dilemas da Abertura Política* (Pôrto Alegre: Sulina, 1982), p. 14.

66. Ibid., pp. 14–15.

67. Bolivar Lamounier, "Expansão e Institucionalização das Ciências Sociais no Brasil: Um Estudo Preliminar," unpublished manuscript, 1982, cited by Otávio Guilherme Velho, "Processos Sociais no Brasil pós-64: As Ciências Sociais," in Bernardo Sorj and Maria Hermínia Tavares de Almeida (eds.), *Sociedade e Política no Brasil Pós-64* (São Paulo: Brasiliense, 1983), p. 246. See also Bolivar Lamounier, "A Ciência Política no Brasil: Roteiro para um Balanço Crítico," in Bolivar Lamounier (ed.), *A Ciência Política nos Anos 80* (Brasília: Editôra da Universidade de Brasília, 1982), pp. 407–435.

68. Lamounier in ibid., p. 247.

69. Velho in ibid., pp. 251–261.

70. See CAPES (Coordenação de Aperfeiçoamento de Pessoal de Nível Superior), Ministério de Educação e Cultura, *Pós-Graduação: Catálogo de Cursos, 1980*, vol. 4, *Ciências Sociais* (Brasília: CAPES, 1982), pp. 25–70.

71. I have in mind the work of such people as Alexandre de Souza Barros, Antônio Octávio Cintra, Benício Schmidt, Bolivar Lamounier, Celso Lafer, Edmundo Campos Coelho, Edson Nunes de Oliveira, Eli Diniz, Elisa Reis, Fábio Wanderley Reis, Gláucio Soares, Hélgio Trindade, José Murilo de Carvalho, Maria do Carmo Campello de Souza, Maria Helena Moreira Alves, Maria Hermínia Tavares de Almeida, Malori Pompermayer, Olavo Brasil de Lima Júnior, Paulo Sérgio Pinheiro, Renato Boschi, Simon Schwartzman, Vilmar Faria, and Wanderley Guilherme dos Santos. This list does not claim to be comprehensive. Still others working in the area of Brazil's foreign relations are noted below in note 81.

72. Otávio G. Velho, "Processos Sociais no Brasil Pós-64: as Ciências Sociais," p. 245.

73. See note 12 above.

74. Velho, "Processos Sociais," p. 260, emphasis in original.

75. Ibid., pp. 249–261.

76. Ibid.

77. Lamounier, "Representação Política"; José Murilo de Carvalho, *A Construção da Ordem: A Elite Política Imperial* (Rio de Janeiro: Campus, 1980); Simon Schwartzman, *Bases do Autoritarismo Brasileiro*, 2d edition (Rio de Janeiro: Campus, 1982); dos Santos, *Kantianas Brasileiras.*

78. See Mark Osiel, "Going to the People: Intellectuals and Popular Culture in Brazil," unpublished paper, Harvard University and Universidade de São Paulo, August 1983.

79. See Scott Mainwaring, "The Catholic Church and Politics in Brazil, 1916–1982," unpublished Ph.D. dissertation, Department of Political Science, Stanford University, 1983. A revised version is forthcoming from Stanford University Press.

80. Gerson Moura and Maria Regina Soares de Lima, "Relações Internacionais e Política Externa Brasileira: Uma Resenha Bibliográfica," *Boletim Informativo e*

172   Robert A. Packenham

Bibliográfico de Ciências Sociais (O BIB), Rio de Janeiro, no. 13 (1st Semester 1982): 5.

81. I have in mind such people as Alexandre de Souza Barros, Carlos Estevam Martins, Celso Lafer, Gerson Moura, Maria Regina Soares de Lima, Mônica Hirst, and Walder de Góes. My list is very short. For a much longer and more informed list, as well as a very useful, detailed bibliography and a good short bibliographical essay on these matters, see ibid., pp. 5–36.

82. For example, Golbery do Couto e Silva, *Geopolítica do Brasil* (Rio de Janeiro: José Olympio, 1967); Carlos de Meira Mattos, *Brasil: Geopolítica e Destino* (Rio de Janeiro: José Olympio, 1975); José Osvaldo de Meira Penna, *Política Externa: Segurança e Desenvolvimento* (Rio de Janeiro: Agir, 1967); idem, *Psicologia do Subdesenvolvimento* (Rio de Janeiro: APEC, 1972); idem, *Em Berço Esplêndido: Ensaios de Psicologia Coletiva Brasileira* (Rio de Janeiro: José Olympio, 1974); idem, "The U.S. As Scapegoat: A Psychological Approach to Foreign Policy Problems," *Catholicism in Crisis* (July 1983): 30–34.

83. Hélio Jaguaribe, *Political Development* (New York: Harper and Row, 1973), esp. chapter 26; idem, *Brasil: Crise e Alternativas* (Rio de Janeiro: Zahar, 1974); idem, *Introdução ao Desenvolvimento Social: As Perspectivas Liberal e Marxista e os Problemas da Sociedade não Repressiva* (Rio de Janeiro: Paz e Terra, 1978); Celso Furtado, "Dependence in a United World," *Alternatives 8* (1982): 259–284.

84. Furtado, "Dependence in a United World." This summary draws on the editor's precis on p. 259.

85. *Jornal do Brasil*, August 11, 1982, p. 4.

86. *Revista do PMDB* 1, no. 1 (July 1981): 7–8.

87. During interviews with Brazilian scholars in Rio de Janeiro, São Paulo, and Brasília in 1982 and especially in 1983, I was told frequently that the new tendencies were more or less permanent and that a return to the earlier pattern of Marxist dominance was most unlikely, if not impossible.

88. According to Warren Hoge, Brizola's performance "has been a study in how to be a politician, something that has been out of style in Brazil for the past two decades." According to Hoge, Brizola has also been remarkably understanding of and empathetic toward his erstwhile enemies, the Brazilian military: "We civilians," Hoge quotes Brizola as saying, "have to understand the armed forces, and the Brazilian left and many liberals have been blind about it. This is not Central America, and the military here is not Somoza's national guard. They represent in our history a kind of skeleton that keeps the national organism on its feet. They are the best defined national structure." Warren Hoge, "Brazil's Governors Find Coffers Bare," *New York Times*, July 7, 1983, p. 4.

89. Quoted in Hoge, Ibid.

90. See note 86.

91. For details, see "Esquerdas Convivem na Oposição," *Jornal do Brasil*, August 22, 1982, 1aCaderno, p. 5.

92. Ibid.

93. See Simon Schwartzman, *Ciência, Universidade e Ideologia* (Rio de Janeiro: Zahar, 1981), p. 143.

94. Quoted in Kahl, *Modernization, Exploitation, Dependency*, p. 184.

95. Bresser Pereira, "Seis Interpretações sôbre o Brasil," p. 298.

96. dos Santos, *Kantianas Brasileiras*, pp. 13–14, emphasis in original.

97. On the other hand, these relationships do not always operate in the ways we expect them to. For instance, the most repressive political phase (1968–1974) was accompanied not by the most severe economic strains but by the so-called economic miracle; moreover, political *distensão* and *abertura* occurred not in the most "favorable" economic climate but in a period of slowing growth followed by stagnation. Indeed, it would be more correct to say that *abertura* was enhanced by a weakening economy, which eroded support for the regime among powerful economic groups that had earlier supported it. So the relations between these external and internal macrovariables, and the consequent prospects for neo-liberalism, are complex.

98. Among the most important such works are Faoro, *Os Donos do Poder;* Roberto da Matta, *Carnavais, Malandros, e Heróis: Para uma Sociologia da Dilema Brasileira* (Rio de Janeiro: Zahar, 1978); Schwartzman, *Bases do Autoritarismo Brasileiro;* Carvalho, *A Construção da Ordem;* dos Santos, *Kantaianas Brasileiras.*

99. Juan Linz and Alfred Stepan (eds.), *The Breakdown of Democratic Regimes* (Baltimore: The Johns Hopkins University Press, 1978), especially volume 1, passim, and volume 3, pp. 116–120 and 142–143.

100. Quoted in "The Battle for Southern Europe," *The Economist*, August 10, 1974, p. 15.

101. Schwartzman, *Ciência, Ideologia, e Universidade*, p. 143.

102. Pedreira, *Março 31*, pp. 146–150; Cardoso, *As Idéias e seu Lugar*, pp. 90–101.

103. Cardoso, Ibid.

104. See note 87.

105. Cardoso, *Democracia para Mudar*, p. 84.

106. Cardoso as quoted in "Lições da Política," *Isto É*, Ano 8, no. 380 (April 4, 1984), p. 23.

107. Cardoso, *Idéias e seu Lugar*, p. 107.

108. Bresser Pereira, *Seis Interpretações sôbre o Brasil.*

109. Robert da Matta, "Sôbre a Questão da Cidadania num Universo Relacional," paper delivered to the Conference on Opportunities and Constraints in Peripheral Industrial Society: The Case of Brazil, Stanford-Berkeley Joint Center for Latin American Studies, Berkeley, January 30–February 2, 1984. More generally, see idem, *Carnavais, Malandros, e Heróis.*

110. See note 1 above.

111. According to the Stanford historian David M. Kennedy, *Stanford Observer*, May 1982, this is what André Malraux said to President John F. Kennedy in 1962.

5

Transitions Through Transaction: Democratization in Brazil and Spain

Donald Share and Scott Mainwaring

In the 1970s, scholarly interest was focused on authoritarianism and the breakdown of democracy, but recently the question of transitions from authoritarianism to democracy has become a central theme in comparative politics. The emergence of democratic regimes in Spain, Portugal, Greece, Peru, Ecuador, Bolivia, Argentina, Brazil, and Uruguay has made the transition from authoritarianism to democracy one of the outstanding political issues of our time. Yet despite the evident importance of these transitions, only recently has much been written on the topic. Consequently, there is ample space for further historical, theoretical, and comparative contributions.[1] This chapter is especially geared toward the comparative dimension of the task.

Previous chapters in this volume have discussed various aspects of political liberalization in Brazil. This chapter has a different purpose: to analyze aspects of the logic of a form of transition from authoritarianism to democratic rule that we term "transitions through transaction" and to place the Brazilian case in comparative perspective with Spain.

The term "transitions through transaction" refers to cases in which the authoritarian regime initiates the transition, establishes some limits to political changes, and remains a relatively significant electoral force during the transition.[2] The term "transaction" connotes negotiation (usually implicit) between elites of the authoritarian regime and the democratic opposition. But this negotiation does not take place among equals; the regime takes the initiative in beginning liberalization, and during most of the process it remains in a position to significantly influence the course of political change.

However, it is also important to emphasize that the level of regime control is relative. There is a genuine process of negotiation; the opposition can win significant victories that redefine the political struggle. In neither Brazil nor Spain did the authoritarian regime completely determine the nature of the transitions; on the contrary, the liberalization process inherently allowed opposition forces to amass some weight in the political struggle. Furthermore, in both cases, the regime's control declined as the transitions progressed; in Spain, this decline occurred after the elections of June 1977, and in Brazil the decline accelerated after 1982.

In Spain, after forty years of franquist authoritarianism, a full-fledged parliamentary democracy has emerged. Between Francisco Franco's death in November 1975 and the implementation of a democratic constitution in December 1978, members of the franquist regime initiated a democratic reform through the existing authoritarian political structures. Since 1975 the franquist regime has been largely dismantled, a democratic constitution has been written, a competitive party system has emerged, and there has been an alternation of political power and a consolidation of democracy at all levels of Spanish politics.[3]

In 1974 Brazil's military regime began to promote a slow and gradual liberalization. Challenges to its authority notwithstanding, the military government exercised significant control over this liberalization process until 1983, when the government began to experience a more rapid erosion. Indeed, by late 1983 the Brazilian case no longer clearly approximated the ideal type of a transition through transaction. This liberalization process eventually culminated in the indirect election of a civilian president from an opposition party, Tancredo Neves, in January 1985. Although it remains to be seen how stable this fledgling democracy will be and how fully it will eliminate the remnants of military rule, Neves's election marked the demise of the most successful and enduring bureaucratic-authoritarian regime in Latin America.[4] Neves died before being inaugurated, but his legal successor, Vice-president José Sarney, was sworn in as president and carried on the democratization process.

Although Brazil's transition to democracy was more protracted and is far more recent and uncertain, the two transitions had significant similarities. All political transitions are characterized by constant negotiation, unexpected changes, and unforeseen circumstances, but compared to the norm, in both Spain and Brazil elites controlled important aspects of political change. They excluded some actors, insisted on impunity for regime leaders, and blocked radical changes.

The Spanish and Brazilian cases are among the few contemporary transitions through transaction, and they also stand out because of the relatively low level of violence and the relative degree of stability. These two cases may suggest a desirable alternative for authoritarian elites who wish to minimize the risk, uncertainty, and cost of democratization while still moving away from authoritarian rule. At the same time, it is our contention that transitions through transaction, although seemingly more stable, are difficult to achieve and can only be effected under certain conditions. Furthermore, we argue that this form of transition is likely to entail some political, economic, and social costs.

By comparing these two important and potentially influential examples we hope to shed some light on aspects of the logic of transitions through transaction. We begin by addressing the paradoxical question of why authoritarian elites undertake democratic transition. We then examine the question of the conditions that make possible this type of transition. Finally, we discuss some of the costs and benefits associated with transition through transaction. In addressing all of these questions we analyze some of the major similarities and differences between the two cases.

Democratization and Transition Through Transaction

Before discussing the Brazilian and Spanish transitions to democracy, it is necessary to define briefly some basic terms.[5] By democracy, we mean a political regime with free competitive elections, without major proscriptions, and with universal adult suffrage. Democratic regimes afford freedom of speech and the press, freedom of political association, and individual rights. There are competing definitions of democracy that focus on outcomes rather than procedures, but we believe that there are good reasons for focusing on these institutional arrangements. Although these institutions ensure neither full governmental responsibility nor socioeconomic justice, they do ensure the basic rights and political competititon that are essential to democracy as we understand it. Although this definition suffices to characterize a liberal democracy, democracy can always be expanded, both in competitiveness and participation.[6]

Democracy implies the possibility of an alternation in power. In this sense, a transition to democracy involves more than a liberalization of an authoritarian regime. Liberalization refers to a decline in repression and the reestablishment of most basic civil and political rights but without permitting competitive elections that would allow for an alternation in power. Democratization refers to the establishment of institutional arrangements that make possible such an alternation. Transitions to democracy involve both liberalization and democratization.

These definitions are important because they point to a major difference between Brazil and Spain. Although franquism was unquestionably an authoritarian regime until the dictator's death, inchoate liberalization in Spain began in the late 1950s. Democratization began only with the accession of King Juan Carlos in November 1975. The transition was complete, though democracy was not consolidated, with the popular approval of a democratic constitution in December 1978. Compared with the Brazilian case, Spain's transition to democracy was relatively rapid and had clearer beginning and ending points.

In Brazil, liberalization began in 1974 with the presidency of General Ernesto Geisel and continued until 1985. Democratization began in 1980 with the party reform and the promise of open, competitive elections for state governors in 1982, which allowed for the first competition for major decisionmaking arenas since the coup. The empowering of José Sarney as acting president in March 1985 marked the inauguration of a liberal democratic regime, but democratization in Brazil has not gone as far as in Spain. The continuing existence of the constitution established by the authoritarian regime, the use of repression in many regions of the country, and the strength of authoritarian forces are among the most significant limits to a more complete democratization. In comparative perspective, Brazil's transition was singularly slow and protracted.

In order to understand better the specific qualities of transitions through transaction, it is useful to locate them within the universe of non-revolutionary transitions to democracy. In the classical cases of democratization (England, the United States, Scandinavia, and other Northern European countries), an oligarchic regime gradually extended participation and contestation over a long period of time, often involving centuries of incremental change. Some South American countries (Chile, Uruguay, and Argentina) followed this evolutionary path in the late nineteenth and early twentieth centuries, but this classical route is probably historically closed.

Democratization in the classical cases occurred in a context of limited popular mobilization, limited or non-existent cultural legitimacy of democratic institutions, and limited global interdependence and external influence in domestic politics. This context facilitated a gradual, elite-controlled democratization that seems highly unlikely in today's world. It is worth noting, however, that contemporary transitions through transaction share a major similarity with these classical cases—entrenched elites control much of the democratization process. Like the classical cases, transitions through transaction involve considerable continuity of political structures, elites, and practices.

Types of Transitions to Democracy

Transitions through transaction are neither the only nor the most common form of democratic transition. According to the amount of control authoritarian elites exercise, we can analytically distinguish between three ideal types of transitions to democracy. These ideal types are deductive constructs and no case will completely conform to them.

The most common type is a *transition after regime breakdown or collapse*, in which the authoritarian elites exercise almost no control. Whether through military defeat at the hands of an external force or profound internal crisis, these regimes become thoroughly discredited and delegitimized. This type of transition to democracy involves significant institutional changes and a rupture in patterns of political authority. Examples include Germany, Italy, and Japan after World War II; Greece and Portugal in 1974; and Argentina in 1982–1983.

In a second ideal type, *transition through extrication,* the authoritarian elites set limits regarding the form and timing of political change, but are less capable of controlling the transition beyond the moment of the first elections. These authoritarian regimes withdraw from power because of their low level of legitimacy and internal cohesion but still manage to retain some control of the transition. Although it is appropriate to speak of the erosion of these regimes, they manage to avoid a breakdown or collapse. For a variety of reasons, including a lack of popular support, the authoritarian leadership decides to extricate itself from power. As is the case with transitions through transaction, democratization involves negotiation between regime and opposition, but the terms of negotiation are less favorable to the regime. Examples would include Peru (1980), Bolivia (1979–1980), and Uruguay (1982–1985). By 1983–1984, the Brazilian case began to assume some features of transition through extrication.

The third ideal type, and the one with which we are concerned, is *transition through transaction*. Elites from the authoritarian regime initially control most aspects of the transition. In contrast to situations of regime collapse, they initiate the process of liberalization. Liberalization and democratization come about as choices made fundamentally by the regime. Popular mobilization, foreign pressures, and domestic opposition may be important, but in the initial phase they are secondary factors in shaping the process. Over time, the regime's control declines noticeably, but authoritarian elites still exercise greater capacity to shape the broad contours of the political process than in other types of transition.

The Exercise of Control in Transitions Through Transaction

One important element of control in transitions through transaction is the timing of political change. By regulating the pace of implementing reforms, authoritarian elites attempt to guard against losing control. Even though they may be committed to reestablishing democracy, they believe it is necessary to effect reforms in a gradual way. Incremental change elicits less resistance within the authoritarian coalition and prevents disaffected interests from unifying in opposition to democratization. The gradual character of the transition fosters the perception that order and stability are intact.

Although the Spanish transition transpired in a relatively short time period, President Adolfo Suárez staggered political reform when possible.[7] Despite the uncertainty and improvisation inherent in all regime change, democratization involved a well-paced set of reforms whose timing was, for the most part, determined by the regime in the period before the 1977 general elections. These changes began with the initial limited amnesties in the summer of 1976 and continued through the constitutional reform and popular referendum of late 1976, the legalization of the Spanish Communist Party (PCE) in April 1977, the dismantling of franquist institutions in May 1977, and the parliamentary elections in June of that year. By staggering the reforms, Suárez avoided antagonizing too many sectors of the franquist regime simultaneously. The last set of democratic reforms provoked open hostility from the military and other franquist hardliners, but the president had already gained considerable momentum and popular support.

Although the timing of liberalization in Brazil changed in response to opposition demands, that country's leaders conducted a process of reform that spanned more than a decade. Major highlights of this process included the relaxation of repression in 1974, the political amnesty and reestablishment of major civil liberties in 1979, the direct gubernatorial elections in 1982, and the election of an opposition president in 1985. There were some reverses in democratization and some unplanned advances, but until 1983 the regime's ability to limit change was significant.

In addition to controlling the timing of democratization, regimes undergoing transition through transaction are likely to insist upon excluding some actors from the transition. Where authoritarian regimes come to power with the purpose of defeating a perceived leftist threat, for a protracted period of time the leaders are likely to view the left as an enemy with whom no negotiation is possible. Even though time may erode the sense of threat, most of the regime still views the left's reincorporation with hostility. The possibility of negotiating with the left depends on the timing and intensity of previous leftist mobilization. The insistence upon prohibiting the left from politics tends to be greatest where the perceived threat was strongest and where the memories of those threats are most vivid.

In both Spain and Brazil the decision to democratize was contingent on guarantees of the Communist left's exclusion. In the initial phases of Spain's democratization there was a consensus among regime reformers and the moderate democratic opposition that the Communist left would be excluded. Suárez's decision to legalize the Spanish Communist Party six weeks before the June 1977 elections shocked and disappointed virtually the entire franquist elite, which had supported democratization under the condition that the extreme left be permanently proscribed.[8] In Brazil, the circumscription of the Marxist left lasted longer and was more extensive. The Marxist parties remained illegal until May 1985, and to the end of military rule there continued to be sporadic repression against the Marxist left, the Catholic left, and popular leaders.[9]

A third area of control concerns policy outputs. Some vital questions concerning economic, social, and political life are proscribed from the agenda. In transitions through transaction initiated by conservative authoritarian regimes, we can expect regime leaders to rule out structural socioeconomic change. In Spain, for example, the 1978 constitution explicitly guaranteed the preservation of a capitalist economy. In both countries, agrarian reform was excluded from the agenda. Neither transition was accompanied by any attempt to radically improve income distribution or to significantly change the model of development. This was especially evident in Brazil, where the plight of urban marginals and peasants was relegated to a back burner.

Transitions through transaction also rule out punitive measures directed against leaders from the authoritarian period, regardless of their involvement in repressive activities. Authoritarian leaders will not initiate democratization unless they are assured that they will not be prosecuted. In Spain and Brazil there have been almost no cases of punishment or forced exile of authoritarian leaders. This contrasts markedly with many cases of regime collapse (Germany and Italy, 1945; Greece and Portugal, 1974; Argentina, 1983) where some leaders from the previous regime have been brought to trial or forced to leave the country.

In transitions through transaction, the authoritarian leadership continues to enjoy a meaningful level of popular support. As a result, elections offer the possibility of retaining some power. Even if they do not win open competitive elections, the authoritarian regime's elites will be a serious electoral force. This ability to compete in open elections is the primary factor distinguishing these transitions from transitions through extrication. The authoritarian leadership's confidence in its ability to fare well in democratic elections explains its concern about the minutiae of electoral laws.

The franquist elite bargained energetically to achieve an electoral law that would favor conservative, rural Spain and that would benefit large parties and widely recognized politicians. In Brazil, the manipulation of electoral laws to favor the regime went to extremes. The government altered the electoral laws substantially in 1977, 1978, 1981, and 1982, attempting to enhance its own situation. In 1979 the regime felt that it would fare better against a divided opposition, so it imposed party reform that split the opposition. By late 1981, it realized that the opposition parties would unite against the regime, so it issued another decree preventing electoral alliances. The representation system set up by these manipulations of electoral laws enabled the regime to retain a large majority in the Senate despite the opposition's majority of the popular vote.[10]

The fact that these regimes believe they can compete in elections minimizes their fears about democratization and maximizes their sense of control. This provides some security and reduces the risks of democratization for the entire authoritarian coalition. Eventually, the authoritarian elites with the best electoral prospects begin to have an active stake in the holding of elections. Consequently, these elites stand to lose a great deal in the event of an authoritarian involution. Under these circumstances, although the hardliners may continue to threaten a coup, the prospects for a long-term reversal diminish. The authoritarian leadership committed to elections then shares a significant interest with the moderate democratic opposition, creating a potential schism in the authoritarian coalition. These leaders are likely to attempt to isolate the authoritarian hardliners, both to diminish the prospects of an involution and to further their own electoral goals by distancing themselves from the far right.[11] President Geisel's firing of General Sílvio Frota, minister of the army, in 1977, because Frota threatened the liberalization process, was one key case of marginalizing the far right in Brazil. In Spain,

President Suárez's decision to form a center-right electoral coalition in the spring of 1977, displacing the rightist Popular Alliance, also exemplifies this marginalization.

Continuity During the Transition

One of the consequences of the significant level of control over the transition is the continuity in many areas from the authoritarian to the democratic period. Although there is likely to be some elite turnover, especially with the marginalization of the hardliners, some high level elites from the authoritarian period retain positions of prestige and power. In the democratic period, Spain's chief of state and first two heads of government were strongly identified with the franquist regime. Eight years after the first democratic elections, Spain's second largest political party was headed by Manuel Fraga Iribarne, a top cabinet minister under Franco. In Brazil the continuity of elites from the blatantly authoritarian period throughout the whole transition was pronounced. There was a major turnover of elites in March 1985, but even so, the new president, original minister of economics, and minister of communications, among others, had occupied major positions in the military regime. The leaders of the transition helped engineer the coup in 1964 and occupied important positions during most of the regime. President João Figueiredo (1979–1985), who oversaw Brazil's *abertura*, was previously head of the National Intelligence Service (SNI), the secret service apparatus that was the core of the most repressive side of the regime. Figueiredo's minister of planning, minister of the interior, minister of social welfare, and chief of the civilian cabinet all held cabinet positions during parts of the 1960s and 1970s.

Continuity can also be witnessed in major social institutions. In transitions initiated by conservative authoritarian regimes, democratization requires at least tacit consent from the armed forces. This situation may constitute a serious obstacle as the military is generally a key component of the authoritarian coalition and frequently opposes democratic change. Its control over the means of coercion gives it a special ability to impede the transition. As a result, transition through transaction requires a modus vivendi between the armed forces and the government, usually in the form of a guarantee of the continuation of military autonomy. Unlike cases of regime collapse in which the military is discredited, transitions through transaction initially do not significantly alter the military's position of power.[12]

The role of the military posed difficult problems in both Brazil and Spain. Both countries' armed forces constituted the outstanding threat to democratization; military hardliners repeatedly threatened to reverse the process. In Spain, the 1981 coup attempt came close to undermining the democracy. Were it not for the intervention of King Juan Carlos, Spain's highest ranking military official, the plot might have succeeded.

Brazil's armed forces presented a more constant if less dramatic threat to democratization.[13]

We can also expect transitions through transaction to exhibit considerable continuity in political structures and institutions. Legislatures, constitutions, and judiciaries may all remain essentially unchanged during an initial period. For example, there was a continuity in the office of head of state between franquism and democracy since Franco designated his own successor in 1969. Brazil's democratization has not yet included the writing of a new constitution, scheduled for 1986 or 1987, and in both countries the bureaucracy changed only slightly.

Continuity is also manifested in the fact that the legitimacy of the authoritarian period is not attacked retrospectively. In transitions through transaction, the democratic leaders are unlikely to assail the policies, symbols, and leaders of the authoritarian regime. The transition leaders may actively draw upon their linkages to the authoritarian regime as a means of winning "retroactive legitimacy," even while attempting to obtain support based on their newly found democratic ideals.[14] In Spain, the transition did not challenge the substantial reservoir of positive memories regarding the previous regime, and a large percentage of the population continues to view that period favorably.[15]

Limits to Control and Continuity

Thus far we have emphasized the authoritarian regime's control over the transition and continuity between the democratic and authoritarian period, but there are limits to this control and continuity. Even though transitions through transaction afford more stability and security, all transitions involve significant risks and uncertainties. Furthermore, no government completely controls major political changes. Democratization can take on a dynamic of its own; it can be reversed, stalled, or accelerated. Unforeseen events can alter the democratization process in unpredictable ways, and there are predictable ways in which the regime's control will erode as democratization proceeds.

Liberalization inherently involves marginalizing the hardliners and constructing a dialogue with the moderate opposition. This process gives the opposition greater influence over subsequent political events. With the first democratic elections, a variety of new forces enter the political picture in new ways, with uncertain consequences. After these elections are convoked, any involution runs a greater risk of contravening the expressed wishes of the population. Once elections become the mechanism for selecting leaders, elites must take into consideration popular demands and public opinion. Even if the authoritarian regime initiates the transition with considerable popular support, it will have to adapt its style and policies to the new political environment.

Leaders of the transition may also develop autonomy and direct the process in a different direction than the original democratizing coalition had foreseen. Authoritarian regimes afford considerable leeway to top elites who subsequently may employ this power as they choose, within some limits. President Suárez's behavior during the Spanish transition clearly illustrates this point. Suárez pushed the transition much further than almost anybody—opposition and regime alike—would have expected. His surprise appointment in July 1976 was met with widespread skepticism on the part of democratic opposition leaders. The regime right supported his appointment precisely because of his impeccable franquist credentials and felt deceived when Suárez took democratization further than expected.[16]

In Brazil, even between 1974 and 1982, democratization often surpassed the limits authoritarian leaders hoped to establish. The regime did not expect the results of the 1974 elections, when the opposition did much better than predicted. Between 1977 and 1980, the resurgence of popular mobilization caught the leadership by surprise.[17] In devising the 1980 party reform, the government expected the emergence of a centrist opposition party with which it could ally. A centrist party (the Popular Party) did emerge, but it quickly developed an opposition stance not foreseen by the government. This development scuttled the government's electoral plans, forcing it to elaborate a new strategy.

By 1984, Brazil's transition had become an old and tired one. After successfully establishing limits to political change until early 1983, the regime finally began to erode beyond its control. The most important manifestations of this erosion included emergence of a major schism within the regime, the refusal of the official party to endorse the government's wage policies in October 1983, Figueiredo's decision to avoid intervention in selecting the regime's candidate for president, massive defections from the regime in 1984, widespread mobilization for direct elections in early 1984, and the ongoing economic crisis.[18]

Just as there are limits to the authoritarian regime's ability to control the transition, so too are there limits in the continuity between the authoritarian and democratic periods. Most important, the very existence of democratic elections means that there are new mechanisms for legitimizing the exercise of political power. Blatantly authoritarian practices are no longer permissible, and leaders are subject to a greater accountability. Some of the most characteristic aspects of authoritarian rule, like institutional repression, torture, and censorship, greatly decline. Even though the transition to democracy does not necessarily lead to changes in economic policy, significant alterations may occur.

Although the military may remain an important actor, we can expect some demilitarization of politics. Sectors of Spain's armed forces have continued to threaten democracy, but under prime ministers Leopoldo Calvo Sotelo and Felipe González, the military has been gradually brought under civilian control. In Brazil, presidents Geisel and Figueiredo initiated a pattern of disengaging the armed forces from the government. In its first months in power, the Sarney administration indicated it planned to attempt to complete this process. However, although the military is no longer in power, it continues to be an important and relatively autonomous political force, more so than in Spain.

In both countries, no area more clearly reflects the positive aspects of democratization than culture and education. In Brazil, after years of censorship and repression against institutions of higher education, Figueiredo appointed a young, liberal university professor as minister of education, ended censorship, allowed university professors who had been dismissed for political reasons to reapply for their old jobs, terminated the open presence of the security apparatus in the universities, permitted increasing university autonomy, and tolerated unionization and even strikes among teachers and professors. In Spain, democratization gave rise to a cultural renaissance, including a rediscovery of the regional languages and literature, and a revitalization of the media. Spain has become an international center for literature, film, music, and the arts.[19]

Reasons for Initiating Transitions Through Transaction

Figure 5.1 outlines our scheme of reasons why an authoritarian regime might democratize. As this figure indicates, the move toward democracy may be a necessity or a choice. In this chapter we focus on democratization by choice, because by definition transitions through transaction result from a choice by regime elites, even if declining internal cohesion or limited legitimacy are factors in that choice. This means that factors such as mass mobilization, international pressures, and economic success or failure are initially less important.

There is a striking paradox here: Why would an authoritarian regime decide to alter the very rules of the game that have sustained it? A first possibility is that some members of the authoritarian coalition always had the intention of defusing a threat and restoring democracy after an interregnum.[20] The Brazilian situation illustrates this point; many high-ranking officers had always hoped for an eventual return to democracy. The two decades of authoritarian rule were marked by constant tension between those generals who perceived the regime as long term and wanted a rupture from the democratic past and those who wanted to restore order and return to the barracks. Although the former pushed the military into staying in power for more than two decades, they could never effect a full break from democratic institutions. Consequently, the history of the regime was one of compromise between hardliners and the moderate authoritarians over the issue of democratic institutions.

Unlike the Spanish case, the Brazilian regime always retained some institutional continuity from the preceding democratic period. Former political parties were abolished, but in 1965 the government created regime and opposition parties that continued to function until the 1979 party reform. Even though the opposition party suffered significant repression, it was always a source for channelling some demands. The constitution was rendered less democratic but was never abolished.

FIGURE 5.1

Reasons Why Authoritarian Regimes Democratize

I. BY NECESSITY

    (Democratization
    through Collapse
    or Extrication)

II. BY CHOICE

    (Democratization through
    Transaction)

A. The initial idea was to correct
   unacceptable aspects of the
   previous regime and then
   reestablish democracy.

B. The advantages of staying in power
   and the costs of democratizing
   diminish.

   1. The costs of staying power
     increase because of:
     a. A succession crisis.
     b. Declining military
       cohesion.
     c. Declining legitimacy:
       (i) "Negative legitimacy"
          declines in value.
      (ii) Limited legitimacy of
          authoritarianism since
          World War II.

   2. The costs of democratizing
     decline because of:
     (i) Elimination of
       perceived threat.
     (ii) Establishment of socio-
       economic order.

Congress functioned throughout almost the entire authoritarian period. Even at the apex of authoritarianism, military leaders employed a democratic discourse. Between 1969 and 1974, military hardliners considered institutionalizing the regime in a more authoritarian direction, but they met excessive internal military opposition. This continuity in democratic rhetoric and institutions later facilitated the transition to democracy.[21]

In Spain the break from the past was more complete than in Brazil. After the civil war, Franco destroyed all aspects of the previous democratic regime. His movement was influenced by the antidemocratic emphasis of fascism during a time when democratic institutions did not have the same legitimacy as in the post-war period. The republic was replaced by a monarchy and a federal system by a centralized one. The Nationalists eliminated elections and parties, abolished the republican constitution, and introduced a new flag and national anthem. The entire franquist coalition shared a rejection of parliamentary democracy, although there was less consensus regarding the regime's ultimate political direction. The regime's long-term intentions were evident in the constitutional provision that made Franco dictator for life. Only in the 1960s did the regime attempt to construct a democratic facade and introduce a democratic discourse.[22]

Rising Costs of Continued Authoritarian Rule

The second major possibility is that the costs of staying in power increase and the costs of democratization decline. Over the course of time, contemporary authoritarian regimes in the Western world face a number of challenges that alter the costs and benefits of staying in power. Three of the most common and important challenges are leadership succession, erosion in elite cohesion, and declining legitimacy.

Leadership succession has differing consequences from authoritarian regime to authoritarian regime, but in all cases it presents a serious problem. Whereas democratic regimes have defined procedures for selecting new leaders, this process is more uncertain and often creates political infighting in authoritarian regimes, precisely because they lack institutionalized forms of political recruitment. At best, top leaders make policy in consultation with the major partners of the authoritarian coalition, and the decisionmaking process is more closed and arbitrary than in democratic regimes. The executive tends to have more power in authoritarian regimes. These systems are generally so top-heavy that any change at the apex has major reverberations and easily constitutes a regime crisis. Authoritarian regimes are based on carefully balanced coalitions of interests. Frequently a single leader is responsible for maintaining this equilibrium, so the death or demise of the leader may provoke a struggle among disparate factions.

The intensity of the crisis resulting from leadership succession depends on a number of factors. Succession is more traumatic in personalized regimes, especially when power has been exercised by a single charismatic leader. The crisis is also more severe when the leader held power for an extended period and/or was responsible for founding the regime. For a regime facing a succession crisis, democratization may be a desirable alternative because of the impossibility of reaching a consensus within the regime concerning a new leader.

Military authoritarian regimes almost invariably face tensions that can easily cause an erosion of elite cohesion. There is generally a conflict between the military as institution and the military as government. The military as institution requires autonomy and depends on a professionalization that is above politics. Being in government prevents such autonomy and almost always politicizes the armed forces. It entails serious risks because political setbacks and mismanagement may compromise the autonomy and image of the entire military. Although a military government may safeguard some interests of the armed forces, over time it may damage others, especially the internal cohesion so essential for a professionalized military. Few military regimes in the contemporary Western world have successfully resolved this tension. In this context, democratization often appears to be the best way to avoid further erosion of military cohesion. It offers the benefits of returning to the barracks while affording the possibility of exercising enough control over the transition to guarantee the military's institutional interests.

A long-term decline in legitimacy may also induce democratization through transaction. Authoritarian regimes generally derive part of their initial legitimacy from their ability to counteract a perceived threat. Their capacity to guarantee order, restore faith in the economy, or eliminate a "subversive" threat accounts for much of their support. Much of the authoritarian coalition supports the regime principally out of a dislike for the previous regime. Thus a primary source of legitimacy is based on opposition to the earlier democratic system. Over time these negative forms of legitimacy tend to weaken as memories of democratic "evils" dissipate. Order and stability, once highly valued, may come to be taken for granted. The defeat or disappearance of the "subversives," which initially helped legitimate authoritarianism, become less important as time passes. The negative legitimating factors, which allowed disparate forces to support authoritarianism, do not provide a basis for agreement about a positive direction.[23]

As time passes, even well-established authoritarian regimes usually begin to lose their active support. Authoritarian regimes discourage mobilization but in doing so also deprive themselves of a reservoir of active support. Although democratic regimes enjoy procedural legitimacy, authoritarian regimes rely heavily on economic performance or charisma after the negative sources lose their appeal. But performance is a fickle basis of legitimacy; poor performance can shatter it and good performance may eventually be taken for granted.[24]

Authoritarian regimes initially enjoy the support of some relatively uncommitted "semidemocratic" political forces. These forces are willing to adhere to authoritarianism when their interests are threatened, but once the threat is overcome they no longer support authoritarian rule. Some even join the democratic opposition, and others feel no compelling interest in the continuation of authoritarianism. The decline of legitimacy is compounded by the emergence of a new generation of young citizens that does not have the same fear of democracy and that may view democratic rule as a cure for the ills of authoritarianism.

Finally, it is difficult to cultivate legitimacy for authoritarian rule in the contemporary Western world. Authoritarian rule was delegitimated after the defeat of the Axis powers in World War II. Conversely, democratic institutions and practices have become widely accepted. Although this has not precluded authoritarian rule, it has made authoritarianism more difficult to legitimate. As a consequence, most contemporary authoritarian regimes do not completely reject democratic values. They may act undemocratically, but they often retain aspects of democratic institutions and discourse. This situation generates contradictions and creates problems for long-term institutionalization of authoritarian rule.

Just as the benefits of authoritarian rule tend to decline over time, the costs of democratization through transaction may also decrease. Once stability is restored and once the perceived threat is contained, a return to democracy may be more acceptable. Conversely, if the regime fails to contain political challenges and establish socioeconomic order, the perceived costs of democratization increase. Paradoxically, then, it may be easier for a stable and relatively popular authoritarian regime to promote democratization than for less successful ones, even though the unsuccessful ones have a more urgent need to expand the channels of communication with civil society.

Reasons for Democratizing: Brazil and Spain

Authoritarian regimes may initiate transitions to democracy in response to any combination of the challenges mentioned above. The Brazilian and Spanish regimes demonstrate some similarities and some differences in the kinds and intensity of challenges faced and in the reasons they ultimately democratized. In both cases all four reasons for democratization were present, although to varying degrees.

In twenty-one years of military rule in Brazil, five presidents governed and each willingly agreed to relinquish power after a single term. This regularized succession is exceptional for an authoritarian regime. Nevertheless, even in the Brazilian regime, which so successfully and regularly handled the issue, all four successions generated significant internal military conflicts. Between 1965 and 1967 there were constant conflicts over who would replace President Humberto Castelo Branco. In 1969 a severe conflict took place over the succession question, pitting the hardliners against the moderates.[25] In 1974 this scenario reproduced itself, but this time the moderates won out. In 1977 General Frota led a group of hardliners who opposed the candidacy of Figueiredo in vain. In 1978 the opposition party's presidential candidate was a dissident general, so the electoral campaign could have split the armed forces. In 1983 and 1984 three government party leaders competed for the official party's presidential nomination, again dividing the regime. Even though these succession problems were not the major reason for initiating the transition, the conflicts resulting from leadership change contributed to the military's decision to return to the barracks.

In Spain, the succession problem was more crucial. Franco governed for almost forty years without any intention of relinquishing power. In fact, the dictator purposely avoided the question of succession for decades to avoid antagonizing some members of the authoritarian coalition. In 1947 Franco made Spain a monarchy, but he retained the role of chief of state for life and reserved the right to appoint his successor at an unspecified date. Only in 1969 did Franco name Juan Carlos as heir to the throne, and even then the fact that the prince was young, inexperienced, and a political unknown cast continuing doubt over the succession. Until 1973 the positions of head of state and head of government were held by Franco. The appointment of Admiral Luis Carrero Blanco to the presidency in 1973 was Franco's first real delegation of power. Previously, Franco had systematically prevented the emergence of any autonomous leader who might have filled his shoes. The fact that Franco waited so long to address the issue deprived this regime of a well-established leader at the time of his death and made succession a more traumatic problem. Had Carrero Blanco not been assassinated shortly after his appointment, he might have been able to assert himself as the principal guardian of Spanish authoritarianism. As it was, the regime lacked a leader capable of maintaining an equilibrium in the authoritarian coalition.

A significant part of the legitimacy of Spanish authoritarianism derived from Franco's leadership. Not only had Franco governed for forty years, his victory in the civil war and his sheer perseverance endowed him with an almost mythical quality. Although hardly a flamboyant leader, Franco commanded respect from and intimidated all the coalition partners of the regime. For all of these reasons, Franco was an irreplaceable leader whose death created a serious crisis, even though succession was not the only factor behind the decision to democratize.

The potential for erosion of military cohesion was more important in the Brazilian regime's decision to democratize than in the Spanish case. The Brazilian military directly governed the country, even though there were more high-ranking civilian leaders than in the recent Argentine (1976–1983) or Chilean (1973–present) regimes. Although the Brazilian military maintained significant cohesion, high-ranking military leaders feared that continuing control of government would damage the military institution. They responded in part by reducing direct military involvement in politics. The Figueiredo administration made efforts to civilianize the regime, and the military did not work to control the 1985 presidential succession.

The armed forces also responded by creating autonomous military institutions that continue to be responsible for national security. The most important example was the National Intelligence Service (SNI), a state apparatus autonomous from the rest of the military, yet largely controlled by military leaders who made their career in the SNI. Its existence facilitated the separation between the military government and the armed forces as an institution, thereby enabling the military to maintain a high profile in the upper echelon of the state without politicizing the armed forces as a whole. As a result, it helped avoid the delegitimation of the armed forces that is characteristic of many transitions from military rule. Although fears about military unity provided one motive for initiating a return to the barracks, the most significant opposition to liberalization also came from within the armed forces.

The fear of declining internal cohesion in the Spanish military was not a factor in the transition to democracy. Although the armed forces played an important role, Franco's government was not a military regime, so the conflict between military as institution and military as government did not exist. For a number of reasons, the Spanish military enjoyed a high degree of internal cohesion throughout the regime. All the loyalists and most moderates were eliminated from the military after the civil war. As opposition emerged from within the military, Franco was quick to smash it. The dictator maintained strict respect for the military's autonomy and avoided policies that could endanger military unity. In the twilight of franquism, the military remained solidly united behind the dictator and was the major bulwark of authoritarianism. Rather than supporting a return to democracy, the military was—and is—the chief obstacle for democratization.

Both authoritarian regimes experienced a long-term decline in legitimacy, even though both continued to enjoy considerable support. In Brazil, this long-term decline was manifested in electoral returns and the defection of some partners in the original authoritarian coalition. The 1974 elections made apparent a widespread opposition to authoritarianism. The regime was badly defeated in the major metropolitan areas that had been the primary beneficiaries of rapid, uneven growth. Both the regime and the opposition alike read the electoral results as a partial repudiation of military rule.[26] Around the same time, the industrial bourgeoisie of São Paulo began to criticize the government and to call for a return to democracy.

After having initially supported the 1964 coup, the Catholic church, which enjoys unparalleled moral legitimacy in the society, became the leading source of opposition. Important voices of middle-class Brazil, like the Order of Brazilian Lawyers and the Brazilian Press Association, criticized human rights abuses and demanded a restoration of democracy. U.S. President Jimmy Carter's human rights policies and West European support for democracy reinforced the opposition to authoritarianism. None of these factors directly led to the democratization process, but all of them contributed to an erosion of support for the regime, which partially shaped the decision to liberalize.[27] At the same time, however, it should be emphasized that until 1982 the Brazilian government enjoyed unusual support for an authoritarian regime. The massive defections of former regime supporters in 1984 finally changed this situation.

Since the 1950s, Spanish authoritarianism also suffered from a decline in legitimacy. Initial opposition to franquism was centered in the universities and intellectual circles. Gradually, however, the desire for liberalization extended to important members of the franquist coalition, such as the Catholic Church. As the first generation of authoritarian leaders was replaced by younger Spaniards in the 1950s and 1960s, the need to liberalize the regime became widely accepted by much of the franquist elite. The liberal press law of 1966, the direct election of some legislators in 1967, and measures designed to allow limited political competition were some responses to this desire for liberalization.

In the late 1960s and early 1970s, a number of periodicals associated with the moderate democratic opposition, such as the Catholic *Cuadernos Para el Diálogo* and the liberal *Cambio 16*, enjoyed widespread circulation, even among the franquist elite. Workers and employers alike bypassed the inefficient vertical syndical structures, and the Communist-led workers commissions made important gains. Attempts to institutionalize authoritarianism and sell it as an "organic democracy" reflected the generalized acceptance of a democratic discourse. During most of the Franco period, democracy was the exception to the rule in Southern Europe, but by 1975 Spain had the only remaining authoritarian regime. *Europeísmo* became a euphemism for the acceptance of democracy and the delegitimation of authoritarian rule.[28]

Finally, in both countries the perceived costs of democratization had declined. Many Brazilian civilian and military leaders had always viewed the regime as transitory, leading back to democracy. The most important condition for initiating the transition was political stability, though for many people, economic stability was also a condition. By 1973, both conditions were satisfied. The regime had annihilated the guerrilla left, crushed the popular movements, and domesticated the rest of the opposition. Between 1967 and 1974, the economy grew at one of the fastest rates in the world, and inflation slowed to 20 percent per year, from almost 100 percent in 1963–1964. The "economic miracle" ended in 1973, but even so, the GNP expanded at a rate of 7 percent per year between 1974 and 1980. In this favorable context, the authoritarian leaders were confident that they could initiate political liberalization with minimal risks. In doing so, they could also resolve the problems accruing from declining legitimacy and concerns about military cohesion.

The Spanish regime also enjoyed considerable political and economic stability in 1975. The regime had survived the domestic and foreign challenges of the post-war period and was well entrenched. Franco had overseen the economic "miracle," a period of unprecedented economic growth between 1960 and 1970. A new and relatively wealthy middle class, the direct beneficiary of this growth, augured well for the creation of a political center. Opposition to authoritarianism existed but never exceeded the regime's ability to control it. Yet although the perceived costs of democratization had declined, there continued to be risks. The international economic crisis adversely affected the Spanish economy, bringing the "miracle" to an end. The Communist Party, the bête noire of the hardline franquists, was the strongest and best organized force within the opposition. After years of franquist suppression of regional autonomy, the movements for Basque and Catalán separatism had grown stronger. Terrorism, the scourge of the Spanish military, was well rooted in the Basque provinces.[29]

Conditions for Transition Through Transaction

For many reasons, democratization through transaction may be a desirable alternative for authoritarian regimes. It can resolve the tensions created by succession problems, declining internal cohesion, and eroding legitimacy. At the same time, a transition through transaction affords authoritarian elites a means of continuing to establish limits and shape the outcomes in the new democracy. These elites must make some concessions, but they can also benefit from managing the transition.

Although transition through transaction is often an appealing alternative, it is very difficult to effect. Many authoritarian regimes attempt transitions through transaction, but few succeed. Most cases of transition through extrication and some cases of transition after collapse initially began as attempts to control transitions through transaction. The elites, however, lacked the conditions and/or skill to exercise the requisite level of control. For example, the Argentine military governments of 1966–1971 hoped to remain in power for a protracted period. General Alejandro Lanusse, who became president in 1971, realized that the military lacked the support necessary for long-term rule and attempted to negotiate a transition through extrication. Serious schisms within the armed forces, dramatic mass mobilization, the eruption of. guerrilla warfare, and Juan Perón's determination to discredit the military government ultimately led to a collapse of the regime, which was unable to enforce even the most basic limits to the transition.[30]

Transitions through transaction require a delicate balance between regime and opposition forces. Convincing the moderate authoritarian elites to support a transition to democracy requires assuring them that their paramount interests will be safeguarded. Transition leaders must marginalize regime hardliners, who generally control the coercive apparatus and consequently have the capacity to undermine democratization. A first major tension in the transition revolves around this need to court the moderate authoritarians while marginalizing their hardline colleagues. Second, transitions through transaction must obtain the support of the opposition even though it stands to gain little in the short term. The need to appease significant elements of the authoritarian coalition may undermine the confidence of opposition leaders, who then become less willing to accept the limits imposed by the regime. Opposition leaders must walk a tightrope between demanding a more rapid and thorough transition, and accepting important limits so as to avoid provoking an involution.

A third major tension arises from the need to make some concessions to the opposition while continuing to control the most important aspects of the transition. The concessions must be limited enough in the short run that the hardliners and authoritarian moderates do not torpedo the transition, yet significant enough that they move the country in a democratic direction. In summary, governments overseeing transitions through transaction must know how to use both the accelerator and the brake of reform. If the transition through transaction is carried out with excessive haste or delay regarding the relationship of political forces, democratization is imperiled.

These considerations raise the question of the conditions necessary for successful transition through transaction. In the remainder of this section, we discuss five such conditions.

I. Transition through transaction requires that the authoritarian regime be well established and widely supported.[31] As is evident from our discussion, democratization through transaction is unlikely to emerge from weak authoritarian regimes. Authoritarian regimes that lack significant support are unable to control a transition. They may be able to remain in power through maintaining authoritarian rule, but if they hope to relinquish power, the best they can do is to negotiate an extrication. In situations of weakness, it is hard to convince regime forces that their interests will be safeguarded and that the transition will be limited. Likewise, it is difficult to persuade the opposition to accept a transition initially dictated from above when it believes it can topple the regime in the short run.

One manifestation of the level of support an authoritarian regime enjoys is its capacity to create a competitive political party during the transition. The creation of a party shows regime confidence in its popular support. Frequently, however, authoritarian regimes significantly overestimate their following. The absence of visible protest, a result of the suppression of institutionalized means of resolving conflict, leads them to equate silence with consent. The fact that there have been no competitive elections enables them to overestimate their electoral strength. This kind of miscalculation has occurred in many transitions, including those in Argentina (1971–1973) and Bolivia (1978–1980).

Both the Spanish and the Brazilian regimes were well established and widely supported. Both regimes had been in power for decades and had uncontested control of the government, and neither regime ever came close to collapsing. The demise of Portuguese authoritarianism in 1974 shows that longevity does not ensure the capacity to control a transition to democracy, but only a well-established regime has the authority to do so.

The Spanish and the Brazilian regimes are among the few authoritarian regimes to create parties that have fared well in democratic elections. The Brazilian regime party, ARENA (National Renovating Alliance), created in 1965, was the majority party in the lower house until the party reform in 1979. Although its successor, the PDS (Democratic Social Party), briefly lost its absolute majority in November 1981 and lost it for good after November 1982, it remained the largest party until the massive defections to the newly created Party of the Liberal Front (PFL) in 1985. In the Senate, the government party retained an absolute majority until 1985. In the 1982 elections, the PDS won a majority of the states and earned enough electoral college votes to seemingly assure victory in the 1985 indirect presidential election. Aided by electoral engineering and occasional fraud, until 1984 the PDS successfully used the deeply rooted clientelistic traditions throughout Brazil's lesser-developed regions.

Authoritarian elites in Spain took much longer to create a party and were unable to agree on a single electoral vehicle. While a number of franquist political associations were formed after 1974, a full-scale political party, the Popular Alliance (AP) was not established until early 1977. This party included much of the prominent franquist elite, including a number of top cabinet ministers. However, many reformist leaders of the regime, including President Suárez, refrained from participating in AP and later founded a competing electoral coalition, the Union of the Democratic Center (UCD), with members of the moderate opposition. The major question in the June 1977 elections revolved around which regime party would win control of the government. UCD's victory in the first two democratic elections was followed by a spectacular demise. Since 1982, AP has replaced it as the major party of the right. As the second largest party in Spain, AP continues to be heir of the franquist past.[32]

II. Transitions through transaction require that the authoritarian regime be capable of controlling "subversive" threats. Containing some opposition forces, especially those committed to overthrowing the system, is a major goal of most authoritarian regimes. Democratization only becomes an attractive alternative if these perceived "subversive" forces have been vanquished. No significant partners in the authoritarian coalition will support democratization so long as there are clear prospects for the reemergence of such forces in the democratic regime.

The crushing of the guerrilla left was an indispensible condition for political liberalization in Brazil. The regime came to power largely to defeat a perceived leftist threat. However, significant parts of the left radicalized in response to the initial repression. This radicalization provoked a further increase in repression, and by 1973 the government had decimated the left. By as early as 1968, it had completely contained the popular movements that it also perceived as a threat. Thus, by 1973, the military believed it could liberalize without facing any significant leftist opposition. Throughout the eleven years of liberalization, the government continued to repress parts of the left, making clear the limits of democratization. For the most part, as described in Chapter 4, the left that has emerged from this repression has become more committed to democratic values, a transformation that has also facilitated the transition.[33]

Leftist opposition to the franquist regime was extinguished by the late 1940s and only in the late 1950s did significant anti-franquist movements reemerge within Spain. The major leftist party, the Spanish Socialist Workers Party (PSOE), virtually ceased to exist. Most democratic leaders were in exile awaiting the overthrow of Franco by the Allied Powers. The security forces periodically decimated the ranks of the opposition, limiting its cohesiveness and mass appeal. In the 1960s the Communist party made inroads among workers and students and became the best organized and most effective opposition force, but it never constituted a serious threat to Franco. The repression was especially directed at PCE leaders and was successful in keeping the party underground. Beginning with the PCE's adoption of a national reconciliation policy in 1960, major leftist parties abandoned strategies based on the overthrow of franquism. Despite the increase of antifranquist demonstrations in the 1970s, no opposition activity ever exceeded the ability of the franquist repressive apparatus to respond. On the eve of Franco's death, the left was weak and divided. The specter of terrorism was the major security problem facing the regime, but it was largely confined to the Basque Country.

As the reformist coalition changes and as hardliners are marginalized, the definition of "subversive" threats may change. For example, the Suárez governnent was able to redefine "subversive threats" to include the Socialist party and eventually the Communists in the political process. In Brazil, in May 1985 the Communist parties had the chance to gain legal status.

III. In transitions through transaction, the democratic opposition must accept some limits and rules set by the authoritarian regime. The opposition may be able to challenge the regime but is not strong enough to topple it. Consequently, it is more prone to avoid confrontational strategies. If the opposition actively pursues radical change it runs the risk of provoking an authoritarian involution. Having suffered through periods of repression, opposition leaders may prefer to accept the limits and rules of a transition through transaction.

While radical opposition demands threaten transition through transaction, any democratic opposition must challenge some aspects of authoritarianism. Thus, there are limits to the opposition's willingness to accept the regime's rules, even in transitions through transaction. The opposition must push an essentially authoritarian regime toward democratic change but do so as a loyal opposition. Opposition leaders must operate as if they were in a democratic system but without enjoying any of the guarantees afforded by a democracy. Simultaneously, they must contend with sectors of their own constituency that demand more rapid change and that oppose negotiation with the authoritarian regime.

In the initial stages, the Brazilian opposition was in no position to overthrow the regime, so there was no question of rejecting a controlled democratization in favor of a more ambitious strategy. The opposition continuously faced the dilemma of pushing for change while avoiding an involution. When the *abertura* began, the opposition party (MDB— Brazilian Democratic Movement) had been seriously weakened by years of repression. Most of the remaining MDB leaders represented conservative positions within the opposition. The decimation of the left and government repression of popular movements reinforced the opposition's weakness and its tendency to accept limits established by the regime.

After the 1974 elections, the MDB gradually acquired a more progressive profile and became more willing to confront the regime. Nevertheless, it continued to accept some basic parameters of transition through transaction, even while challenging blatantly authoritarian measures. This cautious tendency was reinforced by selective repression against more combative leaders, which had the effect of dampening opposition demands as a whole. Only after the 1978 elections did a significantly more assertive opposition emerge in Congress. After the party reform in 1979–1980, the small Workers Party (PT) promoted radical change and rejected the government's slow pace of reform, and the largest opposition party, the Party of the Brazilian Democratic Movement (PMDB), demanded substantial change. Following the 1982 elections, the PMDB moved in a more cautious direction, but the 1984 mobilization for direct presidential elections and the military regime's crisis encouraged a more ambitious opposition.

The Spanish opposition abandoned attempts to overthrow the regime in the 1960s, but it continued to harbor illusions of a regime collapse, followed by a *ruptura democrática* (a democratic break) in which all democratic forces would form a provisional government. After Franco's death, the democratic opposition remained stubbornly attached to this strategy. President Carlos Arias's failure to enact a genuine democratic reform and his inability to convince the opposition of his sincerity contributed to this intransigence.

After July 1976 President Suárez's capacity to implement reform and his success in initiating a dialogue between the regime and opposition began to weaken the opposition's hostility to a transition through transaction. Between July 1976 and January 1977 most of the opposition dropped the demand for a provisional government and spoke instead of a *ruptura pactada* (a negotiated democratic break). This change of position was motivated by Suárez's success in building a consensus within the franquist regime in support of a transition through transaction.

The most important sign of this consensus was the overwhelming passage of the Political Reform Law by the franquist legislature in November 1976. In a referendum held one month later, the Political Reform Law won a massive popular endorsement. Although the major opposition officially advocated abstention in the referendum, it did not campaign actively against the Political Reform Law. Opposition leaders consistently called for greater civil liberties, legalization of all parties, the dismantling of the franquist state apparatus, and more rapid reform. Yet by participating in the June elections and by agreeing to avoid all attacks against the monarchy or the franquist past, the opposition implicitly accepted Suárez's transition through transaction. Finally, throughout the entire transition period, opposition leaders repeatedly called for calm and moderation, a factor that contributed to the success of the Suárez reforms.

IV. Transitions through transaction require limited levels of mass mobilization. A high level of mobilization makes a negotiated transition extremely unlikely, both because the regime fears the consequences of a more open system and because the opposition is unwilling to accept the regime's conditions.[34] When levels of mass mobilization are low, authoritarian leaders are less likely to fear democratization. High levels of mobilization may raise fear of disorder reminiscent of that which preceded the authoritarian takeover. Such mobilization also favors the unacceptable prospect of a leftist victory in elections.

In highly mobilized societies, it is more difficult for opposition leaders to accept the regime's rules for the transition (Condition III). High mobilization suggests that the authoritarian regime is weak, so the opposition is more likely to attempt to topple the regime. Furthermore, under these conditions opposition leaders frequently have difficulty containing grassroots demands for rapid change. They are less insulated from their constituency and more constrained in their negotiations with regime leaders.

Brazil's political history has been characterized by low levels of popular mobilization; the popular sectors have been consistently marginalized from participation in major political decisions. This pattern eroded in the years immediately preceding the 1964 coup, but the increasing popular mobilization was a significant factor behind the military intervention. Popular leaders were a primary object of repression during the early phases of the regime, and by late 1968 the popular movements were well under control. Between 1968 and 1978, the labor movement did not organize a single major strike, and peasant organizations were even more silent. When the *abertura* began, there had been no major popular protests for several years, a fact that gave the military the confidence to ease the repression. During the subsequent course of the *abertura*, the government continued to repress the strongest movements.[35] This pattern of limiting popular mobilization was broken in the first four months of 1984 when the campaign for direct presidential elections peacefully mobilized millions of Brazilians.

Historically, Spain has had higher levels of mass mobilization. The Second Republic was one of the most highly mobilized regimes in history, which partially explains the intensity of the authoritarian reaction. Franco discouraged political mobilization and was successful in demobilizing and depoliticizing the masses.[36] Although opposition labor activity steadily increased in the 1960s and 1970s, at no time did a strike paralyze a major sector of the economy. Political demonstrations, especially in the Basque Country and Catalonia, were on the rise in the years surrounding the transition, but the opposition remained weak and fragmented. Franco's death evoked no mass mobilization, a fact which astounded most observers. Opposition leaders felt little mass pressure to wage their political struggle in the streets, a strategy they feared would only provoke an authoritarian involution.

V. Transitions through transaction require skillful leadership. Transitions through transaction can occur only under certain conditions, but even where all of these conditions obtain, they do not ensure that a transition through transaction will result. As this kind of transition does not automatically derive from any set of preconditions, it requires a willful choice even if favorable conditions are present. Poor leadership, in either the regime or opposition, can bungle the most propitious opportunities.[37]

The leadership qualities that facilitate transitions through transaction include a willingness to promote democratization, a capacity to negotiate and persuade, and an ability to sustain the momentum and regulate the timing of the reform. Given the difficulty in balancing the competing demands of different regime and opposition forces, skillful leadership is crucial. Leaders of transitions through transaction must be able to sell the transition as the optimal solution for most of the regime and opposition. This involves persuading authoritarian forces to accept democratization and convincing the opposition to accept limits. The momentum of the transition must be sustained despite the many obstacles that emerge. Leaders must regulate the timing of reforms to avoid excessive hostility.

President Arias's failure to effect a transition through transaction between December 1975 and June 1976 and Suárez's subsequent success illustrate the crucial role of leadership in the Spanish transition. Arias proved unable to convince either the regime hardliners or the democratic opposition to support the transition. His poor oratorical skills and lack of tact made him a poor choice to lead the transition, and his lack of conviction about the desirability of democracy was manifested in constant vacillations. Arias failed to initiate a dialogue with the democratic opposition, which he distrusted and despised. Because the president proved unable and unwilling to confront the right wing "bunker" with which he sympathized, he never dispelled his image as a hardline franquist.

Under essentially similar conditions, Suárez's superior leadership skills and his greater desire for democracy made the transition possible.[38] His youth appealed to an entire generation of Spaniards who had not experienced the civil war. His franquist credentials won him initial confidence from regime hardliners. His charisma gave him undeniable popular support and facilitated the victory of the center-right in 1977. Suárez's political style was markedly different from that of his predecessor. He felt comfortable negotiating with the democratic opposition, even the PCE, and did not share Arias's anti-Communist feelings. He convinced the military and many doubtful franquists that a transition through transaction offered the best solution to a regime crisis, and that strict limits would be respected. He employed a combination of persuasion, negotiation, and coercion to convince the franquist Cortes (the legislature) to support the transition. His ability to sustain a steady, rapid pace for the transition kept both the hardliners and the democratic opposition off guard. Finally, Suárez's willingness to break past promises and to exceed the established limits of the reform was instrumental in his success.

The importance of leadership is also underscored by the role of King Juan Carlos.[39] Initially considered awkward and inept, the King proved to be a prudent leader. When it became apparent that Arias could not effect a transition through transaction, the monarch removed him and appointed Suárez. Both the King and Suárez cultivated dual images throughout the transition. On the one hand, they were always careful to express their respect for franquist traditions and procedure. On the other hand, both leaders were unequivocal in their public support for democratization. This balancing act required careful behavior, ambiguous public statements, and occasional duplicity.

Although the Brazilian transition did not have any leaders of the stature of Juan Carlos or Suárez, President Geisel, former Chief of the Civilian Cabinet Golbery do Couto e Silva (the regime's outstanding ideologue since 1964), and former Justice Minister Petrônio Portela all contributed toward striking a balance between introducing some reforms and maintaining significant control. They marginalized the far right, won considerable popular support (until 1983) despite authoritarian measures, and sometimes anticipated opposition demands in promoting change. Nevertheless, after Golbery's resignation in 1981, the Brazilian regime lacked the strong leadership that characterized the earlier part of the transition, and official guidance of the process weakened accordingly.

Interrelationships

The five conditions discussed above are interrelated. For example, well-established authoritarian regimes (Condition I) are more likely to control "subversive" threats (Condition II). The democratic opposition will more likely accept limits (Condition III) where Conditions I and II obtain. The presence of skilled leaders (Condition V) facilitates the opposition's acceptance of limits (Condition III). Other conditions beyond those we have discussed may facilitate the transition, but they are not necessary. For example, the greater longevity of an authoritarian regime may make transitions through transaction easier by dampening past fears and by creating a generational turnover.

In contrast to some other scholars, we have intentionally omitted discussion of economic and international factors as necessary conditions for a transition through transaction.[40] There is no predictable relationship between the economic environment and the ability to effect transitions through transaction. A favorable economic situation may give authoritarian elites the confidence necessary to begin a transition, but it may also provide a justification for remaining in power. An economic crisis often creates problems for a transition to democracy, but it can also contribute toward the erosion of authoritarianism. Appositely, the Spanish transition began in a period of economic crisis, whereas the Brazilian transition began in what was still a relatively prosperous period. Although an economistic explanation of the liberalization process is inadequate, in both Brazil and Spain, modernization helped generate pressures for democratization.

An international environment that actively encourages democracy facilitates democratization, but it is not a necessary nor a sufficient condition.[41] Democratization can occur in an unfavorable international climate just as authoritarian regimes can survive a hostile environment. Authoritarian regimes either can be well insulated or can use foreign pressure to enhance their legitimacy. International ostracism can make the elites more insecure, more nationalistic, and less willing to democratize. For example, the franquist regime survived the international isolation of the 1940s and early 1950s. Throughout the regime's history, Franco was successful in converting foreign condemnation into political capital.[42]

Differences in Transitions Through Transaction: Brazil and Spain

One of the fundamental postulates of this chapter has been that there are significant similarities between the Spanish and the Brazilian transitions. Nevertheless, we have also emphasized differences between democratization in Brazil and Spain. Figure 5.2 summarizes some outstanding differences mentioned in previous sections.

In this section we analyze reasons for the greater rapidity and completeness of the Spanish transition. The question of how the transition evolved is analytically distinct from the issue of conditions for democratization through transaction. As we argued above, both Spain and Brazil enjoyed favorable conditions for a transition through transaction. However, three main factors in Spain were conducive to a more rapid and complete transition.

Although both transitions had skilled leaders, these leaders had different orientations. The Spanish leaders were more genuinely reform-oriented than their counterparts in Brazil. The transition to democracy in Spain was led by a generation of younger leaders, notably King Juan Carlos and President Adolfo Suárez, who implemented a transition through transaction that exceeded the wishes of the moderate authoritarians. By contrast, in Brazil the same people who led the authoritarian period oversaw the transition. The military controlled the selection of presidents so as to perpetuate a gradual, conservative transition. The leaders of the transition were fundamentally concerned with devising ways to limit change and prolong their power, even while introducing some reforms. Even if a genuinely democratic general had been selected

FIGURE 5.2

Some Differences Between Democratization in Brazil and Spain

Aspects of the Authoritarian Regime Affecting Democratization	Brazil	Spain
Type of previous regime	Military	Personal dictatorship
Continuity between previous democratic regime and authoritarian regime	Moderate	Almost none
Longevity of authoritarian regime	21 years	39 years

Aspects of the Transition:		
Pace of democratization	Gradual	Rapid
Leaders of transition	Founders of regime	New generation
Orientation of transition leaders	Authoritarian	Reform-oriented
Party options for leaders of the authoritarian regime	Rightist regime party (PDS) and, after April 1984, centrist Party of the Liberal Front (PFL)	Centrist regime-opposition party (UCD) and rightist regime party (AP)
Regime's ability to shape the transition	High until 1982; eroded sharply, 1983-1985	High until June 1977

as president, he would have lacked the autonomy to carry the reforms beyond the limits imposed by the armed forces.

This difference in leadership orientation was also reflected in the newly created parties. The Brazilian leaders formed a strictly regime party, whereas the UCD combined elements of the moderate opposition and regime reformists. ARENA/PDS was the party *of* the government, but never the party *in* government, as was the case of UCD. Given the crucial role of leadership in transitions through transaction, this difference between Spain and Brazil was important.

The differences in leadership also help explain the greater erosion of the Brazilian regime during its final two years. The protracted character of the transition and the severity of the economic crisis created major problems for the regime. By 1983 the Figueiredo administration was incapable of dealing with these problems as adroitly as its predecessors. Figueiredo essentially abdicated responsibility for the choice of a successor and for keeping intact the authoritarian coalition. He was far less successful in imposing his vision of the reform than Adolfo Suárez was in Spain.

Earlier we argued that there is no necessary relationship between the economic environment and democratization. Nevertheless, although economic development is not a necessary condition for the establishment of a stable democracy, widespread poverty can hinder the consolidation of a democratic regime. Almost all stable democracies have highly developed economies. In a developed nation there is a large middle class that has a stake in the system, and the government has resources to distribute, helping it to contain sources of instability.[43]

Spain's higher level of development and greater equity facilitated the consolidation of parliamentary democracy after 1975. The economic "miracle" created a large middle class and a consumer society uninterested in radical change. No Western capitalist nation with a comparable level of development had an authoritarian regime.

Brazil is less developed than Spain and has more unequal income distribution. In 1981, Spain's per capita GNP was $5,640, compared to $2,220 in Brazil. The wealthiest 10 percent of the Brazilian population accounted for 50.6 percent of total income, compared to 26.7 percent in Spain. Brazil has eight times as much illiteracy and its infant mortality rate is 7.5 times greater.[44] The extreme poverty found in many regions of the country bolsters authoritarianism since the poorest sectors of the population still tend to accept their fate passively. Large sectors of the elite that have formed the basis for authoritarian rule reject a democratic ethos. The extreme income inequality fosters the continuation of rigid elitism and a well-defined social hierarchy.

A favorable international environment is not a necessary condition for democratization, but it helps. Here again, there were differences between the Spanish and Brazilian cases. Spain's West European neighbors provided consistent support for democratization, and many Spaniards associated democratization with a much desired entry into the European Economic Community. Brazil's international environment was less favorable than Spain's. Spain's fundamental cultural reference point was democratic Europe, whereas Brazil's was the Southern Cone of South America and the United States. During much of the liberalization process, most of Brazil's neighbors had extremely repressive governments. The level of repression in neighboring Argentina, Uruguay, Paraguay, and Bolivia far exceeded that in Brazil, and Peru and Ecuador also had military governments. With the exception of the Carter administration, there has been little or no pressure for democratization from the United States.

Costs and Benefits of Transitions
Through Transaction

The way in which a democracy is inaugurated does not wholly determine its subsequent development but it does establish rules of the game, modes of political interaction, and limits to political behavior and change. Subsequent political struggles can alter these precedents, but, generally speaking, no period of a democracy's life is more important than its inauguration. The transition period also offers the best opportunity to change past traditions, even though these traditions continue to shape the new regime.

All forms of transition to democracy have costs and benefits relative to each other. On the positive side, successful transitions through transaction offer a relatively peaceful means of establishing democracy since both the regime and the opposition accept the basic rules of the game. Because the regime controls the basic aspects of the transition, it can intimidate most violent opposition. In addition, the population remains relatively demobilized, depriving political extremes of mass support. Transitions through transaction are also more likely to establish a stable democracy, an objective that few countries have achieved since 1950. This kind of transition facilitates the institutionalization of the politics of compromise, thereby initiating democratic means of resolving conflict. Because transitions through transaction include all major political actors, antidemocratic coalitions are less likely to develop. The moderation necessary during the transition may carry over to the democratic period, decreasing the likelihood of immediate polarization.

On the negative side, transitions through transaction afford less opportunity for a sharp break from the authoritarian past. The actors responsible for authoritarian rule, including abusers of human rights, continue to be present on the political scene. Authoritarian forces may be weakened and some ex-authoritarians may become conservative democrats, but others pose an ongoing threat to the democratic system. The immunity granted them during the transition may encourage them to act against the democratic system. The bitterness of the hardliners, caused by their marginalization from politics, may exacerbate this tendency.

Although transitions through transaction seem more likely to produce stable democratic regimes, the initial phases of this democracy are likely to be fragile and conservative. Until the democratic system has taken root, the military will remain a threat. Because of low levels of mobilization and weak political structures, there is little effective opposition to an authoritarian involution. The demobilization of society also gives the nascent democracy an elitist character. The absence of major socioeconomic change makes it impossible to resolve some fundamental questions like agrarian reform and inequitable income distribution. These initial costs of transitions through transaction may decline over time; the critical question is the extent to which the democracy can break from its conservative, elitist origins to become more broadly representative.

Costs and Benefits in Spain

Both Spain and Brazil have demonstrated some of these costs and benefits, but Spain has been more successful in moving away from its authoritarian past. The outstanding benefit of the Spanish transition has been the development of a stable parliamentary democracy. Electoral competition has resulted in the alternation of power between parties of the center-right and the center-left. The parliamentary monarchy has attained a new democratic legitimacy.[45] Elites have learned to reach compromises over contentious issues and have been able to avoid politicizing potentially divisive issues.

The transition through transaction has ended the historical—and often violent—confrontation between the "two Spains"—one that was conservative, authoritarian, clerical, and rural, and the other that was liberal, republican, anticlerical, and urban. The new constitution, often referred to as the "constitution of consensus," represents one example of how elites compromised on the most important issues that have traditionally divided Spaniards. The menacing church-state conflict was resolved by article 17, which guarantees freedom of religion and explicitly rejects a confessional state but nevertheless recognizes the special role of the Catholic Church. The equally contentious question of regionalism was largely resolved by officially recognizing the right to regional autonomy while stopping short of establishing a federal system.

The constitution establishes a market economy but allows for significant state intervention in the "direction, coordination, and exploitation of enterprises when the general interest demands it." It calls for civilian control over the armed forces but acknowledges the military's duty to "guarantee the sovereignty and independence of Spain, and to defend its territorial integrity and the functioning of the constitution." All parties and organizations were dissatisfied with some aspects of the constitution, but almost all Spaniards have accepted it as a reasonable compromise.[46]

The ability of elites to compromise on the rules of the game has carried over to the socioeconomic sphere. The transition took place during a severe international economic recession.[47] The uncertainty surrounding the regime change had exacerbated an already critical economic situation in Spain. Suárez had paid almost exclusive attention to political problems and had neglected the economy, fearing that attempts to implement economic reforms would imperil the political reforms. After the first elections, however, it was no longer possible to delay taking action. The inflation rate in 1977 (26.4 percent) was almost double that in other OECD countries. By late 1977 almost one million Spaniards were unemployed and the balance of payments deficit reached an alarming five billion dollars.

Suárez was caught between the opposition of the right, including much of his own party, to any economic reforms, and the demands of the leftist opposition for a progressive economic program. Faced with the prospect of a "hot autumn" that might trigger a military coup, government and leftist opposition reached a broad social accord known as the Moncloa Pacts. These negotiations earned Suárez the left's support for an austerity program in exchange for his promise of a substantial reform of the fiscal system, an increase in certain social expenditures, and a more rapid devolution of power to the regions and the trade unions. By reaching an accord between the center-right and the center-left and by marginalizing both extremes, the Moncloa Pacts minimized the prospects for an authoritarian involution and established a precedent for elite negotiation and compromise.[48]

The logic of transition through transaction in Spain contributed to the moderation of the party system and consequently to the prospects for alternation in power. On the one hand, the transition through transaction required that the democratic opposition moderate its demands and accept the regime's limits. This helps explain why the PSOE underwent a dramatic metamorphosis, transforming itself from one of Western Europe's most radical Socialist parties in 1977, to one of its most cautious leftist parties.[49] On the other hand, the regime right had to prove its democratic credentials to the Spanish electorate and could not afford to appear too rightist. From June 1977 to February 1981, Suárez's UCD acted in a manner befitting a social democratic party rather than a conservative one. In fact, Suárez's centrism eventually alienated him from the UCD right and led to the disintegration of the coalition. The more conservative Popular Alliance (AP) has since replaced UCD in Spain's party system, but it has also come to avoid political extremism for electoral reasons and because it has integrated conservative sectors of UCD. AP has become a conservative loyal opposition party and has distanced itself from its franquist origins.

Although the benefits of Spain's transition to democracy stand out, two important costs are evident. The regime has had difficulty restraining the military, which has been the staunchest opponent to democratization. The legalization of the Communist party, the granting of autonomy to Catalonia and the Basque Country, and the dismantling of the National Movement were all viewed by the armed forces as broken promises. After the first democratic elections, military hostility to democracy steadily grew. In early September 1977 plans for an authoritarian involution were initiated within the armed forces. In the fall of 1978, a major coup plot was uncovered, but military courts handed down light sentences to the conspirators. Attempts by hardline sectors of the military to undermine democracy culminated in the coup attempt of February 23, 1981. Since the discovery of another military conspiracy on the eve of the 1982 elections, the armed forces have maintained a lower profile.[50] Nevertheless, the specter of military intervention has contributed to what has been described as Spain's "conditional democracy."[51]

A second cost associated with transition through transaction has been a continuity in the low levels of mobilization and participation. Transition through transaction has done little to encourage mobilization. In contrast to revolutionary Portugal, which experienced a surge of mobilization, in Spain democratization was initially controlled by authoritarian elites and did not involve the masses. The constitution was written behind closed doors by party representatives, and the Moncloa Pacts were negotiated without participation by trade unions or entrepreneurial groups. Spain continues to have the lowest rate of voter turnout in Europe, and recent survey data demonstrate that comparatively low levels of political participation have accompanied the democratization process.[52]

The long-term impact of low levels of mobilization is difficult to assess. Spaniards may not actively participate in the democratic system in large percentages, but they overwhelmingly express their support for the new regime. Although it is possible to view the absence of an immediate popular response to the coup attempt of 1981 as a sign of weakness of the new regime, the ability of elites to contain the crisis compensated for the popular passivity. As long as elites are able to rally to the defense of the regime, low levels of mobilization may not present a serious danger for democracy.[53] Nevertheless, low levels of participation may adversely affect the quality of a democracy. Participation helps encourage governmental responsiveness to the citizenry and facilitates the development of a democratic political culture.[54]

Costs and Benefits in Brazil

Any discussion of costs and benefits of transition through transaction in Brazil is necessarily tenuous because the democratic regime is so new. From our perspective, the very emergence of a liberal democracy that may become stable is an important and desirable outcome of the transition. Nevertheless, there are reasons to believe that whereas Spain shows the potential for a deepening of democracy after a transition through transaction, Brazil's democracy may be more affected by the negative features of transitions through transaction.

The transition's very length points to a negative feature of the democratization process in Brazil. Some key elements of the most repressive period, including the National Intelligence Service and the law of national security, were intact at the start of civilian rule in March 1985. The military regime embellished the constitution with some authoritarian provisions—sometimes promulgated in unconstitutional ways—designed to enhance the conservatives' role in the new system. The armed forces retain significant autonomy and power in politics.

Probably the most deleterious effect of the transition was the exacerbation of Brazil's traditional pattern of elitist politics. Especially in rural areas, the military regime intentionally excluded the popular sectors from meaningful participation in politics. Although the regime encouraged change that satisfied some demands of middle-class urban Brazil, it continued to exercise considerable repression against the popular classes. In vast areas of the country, especially the Amazon and the Northeast, political liberalization had little effect. Landowners continued to exercise virtually unchecked authority, and the state generally reinforced rather than challenged these patterns of private repression and control. In practice, the popular sectors still lack most of the basic rights of citizenship. Popular participation in politics is very limited, and there is widespread apathy about politics, even about the very establishment of democracy. Most of the popular sectors believe—and historically have reason to— that politics does not affect them.[55]

The economic consequences of this elitist system are as striking as the political. Despite Brazil's level of development, millions of people live in abject poverty. Income distribution ranks among the worst in the world; in 1980, the bottom 50 percent of the population received only 12.6 percent of total domestic income.[56] Regional inequalities are also extreme. The states of São Paulo, Santa Catarina, and Rio Grande do Sul are among the wealthiest parts of Latin America, whereas the Northeast is among the poorest. Per capita income in São Paulo state is approximately eight times that of the poorest state.[57] Political liberalization did little to alter the egregious inequalities that characterize the society, and the antipopular effects of the economic model were reinforced by the severe recession that began in 1980.

Not only did the authoritarian regime succeed in controlling many aspects of the liberalization process, it also reinforced elitist patterns well entrenched in the country's political traditions.[58] Only favorable conditions and exceptional democratic leadership could challenge the elitism and inegalitarianism that have been at the root of Brazil's authoritarianism. These factors suggest that the cautious and elitist pattern established during the transition may be difficult for the new democracy to break, at least in the medium run.

None of this means that political liberalization has been without positive consequences. The reestablishment of formal civil liberties, the more competitive character of political life, the sharp reduction in torture and elimination of political killings, and the revitalization of cultural life are among the positive changes of the last decade. Furthermore, a break from the authoritarian past may still come, enabling a new cadre of leaders to challenge effectively the elitist political traditions and economic inequities.

Acknowledgments

The Office of Advanced Studies at Notre Dame helped support our work. We benefited from thoughtful readings by Gabriel Almond, Karen Bernstein, Eli Diniz, Caroline Domingo, David Fleischer, César Guimarães, Peter McDonough, Guillermo O'Donnell, Ronald Schneider, Wayne Selcher, Thomas Skidmore, and Eduardo Viola.

Notes

1. The most important work is Guillermo O'Donnell, Philippe Schmitter, and Laurence Whitehead (eds.), *Transitions from Authoritarian Rule: Southern Europe and Latin America* (forthcoming). A seminal contribution was Dankwart Rustow, "Transitions to Democracy: Towards a Dynamic Model," *Comparative Politics* 2 (April 1970): 337–363. On transitions from bureaucratic-authoritarian regimes, see Guillermo O'Donnell, "Notas para el estudio de procesos de democratización política a partir del estado burocrático-autoritario," *Estudios CEDES* 2, no. 5 (1979); and Guillermo O'Donnell, "Tensions in the Bureaucratic-Authoritarian State and the Question of Democracy," in David Collier (ed.), *The New Authoritarianism in Latin America* (Princeton: Princeton University Press, 1979), pp. 285–318. For different collections of articles, see John Herz (ed.), *From Dictatorship to Democracy* (Westport: Greenwood Press, 1982); and Alain Rouquié, et. al. (eds.), *Como Renascem as Democracias* (São Paulo: Brasiliense, 1985). A recent analysis is Samuel Huntington, "Will More Countries Become Democratic?," *Political Science Quarterly* 99 (Summer 1984): 193–218. One of the best comparative articles is Juan J. Linz, "Some Comparative Thoughts on the Transition to Democracy in Portugal and Spain," in Jorge Braga de Macedo and Simon Serfaty (eds.), *Portugal Since the Revolution: Economic and Political Perspectives* (Boulder, CO: Westview Press, 1981), pp. 25–45.

2. This term was first employed by Giuseppe Di Palma in his "Founding Coalitions in Southern Europe: Legitimacy and Hegemony," *Government and Opposition* 2 (Spring 1980): 166.

3. On the Spanish transition see Jorge de Esteban and Luis López Guerra, *De la dictadura a la democracia: Diario político de un período constituyente* (Madrid: Universidad de Complutense, Facultad de Derecho, 1979); Raymond Carr and Juan Pablo Fusi, *Spain, Dictatorship to Democracy* (London: George Allen and Unwin, 1981); Edward Malefakis, "Spain and its Francoist Heritage" in Herz (ed.), *From Dictatorship to Democracy*, pp. 215–230; and Donald Share, "Transition Through Transaction: The Politics of Democratization in Spain, 1975-1977" (Ph.D. Dissertation, Stanford University, 1983).

4. On the Brazilian transition, see Fernando Henrique Cardoso, *Autoritarismo e Democratização* (Rio de Janeiro: Paz e Terra, 1975); Wanderley Guilherme Dos Santos, *Poder e Política: Crônica do Authoritarismo Brasileiro* (Rio de Janeiro: Forense-Universitária, 1978); José Álvaro Moises, "Crise Política e Democracia: A Transição Difícil," *Revista de Cultura e Política* 2 (August/October 1980): 9–37; Sebastião Velasco e Cruz e Carlos Estevam Martins, "De Castello a Figueiredo: Uma Incursão na Pre-História da 'Abertura'," in Velasco e Cruz, et. al., *Sociedade e Política no Brasil pós-64* (São Paulo: Brasiliense, 1983), pp. 13–61; Paulo Krischke, (ed.), *Brasil: Do Milagre à Abertura* (São Paulo: Cortez, 1983); and

Fábio Wanderley Reis, "Mudança Política no Brasil: Aberturas, Perspectivas e Miragens" (forthcoming).

5. The definitions of liberalization and democratization are taken from Eduardo Viola and Scott Mainwaring, "Transitions to Democracy: Brazil and Argentina in the 1980s," *Journal of International Affairs* 38 (Winter 1985): 193–219. The typology of transitions to democracy also draws upon this article.

6. The possibilities and difficulties of expanding democracy is a leading theme in the works of Robert Dahl. See especially *Polyarchy* (New Haven: Yale University Press, 1971), pp. 1–16; *After the Revolution?* (New Haven: Yale University Press, 1970); and *Dilemmas of Pluralist Democracy* (New Haven: Yale University Press, 1982).

7. For a treatment of the Spanish transition which emphasizes Suárez's intentional staggering of reforms, see Frederico Ysart, *¿Quién hizo el cambio?* (Barcelona: Argos Vergara, 1984).

8. On the legalization of the PCE see Joaquín Bardavío, *Sábado Santo Rojo* (Madrid: Ediciones Uve, 1980).

9. On the continuation of repression against peasants, see José de Souza Martins, *Expropriação e Violência: A Questão Política no Campo* (São Paulo: Hucitec, 1980); José de Souza Martins, *Os Camponêses e a Política no Brasil* (Petrópolis: Vozes, 1981); and Octávio Ianni, *A Luta pela Terra* (Petrópolis: Vozes, 1978). On repression against the progressive Church, see Scott Mainwaring, *The Catholic Church and Politics in Brazil, 1916–1985* (Stanford: Stanford University Press, forthcoming). Documentation of repression against peasants and the progressive Church is available through the Comissão Pastoral da Terra; see, for example, the two-volume publication, *Denúncia: Caso Araguaia-Tocantins* (Goiânia: Comissão Pastoral da Terra, 1981).

10. On the government's manipulation of electoral laws, see David Fleischer, "Constitutional and Electoral Engineering in Brazil: A Double-Edged Sword— 1964–1982," *Journal of Inter-American Economic Affairs* 37 (Spring 1984): 3–36.

11. Guillermo O'Donnell and Philippe Schmitter address this theme in *Political Life After Authoritarian Rule*, Volume I of O'Donnell, Schmitter and Whitehead (eds.), *Transitions From Authoritarian Rule*.

12. Although not specifically focused on transitions through transaction, a good discussion of the dilemmas of controlling the military in transitions from authoritarian rule is Alain Rouquié, "Demilitarization and the Institutionalization of Military-Dominated Politics in Latin America," Latin American Program, Wilson Center, Working Paper 110 (1982).

13. Two good treatments of the Spanish military are Kenneth Medhurst, "The Military and the Prospects for Spanish Democracy," *West European Politics* 1 (February 1978): 42–59; and Pedro Vilanova, "Spain: The Army and the Transition" in David S. Bell (ed.), *Democratic Politics in Spain* (London: Frances Pinter, 1983), pp. 147–164. On the Brazilian military and the liberalization process, see Alfred Stepan's contribution to Stepan (ed.), *Democratizing Brazil* (forthcoming); and René Armand Dreifuss and Otávia Soares Dulci, "As Forças Armadas e a Política," in Velasco e Cruz, et. al., *Sociedade e Política no Brasil pós-64*, pp. 87–117.

14. For a discussion of the notion of retroactive legitimation, see Giuseppe Di Palma, "Derecha, izquierda o centro?: Sobre la legitimación de los partidos en el sur de Europa," *Revista de derecho político* 6 (Spring 1980): 133–145.

15. For example, a 1979 survey showed that about 25 percent of the respondents evaluated Franco's rule favorably, and a similar percentage felt

"neutral" about the dictator. See Juan J. Linz, et. al., *Informe sociológico sobre el cambio político en España, 1975–1981* (Madrid: Euramérica, 1981), p. 588.

16. Much of this discussion draws on Share's "Transition Through Transaction."

17. There is a substantial literature on these popular movements, including Renato Raúl Boschi (ed.), *Movimentos Coletivos no Brasil Urbano* (Rio de Janeiro: Zahar, 1983); Paulo Singer and Vinícius Caldeira Brant (eds.), *São Paulo: O Povo em Movimento* (Petrópolis: Vozes/CEBRAP, 1980); José Álvaro Moises, et. al., *Alternativas Populares da Democracia* (Petrópolis: Vozes/CEDEC, 1982); and John Humphrey, *Capitalist Control and Workers' Struggle in the Brazilian Auto Industry* (Princeton: Princeton University Press, 1982).

18. On this erosion, see Luíz Gonzaga de Souza Lima, "Notas sôbre a Crise Brasileira" (unpublished paper, 1983); Scott Mainwaring, "The Transition to Democracy in Brazil" (forthcoming); and Thomas Skidmore's contribution to Stepan (ed.), *Democratizing Brazil*.

19. On the cultural renaissance in Spain see Nissa Torrents, "Cinema and Media after the Death of Franco," in Christopher Abel and Nissa Torrents (eds.), *Spain: Conditional Democracy* (London: Croom Helm, 1984), pp. 100–114.

20. Here we are only concerned with regimes which attempt to establish themselves in power. We do not include what Alfred Stephan has called the "moderating pattern," where the military's sole purpose for intervening is to contain a threat and quickly restore democracy. On this point, see Alfred Stepan, *The Military in Politics: Changing Patterns in Brazil* (Princeton: Princeton University Press, 1971). For example, before 1964 the Brazilian military often acted as a short-term "moderator." This pattern differs markedly from the Latin American military interventions inspired by the national security doctrine in the 1960s and 1970s. In these latter cases the military intervened with the intention of remaining in power for a protracted period of time.

21. Among the most important sources on the Brazilian regime are Peter Flynn, *Brazil: A Political Analysis* (Boulder: Westview Press, 1979), pp. 308–515; Alfred Stepan (ed.), *Authoritarian Brazil: Origins, Policies, and Future* (New Haven: Yale University Press, 1973); Thomas Bruneau and Philippe Faucher (eds.), *Authoritarian Capitalism: Brazil's Contemporary Political and Economic Development* (Boulder: Westview Press, 1981); and Maria Helena Moreira Alves, *State and Opposition in Military Brazil* (Austin: University of Texas Press, forthcoming).

22. Some good overviews of the franquist regime are Kenneth N. Medhurst, *The Government of Spain: The Executive at Work* (Oxford: Pergamon, 1973); José Amodia, *Franco's Political Legacy: From Dictatorship to Facade Democracy* (London: Allen Lane, 1977); E. Ramón Arango, *The Spanish Political System: Franco's Legacy* (Boulder: Westview Press, 1978); and José Antonio Biescas and Manuel Tuñón de Lara, *España bajo la dictadura franquista (1939–1975)* (Barcelona: Labor, 1980).

23. On this point, see Bolivar Lamounier, "O Discurso e o Processo: Da Distensão às Opções do Regime Brasileiro," in Henrique Rattner (ed.), *Brasil 1990: Caminhos Alternativos do Desenvolvimento* (São Paulo: Brasiliense, 1979), pp. 88–120.

24. On these features of authoritarian regimes, see Juan J. Linz, "An Authoritarian Regime: Spain" in E. Allardt and Y. Littunen (eds.), *Cleavages, Ideologies, and Party Systems* (Helsinki: Academic Bookstore, 1964).

25. Ronald Schneider chronicles the internal military tensions of the 1964–1970 period in *The Political System of Brazil: Emergence of a 'Modernizing' Authoritarian Regime, 1964–1970* (New York: Columbia University Press, 1971);

and in "The Brazilian Military in Politics," in Robert Wesson (ed.), *New Military Politics in Latin America* (New York: Praeger, 1982), pp. 51–77.

26. On the 1974 elections and their impact, see Bolivar Lamounier and Fernando Henrique Cardoso (eds.), *Os Partidos e as Eleições no Brasil* (Rio de Janeiro: Paz e Terra, 1976).

27. On the regime's difficulties in creating the long-term bases for stable authoritarian rule, see the prescient article by Juan J. Linz, "The Future of an Authoritarian Situation or the Institutionalization of an Authoritarian Regime: The Case of Brazil," in Stepan (ed.), *Authoritarian Brazil*, pp. 233–254. Philippe Schmitter also signaled some of the difficulties of long-term institutionalization, although his assessment differed from Linz's. See "The 'Portugalization' of Brazil?," in Stepan (ed.), *Authoritarian Brazil*, pp. 179–232. On the Church's opposition to military rule, see Mainwaring, *The Catholic Church and Politics in Brazil*; Thomas Bruneau, *The Political Transformation of the Brazilian Catholic Church* (New York: Cambridge University Press, 1974), pp. 177–236; and Helena Salem (ed.), *A Igreja dos Oprimidos* (São Paulo: Brasil Debates, 1981). On the Press Association, see Joan Dassin, "The Brazilian Press and the Politics of Abertura," *Journal of Interamerican Studies and World Affairs* 26 (August 1984): 385–414.

28. On opposition during franquism, see Juan J. Linz, "Opposition In and Under an Authoritarian Regime: The Case of Spain," in Robert A. Dahl (ed.), *Regimes and Oppositions* (New Haven: Yale University Press, 1973), pp. 171–259; and José María Maravall, *Dictadura y disentimiento político: Obreros y estudiantes bajo el franquismo* (Madrid: Alfaguara, 1978); Xavier Tussel, *La oposición democrática al franquismo* (Barcelona: Planeta, 1976).

29. On the regional problem see Kenneth Medhurst, "The Prospects for Federalism: The Regional Question After Franco," *Government and Opposition* 1 (Spring 1976): 180–197. On terrorism, see Stanley Payne, "Terrorism and Democratic Stability in Spain," *Current History* 77 (November 1979): 170ff.

30. On this period in Argentina, see Guillermo O'Donnell, *El estado autoritario-burocrático, 1966–1973: Triunfos, derrotas y crisis* (Buenos Aires: Editorial de Belgrano, 1982); Eduardo Viola, "Autoritarismo e Democracia na Argentina Contemporanea," (Ph.D. dissertation, University of São Paulo, 1982); and William Smith, "Crisis of the State and Military Authoritarian Rule in Argentina, 1966–1973," (Ph.D. dissertation, Stanford University, 1980).

31. O'Donnell makes a similar argument in *El estado burocrático-autoritario, 1966–1973*.

32. On the UCD see Carlos Huneeus, "La Unión de Centro Democrático, Un partido consociacional," in *Revista de política comparada* 3 (Winter 1980–81): 163–192; Luis García San Miguel, "The Ideology of the Unión de Centro Democrático," in *European Journal of Political Research* 9 (1981); and José Amodia, "The Union of the Democratic Centre," in Bell (ed.), *Democratic Politics*. On AP, see Jorge de Esteban and Luis López Guerra, *Los partidos políticos en la España actual* (Barcelona: Planeta, 1982), Chapters 4 and 5.

33. On the evolution of the Brazilian left since 1964, see Leandro Konder, *A Democracia e os Comunistas no Brasil* (Rio de Janeiro: Graal, 1980); Denis Moraes and Francisco Viana (eds.), *Prestes: Lutas e Autocríticas* (Petrópolis: Vozes, 1982); Wladimir Pomar, *Araguaia: O Partido e a Guerrilha* (São Paulo: Brasil Debates, 1980); Herbet José de Souza, "Betinho," in Pedro Celso Uchoa Cavalcanti and Jovelino Ramos (eds.), *Memórias do Exílio: Brasil 1964/19??* (Sao Paulo: Livramento, 1978), pp. 67–112; and Moises Vinhas, *O Partidão* (São Paulo:

Hucitec, 1982). On the reevaluation of democracy, see Bolivar Lamounier, Francisco Weffort, and Maria Victória Benevides (eds.), *Direito, Cidadania e Participção* (São Paulo: Tao, 1981), pp. 230–257.

34. This point is illustrated in much of contemporary Central America (Nicaragua until 1979, El Salvador, and Guatemala). Given the high levels of mobilization and the mutual distrust between regimes and oppositions, transition through transaction is extremely unlikely.

35. On the labor movement between 1964 and 1974, see Kenneth Paul Erickson, *Sindicalismo no Processo Político no Brasil* (São Paulo: Brasiliense, 1979); and Kenneth Mericle, "Conflict Regulation in the Brazilian Industrial Relations System," (Ph.D. dissertation, University of Wisconsin, 1974).

36. For evidence of the depoliticization of Spanish society in the late franquist period, see Amando de Miguel, "Spanish Political Attitudes, 1970," in Stanley Payne (ed.), *Politics and Society in Twentieth Century Spain* (New York: New Viewpoints, 1976), pp. 208–232; Rafael López Pintor, *La opinión pública española: del franquismo a la democracia* (Madrid: CIS, 1982), pp. 92–93; and Antonio López Pina and E. Aranguren, *La cultural política de la España de Franco* (Madrid: Taurus, 1976), Chapter 4.

37. Although it focuses on regime breakdown, Juan J. Linz, *The Breakdown of Democratic Regimes: Crisis, Breakdown, Reequilibration* (Baltimore: Johns Hopkins, 1978), provides an interesting discussion on the importance of leadership. For an introduction to the literature on political leadership, see also Glenn D. Paige, *The Scientific Study of Leadership* (New York: Free Press, 1977); and Dankwart A. Rustow (ed.), *Philosophers and Kings* (New York: Brazilier, 1970).

38. On Suárez's role in the transition, see Gregorio Morán, *Adolfo Suárez, historia de una ambición* (Barcelona: Planeta, 1979).

39. On Juan Carlos's role in the transition see Joaquín Bardavío, *Los silencios del Rey* (Madrid: Strips, 1979).

40. For a similar point, see Wanderley Guilherme dos Santos, "A Ciência Política na América Latina: Notas Preliminares de Autocrítica," *Dados* 23, no. 1 (1980): 15–27. For examples of scholars who attributed democratization to pressures created by economic development or, conversely, by an economic crisis, see Nicos Poulantzas, *La crisis de las dictaduras* (Madrid: Siglo XXI, 1976); Guy Hermet, "Spain under Franco: The Changing Character of an Authoritarian Regime," *European Journal of Political Research* 4 (1976): 311–327; and James R. Kurth, "Industrial Change and Political Change: A European Perspective," in David Collier (ed.), *The New Authoritarianism in Latin America*, pp. 319–362.

41. On international conditions favorable to democratization, see Richard Falk, "The Global Setting and Transitions to Democracy," Latin American Program, Wilson Center, Working Paper 99 (1981). Specifically on ways the United States can foster democratization, see Guillermo O'Donnell, "Estados Unidos, América Latina, democracia: Variaciones sobre un viejísimo tema," Kellogg Institute, Working Paper 19 (May 1984).

42. On the foreign relations of franquist Spain see José Mario Armero, *La política exterior de Franco* (Barcelona: Planeta, 1978); and R. Richard Rubottom and J. Carter Murphy, *Spain and the United States Since World War II* (New York: Praeger, 1984).

43. On the relationship between levels of economic development and democracy, see Seymour Martin Lipset, *Political Man: The Social Bases of Politics* (Garden City: Anchor Books, 1963); and Dahl, *Polyarchy*, pp. 62–80.

44. World Bank, *The World Bank Development Report, 1983* (New York: Oxford University Press, 1983).

45. See Linz, *Informe sociológico*, pp. 616–618.

46. On the constitutional compromise in Spain see Bonifacio de la Cuadra and Soledad Gallego-Díaz, *Del consenso al desencanto* (Madrid: Saltes, 1981); and Joaquín Aguirre Bellver, *Así se hizo la Constitución* (Valencia: S.N., 1978).

47. For a good treatment of the political economy of this period, see Pedro Schwartz, "Politics First: The Economy After Franco," in *Government and Opposition* 11 (Winter 1976): 84–103.

48. A critical analysis of the Moncloa Pacts is Curro Ferraro, *Economía y explotación en la democracia española: Análisis de los pactos de la Moncloa* (Bilbao: Zero, 1978).

49. This argument is developed in Donald Share, "Two Transitions: Democratisation and the Evolution of the Spanish Socialist Left," *West European Politics* (January 1985): 82–103.

50. See José Luis Morales and Juan Celada, *La alternativa militar: El golpismo después de Franco* (Madrid: Editorial Revolución, 1981); and Paul Preston, "Fear of Freedom: The Spanish Army after Franco," in Abel and Torrents (eds.), *Spain: Conditional Democracy*, pp. 161–185.

51. This term is used in the preface and title of Abel and Torrent's recent work, *Spain: Conditional Democracy*.

52. José María Maravall, *La política de la transición* (Madrid: Taurus, 1981), Part 2; Peter McDonough, Antonio López Pina, and Samuel H. Barnes, "The Spanish Public in Political Transition," *The British Journal of Political Science* 11 (January 1981): 49–79; and Samuel H. Barnes and Antonio López Pina, "Political Mobilization in Old and New Democracies: Spain in Comparative Perspective," paper delivered at the 1982 annual meeting of the American Political Science Association (Denver: September 2–5, 1982).

53. Indeed, some scholars argue that high levels of participation may endanger democracy. See the controversial work by Michel Crozier, Samuel Huntington, and Joji Watanuki, *The Crisis of Democracy* (New York: New York University Press, 1975).

54. The role of participation in invigorating democracy is a leading theme in democratic theory. See, for example, C. B. MacPherson, *The Life and Times of Liberal Democracy* (New York: Oxford University Press, 1977); Carole Pateman, *Participation and Democratic Theory* (Cambridge: Cambridge University Press, 1970); and Claus Offe, "New Social Movements as a Meta-Political Challenge" (forthcoming). A work questioning the quality of Spanish democracy is Juan Luis Cebrián, *La España que bosteza* (Madrid: Taurus, 1980).

55. On popular attitudes towards politics, see Teresa Pires do Rio Caldeira, *A Política dos Outros* (São Paulo: Brasiliense, 1984); and her "Para quê Serve o Voto? As Eleições e o Cotidiano na Periferia de São Paulo," in Bolivar Lamounier (ed.), *Voto de Desconfiança: Eleições e Mudança Política no Brasil, 1970–1979* (Petrópolis: Vozes/CEBRAP, 1980), pp. 81–116; Janice Perlman, *The Myth of Marginality: Urban Poverty and Politics in Rio de Janeiro* (Berkeley: University of California Press, 1976); Anthony Leeds and Elizabeth Leeds, *A Sociologia do Brasil Urbano* (Rio de Janeiro: Zahar, 1978); and Lícia Valladares, *Passa-se uma Casa* (Rio de Janeiro: Zahar, 1978).

56. Instituto Brasileiro de Geografia e Estatística, *Censo de 1980*.

57. These regional inequalities are discussed by Clóvis Cavalcanti, "Tristes Processos Econômicos: O Padrão Recente de Desenvolvimento do Nordeste," (mimeo, 1979); and Roberto Cavalcanti de Alburquerque and Clóvis Cavalcanti, *Desenvolvimento Regional no Brasil* (Brasília: IPEA, 1976).

58. These traditional aspects of Brazilian political culture are analyzed in Raimundo Faoro, *Os Donos do Poder* (Pôrto Alegre: Globo, 1958); Wanderley Guilherme Dos Santos, *Ordem Burguesa e Liberalismo Político* (São Paulo: Duas Cidades, 1978); and Simon Schwartzman, *Bases do Autoritarismo no Brasil* (Rio de Janeiro: Campus, 1982).

6

Brazil's Political Future

Ronald M. Schneider

Economic forecasting has a long history of evolution and progress, by now being used widely in the business world as well as being fully accepted in academic spheres. This is not the case, however, with political forecasting, a field in which qualitative judgments still predominate, based upon experience as perceived by the analyst—often filtered through ideological preferences and almost always distorted by subjective considerations. Efforts at predictions stemming from gaming or computer-assisted simulations fall afoul of the basic fact that politics, though a process of purposeful collective action, is not at all a matter only of objectively rational decisions within an essentially fixed framework. Indeed, not only are there the complicating factors of human frailties and perceived versus objective reality, but unexpected (albeit not always unforeseeable) "accidents of history" do occur in national as well as individual lives.[1]

One of the most fundamental problems with political forecasting lies in the often indirect and generally delayed relationship between developments in the economy and their reflection in the political realm. This is in large part a result of the fact that much of economic change is mediated through its societal impact—as changes in the economy affect groups in society and lead to modifications in their demands as expressed in the political process. Then, too, basic economic developments profoundly affect in a secular manner the size and strength of society's constituent elements. Although the political ramifications of this may well be delayed and at times diverted, over the longer haul such fundamental modifications of society impinge upon or condition political decisionmaking, which after all deals essentially with who gets what at the expense of whom. In light of the fact that social changes affect decisionmaking, any valid effort to analyze the impact of economic performance upon politics, and to go from there back to policy decisions affecting the economic actors, must take into account social change—and do this in more than just an offhand and passing manner.

Such a wedding of economic, social, and political factors through an integrated analysis of their interrelationships in the real-world Brazilian context has been the central objective of a long-term and continuing research effort on my part. The approach I have evolved involves a six-

217

step process beginning with an evaluation of Brazilian development from the post-World War II period through 1984. This is followed by examination of the many groups significantly involved in political decisionmaking in Brazil in terms of past, present, and probable future alignments and policy orientations. The third step is to assess the interplay of economic, political, and social factors bearing upon these groups as the effort to establish a viable, representative, and competitive political system continued during 1985 amidst the release of pent-up demands for greater social justice and increased economic benefits after two decades of authoritarian and quasiauthoritarian rule. Subsequently, by defining a comprehensive set of future economic contexts for the 1987–1988 period, I am then able to derive a series of alternative political scenarios embodying the probable sociopolitical situation under each possible economic context. Finally, by estimating the relative probabilities of the scenarios, it becomes possible to calculate the likelihood of varying degrees of political change in a much more systematic manner than has hitherto been the case in political forecasting.

Such an enterprise obviously generates wide-ranging data requirements going considerably beyond the existing literature. A key aspect of my approach is to meet the need for a high level of expertise on both the process of decisionmaking in Brazil and the dynamics of each of the principal groups and institutions out of my own long experience with these subjects. As a baseline, I have gone back through the vast amount of material I have gathered over the past thirty years to calculate relative numbers for the influence of each actor on the total range of major policy decisions at each significant point in time. The results are summarized in Table 6.1, with explanation of the groups included coming later in the chapter. Although certainly not as precise as economic time-series data, nor even as electoral results, this approach constitutes a great improvement over partial and generally implicit qualitative comparisons, which are undercut by a lack of consistency and compatibility stemming from the different framework and point of view of each observer and analyst—the situation heretofore prevailing in studies on Brazilian politics.[2]

Although future changes may be far from straight-line projections of the last quarter century, prediction must begin with an examination of trends during the past generation—a volatile period embracing the crisis of the early 1960s, the drastic regime change of 1964, a protracted series of variations of authoritarianism, and a transition back to competitive civilian politics spanning (in its several stages) a full decade.

The Environment of the Political Process

Brazil is a complex, newly industrialized country going through a process of transition from authoritarian rule to institutionalization of

TABLE 6.1
Power Proportions of the Politically Relevant Groups Over Time

	1961	1965	1969	1973	1977	1981	1984
1. Presidency	12	12	10	11	10	11	10
2. Military Moderates	10	22	20	26	25	20	17
3. MDB/PMDB[a]	8[b]	2	1	2	3	4	6.5
4. Bureaucracy	4	8	13	12	11	9	7
6. Industrialists	6	5.5	4	4	5	6	5.5
7. Church Moderates	5	4	3	3	3.5	4	4
8. Banking	4	3	2	2.5	3	4	4
9. Unions	4	1	0.8	0.7	1	1.3	1.5
11. Commerce	4	3	3	3.5	4	4	3
12. Middle Class	5	2	1.5	1.5	2.5	3	2.5
13. International Banks	3	2.5	2	1	1	3	5
14. Int'l. Fin. Orgs.	4	3.3	2	1	1.5	3	6
15. ARENA/PDS[c]	7[d]	7	3	3	4	5	7
16. Military Hardline	3	10	20	13	10	7	4.5
17. Church Left	2	1.3	0.9	1	1.6	2.3	2.5
18. U. S. Government	3	5	4.5	4.5	4	4.5	3
19. Agriculture	3	2	1	1	1.6	1.6	1.6
20. Multinationals	4	4.5	6.5	6.5	3.5	3	2.7
21. PDT	-	-	-	-	-	0.1	1.2
22. Left Radicals	4	0.5	0.3	0.3	0.4	0.5	0.7
23. Students	2	0.1	.05	.05	0.1	0.3	0.5
24. PT	-	-	-	-	-	0.1	0.8
25. Right Radicals	0.1	1	1.3	1.3	1.5	1.3	1.1
26. PTB	-	-	-	-	-	0.1	1.1
27. Rural Workers	2	0.2	0.1	0.1	0.15	0.25	0.3
28. Urban Marginals	0.9	0.1	0.05	0.05	0.1	0.15	0.3
29. OPEC, et. al.	-	-	-	1	2.5	1.5	0.8

[a] Includes those elements now considered as group 10, PMDB Left.
[b] PTB plus pro-Goulart elements of other parties.
[c] Includes present group 5, PFL.
[d] Weight of center-conservative parties in opposition to the incoming Goulart government.

open competitive politics. Sustained very high economic growth rates from 1968 through 1980 transformed much of Center-South Brazil into a quasi-European society, while at the same time leaving tens of millions living as subsistence farmers or urban poor. Fifth in the world in area and sixth in population (which will reach 140 million by the end of 1986), Brazil is filled with dramatic contrasts and contradictions. Observers' attention usually focuses upon the differences between São Paulo with its massive and sophisticated industrial complex and the backwards Northeast with its starving masses. Yet besides the great urban centers or the retarded rural areas, there is a very important "in between" Brazil of the middle-sized cities and their regional hinterlands. Indeed, this "in-between" Brazil may prove to be the key to a future of stability rather than of turmoil.

The Nature of Brazilian Development

Brazil of the mid-1980s is a much more complex nation than it was when the military came to power in April 1964. It is even more strikingly different than when its great authoritarian populist Getúlio Vargas took his own life in August 1954, frustrated by the complications of governing an increasingly urban and industrializing country—one which had changed substantially even in the short time since his previous experience as its president (from 1930 to 1945). In fact, when the abrupt and unsystematic effort to dismantle Vargas's authoritarian *Estado Nôvo* took place in 1945–1946, Brazil was a country of just over 46 million inhabitants with an electorate still below 7.5 million—less than one-eighth the present number of voters. Since that time population has virtually tripled, while at the same time Brazil has passed through an economic and social transformation roughly analogous to that experienced by Germany during the Bismarckian era (1862–1890). Brazil is now, relative to 1945, a quite complex, largely urban and industrial nation undergoing rapid social change as literacy rates have risen significantly under the post-1964 regime and the number of university students has multiplied more than tenfold to over 1.4 million.

In 1962, following Juscelino Kubitschek's centrist democratic administration with its motto of "Fifty Years' Progress in Five," Brazil's population was something over 75 million—a figure now easily surpassed by the five most populous of its twenty-three states—and there were 18.5 million registered voters. By 1970, with the technocratic-military regime entrenched in power and the "economic miracle" in full swing, Brazil's population had climbed to just over 93 million, and during the next decade it would grow by an additional 26 million—a figure almost equal to the population of either Argentina or Colombia (the second and third most populous countries of South America). Even with a declining rate of population growth during the ensuing decade and a half, this has led to the present situation in which Brazil's population increases by the equivalent of an Uruguay every year, and over 1.4 million new jobs are needed annually to absorb the young people coming into the work force.

With the present electorate surpassing 60 million and expanding apace, Brazil's continued political development requires institutionalization adequate to the growing demands for effective participation. But never in Brazilian history has the party system satisfactorily performed its role in this regard. From the manipulated two-party system of the Empire (1822–1889), through the perverted electoral machines of the Old Republic, to the absence of parties in the *Estado Nôvo*, followed by the excessive fragmentation of the 1946–1964 period, and, finally, with the straightjacket of an artificial two-party system finally laid to rest in 1979–1980, this failure of the Brazilian party system has always been the case. Under such circumstances, the Church and the armed forces have often been viewed as the only real national institutions—and to a considerable extent this continues to be true.

Much more has changed in Brazil during the past generation than just its political demography and the prospect of an adequate party system at long last. New industries have sprung up alongside old, and new crops such as soybeans and oranges have pushed coffee from its dominant position. Agricultural products, which as recently as 1970 still constituted 60 percent of Brazil's exports, dropped to under 40 percent in 1984—but this was out of over $27 billion total foreign sales compared to less than $8 billion in 1970, so the value of agricultural exports actually more than doubled (while non-agricultural sales increased five-fold).

These economic changes have been reflected in society, as a much more complex and differentiated stratification system has come into being. The economically active population rapidly reached, then exceeded, 50 million, and even in the aftermath of recession the country's GNP approximates $300 billion. In a nation where tens of millions are still engaged in subsistence agriculture, quite sophisticated arms (Brazil is the sixth largest exporter of such materials in the world), aviation, and electronics industries have come into existence. And a nation where until recently charcoal was still a basic energy source now boasts the world's largest and third largest hydroelectric projects, an oil production that at over 600,000 barrels a day is much more than triple that of 1979, and a vast program of using alcohol for fuel. Yet at the same time Brazil staggers under a foreign debt of roughly $100 billion and an annual inflation rate that exceeded 230 percent in 1985.

Nationalism remains perhaps the most difficult element to assess and the one with the greatest potential for catalyzing a significant transformation of the present political scene. Once quite strident (during the 1950s and early 1960s), politically relevant manifestations of radical nationalism have been muted since 1964. By all meaningful historical and comparative standards, Brazilian nationalism of the "negative" or xenophobic variety is remarkably low—even through the 1982 election campaign and the economic stringencies linked to the world recession, as well as the protracted saga of Brazil's dealings with the IMF. There remains, however, considerable potential for a marked upswing of such sentiment, perhaps once again focused against the spectre of "Yankee imperialism." The key variable in this respect is the ability of radical left elements to convince significant components of the Brazilian population that the United States is chiefly responsible for Brazil's economic woes. So far they have made little headway in this regard, with exponents of such a message generally faring poorly at the polls in November 1982 and losing ground to essentially moderate elements within the major opposition party—now the chief government party—during 1983 and 1984.

Overall, the elections held in November 1985 reflected the limited short-range prospects for a successful nationalist political mobilization—

in good part related to the improved economic climate beginning in the second half of 1984. During the pre-1964 period Congress played a major role in building a broad nationalist political mobilization with the so-called "Nationalist Parliamentary Front" cutting across the confusing multiplicity of party lines characterizing that period. The present Congress provides but very limited prospects in this regard, and radical elements have not been able to utilize Parliamentary Investigating Commissions (CPIs) to further ultranationalist ends. Should the economic situation deteriorate seriously in mid-1986 and a breakdown occur in negotiations for debt rescheduling, capabilities to do so would be enhanced, although much of this would be transferred to the electoral arena. In such a case the possibility of major gains for the left in the November 1986 elections would be very real, and any sweeping reformulation of the party system as a result of presidential succession rivalries by 1987-1988 could alter the political balance which now heavily favors the centrists. In this respect the inability of Tancredo Neves to assume the presidency (culminating in his death on April 21, 1985) could still conceivably result in presidential succession being moved forward, albeit there is also the possibility of President Sarney's term continuing to 1989-1990.

Demographic Factors

The spectre of "Belindia," with an urban, modernized region swallowed up by a vast backward hinterland with overpopulated cities but little industry (à la India), popularized in the 1970s by Edmar Bacha and other left-of-center economists, is a misleading oversimplification of the Brazil of the 1980s. Brazil is not just a classic dual society, but rather consists of at least three major socioeconomic divisions with profound political significance: the Brazil of huge metropolitan centers; the Brazil of the countryside and small towns; and the too-often forgotten Brazil, that of a hundred nongargantuan cities and their subregional hinterlands. This latter is now the fastest growing and changing of the three Brazils, overtaking the great urban centers that played a similar role during the past generation.

In 1986, in addition to the 40 million people dwelling in the ten major metropolitan regions, nearly 7 million Brazilians live in the fourteen state capitals, which have populations of from 200,000 to 850,000, and more than 6 million live in other cities in this size range. It would be a mistake to believe that these more than 50 million people make up the total of Brazil's city dwellers and that the other 80 million live in small towns or in the country. A rapidly burgeoning strata of Brazil's municipalities are provincial cities in the 100,000 to 200,000 bracket—often complete with all the essential urban attributes and important roles as regional centers in the less densely populated areas of the country. Each has a hinterland with one to five times its population, so perhaps another 15 to 20 million persons live in these areas.

Labor Force, Income Distribution, and Education

The profound transformation experienced by Brazilian society over the past quarter century, already viewed in terms of population factors and their political implications, has also affected those areas in which the government's economic policies have a direct differential impact—favorable or unfavorable—upon different social strata and thus are likely to trigger significant political feedback. Most salient of these areas are income distribution and education.[3]

As of 1984 some 1.6 percent of Brazil's 53.7 million economically active population (EAP) could be considered well-off to rich by Brazilian standards, that is, earning over twenty times the legal minimum wage. (The minimum wage was pegged at about $67 a month following a 100 percent rise on May 1, 1985, but dropped to under $40 before the next semiannual readjustment in November.) This segment of the population shared nearly 18 percent of total income. A substantial upper-middle class was composed of the just under 1.9 million individuals earning from ten to twenty minimum wages. This group received nearly 16 percent of total income, so about 5.1 percent at the top of the social pyramid received almost 34 percent of all income. Solidly in the middle class by Brazilian standards were also the nearly 4.6 million individuals earning from five to ten minimum wages. Although they make up just 8.5 percent of the EAP, they received more than 20 percent of total income. Transitional between this lower-middle class and the upper strata of the working class were the more than 6.1 million individuals earning from three to five minimum wages. Constituting 11.3 percent of the work force, they pulled down just about 15 percent of the total income. Thus, the slightly under 13.5 million persons (25.2 percent of the EAP) who earned at least a reasonable living in Brazil totaled around 69 percent of total income.

By way of stark contrast, the working-class component substantially above the poverty level (earning two to three minimum wages) numbered over 6.6 million and received just over 10 percent of the income, compared to their 12.3 percent proportion of the EAP. Just out of the ranks of the poor, at least in the Brazilian context, were 13.2 million individuals earning from one to two minimum wages for approximately 12 percent of total income (although they made up some 24.4 percent of the EAP). The 38.2 percent of the work force being paid less than minimum wage was composed of 11.5 million earning above one-half the rate and 9.1 million getting by on less than this meager amount. The former totaled some 6 percent of the country's incomes, whereas the latter aggregated only around 2 percent—in chilling contrast to the more fortunate minorities discussed above.

Yet these figures, jolting as they are, reflect substantial improvement through the 1970s. In 1970 no fewer than 60 percent of the EAP was below minimum wage, and the distribution of a significantly smaller economic pie was even more sharply skewed. After that date the greatest change came in the strata earning two to five times the minimum wage, a group that nearly doubled from 12.7 percent of the work force in 1970 to 23.6 percent in 1984. Taking total households, rather than individuals, into account (including the subsistence sector and the unemployed), no fewer than 69 percent had to get along on less than one-half the minimum wage in 1970, a figure that dropped sharply to just under 41 percent a decade later. Again with respect to total households, as of 1984 just over half the population—some 68 million individuals—consisted of families with incomes under three times the minimum wage. The government considers about 40 million of these to be "poor" and intends to address their needs through substantially augmented social programs in the 1986 budget.

The positive developments in the socioeconomic sphere during the 1970s were made possible only by the exceptional economic growth that occurred in spite of the energy crisis. The sustained high GNP growth rates of the late 1960s carried over into the 1970s at the same time as population growth followed a slow but steady decline. The economic growth of 8.3 percent in 1970 was exceeded in each of the next four years with phenomenal rates of 12.0, 11.1, and 13.6 percents preceding 1974's rate of 9.7 percent. Even during the adjustment to skyrocketing oil prices, the Brazilian economy continued to expand: 5.4 percent in 1975; climbing to 9.7 percent in 1976 before dropping to 6.7 percent the next year and 6.0 percent in 1978; rallying to 6.4 percent in 1979 and hitting 7.2 percent to open the 1980s. But the time of reckoning was at hand, and the negative 1.6 percent of 1981 combined with low growth of roughly .9 percent in 1982 more than negated the gain of 1980 in per capita terms, leaving 125 million Brazilians dividing a GNP of somewhat under $300 billion for an average of about $2,300. But this included São Paulo state, with nearly the population of Argentina or Colombia, enjoying a per capita income of $4,500, while for the rest of the country the figure was only slightly in excess of $1,800.

The picture of the field of education is very mixed. According to the 1982 *Pesquisa Nacional por Amostra de Domicílios* (*PNAD*), in the country as a whole some 86 percent of seven-year-olds were enrolled in the first year of school as against only 67 percent in 1970, but a high proportion continue to drop out in the primary ranks. Indeed, for 21.3 million in elementary schools there were only 2.6 million in secondary schools (with nearly 1.4 million more enrolled in higher education). Moreover, some 22 million persons over seven years of age had never attended school, and—although the index of illiteracy fell from 34 percent to 26 percent between 1970 and 1982—the total number of those over seven who could not read or write rose slightly (from 25.2 million to 25.8 million). Then too, against São Paulo's "official" illiteracy rate of under 4 percent, Alagoas still had more illiterate inhabitants than literate ones. More to the point, no progress in this field had been made since the mid-1970s, and at least 25 million individuals considered literate could not usefully read or write.

Regional variations are vast and cruel, with 46 percent of the population in the Northeast illiterate and almost 60 percent of the primary school-age children not enrolled in classes, compared to a national figure of 34 percent. Thus, although the educational situation has clearly improved in the cities and continues to do so—particularly in Rio de Janeiro and São Paulo—little if any headway has been made in the countryside, with a rural illiteracy rate of some 53 percent. Clearly, improvement during the rest of the 1980s of this lamentable situation will rest chiefly upon expansion of educational opportunities in smaller cities and towns. Tax resources can be transferred to these centers, but really rural areas lack the requisite political clout to call attention to the absence of schools and teachers.

There remains a substantial racial factor in the distribution of income and educational opportunities, one which over time may have political ramifications. Although 28 percent of the white working population earns less than minimum wage, this rises to 47.5 percent for brown-skinned and to 52.5 percent for blacks (according to official IBGE figures). Some 48.2 percent of whites in the work force take home from one to five times the minimum wage. For browns and blacks alike this proportion is only 37 percent, with nearly two-thirds of these in the one to two minimum wages bracket, compared to just over one-half among their white counterparts. At the other end of the scale, over 13 percent of whites earned more than five minimum wages, whereas for brown-skinned this was only 3.6 percent and for blacks a meager 2 percent.

It has been estimated that each 1 percent of GNP growth in Brazil yields 0.4 percent in terms of new employment opportunities, and that at this rate Brazil needs at least 6 percent real annual growth in the economy to create the over 1.4 million jobs required each year to provide for the 2.5 percent yearly increase in the work force caused by young people coming into the job market. (Fifty percent of the population is below twenty-one years of age.) Although the Sarney government has been giving attention to how the creation of new jobs could be increased more effectively, 5.5 to 6 percent GNP growth in the years immediately ahead would do little more than maintain present rates of unemployment and reverse the rapid growth of the "hidden" underground economy of odd jobs that has characterized the early 1980s.[4] These considerations are at the root of government determination to maintain economic growth and reject highly recessive measures to combat inflation.

As it is, there is a sharp division within the labor force between the 25 million wage earners whose labor cards have been signed by employers and who thus get the benefits due them under social legislation and the estimated 27 million who are deprived of those advantages either because their employers have not seen fit to so register their employment or because they work for themselves or lack fixed jobs. Indeed, workers without labor cards are the rule in rural areas, with 80 percent lacking such registration, compared to only 40 percent in the urban sectors.

Then, too, Brazil has at least 10 million unemployed and seriously underemployed (depending upon how the latter term is defined). Because of the desperate economic situation of unregistered, unemployed, and underemployed workers, the relative political passivity of the 1970s and early 1980s, marked only by sporadic unrest in the largest urban centers and a rise in the crime rate, will not likely survive a long-continued recession in the years ahead.

Income for most sectors of society took a real beating in 1983, following erosion the preceding two years, in what was arguably the worst economic year for Brazil since at least 1930. Negative growth of 3.2 percent brought the GNP back to second quarter of 1980 levels, which in per capita terms—given the approximately 2.4 percent annual population increase—meant income remained at first quarter of 1978 levels. This seriously eroded the progress made toward more equitable distribution of income between 1970 and 1980, but recovery to 4.5 percent GNP growth during 1984 stemmed the negative effects of the 1981-1983 recession. Indeed, the 1984 growth brought the GNP back to just above the end-of-year 1980 peak, and raised per capita incomes to at least the third quarter 1978 level. Thus, the recession with its sharp rise in unemployment did stop the ongoing surge of upward social mobility and hit the new middle class particularly hard. Yet the combination of a substantial beginning of economic recovery and the anticipated transition to a popular civilian government undercut the resulting social unrest during the second half of 1984 and the early months of 1985—gains which were to be consolidated during the rest of the year.

Impact of Socioeconomic Changes
Upon Political Affiliations

To this point such fundamental social trends as urbanization, demographic growth, education, and class structure have been related to factors of macroeconomic development, especially labor force and income distribution. The passing references to levels of social unrest, the rapid expansion of the electorate, and the political party system must be supplemented by consideration of such links between the socioeconomic transformation and political developments as the changing social bases of political parties. Moreover, understanding of the societal genealogy of the present parties provides a point of departure for assessing future changes in political alignments. Although space limitations prevent detailed discussion here, the chapters by Selcher and Fleischer have shown that none of the present parties are direct linear descendants of any of the pre-1964 ones. Then, too, current alignments are still subject to substantial modification in the crucible of the 1986 national balloting and the ensuing presidential succession.[5]

Trends in the Major Politically Relevant Groups

Given the increased—and still increasing—complexity of Brazilian society, combined as it is with political structures lacking firm popular roots, the possibilities of future political alignments remain fluid. Over the next five to seven years at least, no essentially new social groupings of significance are likely to emerge. The most important trend will be the continued growth of some of those whose roots go back well into the transformations of the Kubitschek years (1956–1960) and that grew during the period of authoritarian rule as a result of continued economic development, although in most cases their avenues of political participation were curtailed.

Constituent Elements of the Brazilian Game

The composition of future political alliances in Brazil will be conditioned by a variety of factors—some have already been discussed, and others will be treated subsequently. Nonetheless, the basic starting point for analysis is the present array of political forces (as of 1985), their relationships, and trends among them during recent years. They must not only be examined with respect to internal dynamics and the effect upon them of social and economic changes, but also with regard to their perceptions of how the system (including the rules of the game) is evolving. Any adequate analysis of Brazilian politics, much less a model of significant predictive value, requires consideration of two dozen relevant internal groups and their strengths, resources, leadership, world views, internal divisions, tactics, interrelationships, and positions on key issues. In terms of power, as reflected in their weight in shaping decisions on national policy, and including significant external actors, I rank them as follows.[6]

1. The Presidency (Planalto). Composed of the president and his closest associates (Private Secretary Jorge Murad, Marcos Vinícius Villaça, Special Advisor Célio Borja, International Affairs Advisor Rubens Ricúpero, Civil Cabinet Chief Marco Maciel, and National Intelligence Service Chief Ivan de Souza Mendes), the Presidential Palace group is concerned with maintaining a coherent policy line over both the score of other civilian ministries and the powerful state enterprises—particularly on budget and fiscal matters—and maintenance of a basic unity of the political alliance upon which the administration rests. This problem was accentuated by the trauma of Tancredo Neves's death and the increased rivalry between the parties supporting the government in Congress.

2. Military Moderates. Composed of the mainstream of the armed forces, they generally support the chief executive, albeit at times with some misgivings expressed within the government by the service ministers. Rivalry among the branches has been muted, but is still a potentially divisive factor, as are generational variations and differences between

the officer corps and permanent cadres of noncommissioned officers. The military moderates were crucial with regard to the process of "transition from above," particularly during the recent presidential succession—in which they favored an "honorable" disengagement from direct involvement in running the government.

3. Party of the Brazilian Democratic Movement (PMDB). The largest component of the Congress, with well over 200 federal deputies and just about a third of the Senate as well as nine governors, it contains several fairly distinct wings ranging from centrist/liberal (out of the old Popular Party—PP) to representatives of radical left movements including a few Communists. Cleavages that were already marked in several of the major states where the party holds power have been accentuated as maneuvering for the 1985 mayoral and 1986 national elections was added to very real substantive programmatic differences. Moreover, Tancredo Neves was key to PMDB cohesion, and his absence became felt quickly and acutely. Thus, for future-oriented analysis the essentially moderate PMDB governors are included in this group along with those elements who supported Neves against the more radical wing of the party as far back as the December 1983 national convention (which saw the moderates gain control of the party by a substantial margin), giving this group around 160 federal deputies and at least 20 senators. Party President Ulysses Guimarães still belongs with this group, although he also has fairly strong ties to the party's left wing.

4. Government Officials (Bureaucrats). At the core of this group are the higher-level personnel of the vast state administrative machine, especially the many government-run economic enterprises, but also including policy-making positions in the regular ministries. At a lower level, a basic tension exists between those 500,000 individuals in "direct" administration and the nearly 1.5 million employed by the roughly 400 mixed-capital state economic entities, a tension that has been rooted in the exceptional financial and material benefits enjoyed by the latter, benefits that are now being curbed as part of the government's austerity program. There are also several million public employees at the state level, but they do not generally have much effect on national policy. Rivalry exists between the development-oriented "spending" ministries (such as Interior, Agriculture, Transportation, Communications, Commerce and Industry, Social Welfare, Labor, and Education) and the fiscal watchdogs of Planning, Treasury, and the Central Bank.

5. The Party of the Liberal Front (PFL). Founded in the late stages of the presidential succession process by the leading moderate figures of the then-governing PDS, it is the junior partner to the PMDB in the present administration. Aside from José Sarney (who for technical reasons formally affiliated with the PMDB), its leaders include cabinet members Aureliano Chaves, Marco Maciel, Jorge Bornhausen, and Roberto Abreu Sodré as well as most of the governors of the Northeast. Still growing at the expense of the PDS, it has over 125 federal deputies and 24

senators, with Communications Minister Antônio Carlos Magalhães and Rio Grande do Sul Governor Jair Soares among the most recent converts.

6. Industrialists. Divided by sector and often by regional differences, this group frequently finds its major policy expression through the Federation of Industries of the State of São Paulo (FIESP) rather than the more bureaucratic National Confederation of Industries (CNI) in which the voice of small states generally prevails (although CNI president, Senator Albano Franco of Sergipe is seeking to become accepted as more of a national spokesman). This sector's electoral support goes to the PFL, the PMDB moderates, the PDS, and in some cases the PTB.

7. Mainstream of the Catholic Church. The middle-of-the road majority of the hierarchy and traditional lay Catholics generally reject the increasing political activism of the progressive wing and the Ecclesiastical Base Communities (CEBs) and support centrist and conservative political movements and leaders.

8. Banking Community. Heavily concentrated in São Paulo and Rio de Janeiro, it is generally led by the biggest of Brazil's private banks such as Bradesco, Unibanco, and Itaú. Basically this sector also incorporates the insurance industry, given the close links of major insurance companies with Bradesco and Unibanco. As with the industrialists, with whom they have a variety of ties, many bankers support the PFL, with others preferring the PDS, and a few the PMDB.

9. Labor Movement. Consisting primarily of the urban trade unions, it is composed of both elements linked to specific political parties and those advocating action outside the party arena. Traditionally it has been manipulated through the structures inherited from the corporatist regime installed during the 1930s by Vargas. (As this sector is in considerable flux, it will be discussed in detail in the subsequent section.)

10. PMDB Left (Authentics, Progressives, or Independent Left). This very vocal group is made up of those elements of the PMDB whose opposition to the military regime goes back through the entire 1964–1984 period. It has relatively little representation in the first echelons of the government and has fairly consistently lost out in intraparty contests since Tancredo Neves and others of the short-lived PP merged with the old MDB during the 1982 campaign. This group is very antagonistic toward the PFL and has often voted against the Sarney government, even on crucial issues. Depending upon the issue at hand, members of this group make up between one-fourth and one-third of the PMDB's congressional delegation (50 to 65 deputies). It must be considered as a separate group, as it is seeking to oust most of those currently in power at the state level through the 1986 elections.

11. Business Community. Composed of those in commerce rather than in production, it is set apart in Brazil from the Industrialists (No. 6) and Bankers (No. 8) by the existence of separate sectoral organizations through law since the corporatist regime of the 1930s. It is represented by the ponderous National Confederation of Commerce (CNC) and by

the Rio de Janeiro-based National Association of Chambers of Commerce catalyzed by the very policy-oriented Ruy Barreto. The major potential internal division is between those internally oriented and those selling abroad (the latter are largely represented by the Brazilian Association of Exporters, AEB).

12. The Middle Class. Although voting for one party or another at election time—often with quite ambivalent feelings—the growing Brazilian middle class has not put down permanent political roots. Composed of a number of sectors running down the stratification system from well-to-do liberal professionals to low-level clerical workers, it is really an amalgam of societal groups caught in between the elites and the masses. Its political potential is increased to the degree that competitive electoral politics have again become an important decisional factor. Its components are highly sensitive to threats to their often tenuous upward mobility posed by economic hard times, and, having suffered heavily during the 1981–1983 recession, the middle class is acutely attuned to signs of another downturn.

13. The International Banking Community (IBC). Led by the major U.S. banks, this group also includes private banks of Western Europe and Japan—and these latter do not always see eye to eye with Wall Street in assessing the Brazilian situation. The group's influence is limited by the fact that many of its members are so over-exposed in Brazil as to jeopardize their solvency should Brazil opt for a moratorium, much less repudiate its debt. Yet short of such an unlikely extreme development, the banks exercise a heavy restraining influence on Brazilian economic and fiscal policy in light of the government's need for the banks' cooperation in rescheduling massive principal payments.

14. International Financial Organizations (IFOs). The IMF, the World Bank, and related institutions have seen their previously marginal influence on Brazilian affairs vastly enhanced since late 1982 by the salience of the debt problem, but they must face nationalist hostility that could—under certain circumstances—inhibit a Brazilian administration from being cooperative.

15. The Democratic Social Party (PDS). It provided the Figueiredo government's majority in Congress and at the state level, but was badly split over presidential succession and now has only about 70 federal deputies and some 13 senators responsive to its divided leadership. Still substantially influenced by defeated presidential candidate Paulo Maluf, its future prospects are negatively affected by the fact that it has lost almost all of its governors, chiefly to the PFL.

16. Military Hardline (*Linha Dura*). This group is composed of that faction of the armed forces that is wary of the recent transition and lacking in confidence in the civilian government. It ranges from some followers of ex-President Emílio Médici (1969–1974) through elements as conservative as the Right-Wing Terrorists (No. 25), but with greater scruples concerning legality.

17. Church Progressives. Advocates of "Theology of Liberation" and political activism on behalf of the masses, this group is strongest in the middle and lower ranks of the hierarchy and has popular support through its organization of Ecclesiastical Base Communities (CEBs). It has been aligned in many areas with the PT (No. 24).

18. U.S. Government (USG). It is influential chiefly because of Brazil's onerous foreign debt problem and the key role of the United States in Brazilian trade, this power coming after a period in which its policy influence had been sharply decreased by progressive reduction of Brazil's economic dependence.

19. Agricultural Producers. Although far less important today than in the past, they represent the large-scale commercial production of major export crops and staples of the domestic food supply. Essentially these elements are conservative but subject to being "bought" by preferential treatment for each segment's chief product. Their priority concerns are positions on the directorates of the government agencies vitally affecting their well-being, particularly the Brazilian Coffee Institute (IBC), the Sugar and Alcohol Institute (IAA), and the Agricultural Credit Department of the Bank of Brazil. They are represented by the National Confederation of Agriculture (CNA) and the Brazilian Rural Society, the former headed by Flávio Brito and the latter by Flávio Telles.

20. Multinational Corporations. They are influential largely to the extent that their investment and export programs help ameliorate the country's critical balance of payments problems. As shown by such decisions as 1984's restrictive "informatics" law, their political importance has been greatly exaggerated by many writers, generally for ideological purposes, but this does not mean that they would be impotent in situations in which the government might be far weaker than it is at present.

21. The Democratic Workers Party (PDT). This party is the instrument of Rio de Janeiro Governor Leonel Brizola, and its future growth is inextricably wound up with his aspirations to national leadership. The November 1985 mayoralty elections in capital cities provided a crucial test of its efforts to "go national," with victories in Rio de Janeiro and Pôrto Alegre confirming its strength in these two centers, but failing to make a strong showing in other major cities (except Curitiba). In Congress it has 3 senators and 27 deputies.

22. Radical Left-Wing Political Movements. These include intellectual advocates and range widely with respect to degree of radicalism and attitude toward the use of force. Fragmented and fractionalized, the movements' major components are presently very concerned about what to do with newly regained legal status and how to exploit the greater tolerance for propaganda and agitational campaigns that the return to democratic civilian government has entailed.

23. University Students. Very quiet politically following the wave of repression in 1969–1970, Brazil's university students number roughly

1.4 million and contain a politically militant minority. The National Union of Students (UNE) has recently been legalized (after a period of being non-legal rather than illegal), and dreams of having an impact comparable to the late 1950s and early 1960s. Fragmented ideologically, the elements active in student politics have ties to Radical Left organizations (No. 22), the PT (No. 24), and to a lesser extent the Church Progressives (No. 17).

24. The Workers Party (PT). In considerable disarray for some time after its poor showing in the 1982 elections, this young party still rests on the charisma of metalworkers' leader Luís Inácio ("Lula") da Silva and its appeal to intellectuals lacking any other really socialist alternative. Its base in São Paulo contains at least eight or nine left-wing ideological currents, rival one with the other, but each too weak in numbers to exist as open and independent political movements. It showed respectable strength in the November 1985 balloting in São Paulo, Fortaleza, Goiânia, and Vitória, but is still almost nonexistent where the PDT is strong (and like the PDT has no significant support in Minas Gerais or Bahia).

25. Right-Wing Terrorists. Presently at low ebb, this group includes both reactionary elements willing to resort to force and their protectors within the security apparatus, military and civilian. It is significant chiefly to the degree that it can find common cause with the Military Hardline in a deteriorating political situation. Hence it is on the alert for opportunities to manufacture a crisis or to induce polarization.

26. The Brazilian Labor Party (PTB). Lacking control of any state government and having no national leader, this party became a very minor factor in Congress, with half of its members leaving for other parties in mid- and late 1984. It can now build in São Paulo upon the election of ex-President Jânio Quadros as mayor in November 1985, and flourish as a haven for scattered elements lacking space within any of the larger parties.

27. Rural Workers and Subsistence Farmers. Lacking organization and virtually unrepresented by the Labor Movement (No. 9), this sector has nothing going for it politically except numbers. The transition to democratic rule has provided increased opportunity for efforts to organize and demonstrate for improved wages and working conditions, particularly in more developed areas such as São Paulo, but mobilization on a national level will take time. Although it has a fairly long history, the National Confederation of Agricultural Workers (CONTAG) has yet to prove its effectiveness.

28. Urban Marginal Population and Slum Dwellers (*Favelados*). Largely unorganized and frequently politically inarticulate, they are still, on a national scale, significantly more subject to manipulation by political bosses and populist leaders than to radical agitation, but this is already changing in some of the industrial suburbs of São Paulo and in Rio de Janeiro's "Baixada Fluminense," the belt of working-class communities surrounding the more prosperous city and its affluent southern suburbs.

29. OPEC and Other Supplier Countries. Their once perceptible influence has been diminished by the sharp reduction in Brazil's need for imported oil resulting from greatly augmented domestic production and substitution of alcohol for gasoline. This has enabled Brazil to shift purchases toward those countries willing to buy Brazilian exports (especially armaments) and contract for Brazilian services.

Trends Bearing Watching

Systematic analyses of the dynamics of each of these groups along the lines of the nine factors defined as most relevant (strength, resources, tactics, leadership, program, worldview, cohesiveness, interrelationships, and perceptions of the political system's functioning) is a task beyond the scope of this chapter—albeit one that I have carried out. Here there will be only a focused discussion of selected facets of each of the internal groups to the degree necessary to support subsequent analysis dealing with the probable impact of different economic futures upon their political alignments and power capabilities.

Group No. 1, the Presidency, which throughout the past quarter century has possessed from 10 to 12 percent of political decisionmaking power, has gained in influence by the added legitimacy of being headed by civilians enjoying broad popular support. Thus, at present it would appear to be the leading single actor with some 15 percent of political power, but this is highly dependent upon continued public perceptions of its effectiveness and responsiveness to the aspirations of the broad range of social sectors that supported the Democratic Alliance in its unseating of the military and PDS establishment. Certainly the tragic removal from the scene of Tancredo Neves, combined with Sarney's reluctance to replace ministers, undercut the cohesiveness of the administration's original inner circle (as Civil Cabinet Chief José Hugo Castelo Branco was reduced to a technical role, Finance Minister Francisco Dornelles not only ceased to have hegemony in the economic sphere, but was replaced in August 1985 by Dilson Funaro, and a new strata of special assistants came to enjoy greater direct access to the president than did most ministers). Certainly the major cabinet revamping of early 1986 provided this group with greater vitality and coherence.

Group No. 2, the Military Moderates, have also been affected by the changes accompanying *abertura* and democratization. This group probably possessed by itself some 25 to 30 percent of all mobilizable power within the closed system of making and enforcing national decisions at the end of the 1960s and through the early 1970s.[7] It witnessed a steady decrease in its once near-hegemonic role after Ernesto Geisel started decompression in 1974 and the presidency clearly became a more autonomous actor. During the same time, however, its relative weight within the military establishment increased as first Geisel, then João Figueiredo, earned the support of elements previously leaning more toward hardline positions. The present high commands of the three services are predominantly composed of moderates, many of whom originally favored the selection of Aureliano Chaves to be Figueiredo's successor. Although the leaders of the officer corps accepted first Neves, then Sarney, and demonstrated considerable loyalty to them, this relationship is not what it was when the presidents were senior four-star generals (as was the case from 1964 through 1984).

By the same token, group No. 16, the Military Hardline, during the latter part of the Costa e Silva administration and the early Médici years (1968–1972) probably held up to 20 percent of the system's aggregate power, but it has declined sharply relative to the more moderate elements of the armed forces as well as in relation to nonmilitary power contenders. Thus, from a high of perhaps 40 percent of total political power during the 1969 to 1971 period, these two military groups have declined to the level of under 15 percent, with around 13 percent in the hands of the moderates.

Group No. 4, the Bureaucrats, has also lost significant power with *abertura* and the perceived failure of many economic policies during the early 1980s. Once holder of perhaps as much as 15 percent of total system power capabilities (around 1971), the government officialdom saw a good proportion of this power shift to political parties, particularly after the elections of November 1982. This trend has continued as presidential succession progressed and as Congress has again become a major arena for policymaking. Hence today the administrative hierarchy exercises only about 6 percent of political power.

Most of what decisionmaking power the military and civilian bureaucracies have lost since the heyday of authoritarianism and of the technocratic "Mandarins" has passed into the hands of the political parties and is exercised chiefly through Congress. The big gainer in this respect has been the PMDB (groups No. 3 and No. 10), which had only 2 or 3 percent of power during the first thirteen years of the military regime, rising to about 6.5 percent by 1984. Even at the end of the Figueiredo government this backbone of the opposition was limited by failure to maintain a high degree of effective discipline, the accommodationist tendency of many of its governors, and the ever-present possibility of a major defection to a new centrist party by former Popular Party (PP) elements uneasy with their more leftist colleagues within the PMDB. Yet the presidential succession allowed for the party to assume a coherent position and come to power behind its more moderate leaders. Thus, these essentially centrist Neves-Sarney loyalists (group No. 3) exercise some 9 percent of national decision-making power at present, with the more ideological elements (group No. 10) possessing an additional 3 percent.

The big loser in the party realm is the PDS, which fluctuated between 3 and 7 percent of political power during the 1964-1984 period (chiefly in its earlier guise of ARENA). The rump of the party (group No. 15) is down to only 2 percent as it has not even begun to rally from the shock of "implosion" during the 1984 campaign. The new party that emerged from this process, the PFL (group No. 5) has a healthy 7 percent as it holds key positions in the administration and at the state level, giving the elements that were the PDS in its glory days a total of 9 percent, more than the united party ever exercised in the more authoritarian framework of 1964–1984.

Minor parties have not really gained yet from a return to a competitive representative system. The PDT (group No. 21), which controls only the government of Rio de Janeiro but has the country's most charismatic leader in Leonel Brizola, has some prospects to evolve into a broader-based socialist party in the future. For now it has a bit over 1.2 percent of total exercisable political power in Brazil. The PT (group No. 24), received only 3 percent of the valid vote in the 1982 elections and provides cover for a number of organizations of the radical, but not necessarily violence-oriented, left. Because of its ties to the progressive wing of the Church and Lula's national projection, it has a future, but weighs in presently at about 0.9 percent of political power. The PTB (group No. 26) has a difficult task ahead to carve out a place as more than an auxiliary of the PFL. Its 0.7 percent rating stems from the occasional value of its handful of votes in the Chamber of Deputies and its nominal control of the São Paulo city government. Yet the PTB and smaller parties that might gain seats through the 1986 elections could become considerably more important in any future situation that undermines the coalition basis of the government. There is a slight chance that Jânio Quadros could become a credible presidential candidate and that the PTB could ride this to growth in 1987-1988.

A significant portion of the power once held by appointed government officials has slipped into the hands of the private sector, especially the Industrialists and Bankers, groups Nos. 6 and 8, which probably possess 5 percent of effective political power each, compared to 2 percent for the Business Community (group No. 11) and less than 2 percent for the Agricultural Producers (group No. 19) whose weight is felt largely through influence in small state governments and the PDS party organizations there. The 1983 decision to make the FIESP president also the first vice-president of the CNI, along with the more dynamic leadership that Roberto Bornhausen has been giving to the Banking Federation, underscore these groups' determination to play a larger role in policymaking. Their support for Neves in the succession fight stemmed largely from a shared perception of failure in economic policy and the consequent need for significant changes. They stand a good chance to increase their influence should the PFL gain in strength, particularly if it could gain control of São Paulo, Minas Gerais, or other major states.

As one of the country's very few truly national institutions, the Catholic Church in Brazil has always been and continues to be an important political factor, although its influence is limited by its deep and apparently deepening internal divisions. Group No. 7, the Mainstream of the Catholic Church hierarchy, dispose of perhaps 5 percent of effective political power, in large part because of their residual hold over much of public opinion. The degree of their power often is not apparent, as group No. 17, the Church Progressives, generally works at cross purposes to its moderate brethren. At the 21st General Assembly of the National Conference of Brazilian Bishops (CNBB) in April 1983, the Progressive Wing managed with some difficulty to reelect Dom Ivo Lorscheiter, Bishop of Santa Maria, Rio Grande do Sul, as president of this organization of nearly 300 prelates for a second four-year term. In what is widely considered the toughest electoral battle in the history of this strategic institution, Dom Ivo was strongly supported by the one hundred-odd members of the left wing of the hierarchy and vehemently opposed by the forty or so convinced conservatives. Less radical than his predecessor and cousin, Aloísio Lorscheider, Cardinal of Fortaleza, Dom Ivo was the recipient of reluctant support by half of the hundred-plus moderates, and then only on the third ballot.

Dom Luciano Mendes de Almeida, perhaps more a progressive moderate than a moderate progressive, was overwhelmingly reelected secretary-general and has continued to play a major role in avoiding excessive polarization of the higher clergy. Yet the deep doctrinal differences focusing upon the Church's political stance and role will likely be aggravated in the years immediately ahead. Whether the 2 percent national power share of the progressives will grow at the expense of the numerically stronger center-conservative elements or whether Vatican backing will prove effective for the latter is a question of no little political significance.[8] As with many other groups, events could lead the centrists to look either leftward or to the right.

The Labor Movement in Brazil, group No. 9, was reduced during 1964–1966 and 1969–1974 to a factor of very limited political significance. *Abertura* has of course enabled the trade union movement to recover most of its pre-1964 political influence (perhaps to the 3.5 percent level). Only in April 1985 did Brazil legally recognize central union organizations. Until recently the National Confederation of Industrial Workers (CNTI), which nominally represents 8 million workers, was the largest entity. In April 1983 the docile Ary Campista won reelection as its president for yet another three-year term by a vote of 38 to 20 over São Paulo metalworkers' leader Joaquim dos Santos Andrade. Campista, then 72, had been president since 1964 and was kept in power by patronage, not popularity with workers or even industrial unions, but in late 1983 he was forced to resign over financial abuses, thus undermining government manipulation of the CNTI. The fifty-nine-year-old "Joaquinzão" has subsequently played an active role, first in the founding of the National Coordination of the Working Class (CONCLAT) and then in its March 1986 transformation into the General Labor Center (CGT). Generally close to the PMDB, the CGT claims over 1,450 affiliated unions and asserts a right to speak for most of organized labor. Its real strength is far less than the 25 million nominal followers its leaders claim.

With Lula now more active as PT party leader than as a union chief, Jair Meneghelli, 38, of the São Bernardo dos Campos metalworkers is representative of the more militantly radical leadership that has formed the Single Center of Workers (CUT), an organization closely tied to the PT, claiming the support of some 1,100 unions, and boasting of representing 12.5 million workers. Rivalry between these two organizations is intense, with the federal and São Paulo state administrations preferring expansion of the CGT rather than further growth of CUT. Still, in spite of the brave assertions of the CUT and CGT leaders, with few exceptions Brazilian unions remain bureaucratic, unrepresentative, and hence unable to effectively channel the aspirations of their rank and file, much less control them. Certainly the credibility of Lula and Meneghelli was undercut by the prolonged strike in which they led the auto workers and related unions in April and May 1985. When it ended after 53 days, these workers had gained little more than the employers had originally been willing to give.

The political power of Rural Workers (group No. 27) and Urban Marginal Population and Slum Dwellers (group No. 28) has been virtually nil since 1964 and is not likely to increase dramatically over the next few years, especially in light of the massive organizational task involved in making them mobilizable, much less effectively mobilized. Indeed, this "critical mass" factor greatly inhibits the degree and rate of change in institution building in Brazil compared to smaller countries. Although some Brazilian social scientists have placed a great deal of emphasis upon neighborhood associations (associações de bairro), their national impact is probably still some years off. In much the same way, peasant leagues (ligas camponesas) were enormously overestimated by many writers as a factor changing Brazilian politics in the late 1950s and early 1960s, and the CEBs and PT were blown out of proportion in the late 1970s and early 1980s. A development that may well have long-range implications of some significance is once again being exaggerated into a "revolutionary" factor with a presumed nearly immediate impact.[9] The fact is that at present both of these core elements of the fabled Brazilian povão (great mass) rate about a .5 percent power ranking. Both groups are likely to become, albeit gradually, more significant actors by the 1990s, but not much before.

The political resources and capabilities of the Radical Left-Wing (group No. 23) in Brazil have been low since 1964 and remain low at present. The Brazilian Communist Party (PCB), a major force in the early postwar period and on the rise in the years just before the military took power, has never recovered from a series of deep internal divisions. First a major schism led to the formation of the Communist Party of Brazil (PCdoB) in 1962 as a reflex of the Sino-Soviet rift, and shortly thereafter came the establishment of the National Liberation Alliance

(ALN) by Carlos Marighella in 1967 under Cuban inspiration. Subsequently the 8th of October Revolutionary Movement (MR-8) gained the support of militant youth through its dramatic series of kidnappings.[10] Finally there was the 1980 ouster of long-time (since the early 1930s) party head Luíz Carlos Prestes over the Eurocommunism set of issues (vanguard versus mass party, conspiratorial activity versus long-run participation in a broad reformist alliance, and so on).

The PCB's membership, down to under 8,000, before its recent legalization, probably does not exceed 20,000. It has little support among the younger generation, either workers or middle-class intellectuals. Secretary General Giocondo Dias is, at 72, not much older than the rest of the Central Committee. Backed by the likes of pre-1964 congressman Hercules Corrêa (59), his traditional (Leninist) faction is challenged within the party by the "Democratic Tendency" (Eurocommunists) of David Capistrano da Costa Filho and Armênio Guedes (66) as well as by a small core of faithful Prestes backers. The PCB has some eight members in Congress, some still under the PMDB label, but with Roberto Freire of Pernambuco, Fernando Santana of Bahia, and Alberto Goldman of São Paulo publicly showing its colors there.

The PCdoB, still headed by seventy-three-year-old João Amazonas, and MR-8, which may have about 3,000 and 4,000 members and active sympathizers respectively, appear to enjoy greater support within radical student movements than the PCB and have infiltrated the left wing of the PMDB in some states, as well as the PT. Also burrowed into the PT and agitating among the same target groups of urban workers and university students are such essentially Trotskyite groupings as OTrabalho, ex-Liberdade e Luta (Libelu); the Convergência Socialista; and the Movement for Proletarian Emancipation (MEP) as well as the Brazilian Revolutionary Communist party (PCBR), the Revolutionary Communist party (PRC), and the Maoist Ala Vermelha. The PCdoB managed in 1982 to elect at least three federal deputies under the PMDB label—Luís Guedes in Minas Gerais, Haroldo Lima in Bahia, and ex-National Union of Students (UNE) president Aldo Arantes in Goiás—all of whom now carry the PCdoB banner openly. Within the PT's small congressional delegation was the PCdoB's Aurélio Peres and former guerrilla José Genoino from São Paulo—now a leader of the Revolutionary Communist Party (PRC)—elected along with ex-nun Irma Passoni of Pastoral Operária (all elected by the lower-class voters in the metropolitan region).

These Radical Left-Wing organizations together account at present for no more than 1 percent of political power in Brazil, plus another less than 1 percent for the student organizations under their control, especially the UNE (group No. 23). At the other extreme are the Right-Wing Terrorist elements of group No. 25 with perhaps 0.7 percent of effective political power. Both of these groups would of course benefit from worsening economic conditions bringing on an outbreak of social unrest with the consequent upsurge of political polarization.

Quite strategic in determining the probable conditions of the next few years is group No. 12, the up-to-now fast-growing Middle Class. Holding at only around 3 percent of political power, largely owing to their lack of organization, these elements are becoming frustrated by the interruptions of their upward social mobility bought on by economic downturns. Having strongly backed the drastic regime change of 1964 and having supported the government during the days of authoritarian rule combined with the "economic miracle," they shifted gradually toward moderate opposition figures in the 1974, 1978, and 1982 elections. That latter year in Rio de Janeiro many of them went a step further and voiced their discontent by voting for Brizola—some really looking for a leader in whom they could deposit their hopes but others just as a form of protest. Yet their ambivalence and political availability is underscored by the fact that many also voted for the PDS's Moreira Franco after first flirting with the candidacies of the PTB's Sandra Cavalcanti or the PMDB's Miro Teixeira.

Nationwide in terms of votes the electoral outcome was a virtual tie between the PDS and the PMDB at just under 18 million votes each (nearly 37 percent of the votes); followed by the PDT with nearly 2.5 million votes (a little under 5 percent), almost all in Rio de Janeiro and Rio Grande do Sul. The middle-class vote was split chiefly among these parties, going to the centrist elements of the government party and the PMDB moderates. The PTB's fewer than 2 million votes (under 4 percent) had a minority element of middle-class voters, whereas the PT's nearly 1.5 million votes (a mere 3 percent, equal to but one-fifth of the blank and null vote) contained some ideologically leftist middle-class student and intellectual support, particularly in São Paulo. The middle class participated very substantially and often enthusiastically in the 1984 campaign for direct presidential elections. The recent mayoralty elections indicate that in the major cities the middle class is behaving differently depending upon the choices available—in Rio de Janeiro turning toward the PFL; staying with the PMDB in Belo Horizonte and Curitiba; backing an old demogogic populist in São Paulo; and dividing in Pôrto Alegre, Recife, and Fortaleza.

Whether the existing political party system will prove adequate to contain and channel these impulses—strong in the working class as well as among the middle sectors—for amplified and more effective participation is extremely doubtful. Indeed, nearly thirty new parties came into being for the 1985 partial mayoral elections. Clearly there are still restless urban middle-class elements similar to those that in the past have given power to the late Adhemar de Barros (twice mayor and twice governor of São Paulo) and to still lively Jânio Quadros (mayor and governor of São Paulo and president, and now mayor again at 69). A nationalist-populist movement, albeit yet without a real leader and with restricted political space, could grow rapidly in and after 1986 should the economic situation again worsen and President Sarney fail to maintain his presently impressive appeal to these groups.

Finally, there are still to be taken into account the international actors: the International Banking Community (group No. 13), the International Financial Organizations (group (No. 14), the U.S. Government (group No. 18), the Multinational Corporations (group No. 20), and OPEC and other supplier countries (group No. 29). The peak of influence over Brazilian policy decisions by these external actors, which totalled some 14 percent of exercisable political power in the beginning of the 1960s, came in 1984 at over 17 percent. By the end of 1985 this had fallen to under 10 percent, chiefly as a result of Brazil's improved capabilities for dealing with its still serious debt problem. Although they certainly can influence Brazilian policy on the economic side, these international forces are far from calling the shots. Thus, the U.S. government has had relatively little success in affecting Brazilian trade policy or its stand on Central America, and the multinationals took a beating on restrictive legislation with respect to computers and related technology.

The IMF has seen Brazil repeatedly fail to implement those parts of its agreements that Brazilian decisionmakers thought would jeopardize economic recovery. Hence early in the Sarney administration an eighth letter of intentions was being worked out—making eight series of modifications in less than two-and-a-half years—but was subsequently scrapped. Yet the IMF seeks to avoid any real rupture, as open defiance by Brazil could be contagious. Similarly, fear of Brazil's moving toward a debtors' cartel is a powerful influence toward persuading U.S. and European banks to reschedule much of Brazil's debt on a long-term basis at more favorable spread and interest rate conditions.

The Current Political Situation

The actors and trends just discussed are very important considerations in forecasting Brazil's political future, but taken alone they tell us much more about what is possible than what is probable. With the transition to competitive politics of an essentially democratic cast so recent and not yet consolidated, it is important to assess the present state of affairs (as of mid-1986) as a benchmark for analyzing future changes. The death of Tancredo Neves before he could take office only underscores the necessity of doing this as coolheadedly as possible, allowing little room for wishful thinking.

With the very rules of the game up for reevaluation and possible modification, a number of misconceptions need to be cleared up and some unnecessary preoccupations put to rest. As has been amply demonstrated in this book from several perspectives, the consecutive processes of decompression, opening, and transition were very largely initiated from above and guided quite effectively by President Geisel during the critical early stages. Figueiredo provided at least adequate leadership until the combination of his progressively more serious health problems and his decision to side with the faction within his government headed by SNI chief General Octávio Medeiros began to lead him toward a series of miscalculations and flawed evaluations. The departure from the government in 1981 of Golbery do Couto e Silva, in many respects the crucial strategist of decompression and *abertura*, was followed by the tactical error of adopting modifications in electoral legislation that resulted in the Popular Party of Tancredo Neves merging with the PMDB.

Thus the 1982 elections resulted in opposition victories in most of the more developed states, in most cases behind PMDB moderates—many of whom came from PP ranks. With the government confident that the 36-seat margin the PDS apparently had in the electoral college would stand up under any strains induced by the choice of a candidate, the opposition turned in late 1983 to a mass mobilization in favor of direct election of the president, a campaign in which PMDB National President Ulysses Guimarães emerged as a popular symbol.

Failure of Figueiredo to define his preference, at least in terms of a particular name, led in early 1984 to significant disaggregation of the government party, reflected also in the cabinet and higher reaches of the bureaucracy. In this context Paulo Salim Maluf, who at 52 had been actively campaigning to gain support of PDS delegates and electors since even before the 1982 elections, continued his relentless drive to force the government to accept him as its candidate. Believing that he could be headed off, key advisors of Figueiredo continued their work of convincing the president that Vice-president Aureliano Chaves had been too independent during the times he had exercised the presidency when Figueiredo was absent undergoing treatment for his serious heart problems. With Medeiros at its core, this group hoped to remain in power behind Interior Minister Mário David Andreazza. Convinced that Chaves would have no real choice but to accept the results of the PDS convention, they apparently discounted the possibility of his precipitating a major schism in the party.

In reality, Maluf—determined, hyperactive, intelligent, but in many ways subject to attack as a nonideological demogogue with limitless ambition—proved capable of winning the PDS nomination, largely through lavish expenditures and promises of future benefits and offices. At almost the same time that the administration successfully turned back (on April 25) the opposition's bid to amend the constitution to provide for direct popular election, Chaves and his backers were already thinking that they might not carry their campaign to the convention, and hence would not feel bound by its outcome. Thus, the candidate with the lowest national popularity quotient moved closer to the nom-ination as the party's most popular figure edged toward destabilizing the whole "controlled" process by reaching some kind of agreement with his fellow Minas Gerais statesman, Governor Tancredo Neves.

Vice-president Chaves enjoyed widespread support among business and industry leaders, as well as being favored by much of the officer corps. Moveover, he was preferred by ex-President Geisel, and the latter still had very substantial weight with important bellweathers of the military establishment. Yet it was to take a series of additional developments to convince Chaves to split with the PDS and break openly with the president, to get many other regime figures to join him, and to be able to transfer his business and military backing to Tancredo Neves. He was aided in eventually doing all of this by Figueiredo's propensity to equate loyalty with defense of even the most unsuccessful of his government's policies. Figueiredo failed as well to see that *abertura* from above required going beyond the hard-core of the 1964 "revolution" to find a candidate who could combine a basic commitment to the major goals of the 1964-1984 regime with an ability to mobilize popular support and channel burgeoning aspirations in directions compatible with those goals.

In this context, the opposition's systematic campaign for a return to direct election of the president, although it was not successful in attaining its express goal, helped significantly to create an environment in which it would not be possible for the government to "add insult to injury" by forcing an unpopular Maluf down the throat of the frustrated masses. Many PDS politicians had to begin to consider seriously the consequences in terms of their 1986 electoral ambitions of supporting a candidate that majority public opinion clearly considered not only the antithesis of their desires, but essentially illegitimate.

Although by mid-1984 the milieu was favorable for a drastic change, this would have to wait until the PDS and PMDB conventions had been held and the choice was clearly narrowed down to Maluf or "Tancredo." (The latter had not yet fully committed himself to stepping down from the Minas Gerais governorship to try for the presidency in a legal framework designed to guarantee the victory of the government's candidate.) Chaves and the liberal wing of the PDS proposed in June that a primary be held to decide the nominee, a move supported by most of the PDS leadership. When Figueiredo backed abruptly away from an initial acceptance of this idea—which had been summarily rejected by Maluf—PDS president Sarney resigned, followed in short order by his immediate successor, Senator Jorge Bornhausen. As a final gesture of a conciliatory disposition, both Chaves and Senator Marco Maciel offered to withdraw from the race if Maluf and Andreazza would do likewise, leaving the president free to name a unity candidate. By this time Antônio Carlos Magalhães, political strongman of Bahia and a staunch Andreazza supporter, had announced that he would vote for Neves in the electoral college if the other choice were Maluf (whom he would shortly thereafter excoriate in a widely disseminated interview in a popular newsmagazine).

Following the handy victory of Maluf in the mid-August PDS convention, the marriage of the "Liberal Front" and the PMDB was first celebrated, then quickly consummated. Under the banner of the "Democratic Alliance," Neves took Sarney as his vice-presidential running mate, and the bandwagon began its transformation into a steamroller.[11] The government fought back halfheartedly by dismissing some office-holders who refused to back Maluf, and right wing military elements sought to raise the spectre of the radical left coming to power should Neves be elected. But these efforts were more than offset by the adhesion of all but one of the PDS governors from the northeast to the Neves-Sarney campaign along with many other former supporters of Andreazza. As public opinion polls consistently showed at least a 60 to 20 percent margin in popular preferences for "Tancredo," state legislatures began one after another to elect pro-Neves slates of electors.[12]

Astutely, Neves insisted in his public pronouncements that he would restore the 1964 movement to its true course, not advocate return to the "pre-revolution" situation. A series of behind-the-scenes meetings with Army Minister Walter Pires de Albuquerque (who had been a classmate of his at the National War College, ESG, back in the 1950s) were skillfully combined by Neves with soundings of senior officers for possible cabinet positions. He sought to neutralize opposition from military elements generally aligned up to that point with the administration, but agreeing that the unpopular Maluf could not be forced down the throats of the public without danger of provoking extreme political indigestion. Then, too, the many pro-Chaves officers exerted pressure on their wavering brethren to accept the faith in the Democratic Alliance candidate demonstrated by ex-President Geisel—who had given his blessing to the vice-president's alliance with Neves. Moreover, a careful calculation as of mid-October showed a probable 377 votes for Neves, a likely 244 for Maluf, with 53 undecided and 12 electors apt to be absent on January 15. From this point on, more and more of the officer corps came to "absorb" the opposition's imminent victory as inevitable, a perspective strongly reinforced by the nation's media.

By mid-November Neves could begin to speak as if he were already president-elect, announcing the main pillars of his projected *Nova República*. For his part Figueiredo grumpily accepted the fact that he was already in many ways a lame duck and began to reconcile himself to the historic role of the man who had fulfilled his promise to bring democracy to Brazil by the end of his term. As the SNI estimated Neves's lead at 200 votes and still rising, moderate PDS leaders redoubled their efforts to disassociate themselves from Maluf's strident but hopeless campaign.[13] General Newton Cruz, an intransigent hardliner commanding the strategic Brasília garrison, was transferred to an innocuous desk job, depriving the right wing military radicals of their last rallying point. A bitter Maluf, seeing victory slipping away—the victory he had always assumed would be his if he won the erstwhile majority party's nomination—belatedly assumed a more independent stance by criticizing the government and making demagogic promises.

By a vote of 480 to 180 on January 15, 1985, the electoral college made Neves the country's next chief executive and not only turned the ailing and bitter Figueiredo into a "crippled" duck, it rendered the incumbent administration so impotent that it might better be described from that point on as a "comatose, paraplegic duck." Some 271 of the Democratic Alliance's votes came from the PMDB, with the PFL delivering 113 more, and the PDS dissidents chipping in with 55. (Fourteen PDS electors and three others abstained, whereas nine electors—five of them from the PT—were absent.) After nearly twenty-one years of military regimes, Brazil was about to get a civilian government, and a broad-based centrist one to boot. But the mood of national euphoria that preceded, permeated, and followed Carnival turned to one of appre-hension and concern when on the eve of inauguration the president-elect underwent emergency surgery. Thus, with public opinion in a state of near shock, José Sarney was sworn in on March 15, 1985, as acting president at the head of a cabinet Neves had painstakingly put together to see the country through the difficult months ahead.[14]

Consolidation of a competitive representative system after twenty-one years of military rule would have been a difficult task under the best of circumstances, and Neves had carefully attempted to learn the lessons of comparative experience, especially that of Spain a decade earlier. The task involved at its core: (1) working out a viable relationship between the executive and legislative branches of government; (2) decentralizing the immense and ponderous state machinery built up since 1964; (3) restructuring the political party system without returning to the excessive fragmentation that contributed to the protracted crisis of the early 1960s; (4) conducting nationwide elections in November 1986 including all governorships, two senators per state, all federal and state legislators, and mayors and city councilmen in over 4,000 munic-ipalities; (5) drafting and putting into effect a new constitutional frame-work; and (6) seeing the country through the first direct election of a president in almost three decades.

These enormous tasks must be carried out without jeopardizing a still fragile economic recovery and under the cloud posed by the death of the leader in whom most sectors of the Brazilian people had deposited their hopes for a successful democratization. Fortunately, a highly qual-ified, if delicately balanced, government had been put together by a sagacious 75-year-old president-elect before he was laid low on the eve of his scheduled inauguration. Equally important, in his "interim" exercise of the presidency, Sarney, 56, a moderate center-right politician from the Northeastern state of Maranhão, skillfully held together the diverse elements of the Democratic Alliance. In this he had the full backing of all six military ministers as well as those civilian cabinet members personally and politically closest to the stricken president-elect. Yet intense competition, bordering in some cases on confrontation, over the final second echelon appointments provided a preview of what might be expected following Neves's death.

Conflicting ambitions regarding presidential succession have already been unleashed and have resulted in significant tension between those elements of the government supporting the "accidental" president and those following the lead of PMDB National President Ulysses Guimarães, 69, who as President of the Chamber of Deputies is next in line to the presidency and who might well personally like to cut short Sarney's term through a constitutional amendment.[15] Sarney has been obliged to maintain the delicate balance among components of the Democratic Alliance established by Neves. Thus, he kept all but one of Neves's choices through 1985. In February 1986 he carried out a thorough cabinet reshuffling on the eve of announcing a bold and imaginative program for ending Brazil's chronic—and increasingly acute—inflation problem.

What exists conceptually then, in brief, is a situation in which the civilian government's actions will continue to affect the economy and society, with feedback through the multiple political actors incorporated into my scheme of analysis. Hence the next requirement for forecasting is an examination of the present economic situation, concentrating upon the dynamic factors as of mid-1986.

The Economic Context, 1985–1986

The factors that will most profoundly affect political alignments in Brazil over the next few years lie deeply rooted in the economic situation and its societal reflexes. The economic "miracle" of the 1968–1973 period kept many groups mollified in the face of political authoritarianism, and the prolonged process of decompression and opening in the political sphere greatly cushioned the social tensions arising from the worsening economic conditions following the first and second "oil shocks" of 1974 and 1979. After the massive political catharsis of the November 1982 elections and the inauguration of new state administrations in March 1983, the drama of presidential succession at least partially distracted public attention from the unsatisfactory economic conditions. Subsequently, economic recovery, albeit not fully consolidated, and the coming to office of an administration representing a distinct break—but not a radical rupture—with twenty-one years of essentially military rule combined to produce an atmosphere of at least cautious optimism relatively free of unrealistic euphoria.

With the exception of inflation, which ran at 12.6, 10.2, and 12.7 percent for the first three months of 1985, the civilian government inherited a substantially improved and in many ways still improving economic situation. Industrial production was up 7.7 percent in 1984, providing the chief impetus for a 4.5 percent GNP growth (running at better than a 9 percent annual rate in the fourth quarter). Initially dependent upon export expansion, this economic recovery had by then broadened into domestic commerce and agriculture. Unemployment dropped steadily during 1984, and the record trade surplus of just over $13 billion came largely from a nearly 25 percent increase in exports to over $27 billion (with manufactures leading the way).[16] Crucial to this was the U.S. market with sales up nearly 29 percent to $7.7 billion, along with a significant drop in oil imports—for the fourth straight year. Even after massive interest payments, this recovery provided a small current account surplus of about $200 million, allowing some room for an increase in essential imports. Moreover, satisfactory debt negotiations made an increase in foreign exchange reserves from zero (or in some strict accounting actually negative) to the neighborhood of $7 billion by the change of administrations in March 1985.[17]

The first year of the civilian government witnessed substantial progress on most economic fronts despite early contradictions between the policies advocated by the Finance Minister and those pushed by the Planning Ministry (before a synthesis was achieved at the end of August). Thus, although the trade surplus stood at only $1.9 billion at the end of the first quarter, some $10.5 billion was added by the new administration during the next nine months for a year-end, highly satisfactory total of nearly $12.5 billion (on exports of slightly over $25.6 billion and imports exceeding $13.1 billion). Employment rose during the first months of 1985 and picked up dramatically once the protracted metalworkers strike ended in May. Indeed, more than 1.7 million persons were added to the rolls of the employed by years end, with at least 1.3 million of these in the formal economy. Internal consumption became the engine of economic growth, as factory employment rose 6 percent and real salaries nearly 13 percent in the industrial sector. With commerce up sharply in the second semester following a good agricultural harvest, the GNP grew a dramatic 8.3 percent for the year. Indeed, industrial production climbed to above the record 1980 level and per capita GNP came up to within 3 percent of the pre-recession high.

On the negative side, the fight against the dragon of inflation was a temporary casualty of the administration's pursuit of growth. Initially Finance Minister Francisco Dornelles managed to get April 1985 inflation down to 7.2 percent and hold it under 8 percent in May and June. But the effect of price controls subsequently diminished, and modest cuts in the projected 89 trillion cruzeiro public-sector deficit inherited from the Figueiredo administration were not sufficient to greatly relieve its inflationary effects. As Planning Minister João Sayad and most of the PMDB congressional delegation rejected Dornelles' call for orthodox anti-inflationary fiscal policies, and inflation reached a record 14 percent in August, the president decided in favor of the developmentalist option and replaced Dornelles with the more structuralist Dilson Funaro. Subsequently inflation continued at a high rate, pushed by both the financing needs of the deficit (which greatly expanded internal debt) and soaring food prices, as well as continued substantial wage increases, and reached 234 percent for the year.

All this had a substantial impact upon the foreign debt situation. With the government inheriting a condition of non-compliance with the "extended facilities" accord with the IMF, which was due to expire in early 1986, and unwilling for political reasons to accept continued close monitoring of the nation's finances by that international body, it soon scrapped efforts to reach agreement on an eighth letter of intentions and explored instead the feasibility of a short-term "stand-by" agreement. But with foreign exchange reserves moving up past $8 billion, the Sarney administration subsequently decided to forgo any agreement at all for 1985, opting for direct negotiation with creditor banks, facilitated by a vague IMF acknowledgement of the seriousness and feasibility of Brazil's 1986 economic program. This was successfully accomplished by early 1986.

The Sarney government's economic goals for 1986 (as embodied in the three-year development plan issued in late 1985) called for GNP growth of at least 6 percent, led by industry, which was to advance some 7 percent beyond 1985's very substantial recovery. This was to be accompanied by reduction of inflation to an average annual rate of 160 percent and a further drop in unemployment—already down near 4 percent in urban centers. Average real income, which declined 12 percent during the 1981–1983 recession, would continue the catching up well begun in 1985 when the minimum wage rose some 260 percent—more than 25 points above the inflation rate. A trade surplus of $12.5 billion was to be achieved on the strength of exports of about $26.5 billion and imports around $14 billion (which, given the continued drop in oil imports, would allow a rise of nearly $3 billion for other purchases, especially food stuffs and items essential to continued industrial growth).

The major economic cloud hanging over 1986 was the continued high budget deficit and the expansion of the internal debt necessary to finance it. In order to keep growth of the internal debt to 30 percent and reduce the operating deficit from 3.2 to .5 percent of GNP, a program of tax increases, continued containment of public sector expenditures, and additional reduction of domestic interest rates was enacted in December 1985. As inflation soared further during the first two months of 1986, the Sarney government acted decisively on February 28, 1986, decreeing an end to monetary correction and imposing a price and wage freeze, accompanied by provisions for automatic cost of living adjustments, should inflation exceed an accumulated 20 percent.

Thus, for the first time during the life of almost any living Brazilian, the cost of living actually decreased in March. More importantly, savings began to be funneled into productive investment rather than the financial speculation that had become rampant in recent years. The government staked its future on the success of its innovative program to eliminate inflation without sacrificing economic growth and employment. The interim report card would be rendered by the electorate at the ballot box in November.

With the basic secular trends of social change having been established, their relationship to contending political forces explored, and the present economic benchmark sketched, one step remains before analysis of the probable political alignments for the 1986 to 1989 period can be examined. To this end, the following section is devoted to laying out the possible economic contexts for this period.

Alternative Economic Contexts for 1986 and Beyond

The economic scenarios that might lead to different political outcomes may be reduced to five basic possibilities stemming from the actual situation of mid-1986. Although these are partially differentiated by objective criteria in terms of GNP growth, inflation, unemployment, and balance of payments performance, they depend also on perception and mood—the belief among the relevant actors that problems are coming under control or that they are worsening in spite of government policies and efforts.

A. *Reasonable Recovery:* In the first and most optimistic of the alternate domestic economic contexts there would be consolidation of the 1985 recovery, involving substantial fulfillment of the goals previously discussed, including GNP growth on the order of 5.5 percent or better. Inflation would remain a serious preoccupation, but after hitting the 210 percent level in 1983, exceeding 220 percent in 1984, and rising above 230 percent in 1985, would be held to under 60 percent in 1986, and drop to below 30 percent the following year. Underlying this improvement would be a substantial reduction in the public sector deficit with a consequent moderation in expansion of the money supply. Unemployment would continue the decline so evident in 1985, and real income would continue to rise. Moderate export growth would continue to generate trade surpluses adequate to cover interest payments on the foreign debt, which would grow only slightly as relatively little new money would be needed, owing to successful long-term renegotiation of debt payments achieved by March 1987 and extending into the beginning of the 1990s. In short, this would be a continuation and consolidation of the recovery apparent during 1985.

B. *Muddling Along:* The second set of possible economic conditions would involve essentially a reversal of the 1984-1985 recovery, bringing things back more or less into the 1981-1982 situation of stagnation, but not a more drastic deterioration. Brazil would experience difficulty in sharply curbing inflation during 1986, with backsliding in 1987 to the 50 percent range without sharply recessive policies. If those were adopted, there would be little economic growth, implying a stagnation or even renewed decline in per capita GNP. A substantial foreign trade surplus would still be achieved but at the cost of further restricting imports. Unemployment would remain at about the present level in 1986 and likely rise moderately the following year. Disenchantment with the Sarney administration would be evident during the 1986 election campaign, whether or not it sticks with its present set of policies or undertakes a major revamping during another pre-election cabinet shakeup, and the government coalition would see its parliamentary base narrowed during 1987.

C. *Return to Recession:* The third possible economic context would see limited success in the government's economic program coming only at the cost of drastically tougher and tighter policies resulting in a return to the 1983 situation of substantial recession or a return to high inflation, perhaps even in the 75–100 percent range. Unemployment would rise sharply, and trade surpluses would be inadequate for interest payments on the foreign debt. The level of dissatisfaction would rise considerably, with many sources—even among groups originally supportive of the government—sharply criticizing economic policy and calling for abandonment of the adjustment program. Under the first variant of this (C_1, *Holding Firm*) there might be some improvement or at least leveling off of the slide during late 1987, and the government would go into the presidential succession sticking by its guns and maintaining that its policies were correct and about to bring positive results. In a second variation (C_2, *New Game Plan*) the administration would switch essentially to the PMDB left's much more populist and nationalist policies and remake the cabinet in keeping with a shift to the left congruent with the trend in that direction shown by the November 1986 election results.

D. *Recession Deepening into Depression:* The fourth possible economic scenario would see a decline during 1986, much steeper than that sketched above, as either inflation refuses to come down or recessionary policies are adopted that bring back negative growth rates. Unemployment rises even more than in C, and concentration of income and wealth becomes increasingly skewed as significant elements of the lower-middle class slip down the socioeconomic ladder and working-class wages fall far behind the soaring cost of living. Social unrest becomes a part of the daily scene as these groups clamor against the rigorous austerity measures. Under variant D_1, *Hanging Tough*, the government would stick to its policies as the only ones viable given Brazil's debt situation, albeit there would still be a change of faces in many ministries at the end of 1986. Under D_2, *Switching Tracks*, a substantial series of policy changes would be put into effect by mid-1986, with further changes should the proceedings of the constituent assembly go badly for the administration. These would be in the direction of regaining growth even at the risk of runaway inflation and would likely involve significant restrictions on paying the interest on foreign debt.

E. *Prolonged Economic Crisis:* This most pessimistic of short-term economic contexts would involve failure to stem inflation, even through acutely recessionary measures combined with negative GNP growth rates such as Brazil has yet never known. Buffeted between external pressures to abide by an orthodox adjustment program and sharply rising social unrest rooted in growing unemployment, administration

TABLE 6.2
Economic Scenarios for the Future

Scenarios to 1989	Probability
A. Reasonable Recovery	65%
B. Muddling Along	17
C. Return to Recession	10
1. Holding Firm	
2. New Game Plan	
D. Recession Deepening into Depression	5
1. Hanging Tough	
2. Switching Tracks	
E. Prolonged Economic Crisis	3
1. Cutting Losses	
2. Conservative Backlash	

forces would begin to quarrel bitterly over policy, and the PFL would abandon its coalition with the PMDB. Under variant E1, *Cutting Losses*, the government adopts an increasingly nationalistic stance, as it is alarmed by the gains made by the parties of the left. Alternative E$_2$, *Conservative Backlash*, sees the major gains being made instead by a resurgent PDS (probably behind Maluf), with that party arguing that the policies followed by the Figueiredo government had led to recovery and that the Sarney administration had recklessly destroyed these advances. Then, too, Quadros might break with the government to assume the pose of the providential man able to head off the rise of the radical left. This would leave the executive unable to marshal congressional support for its policies and thus would lead toward impasse and immobilization.

Although the ensuing analysis deals in considerable detail with the probable political consequences of each of these economic possibilities should it in fact come to be reality, the economic scenarios are not at all of equal probability. The worse case scenario (E) is fortunately the least likely to be approximated in the real world. As of June 1986, it would appear to have no more than a 3 percent chance of taking place. In sharp contrast, the most favorable economic context, that of coping reasonably well with the very real problems Brazil faces (A), would seem to have at least a 65 percent probability, with that of a relatively mild deterioration (B) coming next at 17 percent. Return to recession (C) follows at about one chance in ten of occurring, with marked depression (D) only around a one-in-twenty proposition. The overall outlook is presented in Table 6.2.

Alternative Political Alignments Under
Different Economic Conditions

Taking into account the nature of the relevant political actors and the processes of socioeconomic change as analyzed in the opening sections of this chapter, the task is now to assess how these would interact under the several possible economic contexts just·outlined. Each of the economic alternatives leads to a distinctive sociopolitical outcome. Thus, if the economy during the next few years approximates alternative A (a reasonably adequate resolution of present problems), we could expect that the distribution of power among the internal groups would change relatively little from that now prevailing and that the present coalition of forces in support of the government would be essentially maintained. Nationalism would remain low, and much of the labor movement would continue to be coopted, compromising, and cooperative. In this context the radical left would have little room for expansion of its activities or a significant deepening of support. Prospects would be good for strong showings by centrists in the 1986 elections and for the 1988 presidential succession to yield a victory for a moderate candidate such as Aureliano Chaves or Marco Maciel. Indeed, Sarney's term might extend to 1990, or he might even be allowed to run for reelection in 1988. If the next president were to come from PMDB ranks, he would likely be an ex-PP type wrapping himself in the Neves mantle. Maluf would be largely forgotten, and Brizola would have failed in 1986 to project himself as a real alternative.

Should the assumptions of alternative B, involving a reversal of the recent recovery, prove closer to the mark, the derivative political scenario would show no drastic shifts in power shares or in basic alignments, at least in the short run. Under alternative A the PFL and PMDB moderates would be almost certain both to retain dominance within the administration and to hold the upper hand in the presidential succession. In case B the PMDB moderates could well come to favor a center-left candidate should the rather unsatisfactory economic conditions continue into the 1987–1988 period with sporadic and anomic urban outbursts punctuating the spreading popular discontent. The left wing of the PMDB would most probably gain in strength, and labor would become more independent of the government. The PFL would by 1988 be seriously weakened, as much of its constituency would be disillusioned with the performance of Sarney, Chaves, and the others in office, and would have lost most of the statehouses it presently controls in the 1986 balloting. The orthodox PDS would find greater receptivity to its more aggressively critical line, and Quadros might begin to be seen by some middle-class elements as a viable alternative. The military moderates, along with their counterparts in the Church, would suffer limited erosion—the former to the hardliners and the latter to the progressives.

Alternative C, a turn for the worse that reaches 1983-level recession characteristics, would lead to some important shifts in the relative influence of the politically relevant groups. Within the Church liberal centrists would move closer to the positions of the progressive wing, which itself would turn more decidedly to the left—and this movement would be duplicated within the labor movement. Rising social unrest would begin to reach rural areas as well as the fringes of the major metropolitan centers. The outcome of the 1986 elections and the subsequent realignment of political forces might well vary between C_1 (*Holding Firm*) and C_2 (*New Game Plan*), but in either case favorable breeding grounds for radical nationalism would be present, albeit with considerable time still necessary for this to have a profound, rather than intermittent, impact upon policy. A marked shift to the center-left, with gains for the PMDB left and minor parties, would be likely in the 1986 voting (should this occur early on), and a center-left to left outcome in presidential succession would become a distinct possibility. If the administration stuck with its policies as being sound in the long run (C_1), the erosion of support would be greater than if it had moved to a more exclusively structuralist stance on economic matters and dropped its remaining fiscal conservatives and vestiges of a monetarist approach as under the assumptions of C_2. Hence the latter strategy would, under the given circumstances, enable the government to maintain a base of support by shifting leftward and subsequently to exert greater influence over the succession, leading perhaps to the election of someone along the lines of Ulysses Guimarães or Paraná's José Richa—who would be stronger contenders under the scenario of context B. In brief, alternative C would result in a condition of containable to fairly serious political erosion rather than drastic regime decomposition.

The largely quantitative shifts of scenario C would be transformed into significant qualitative changes should the fourth set of economic assumptions—involving deepening stagflation and rapidly mounting unemployment—come to be the real situation. Those elements of the working class hitherto still coopted would move toward their more radical brethren, and the middle class, instead of manifesting an increasing ambivalence as under alternative C, would divide between those switching from support of the administration to the leftist opposition and those looking for a right-wing authoritarian saviour to set things straight. A parallel polarization would take place among business, banking, industry, and agriculture under context D, with most of these elements probably turning toward the right. The military moderates, who would suffer serious defections under the less socially devastating conditions of scenario C, under alternative D would find their ranks significantly depleted, with the hardliners the major beneficiaries of this change.

The form and nature of the ensuing political crisis would be conditioned by a number of factors, most directly the choice of the president to stay with essentially a centrist set of policies while making cosmetic changes and shuffling personnel (D_1) as against the alternative of scrapping continuity and adopting a sharply different set of fiscal and economic policies designed to stem the alarming loss of political support (D_2). Although both of these variants would enhance the position of the radical left, they would also lead to a strengthening of the extreme right. The former would still need years to organize a bid for power, and the latter—given the fundamental changes in Brazil by 1987–1988 compared to 1963–1964—would find it very difficult to pull off a successful coup. Thus a long period of tension and uncertainty would be a more likely outcome, probably stretching through 1988 and presidential succession.

Alternative D_2, with a shift to nationalist policies, would involve at heart a quest for political viability at the cost of giving up the fight against inflation. If done in time and with skill, it could allow the administration to exert some influence over succession but very probably behind a more radical candidate than would be possible if the situation had not deteriorated so badly. Indeed, with luck it might be able to engineer the election of a moderate left type acceptable under the circumstances to the military mainliners and possibly able to compete at the polls with a more sectarian candidate of the left or a more demagogic rival (a role reserved for Fernando Henrique Cardoso if he had won the São Paulo mayor's race). Much would depend on whether the PFL were willing to participate in a national union government that far left of center or would prefer to rejoin with the PDS and PTB in an alliance to contest presidential succession. In the latter case the odds would favor the left-of-center candidate—a fact which might begin to stir up coup planning by the hardliners.

Should the worst case, that of a prolonged crisis, come to fit the actual conditions as they develop through 1986 and beyond, it would lead the government past disaggregation to decomposition, as the damage could not effectively be contained at this stage by policy reorientation. Indeed, polarization would reach the regime's very core, with the governmental bureaucracy and the armed forces being affected and with the PFL strongly reflecting these strains. Moreover, should the administration opt for "damage control" by shifting to a nationalist stance (E_1), the PFL would have great problems in continuing to support it. Certainly a break by the PFL would influence important elements of business, banking, and industry as well as the middle class. Church moderates would be losing out to the progressive wing, and labor would be more than just restless—conditions that the radical left would begin to exploit in spite of the residual fears of some older elements that this might spark a right-wing countermobilization and a possible preemptive coup.

The economic crisis and its by then alarming social ramifications would be clearly reflected in the succession process, where the left— likely having experienced substantial gains in the 1986 balloting—would push hard for the election of one of its spokesmen, an event which in turn would greatly increase the probability of a right-wing coup attempt. Thus the succession question could so deeply divide the country as to give rise to a right-wing conspiracy to block a leftist from assuming the presidency, by force if necessary—either by heading off the elections or later in face of the electorate's choice. This right-wing action would clash frontally with a conviction by the radical left that the country was nearing a "prerevolutionary" situation and its consequent determination to resort to violence to prevent "another 1964." Given the transformations that have taken place in Brazil (and the rest of the world) since 1964, these incompatible movements might well lead to a situation of near civil war and protracted strife. To head off such a dismal prospect, it is quite likely that the president, faced with the grim dilemma of giving way to someone sharply to his right or dismayingly far to his left, might well adopt an increasingly strident nationalist tone in hopes of rallying support. The possible success of this Vargas-type strategy (E_1) would depend upon many factors not subject to analysis this far in advance, but the consequences would be grave in terms of the policies that would have to be adopted to give such a stance credibility.

Failure to move to the left—or at least to an anti-American nationalism—under these circumstances would reduce the administration to short-run calculus of survival considerations. Its base of support would by this time have narrowed perilously. Political gains by the right behind a Malufian smoke screen of populist promises or a Quadros-led nostalgia for a return to better days could lead to a center-right coalition (E_2) under which the PFL and even some present PMDB moderates accept one of these conservatives as a lesser evil than someone of the Brizola or Lula stripe. In fundamental ways, then, E_2 would lead to the kind of acute political crisis already discussed as the darkest side of situation D_1 but in even more traumatic conditions of sociopolitical malaise.

The impact of each of these possible courses of events upon the political power of the national policymaking actors is obviously of critical importance to forecasting future political change, which in turn is essential to estimating conditions and levels of risk to Brazil's fragile democratic institutions. In this regard, the results of a great deal of painstaking analysis are summarized in Table 6.3 as assessments of the relative political power of the significant political actors to influence national policy decisions. Examination of these figures provides the first element for forecasting Brazil's political future.

Thus, for example, the Presidency is most likely to experience a wide variation in its political power, depending upon which economic context becomes the real situation, with the Military Moderates also subject to a drastic drop in political power depending on how much the economy worsens. Conversely, the Radical Left stands to gain most from a deterioration in economic conditions—unless this were to lead to a successful right-wing coup, not likely before the end of the decade. This would also be true for the Labor Movement, with the Military Hardliners and the Radical Right doing just about as well should things go badly for the country economically and socially as they would if things went well. Students, Rural Workers, and the Urban Marginal Populations are

TABLE 6.3
Prospective 1987-1988 Power Configurations Under Eight Economic Alternatives

		1986	A	B	C_1	C_2	D_1	D_2	E_1	E_2
1.	Presidency	15	17.5	13	12	12.5	9.5	10.3	8	6
2.	Mil. Moderates	13	12	11	10	9.5	8.5	9	8	7
3.	PMBD	9	10	8	6	6.5	5.3	6	5	4
4.	Bureaucracy	6	6	6	5	5.5	3.8	4.3	3.5	3
5.	PFL	7	7.5	6.5	6.5	6.3	4.5	5	5	3.5
6.	Industry	5	6	5.5	5	4.8	4.2	4.5	4	3.3
7.	Church Moderates	5	5	4.5	3.5	3	3.2	3	2.5	2
8.	Banking	5	5.5	5	4.5	4	3.4	3.7	2.7	2.5
9.	Unions	3.5	3.3	3.8	4	5	6.4	6	7	8
10.	PMDB Left	3	2.5	4	5	5.5	5.5	5.5	6	5
11.	Commerce	2	3.5	3	2.9	3	2.8	2.7	2.7	2.5
12.	Middle Class	3	4	2.5	2	2.3	2.4	2.4	2.5	2
13.	Int'l. Banks	3	2.1	3.5	4	3	2.7	2.6	1.5	2.5
14.	Int'l. Fin. Orgs.	3	2	3.5	4	4	4.3	4	3	5.6
15.	PDS	2	1.5	2.5	4	3.5	3.8	3.5	4	6
16.	Mil. Hardline	1.7	1.5	2.5	4.5	4	5.3	5	6	5
17.	Church Left	2	2	2.3	3.1	3.3	4	3.6	4.5	5
18.	U.S. Govt.	2	1.5	2.5	2.3	1.8	2	1.6	1.7	1.5
19.	Agriculture	1.7	1.4	1.5	1.4	1.3	1.2	1.1	1.1	1
20.	Multinationals	2	1	1.4	1.4	1.1	1	1.3	1.3	1.1
21.	PDT	1.2	.9	1.3	1.7	1.6	4.2	3.7	5.5	6.2
22.	Left Radicals	1	.5	1.2	1.4	1.6	2.8	2.5	3.5	3.8
23.	Students	.9	.5	.6	1	1.3	1.4	1.3	1.4	1.5
24.	PT	.9	.6	1.4	1.6	1.8	2.6	2.4	3.7	4.5
25.	Right Radicals	.4	.3	1.0	1.3	1.5	2.5	2.3	3.3	4.2
26.	PTB	.7	.6	1	.8	1	1.2	1.1	1.1	1.3
27.	Rural Workers	.5	.4	.5	.5	.6	.7	.8	.9	1.1
28.	Urban Masses	.5	.4	.5	.6	.7	.8	.8	.9	1.2
29.	Foreign Suppliers	-	-	-	-	-	-	-	-	-

apt to gain in influence under any circumstances, but would not be of major importance as power factors even under the worst-case scenario by 1989. Among political parties, the PFL and PMDB would benefit from the more favorable economic possibilities, whereas the PDT, PT, and PMDB Left would gain dramatically under the depression and crisis contexts—as would the PDS. The Bureaucracy, Industrialists, Bankers, Businessmen, Mainstream of the Catholic Church, and Middle Class would all have their power seriously cut under the more adverse economic conditions. The influence of the international actors would not vary so directly, since the nationalist variable would enter heavily into account.

Yet power of the groups taken individually is only part of the story; there is also the factor of alignments and coalitions. As of the consolidation of the Sarney government during the latter part of 1985 and early 1986, the alignment of forces supporting it included, in addition to the Presidency (1), most of the Military Moderates (2), the PMDB (3), the vast majority of the Bureaucracy (4), the PFL (5), by far the largest part of the Industrialists (6), nearly all of the Church Moderates (7), the dominant elements of Banking (8), a good share of the Labor Movement (9), the PMDB Left (10), the major components of Business (11), nearly all of the Middle Class (12), some of the Progressive Wing of the Church (17), a significant part of Agriculture (19), many Students (23), and—in a much less organized manner—most of the Rural Workers (27) and Urban Lower Classes (28). Moreover, the External Actors (13, 14, 18, and 20) were at least fairly favorably disposed.

As the PTB (26) was at worst sympathetically neutral, the opposition in early to mid-1986 was restricted on the right to the Malufista PDS (15), Hardline Military (16), much of Agriculture (19), and the Right Radicals (25), plus minority elements in Industry (6) and Commerce (11) and scattered enclaves among the Middle Class (12). Although the PDT (21) and PT (24) were technically not in open opposition to the Sarney government, in reality they were, supported by some of the Unions (9), the Left Radicals (22), part of the Church Left (17), and militant elements of the Students (23), Rural Workers (27), and Urban Marginal Populations (28). This gave the left opposition, as of early 1986, only about 7 percent of effective political power, compared to just under 8 percent for the right opposition. Certainly these were still "honeymoon" figures in a nation celebrating a return to civilian government, but careful analysis indicates that the government would maintain its overwhelming support under scenario A and see it shrink only marginally under scenario B—the two scenarios with at least 80 percent probability of occurring.

Even under the more adverse circumstances of alternative C, the administration would continue to have the support of groups possessing about 64 percent of power capabilities. Should the greater changes in both the power of individual groups and in their alignments forecast under context D and its political scenarios come to be, the government would still hold on to 60 percent of effective power. With the worst case possibilities of alternative E, the administration would retain close to 60 percent of power under variant E_1 and still above 55 percent under E_2. But here this would largely be a result of support by the international actors. In the internal struggle for control of the government rather than influence over policymaking, the situation would be much more even, with the left opposition having 23 and 26 percent of power capabilities under the two possible variations and the right some 17 or 18 percent. Although the government could probably hold on to office, its ability to shape the succession process would very likely be lost. But as the combined probabilities for scenarios D and E come to only one in eight, the outlook for political stability in Brazil is quite strong, with a very good possibility of consolidating a democratic civilian government of an essentially centrist orientation.

In sum, although critical problems remain ahead, Brazil is in a far better position than ever before to use its augmented economic resources to ameliorate the multiple strains in society that are at the root of tensions that could undermine political progress—and have done so repeatedly in the past. This is clearly the priority for the rest of the 1980s and, if accomplished with reasonable success, should allow in the 1990s the more equitable distribution of both material benefits and opportunities that would all but guarantee the viability of a broadly participant and even highly competitive political system.[18]

Notes

1. This study draws heavily upon both an interest spanning four decades in how understanding of the past and present can be translated into sound predictions for the future and my nearly thirty years of close observation of Brazil, a period that embraces the Kubitschek, Quadros, and Goulart governments before 1964 and all twenty-one years of the "revolution." The contrasts between the present period and the early 1960s are based upon many research ventures there, especially the intensive studies I carried out in the field on the 1962 and 1982 elections, the latter as part of an eighteen-report project done in cooperation with the Georgetown University Center for Strategic and International Studies. In all I have made four research trips to Brazil before 1964, five more during the first decade of military rule, ten between 1974 and 1981, and an additional nine visits during the past four years. (Those from 1978 through 1982 were made possible by grants from the PSC-CUNY Faculty Research Program.)

Although I have used all relevant social science literature on Brazil—U.S., Brazilian, and European—and for many years have regularly read four major Brazilian newsmagazines and an equal number of daily papers, the quantifications of effective political power used in this study are rooted foremost in a long-term personal analysis of Brazilian national politics and the decisionmaking process as they have evolved since the mid-1950s. Many of my findings through 1970 have been detailed in *The Political System of Brazil* (New York: Columbia University Press, 1971), while material through 1976 is brought together in *Brazil: Foreign Policy of a Future World Power* (Boulder, Colo.: Westview Press, 1977). My views on the 1976–1981 period are embodied in my chapter in Robert Wesson (ed.), *New Military Politics in Latin America* (New York: Praeger Publishers, 1982).

2. These figures are numerical expressions of what are at root admittedly qualitative judgments. They are, however, based upon a painstaking study of political decisionmaking under each administration since 1960 and the increases and decreases in the relative influence of the various actors over this span of some twenty-five years. They clearly convey incremental changes in this regard more effectively and accurately than would the conventional resort to modifiers (marginally, slightly, moderately, substantially, significantly, and dramatically, not to mention perceptibly, measurably, emphatically, and some of the other "incomparable" words used to describe changes of degree). I hold that such quantifications facilitate identification of trends and concise description of changed relationships among a large number of factors—something reliance upon words generally hinders.

3. As the task here is limited to demonstrating the relationship among economic, social, and political facets of Brazilian development, I will refer only to very basic and salient trends apparent from the Brazilian Institute of Geography and Statistics (IBGE), *Pesquisa Nacional Por Amostra de Domicílios* (PNAD) for

the years 1982, 1983, and 1984. The *PNAD's* data collection is done in October, with publication the following year.

4. The economic side of Tancredo Neves's transition team, the seven-member Comissão para o Plano do Govêrno (Copag), proposed in "Subsídios para a Ação Imediata contra a Fome e o Desemprêgo" that jobs be created by all government organs, giving priority to programs and projects that are labor intensive so as to create a greater volume of employment relative to resources invested. See *Jornal do Brasil,* February 24, 1985. Debate over the size of the underground economy and how to measure it has been inconclusive to date, except in so far as it is clear that its great expansion during the early 1980s did cushion the social impact of the recession as some millions of individuals found such "off the books" employment as being street vendors.

5. This subject is pursued systematically in my essay "Transition Without Rupture: Parties, Politicians, and the Sarney Government," in Julian Chacel, David Fleischer, and Pamela Falk (eds.), *Brazil's Economic and Political Future* (Boulder, Co.: Westview Press, forthcoming).

6. These groups are clearly not mutually exclusive, and admittedly individuals could belong to more than one of them—but this is in keeping with Brazilian political realities. This "untidy" array of groups stems from the fundamental fact that we must deal with both organized sectors of society and political structures participating in the governmental process. Hence the political power ratings given to economic and societal sectors (business, industry, banking, agriculture, labor, rural workers, and so forth) center on their ability as such to affect national policy decisions—no matter how this influence may be exerted, as different political actors possess different types of power capabilities. On the other hand, the power assessments of elements of the political-governmental system are based upon their direct role in the making of such decisions. As Congress is the basic arena of political party activity, it is not included as a separate actor. The executive bureaucracy is, for the decisionmakers there are not in any immediate sense agents of or dependent upon political parties (although they may well be affiliated with them, or even be leading figures within them, given the prevalent Brazilian pattern of movement between appointive and elective office).

7. It may be useful to refer back to Table 6.1, remembering that the figures there are given only at four-year intervals and that here I will at times refer to intervening dates or to longer or overlapping periods.

8. Most useful on the Church is Ralph della Cava, "Catholicism and Society in Contemporary Brazil: Notes for a History in Progress—Part I, The Church and the *Abertura,* 1974–1985," paper prepared for the Conference on Popular Culture and Democratization in Brazil, University of Florida, Gainesville, Fla., April 1985. See also Scott Mainwaring, *The Catholic Church and Politics in Brazil, 1916–1985* (Stanford: Stanford University Press, forthcoming).

9. The *ligas camponesas* and other organizations of rural workers are put into proper perspective in Marta Cehelsky, *Land Reform in Brazil: The Management of Social Change* (Boulder, Colo.: Westview Press, 1978), especially pp. 40–48. See also Joseph Page, *The Revolution That Never Was: Northeastern Brazil, 1955–1964* (New York: Grossman Publishers, 1972). In 1981 and 1982 very many Brazilian social scientists and a large proportion of the U.S. scholarly community interested in Brazil went as far overboard on Lula, the PT, and the CEBs as had been the case with Francisco Julião and the peasant leagues twenty years earlier. Residual traces of this kind of "thinking with the heart, not with the

head" can be seen in Brady Tyson, "Brazil: The Quest for a New Social Contract," in Jan K. Black (ed.), *Latin America: Its Problems and Its Promise* (Boulder, Colo.: Westview Press, 1984), pp. 489–501. No sooner did the PT turn out to be a "paper tiger" in the 1982 elections than the fad shifted to grossly exaggerating the national importance of Brizola.

10. The most useful work on the PCB is Ronald Chilcote, *The Brazilian Communist Party: Conflict and Integration, 1922–1972* (New York: Oxford University Press, 1974). The name Brazilian Communist Party was adopted in September 1961, and shortly thereafter dissidents resolved to retain the old name. Marighella exited from the PCB's Central Committee in December 1966 to take up the armed struggle, and was expelled from the party in September 1967 along with a number of others who founded the Revolutionary Brazilian Communist Party (PCBR). Marighella was shot in November 1969 by government security forces. The MR-8 was originally led by Captain Carlos Lamarca, killed by security forces in September 1971.

11. Of use in reconstructing the course of events in 1984 is Ricardo Noblat, et al., *O Complô que Elegeu Tancredo* (Rio de Janeiro: *Jornal do Brasil,* 1985), an expanded version of a comprehensive reportage put together in *Jornal do Brasil,* January 13, 1985. See also Walder de Góes and Aspásia Camargo, *O Drama da Sucessão e a Crise do Regime* (Rio de Janeiro: Nova Fronteira, 1984) and "A História Secreta da Sucessão," *Veja,* January 16, 1985, pp. 20–55.

12. Had the Liberal Front not undercut the PDS majorities in many state legislatures there should have been at least eighty-one state electors for Maluf; instead the PDS selected only forty-one, and just twenty-three of these ended up voting for the party's candidate. The PFL came away with forty state electors and the PMDB with fifty-one (whereas the PDT chose the six from Rio de Janeiro).

13. Maluf's prospects went from dim to dismal on November 6, when the Superior Electoral Tribunal rejected his contention that "party fidelity" applied to the electoral college. This ended his hopes that votes of those who had been elected on the PDS ticket in 1982 would be automatically counted for him as the party's official candidate (or at least that those cast for Neves would be ruled invalid).

14. The president-elect was very fearful that some conservative groups might attempt to block the handing over of the government to the opposition and PDS "traitors" (as the government viewed Sarney, et. al.) if the truth were known concerning the seriousness of his health problems. Hence he refused to have the intestinal tumor treated until he was on the verge of severe peritonitis with the infection spreading through the intestinal cavity and entering the bloodstream. This, plus some possibly substandard care at the Brasília hospital, led to the combination of intestinal abscesses, lung problems, kidney failure, and cardiac complications that eventually took his life after nearly six weeks of a courageous effort on his part to survive at first just by sheer will power and subsequently on life support systems. During this time a near paralysis seized the new government, broken only on the eve of Neves's death when Sarney decided that it was necessary to begin acting as if he were the permanent, not just the interim, president.

15. In light of Figueiredo's health problems and the Neves tragedy, age is definitely against Guimarães's understandable desire to become president. Almost certainly 1988 would be too late for him in this respect. His surest road would be the departure or removal of Sarney, parallel to Brazil's experience in 1954–

1955 with Vice-president Café Filho succeeding Vargas but subsequently taking leave for "health" problems and not being allowed to resume the presidency when he "recovered" in late 1955. Scheduling presidential elections for 1986 would have held appeal for Guimarães, but would have split the administration wide open.

16. Manufactures at $15.1 billion were up 34 percent from the 1983 total of $11.2 billion and constituted 56 percent of exports. The current account deficit had been $16.3 billion in 1982 (when the trade surplus had only been something over $2 billion), falling to $6.9 billion in 1983 (as the trade surplus rose to nearly $6.4 billion), and disappearing in 1984 with the record $13 billion trade surplus. Armaments and services, especially to Middle Eastern and North African countries (particularly Iraq and Libya), have been among the leading new factors in Brazil's export growth, along with a substantial increase in automobiles and steel.

17. Even after the energy crisis ended Brazil's "economic miracle," GNP growth rates through 1980 remained close to the country's comparatively high historical average at over 7 percent yearly. The recession of the early 1980s was short-lived, embracing only 1981 through 1983. Not only did the 1984 GNP growth of 4.5 percent fully offset the drop of those years but, in conjunction with a more than 8.0 percent rise in 1985, it set the stage for full recovery of per capita GNP by the end of 1986. (A GNP growth of 5 percent in 1986 would be just above the 1980 record.) With the 7 percent growth rates considered feasible for the late 1980s by World Bank studies, real per capita GNP would be up by almost one-seventh during the 1987–1989 period, with the economy having grown nearly 40 percent from 1985 through 1989. National Economic and Social Development Bank (BNDES) projections are for GNP growth rates of nearly 8 percent annually through 1990, which would result in even higher income levels. EAP is expected by most studies to reach 60 million by 1989 (compared to 17.1 million in 1950, 22.8 million in 1960, 29.6 million in 1970, and 45.8 in 1980).

18. On the societal side of the developmental process, the government's intention to deal with the explosive land problem is the most critical element. There are nearly 1,000 areas of land conflict registered by the newly established Agrarian Reform and Development Ministry, and it is estimated that nearly 7 million families require land that they do not have at present—including perhaps as many as 3.3 million migrant harvest laborers (*bóias frias*). The government's ambitious goal is to begin a process that would benefit 35 million people by the year 2000, using over 400 million hectares of private land and some 70 million hectares of government-owned lands. At present there are over 5 million rural landowners, fewer than 30 percent of whom control 86 percent of the privately owned rural acreage, with two-thirds of the 5 million property holders having—in stark contrast—only 8 percent of the territory.

About the Contributors

Enrique A. Baloyra is professor of political science and associate dean of the Graduate School of International Studies of the University of Miami, Coral Gables. He is the author of *El Salvador in Transition* and of numerous articles on the politics of transition to democracy.

David Fleischer is associate professor of political science and chairperson of the Department of Political Science and International Relations at the University of Brasília. He has published numerous studies of Brazilian politics, especially on elites, electoral systems, parties, and legislatures. In 1982 he was named to the select Ministry of Justice commission to draft legislation for a new mixed electoral system. In 1985 he was named special adviser to the First Secretary of the Brazilian Senate, Eneas Faria (PMDB/Paraná).

Scott Mainwaring is assistant professor of government and member of the Kellogg Institute of the University of Notre Dame. His book, *The Catholic Church and Politics in Brazil, 1916–1985*, is in press. He has written a number of articles on social movements and the transition to democracy.

Robert A. Packenham is professor of political science at Stanford University, where he has taught since 1965. He is the author of *Liberal America and the Third World* and of other writings on political development theory, U.S. foreign policy, comparative legislative behavior, social science and public policy, Brazilian political economy, and Latin American Marxism. He has been a Fellow of the Woodrow Wilson International Center for Scholars in Washington, D.C. and a visiting professor at the University of California at Berkeley.

Ronald M. Schneider is professor of political science at Queens College, City University of New York. Author of several books and a number of articles on Brazil, he also writes on Latin America in general and is the editor of Nations of Contemporary Latin America, a series being published by Westview Press.

Wayne A. Selcher is College Professor of International Studies in the Department of Political Science at Elizabethtown College (PA), with research interests in Brazilian politics and foreign policy and in Latin American foreign policies. In addition to many articles and studies, he has written *The Afro-Asian Dimension of Brazilian Foreign Policy, 1956–1972* (1974) and *Brazil's Multilateral Relations: Between First and Third*

Worlds (1978), as well as edited *Brazil in the International System: The Rise of a Middle Power* (Westview, 1981).

Donald Share is assistant professor of political science at the University of Puget Sound. He is the author of *The Making of Spanish Democracy: Transition Through Transaction After Franco* (forthcoming).

Index

DATE DUE